M000159318

MANGA

MANGA

An Anthology of Global and Cultural Perspectives

FAULK CENTRAL LIBRARY
0000202381448
AUSTIN PUBLIC LIBRARY

Toni Johnson-Woods

continuum

2010

The Continuum International Publishing Group Inc
80 Maiden Lane, New York, NY 10038

The Continuum International Publishing Group Ltd
The Tower Building, 11 York Road, London SE1 7NX

www.continuumbooks.com

Copyright © 2010 Toni Johnson-Woods

All rights reserved. No part of this book may be reproduced, stored in a
retrieval system, or transmitted, in any form or by any means, electronic,
mechanical, photocopying, recording, or otherwise, without the written
permission of the publishers.

Library of Congress Cataloging-in-Publication Data
A catalog record for this book is available from the Library of Congress.

ISBN: 978 0 8264 2937 7 (hardcover)
        978 0 8264 2938 4 (paperback)

Typeset by Pindar NZ, Auckland, New Zealand
Printed in the United States of America

Contents

Reading Manga

Manga in the World

Editor's Notes

In Japan, people's names are usually written with the family name first and the given name last (e.g., "Ito Kinko"). However, in this book Japanese names are rendered in a Western format — that is, with the given name first (e.g., "Kinko Ito") — except where indicated in the first endnote.

Commonly used foreign words, such as manga, are not italicized; however, more specific terms such as *shōnen* are italicized upon first mention in each chapter, then generally not italicized thereafter.

Note that the style of presentation by different contributing authors may differ.

At the end of many chapters recommended readings offer manga titles that may be of further interest to the reader.

List of Figures

Introduction

Toni Johnson-Woods

What do Cup O' Noodles, Warren Buffet, and William Shakespeare have in common? [1] They are all manga — that is, Japanese comics. Over the past two decades manga has spread from being a quirky style of comics to being the new comic-book art format. In 2007, Daniel Pink claimed that manga is the "hottest trend in American publishing" (in *Wired Magazine* http://www.wired.com/wired/issue/15-11) with good reason: it was the first year that a manga title was ranking in *USA Today*'s best-seller list (*Fruits Basket*, Volume 16). Around the same time, the media was abuzz with the release of Selfmadehero's Shakespearean manga, and Japan's International Manga Awards. Manga was well and truly internationally accepted. But manga is not an overnight sensation, manga first appeared outside Japan in the 1970s; however it was through *anime* that manga came to the attention of the general populace. Now it is difficult to get away from manga. Borders offer gift cards with a Naturo-esque character, the Bible has been mangafied and the manga sections at bookshops continue to expand. This volume reflects the global impact of manga on comic book scholarship and contains essays from comic book scholars in Australia, Europe and the United States.

MANGA AND COMIC BOOK SCHOLARSHIP

Considerable ink has been spent trying to define comics by Scott McCloud (*Understanding Comics*), Will Eisner (*Comics and Sequential Art*), David Carrier (*The Aesthetics of Comics*), and Roger Sabin (*Adult Comics*).[2] Manga adds yet another layer to the "long and complicated" evolution of comics (Sabin 1993, 1). Even a seemingly self-evident description such as "manga is sequential art" is riddled with exceptions: manga is not always sequential (chronologically, anyway) and some might argue that it is not art. Manga is a visual narrative with a recognizable "sensibility." The term *sensibility* is intentionally vague in order to cover a multitude of options and embraces the stereotypical big-eyed, pointy chinned characters that many people consider the epitome of manga, the Disneyesque style of Osamu Tezuka, and the realistic style of corporate manga. Not all manga looks the same and not all manga has the same philosophical issues or the same readership. If it calls itself manga, then it is manga.[3] What manga is not is *anime*. Though *anime* often evolves from manga, the two are not synonymous.

Since the first cavewoman scratched her story on a wall, humankind has used the visual for storytelling. Egyptian hieroglyphics in tombs immortalize a life, the Elgin Marbles depict battle scenes, and the Bayeux Tapestry retells the Norman conquest of England; painters have re-created Christian mythologies (Michaelangelo's Sistine Chapel) and satirized human foibles (William Hogarth and Thomas Rowlandson). Arguably the first graphic novel was Rudolph Topffer's *Histoire de Mr. Vieux Bois* (1827); the first cartoon "strip" with regular characters was Wilhelm Busch's *Max und Moritz* (1865). The first recognizable American comic character, Richard F. Outcault's Yellow Kid, appeared in Joseph Pulitzer's newspaper *New York World* in 1895. By the end of the 1920s, newspapers and periodicals offered installments of Harold R. Foster's *Tarzan* (1929), Chic Young's *Blondie* (1930), and Chester Gould's *Dick Tracy* (1931). Jerry Siegel and Joe Shuster's Superman premiered in Action Comics' first issue in 1938. By the mid-twentieth century, comics were so firmly entrenched in popular culture, that pop artists Andy Warhol and Roy Lichtenstein celebrated the comic aesthetic in their art.

Despite the censorship and moral panics of the mid-twentieth century, and the disinterest of the 1960s and 1970s, comic books retained a place in the publishing industry. At the end of the 1980s, the graphic novel had injected new life into the format. During the 1990s a concatenation of cultural events saw the rise of visual reading material: the Internet, computer games, graphic novels, and globalization fostered the spread of Japanese popular culture and in particular the introduction of *anime* and manga. The uptake of the graphic novel and the popularity of manga reminded academics and popular culture experts that comics are worthy of further investigation.

Frederik Schodt's *Manga! Manga! The World of Japanese Comics* (1983) was the first book to introduce manga to the non-Japanese and it remains a seminal text for manga investigation. Since then Sharon Kinsella, Paul Gravett, and Anne Allison have all written influential books. Kinko Ito and Fusami Ogi have furthered the study of manga with their academic articles. In the past ten years, manga has become cool.

Manga: An Anthology of Global and Cultural Perspectives is divided into four sections: the first provides an overview of manga history, manga in the United States, and manga genres; the second contains detailed analyses of manga-ka and their material; the third examines manga as a new style of visual narrative; and the final section considers the global outreach of manga.

FIGURE I.1: Manga anthologies and tankōbons. © 2008, Toni Johnson-Woods. Used by permission.

MANGA FORMATS

Manga is delivered in two print formats, the manga magazine and the *tankōbon* (see fig. I.1). The magazines, as Christopher Couch notes (chapter 12 in this volume), have inherited characteristics from their publication forebears: serialized novels and superhero pulps. They contain multiple instalments of serialized stories; for instance, in January 2008 *Square Enix* had over 20 serialized stories in its nearly 900 pages, *Comic Blade* contained 17 stories in 550 pages, and *Morning* crammed 21 stories into 430 pages. Each magazine has a targeted readership. For example, *Weekly Morning* (with its catch phrase "*Morning Gets You Going*") targets an older readership; it favors adult content, and its politics, history, and sporting manga are depicted in a more realistic style.

The paper quality of the magazines is poor (*insatsu senkashi*) because they are made from recycled paper. As one editor recalls, "Manga used to be printed with some colors in them, but it was too expensive, so we started to print only with black ink on some colored paper. This was convenient for both the printing office and the publisher" ("Why Do Manga Magazines Use Colored Paper?"). After the paper is de-inked it is off-white, and publishers then add colors; these colors indicate a change of story. As can be seen in fig. I.1, different magazines adopt different colors: "Seinen magazines opt for a shades from cream to light orange while shōnen magazines and shōjo magazines, prefer intense colors" like yellow, orange, and green ("Why Do Manga Magazines Use Colored Paper?"). Whatever colors are used inside, outside the magazines share the same crammed hypervisual covers — which, surprisingly, blend both Japanese and English words. At around ¥300 for over five hundred pages, manga magazines represent value for money. Though it has been claimed that manga prices have been steadily increasing, analysis has found that this is not the case; in fact, "the price of weekly manga magazines have remained stagnant for the past 30 years" and that manga still sells at "around 0.5 yen per page" ("An Analysis of Weekly Manga Magazines Price for the Past 30 Years").

Still, not everyone buys their manga. It is common to see people crowd around the magazine shelves reading — *tachiyomi* (standing reading), a practice one would assume is frowned upon in the United States and Australia, but this is not the case, as a quick visit to the manga section of any bookstore will show (see fig. I.2).

FIGURE I.2: Readers at manga bookshop. © 2008, Toni Johnson-Woods. Used by permission.

There does not generally appear to be the "collectibility" ethos evidenced among Western comic enthusiasts, many of whom wrap their goods in archival sleeves never to be opened. Recently, though, reissues of "classic" manga have become increasingly popular (Satō, 2006). The reason for this new niche? According to Satō's article, mature fans are keen to fill the gaps from their youth; and there is nostalgia, and, of course, the increase in manga research by scholars. All of the readers whom I interviewed in Japan said they bought their copies at railway stations because they read them over the course of several days during their commutes to work. However, manga can also be purchased in bookstores, from vending machines, or from indigents who collect discarded copies and resell them to new readers. Successful serialized manga are reprinted as tankōbon.[4] They are of a better quality than the anthologies and are similar to paperbacks; they sell in bookshops for around ¥500 each.

If standing at a convenience store reading manga does not appeal, *manga kissa* offers readers a library of manga material. Manga kissa are Internet-style cafés that stock hundreds and even thousands of manga;[6] for around ¥500 per hour, readers can occupy a small cubicle and read manga, use the Internet, play video games, watch DVDs, and so on.[7] Recently manga kissa have attracted unfavorable press attention because they have been used as refuges for the homeless or pick-up joints for prostitutes and because they don't pay royalties or lending rights (*Kyodo News* 2007). Still they continue to grow — from three hundred cafés nationwide in 1998 to two thousand in 2002 (Japan Forum), spreading to Europe, the United States, and Australia.

MANGA'S PLACE IN COMIC CULTURE

Manga differs from Western-style comic books in several salient ways.

Eijiro Shimada of Kodansha claims that "the main difference between manga and comics is that manga focuses on one main character. The reader follows in the footsteps of that character and sees everything through the character's eyes" (Cha 2007). The most obvious visual feature is that manga mimic an Asian reading orientation; that is to say, manga are read from back to front and right to left. The next most glaring difference is that they are largely rendered in black and white, lacking the hypercoloring of Western comics. Inside, the frames are not always neat rectangles lined up equidistant (i.e., four to a line and four lines to a page); there can be one, two, or seven frames on a page. The manga aesthetic embraces a myriad of graphic techniques — the Disneyesque styles of Tezuka, the precision of the *mechas* (robot manga) or the softness of the *shōjo* (girls' manga). Often drawing techniques are mixed on the same page; thus, the same character can be rendered as a full-sized angular person or a small chubby one. The words are

FIGURE I.3 (left): From Queenie Chan, *The Dreaming*, vol. 1.
FIGURE I.4 (right): From Queenie Chan, *The Dreaming*, vol. 1.

few — manga relies more heavily on visual cues and adopts cinematic techniques such as close-ups and freeze frames. Sound effects also add texture
to the story. The use of sound effects is quintessentially Japanese and reflects
the onomatopoeia of the Japanese language (Neil Cohn's chapter discusses
the visual language more fully), in *From Eroica with Love* (a campy James
Bond manga) cars go sweesh and helicopters go kacha. The illustrations
from Queenie Chan's *The Dreaming* demonstrate some of these manga traits
(see figs. I.3 and I.4).

For the first-time Western reader, manga is a visual, textual, and intellectual challenge. Tracking the narrative via an unfamiliar reading system,
Japanese characters,[8] and limited visual cues can leave the newbie manga
reader shaking her head. However, once the skill of "reading" manga is con-
quered, the manga is a rich experience.

Several scholars have explored the issue of Eastern versus Western ways
of reading manga. Mary Grigsby claims that the Japanese are "used to reading pictures" (1998, 67); *Wired* reporter Daniel Pink underwent an experiment conducted by a developmental psychologist who studies how the
eyes and brain collaborate to "process complex images like the mixture of
words and images found in manga" and found that manga readers' eyes "sla-
lomed smoothly from page edge to page edge, rarely stopping at the text. In
fact, there were portions of pages that his eyes never touched — because,

as Nakazawa explained, Keito was either processing the words through his peripheral vision or simply imputing what was there. Like a seasoned skier, he moved with great speed yet remained acutely aware of his surroundings" (Pink 2007).[9] Furthermore, this controversial type of cultural coding is part of research, such as the work done by Richard Nisbett, who claims that East Asians are more "collectivist" and Westerners more "individualist" in their cognitive processes. Neil Cohn's essay on the visual language of manga in this volume (chapter 11) provides a linguistically attuned analysis of manga and its narrative processes; he expands Schodt's hypothesis that manga is another language with a unique grammar.

A brief glance at a manga page demonstrates that manga differs from Western-style comics in many ways. Most obvious is the page layout; not merely reading left to right or whatever system fits within the page (in the above instance the final statement is the solitary bubble on the left-hand page) but following the oddly shaped frames in the correct sequence can be confusing, and sometimes the words don't help. In other words, the narrative flow is not as simplistic as that in Western comics. Also startling is the visual aesthetic: the wide variety of frames, the highly detailed backgrounds which often dwarf the characters, the *chibi* (small renditions of characters which indicate anger or frustration); and the cinematic angles flavour the narratives. Even though the illustrations are in black and white the inking, shading, and toning produce differing effects, as Mio Bryce discusses in chapter 8 of this volume. In many manga, especially historical (*Vagabond*), CLAMP work (*XXX-Holic*), Victoriana-inspired (*The Cain Saga*), and children's (*Dr. Slump*) books, the amount of detail in each frame can be confusing to the eye.

One of the most controversial issues has been the use of the honorifics *sama*, *sensei*, *kun*, and *chan*, among others — Japanese words that give readers subtle clues as to the relationships between the characters. The rather insensitive mishandling of honorifics in early translations concerned American *otaku* who wanted "uncorrupted" texts; as manga fan Stacy Rue explains, American fans want

> to have the same experience with the translated text as the Japanese audience has with the original manga, in a literal rather than figurative sense. And as American fans interact online with manga fans not only in Japan, but in France, Germany, and other Western countries, we are keenly aware that U.S. publishers are under more pressure (both real and imagined) to change or adapt manga to suit the conservative American cultural norms as compared to other translations by Western publishers. So as American otaku, we remain vigilant for any possible alterations, not only to protect the manga but to ensure our ability to participant in the global manga community.[10]

James Rampant (chapter 13) agrees that "what fans want, fans get" in his exploration of the impact of scanlation, the practice of fans' translation of manga into their own languages in which devotees "scan" their favorite manga and translate the Japanese text. It is a thriving underworld that challenges publishing orthodoxy by offering translated material on the Internet free of charge. Obviously there are copyright issues and, of course, it's a problematic area. Even though it is piracy, scanlation has had positive impact. As Rue notes, fans feel protective of their favorite manga, and Rampant demonstrates how the publishing companies have adopted and adapted aspects of scanlated material into their publications.

Another minefield is the issue of essentialism — are manga-style comics written by the British, Australians, Koreans, or Americans truly "manga"? A recent book, *Mangaka America*, celebrates nine artists (Steelriver Studio and Adam Warren, 2006), and "Shakespeare Manga" by Emma Hayley of SelfMadeHero — the UK company that made worldwide headlines with its Shakespeare adaptations — demonstrates that the manga style has success-fully extended beyond the solely Japanese *mangaka*, or comic artist. Hayley's essay in chapter 16 provides a behind-the-scenes glimpse into how her idea progressed to a finished and internationally recognized manga product.[11]

READING MANGA

If you thought manga was "doe-eyed girls with melon-sized breasts, slasher samurai, resilient teenage heroines wielding magical powers and adventurous ninja boys" (Birmingham 2008), then think again. There is manga for every taste, age group, and interest. As such it almost becomes meaningless to try to describe the genres, since for every description there will be a manga that doesn't conform. However, in order to impose some classification on the thousands of titles, genres are handy, if not always accurate, labels. Anthologies are printed by publishers who deliberately target certain readerships;[12] thus, manga are shaped to conform to an editor's expectations. The Japanese manga genres therefore reflect the genre of anthologies in which the manga appear: shōnen (boys' manga, such as *Shōnen Jump* and *Shōnen Sunday*), shōjo (girls' manga, such as *Princess* and *Margaret*), seinen manga (men's manga, such as *Big Comic Spirits* and *Business Jump*) and *josei* manga (women's manga,[13] such as *Be Love* and *Office You*) — and then it starts to get a little more complicated. Below is a list of names commonly used in relation to manga; however, some meanings differ between the United States and Japan, and the terms can and do change over time:

Name(s)	Literal Translation	Description
Dōjinshi	Same person, same magazine	Amateur or fan manga; can be yaoi, shōnen, and seinen.

Gekiga	Dramatic pictures	Adult manga that explores serious topics.
Hentai[15]	Sexual perversion	The most explicit material comes from the United States.
Josei, Redīsu, Redi Komi Redīsu Komikku	Ladies' comics	Adult women's issues as wives and office workers; examples include *Comic Amour* (anthology), *Paradise Kiss*, *Tramps Like Us*.
Kodomo	Children	Includes pronunciation guide as children learn to read.
Mecha	Mechanical	Robots and transformers.
Shōnen-ai	Boy love	Male love stories.
Yaoi	Acronym for Yama nashi, ochi nashi, imi nashi "No climax, no point, no meaning".	Male homosexual stories; Male/male love stories written for women.
Yuri Shōjo-ai	Girl love	Girl/girl love stories.

Aside from the confusing profusion of manga genres, more traditional categories such as romance, fantasy, and science fiction can be and are used to classify manga. In his extensive manga guide, Jason Thompson (2007) assigns each of the more than one thousand manga genres more meaningful descriptors; for example, *Monster* is "Seinen, Thriller" (227) and *Fruits Basket* is "Shojo, Fantasy, Romantic Comedy, Drama" (114). Thompson embellishes the broad publishing categories because they are such umbrella terms.

In their essays in this volume, Mio Bryce and Jason Davis, Jennifer Prough, and Angela Drummond-Mathews point out that the four basic genre labels are by no means indicative of manga readership; the energy and inventiveness of essentially children's fare such as *Dr Slump* and *Dragon Ball* can also make for enjoyable adult reading.

In chapter 2, Bryce and Davis divide about one hundred manga into ten categories such as humor, religion and spirituality, and war. These headings make more sense than the broad age/gender divide because they encapsulate the "sensibilities" of manga better. Bryce and Davis briefly trace the development of each type, identify its major elements, and explore the "salient aspects" within each. For the new manga reader the surprise might be the high number of sports manga. Sabin (1993) nominates sport as the second biggest genre, and claims that this is because sport has been viewed by Japanese society as "a testing of the spirit" (202).

Angela Drummond-Mathews (chapter 3) discusses the plethora of sports manga in her chapter on shōnen manga, "What Boys Will Be." After outlining the rise of different types of boys' manga, she then examines the stories through a Joseph Campbell–influenced mythological framework. She notes the reciprocal nature of readership — boys' manga has added romantic subplots and girls' manga now includes kickass heroines (*Gunslinger*).

Girls' manga is the focus of two chapters. Mark McLelland (chapter 4) delves into one of manga's most curious characters, the *bishōnen*, in which he teases out the cultural influences that have spawned female romance comics that have, at their center, male homosexual love; he concludes that through these "feminine" males, female readers imaginatively refashion their romantic and sexual selves. Tania Darlington and Sara Cooper (chapter 9) explore manga's fluid approach to gender and sexuality.

Three essays in this volume engage with more specific facets of manga. Philip Brophy, the curator of the traveling *Tezuka — The Marvel of Manga* exhibit, looks at the cultural ramifications of mask in Tezuka's manga (chapter 7); and imaginary worlds are the focus of two case studies, Marc Hairston's messianic reading of Hayao Miyazaki's *Nausicaä of the Valley of the Wind* (chapter 10) and Mio Bryce's examination of the themes of Kyōko Hikawa's *Kanata kara* (*From Far Away*; chapter 8).

Much of the scholarship to date has focused on manga genres and readership. However, the creation of manga is equally fascinating, for manga is often the result of collaborative efforts, as one editor describes the process, "the idea for a story is dropped into a deep pool and the artist and editor put a lot of effort into trying to dig it out . . . the pool has to be deep enough for the artist . . . if it's only a shallow pool, you can pull out a little rock easily but that's not real manga" (Cha 2007). In chapter 5 Jennifer Prough presents an industrially attuned examination of shōjo; she draws upon her field research to show the impact of culture and editors upon shōjo narratives, and the success that shōjo has enjoyed in the United States.

MANGA AND THE WORLD

Timothy J. Craig has noted that Japanese pop culture has "attracted a broad street-level following overseas" (2000, 4), and nowhere is this truer than in the uptake of manga. If manga are comics written by the Japanese for Japanese consumption, then how and why have they become such a global media phenomenon? The Internet has obviously fostered the spread of manga. In addition to scanlation sites, there is a Wikipedia manga subset; publishers have websites; and there are multitudes of mangaka who use the Internet to demonstrate their skills.

Nowadays, the "flow" goes both ways — in and out of Japan — and Japanese publishers such as Kondasha seek to inject new life into manga by holding international competitions. In 2006, Kondasha announced its first international manga competition; the following year Eijiro Shimada, editor-in-chief of Kondansha's *Morning Two*, and Yukari Shiiina, president of world-mag.com (a literary agency for non-Japanese manga) visited the San Diego, California, Comic-Con to find new manga talent. In an interview with *Publishers Weekly*, Shimada explains that while he was impressed by the number of manga in bookstores he found the quality disappointing. Too many submissions to *Morning*'s competition were Naruto wannabes. The limitation demonstrated by overseas competitors highlights how little manga is understood. It's supposed to be free and unrestricted, Shimada explains, and Japanese fans are interested in manga from Italy and Germany.

Wendy Siuyi Wong (chapter 20) charts the globalization of manga, and John Lent (chapter 18) concentrates on complex censorship and local cultural issues that the influx of manga has raised in China, Hong Kong, Korea, and Taiwan. Paul Malone (chapter 19) provides an overview of manga in continental Europe and the United Kingdom. Jean-Marie Bouissou, Marco Pellitteri, and Bernd Dolle-Weinkauff (chapter 15) distributed a fifteen-page survey to fans at manga conventions in France, Italy, Germany, and Switzerland; the results show that fans' reasons for reading manga are not as simplistic as one would imagine. Jason Bainbridge and Craig Norris (chapter 14) trace the "flow" of manga into Australia and its impact upon the Australian comics scene.

Another obvious marker of the internationality of manga is the surge in international manga competitions. *Anime* and manga publisher Tokyopop has instigated the Rising Stars of Manga competition in the United States and in the United Kingdom. And, beginning in 2007, the Japanese government has instigated the International Manga Award in order to promote international diplomacy in the belief that popular culture can play a role in diplomacy and that manga can "enhance understanding of Japanese culture" (Ministry of Foreign Affairs of Japan, 2007). The second International Manga Award competition attracted more than double the number of entries than the first had — 368 entries from 46 countries and regions:

Asia: 156
United States: 66
Europe: 114
Pacific Region: 4
Middle East: 23
Africa: 5 (Ministry of Foreign Affairs of Japan 2008)

European countries have also cast their manga nets wider; Spanish publisher Norma Editorial has announced its Third Manga Competition for 2008.

CONCLUSION

That Warren Buffet, Cup O' Noodles, and William Shakespeare all share a publishing format gestures to the wide variety of manga available and the global spread of manga and its commercial, aesthetic, and educational value. What is less surprising is how each culture deals with similar issues; Warren Buffet stars in his own biographical story, whereas in writer Tadashi Katoh and artist Akira Imai's *Project X: Nissin Cup Noodle* the development of the ideal cup of noodles is clearly outlined as a team effort. Today one can buy the manga Bible and Beowulf manga; any story that can be told can be drawn.

Manga's contribution to popular culture is fascinating because it is essentially a comic book, and comic books have always been ignored (at best) and condemned (at worst). Manga has caused moral panics about its violence and sexual content even though it grapples with deep philosophical questions: to be or not to be (*Confidential Confessions*), the nature of war (*Barefoot Gen*), what is it to be male or female (*Yours and My Secret*), the environment (*Nausicaä of the Valley of the Wind*), the essence of evil (*Death Note*), and what it means to be human (*Ghost in a Shell*). It is a complex visual art form, an aesthetic with proven worldwide appeal. Manga is essentially ephemeral entertainment, something to be bought and discarded; yet, for over sixty years it has provided entertainment to millions of people.

Notes

1. See Katoh and Imai 2006; Morio, 2005; and Shakespeare, 2007.
2. *Comics* is shorthand for a variety of visual formats: one-frame gags (*The Far Side*), multiframe strips (*Peanuts),* serialized narratives (*Mandrake*), comic books (*Casper the Friendly Ghost*), and the graphic novel — though the adult content of the graphic novel sets it apart in that it often lacks a "comedic" tone. And, of course, *comics* embraces genres as diverse as the superhero (*Superman*) and teenage life (*Archie*).
3. For a summary of these issues see Meskin 2007.
4. The longest-running manga is Osamu Akimoto's *Kochira Katsushika-ku Kameari Kouenmae Hashutsujo* (This Is the Police Box in Front of Kameari Park in Katsushika Ward). *Kochikame*, as it is commonly known, portrays the comic adventures of policeman Ryo-san; the series has been running in *Shōnen Jump* since 1976. It has appeared in more than 1,100 issues and been reissued in more than 150 tankōbon.
5. Kinokuniya has branches all over the world, including Singapore, Malaysia, the United States, and Australia.
6. For a history of manga kissa see Japan Forum (n.d.), "Manga Cafes."
7. If you check in around midnight, for ¥10,000 you can stay the night.
8. Of course, manga include the *hiragana* and *katakana* Japanese writing systems and *kanji*, which is composed of Chinese ideograms.
9. Stacy Rue, e-mail correspondence with the author, March 29, 2008.
10. A glimpse into the Japanese manga industry appears in Kinsella 2000.
11. Schodt 1996 gives an excellent overview of each publishing house, its publications, and sales figures.

12. For a discussion of the differences between shōjo, young ladies' comics, and ladies' comics, see Ogi 2001.
13. *Hentai* is less frequently used as a descriptor for manga in Japan than it is in the US; for more information see McLelland 2006.

References

Allison, Anne (1996). *Permitted and Prohibited Desires: Mothers, Comics, and Censorship in Japan.* Boulder, CO: Westview Press.
"An Analysis of Weekly Manga Magazines Price for the Past 30 Years" (2007). *Translated by Yurikomama. ComiPress, http://comipress.com/article/2007/04/06/1777.*
Birmingham, Lucy (2008). "Manga's Doe-Eyed Girls, Ninja Boys Woo U.S. Comic-Book Readers." Bloomberg Online, http://www.bloomberg.com/apps/news?pid=20601080&sid=apcSQGNG_Ti8&refer=asia.
Cha, Kai-Ming (2007). "Kodansha Launches Second Manga Contest." *Publishers Weekly,* August 7. http://www.publishersweekly.com/article/CA6466184.html.
Chan, Queenie (2005). *The Dreaming,* vol. 1. Los Angeles: Tokyopop.
"Dealing with Copyright and Plagiarism Issues Part I — Idiot's Guide to Online Copyright Issues" (2007). ComiPress, http://comipress.com/article/2007/06/09/2092.
Gravett, Paul (2004). *Manga: Sixty Years of Japanese Comics.* London: Laurence King.
Grigsby, Mary (1998). "Sailormoon: Manga (Comics) and Anime (Cartoon) Superheroine Meets Barbie: Global Entertainment Commodity Comes to the United States." *Journal of Popular Culture* 32(1): 59–80.
Kyodo News (2007). "Internet Café Survey to Gauge Working Poor." Reprinted in *Japan Times* Online, http://search.japantimes.co.jp/cgi-bin/nn20070414f1.html.
Ito, Kinko (1994). "Images of Women in Weekly Male Comic Magazines in Japan." *Journal of Popular Culture* 27(4): 81–95.
—— (2002). "The World of Japanese Ladies' Comics: From Romantic Fantasy to Lustful Perversion." *Journal of Popular Culture* 36(1): 68–85.
—— (2003). "Japanese Ladies' Comics as Agents of Socialization: The Lessons They Teach." *International Journal of Comic Art* 5(2): 425–36.
—— (2004). "Growing Up Japanese Reading Manga." *International Journal of Comic Art* 6(2): 392–403.
—— (2005). "A History of *Manga* in the Context of Japanese Culture and Society." *Journal of Popular Culture* 38(3): 456–75.
Japan Forum (n.d.). "Manga Cafes from Reading Spot to Relaxation Space." Japan Forum, http://www.tjf.or.jp/eng/content/japaneseculture/27mangakissa.htm.
Katoh, Tadashi, and Akira Imai (2006). *Project X: Nissin Cup Noodle.* Gardena, CA.: Digital Manga.
Kinsella, Sharon (2000). *Adult Manga: Culture and Power in Contemporary Japanese Society.* Richmond, Surrey, England: Curzon.
McLelland, Mark (2006). "A Short History of 'Hentai.'" *Intersections: Gender, History and Culture in the Asian Context* 12, http://intersections.anu.edu.au/issue12/mclelland.html.
Meskin, Aaron (2007). "Defining Comics." *Journal of Aesthetics and Art Criticism* 65(4): 369–79.
Ministry of Foreign Affairs of Japan (2007). "Establishment of the International MANGA Award." Ministry of Foreign Affairs of Japan, http://www.mofa.go.jp/announce/announce/2007/5/1173601_826.html.
Ministry of Foreign Affairs of Japan (2008). "Results of the Entries for the Secomd International MANGA Award." Ministry of Foreign Affairs of Japan, http://www.mofa.go.jp/announce/announce/2008/4/1178958_1000.html.

Morio, Ayano (2005). *Warren Buffett: An Illustrated Biography of the World's Most Successful Investor*. Translated by Mark Schreiber. Singapore: John Wiley and Sons.

Nisbett, Richard (2003). *The Geography of Thought: How Asians and Westerners Think Differently . . . and Why*. New York: Free Press.

Ogi, Fusami (2001). "Beyond *Shoujo*, Blending Gender: Subverting the Homogendered World in *Shoujo Manga* (Japanese Comics for Girls)." *International Journal of Comic Art* 3(2): 151–61.

——(2003a). "Female Subjectivity and *Shoujo* (Girls) *Manga* (Japanese Comics): *Shoujo* in Ladies' Comics and Young Ladies' Comics." *Journal of Popular Culture* 36(4): 780–803.

——(2003b). "Shimizu Isao: A Pioneer in Japanese Comics (*Manga*) Scholarship." *International Journal of Comic Art* 5(2): 216–32.

Pink, Daniel (2007). "This Is Your Brain on Manga"; *Wired*, http://www.wired.com/techbiz/media/magazine/15-11/ff_manga_chiba.

Sabin, Roger. (1993). *Adult Comics: An Introduction*. London: Routledge, 1993.

Sato, Kenichi (2006). "Republication Boom in Classic Manga." Translated by Neuroretardant. Originally appeared in *Yomiuri Shinbun*. Reprinted ComiPress, http://comipress.com/article/2006/07/07/438.

Schodt, Frederik L. (1983). *Manga! Manga! The World of Japanese Comics*. Tokyo: Kodansha International.

——(1996). *Dreamland Japan: Writings on Modern Manga*. Berkeley, CA: Stone Bridge Press.

Shakespeare, William (2007). *Romeo and Juliet*. Adapted by Richard Appignanesi, illustrated by Sonia Leong. London: SelfMadeHero, 2007.

Steelriver Studio and Adam Warren (2006). *Mangaka America*: Manga by America's Hottest Artists. New York: Harper Collins.

Thompson, Jason (2007). *Manga: The Complete Guide*. New York: Ballantine.

"Why Do Manga Magazines Use Colored Paper?" (2006). Translated by Michiko. ComiPress, http://comipress.com/article/2006/10/29/941.

Suggested Manga Reading

Antique Bakery
Addicted to Curry
Death Note
Dr. Slump
Dragon Ball
Even a Monkey Can Draw Manga
From Eroica with Love
Monster
To Terra

Manga and Genres

1

Manga: A Historical Overview

Jean-Marie Bouissou

THE FUTILE DEBATE ABOUT THE ORIGINS OF MANGA

Among Western intelligentsia, educationalists, and parents, manga has long had a reputation for vulgarity, violence, and bad drawing. When it entered the non-Japanese comics market — first in the United States, France, and Italy during the 1980s — most sophisticated Nipponophiles disliked it at first sight because it seemed so foreign to the traditional Japanese culture as symbolized by Confucian morality, Zen gardens, and the *mono no aware* (the pathos of things or the ahh-ness) of cherry blossoms. However, these "Japan lovers" overlooked the fact that the Japanese culture of samurai and aristocratic elites has always coexisted with the hedonist, unbridled, and rebellious popular cultures of Japanese peasantry and townspeople (*chônin*), which makes much room for amusement, tears, drama, romance, and sex and did not bother about morality or "good taste" (Itasaki, 1975; Lehmann, 1982; Seidensticker, 1983; Pons, 1988; Yokoi, 1975). Only since the Meiji era (1868–1912) have the governing elites forced the values and aesthetics of aristocratic and warrior's high culture upon the whole society and suppressed the popular ones (Gluck, 1985; Pons, 1988) — which, of course, remained alive and well underneath the "politically correct" layer of ikebana, tea ceremonies, and stone gardens. This process of forcing an elitism upon national culture during the contemporary period, and the ensuing mix of high and popular cultures, seem to be rather peculiar to Japan. Manga is a by-product of this phenomenon — as a genre where the most gifted samurai hero can fart, burp, get drunk, and cry — that gives to many series an unmistakable and very attractive "politically incorrect" flavor.

When looking for the origins of manga, most authors (among others Groensteen 1991; Schodt 1983) mention the painted narrative scrolls (*e-makimono*), especially the four *Chô-jûgiga* (the Animal Scrolls, twelfth century) by the abbot Toba Sôjô (1053–1140),[1] kept in the Kôzanji shrine near Kyoto. This satirical black and white piece of work portrays aristocrats, priests, and warriors under the guise of rabbits, frogs, monkeys, and other not-so-dignified animals. One may wonder why the much older *Eingakyô*, an anonymous full-color scroll from the Nara period (710–794), which narrates the life of Buddha using a mix of images and text (underneath) — whereas the *Chô-jûgiga* have no text — is never mentioned. Some manga scholars warn against the temptation to link present-day manga to the e-makimono, and Neil Cohn points out that "the dialect of the Japanese Visual Language hardly resembles . . . the graphic system depicted in *e-maki*" (2007, 12). Although of interest for specialists, this debate about filiation misses two very significant points.

The first point is the content, since many themes of the scrolls imagery have also found their way into contemporary manga. Often mentioned in this regard is the Scroll of the Hungry Ghosts (*Gaki Zôshi*, twelfth century), in which the desperate spirits feed on, among other things, human excrement, and other scrolls depicting farting or penis-size contests, one of which is attributed to the abbot Toba himself. In the same vein are contemporary manga that particularly disgusted the Western "Japan lovers," like *Toiretto Hakase* (Professor Toilet) or the (in)famous first martial arts tournament in *Dragon Ball*, in which one of the heroes confronts an opponent who uses farts and stinky genitals as chemical weapons.[2] Also of interest are *Hyakki Yôkai* (The Night Walk of One Thousand Demons, fifteenth century), and countless sketches and drawings depicting *yôkai* (supernatural monsters). These works passed on many oddly-looking but good-natured devilish beings to manga series like Okano Reiko's *Onmyôji* (exorcist) or Mizuki Shigeru's *NonNonBa* (Grandma NonNon), and, more generally, testify to a tradition of familiarity between human and nonhuman beings that lies at the core of manga universes and imaginaries, whereas this mix, although not totally unknown, is less common in the French "bande dessinée" (BD) and American comics.[3]

The second point is the technique. The narrative scrolls — devoid of balloons and frames, but mixing text and drawing as soon as the eighth century — are the first pillar of a rich tradition of graphic narration in Japan. Many ancient cultures outside of Japan also knew graphic narration under various forms: the Egyptians had frescoes, the Aztecs had codices, and the French had the Bayeux Tapestry (eleventh century) which mixed text and drawing more intimately than the Japanese scrolls did (McCloud 1993). Thus, from a theoretical point of view, if one considers only the graphic system, there is no reason to argue that the e-makimono are more the "ancestors" of manga than the Aztec codices or the Bayeux Tapestry are those of Mafalda or Tintin. But from a historical point of view, the tradition of graphic narration collapsed in Egypt and South America — if not in France — whereas the e-makimono remained alive until the Edo period (1603–1867), and was succeeded by other media mixing text and image. This continuity made the Japanese culture familiar with graphic narration, a fact that certainly contributed to the blossoming and social acceptance of manga. Many scholars also relate this "familiarity" to the use of ideograms (Cohn 2007). This debate goes beyond the scope of this chapter. Suffice it to say that even if there is no "linear" relation between e-makimono and manga as far as graphical and narrative techniques are concerned, there is a long tradition of graphic narration in both high and popular Japanese culture.

In addition to e-makimono, manga can be related to other forms of Japanese graphic art. The Zen painting (*zenga*), which debuted in the fourteenth century and blossomed during the first part of the Edo period, often mixes calligraphy and drawing. Zen masters, as a way toward enlightenment, use absurd enigmas to confront their disciples to the inanity of rational thought. In the same vein, the zenga offers many nonsensical pieces of work — a man defecating in a field, looking inside the anus of a horse, or having his buttock burnt by an old woman, with the accompaniment of enigmatic sayings. This tradition reemerged in two genres that flourish in manga whereas BD and comics almost ignore them (with a few underground exceptions like George Herriman's *Krazy Kat*) — the gag manga and the *yaoi* genre,[4] like Yamagami Tatsuhiko's *Gakideka*, Ueda Hajime's *FuliCuli*, or Sawai Yoshio's *Bobobo-Bo Bo-Bobo*. This is not to say that Yamagami and Ueda are the direct heirs of the Zen monks; the relationship between manga and the past graphic arts is more complex than that.

Manga owes much to the urban culture of the Edo period — although, here again, some specialists, such as Tomofusa Kure, see "no more relation between it and the manga than between abacus and computer" (Kure, 1997, II-2; author's translation). After two centuries of bloody anarchy, peace was restored by the authoritarian regime of the Tokugawa shoguns. Big cities flourished and the popular culture of the merchant class and townspeople thrived, introducing woodblock prints (*ukiyo-e*), Kabuki theater, popular illustrated novels and flamboyant "pleasure quarters" like Yoshiwara in Edo (now Tokyo). Manga owes something to each of these older forms of entertainment (Koyama-Richard 2007).

Because of the technical limitations of woodblock printing and the constraints of mass production, the ukiyo-e basically remains the same, without shadows or realistic perspective, not so different from Hergé's *ligne claire* (clear line).[5] The anatomy of characters is simplistic. The faces are typically ovals devoid of realistic features, like white canvas on which only eyes and mouth, albeit minuscule, convey the emotions through expression exaggerated to the point of caricature — something quite familiar to manga readers, especially *shônen* and *shôjo* manga fans.

Kabuki is no more realistic than woodblock prints. The actors don't mimic the sentiments, but "write them" on their faces using heavy makeup and quasi-cartoonish codes — rolling eyes, contorted mouth, tensed faces, and grimaces. They often move with an unrealistic but extremely expressive slowness, and sometimes stop as if frozen. Manga, especially its shônen and shôjo genres, reuses these techniques, which shocked Western educationalists. For example, the first attempts at translating Nakazawa Keiji's *Hadashi no Gen* failed miserably in both the United States and France during the 1980s, although its denunciations of war and the atomic bomb were very "politically correct" at that time. Part of the reason for this failure is that the clownish mimics of Gen seemed completely out of touch with the dramatic topic of the atomic bomb. Gigantic screaming or laughing mouths, tears bursting out like geysers, and arms or legs wrapping round the body to express utmost embarrassment looked out of place, even somewhat obscene in the context of nuclear holocaust.

Kabuki has many features in common with the popular French Grand Guignol of the nineteenth century. Most plays last for hours, sometimes a full day, and the plot is rich in cock-and-bull developments. Drama, violence, and blood are shown on the stage, and many characters die prolonged brutal and gruesome deaths. Plots are inspired by history, but also by dramatic news items from urban life — especially the double suicides (*shinjû*) that resulted from the prohibition of marriage between people of different castes. Edo townspeople also loved the plot spiced with a dose of supernatural and vengeful disfigured ghosts. Once again, manga feeds on this tradition, with its endless stories and multiple interweaving plots, and high dramatic intensity even in pieces for children — for example, the numerous violent deaths in Tezuka Osamu's *Tetsuwan Atomu* (*Mighty Atom* or *Astroboy*) or in *Dragon Ball*.

The news items and daily life of Edo were also the raw materials for *kibyôshi*. These illustrated, cheap "yellow-backed" or "blue-backed" novels, of which more than three thousand titles were published from 1775 until the end of the Edo period, could sell up to ten thousand copies each. Plots mixed drama, sex, fantasy, romance, and humor and were spiced with as much irreverence toward the powers that be as was tolerated by the authoritarian Tokugawa regime. As for the technique, kibyôshi interwove text and images, whereas at that time, Western illustrated books placed the text either beside or under the pictures. Some of the books also featured the first text "balloons" on a few pages. Furthermore, as early as the eighteenth century, the mass production for a popular audience of illustrated books featuring drawing on almost every page and often more drawing than text was nowhere to be found to the same degree in the West at that time.

The "floating world" (*ukiyo*) of the pleasure quarters furnished plenty of raw material to Kabuki, illustrated popular novels, and woodblock prints. For courtesans and their customers, the masters of ukiyo-e produced *shunga* ("spring images"), whose unbridled pornography attest that Japanese culture was much less inhibited than Western culture was as far as the multiple avatars of sexuality were concerned. Scatology, bestiality, and sadism were part of the game. This open-minded attitude toward sex is rooted in the Shintô culture (Bornoff 1992; Lesoualc'h 1968). Contemporary manga also takes the subject of sexuality without taboo, whereas the Western comics industry seems to ignore that sexuality is a major concern for teenagers — and grown-ups as well. Shunga also had a pedagogical function, which manga perpetuates through series like Aki Katsu's *Futari H* — translated in France and elsewhere as *Step Up Love Story* — probably the most enjoyable sexuality "textbook" presently on the world market.

As seen through the eyes of a historian rather than a theoretician of the art of comics, the debate about "the origins of manga" seems rather futile. Rather than use sophisticated conceptual tools in order to either prove or deny filiation between the *Chô-jûgiga* and *GTO* or between the Bayeux Tapestry and *Asterix*, suffice to say that multiple links can be found that relate the contemporary manga to past forms of graphic narration and art: recurrent themes rooted in Japan's cultural background, borrowed techniques, and — above all — a more continuous and richer tradition of graphic narration than in the West.

Manga also owes much to the second encounter of Japan with the West. Years after the warships of U.S. commodore Matthew Perry forcibly entered Uraga Bay in 1853 and forced the Tokugawa to reopen the archipelago to foreigners, during the Meiji era (1868–1912) the rich tradition of Japanese graphic narration was to meet the Western one, and this encounter gave birth to what has been named — for the first time — *manga*.

THE ENCOUNTER WITH THE WEST AND THE BIRTH OF (WHAT WAS NOT QUITE YET) MANGA

The West introduced the technology — offset and lithography printing — that permitted the transformation of the graphic narration into a new type of low-cost mass media, and some Westerners provided the model for such a new media. In that respect, Briton Charles Wirgman and Frenchman Georges Bigot are often mentioned (Schodt 1983, 38). By launching illustrated magazines for Western expatriates — *Japan Punch* (1862) and *Tôbaé* (1887) — they introduced in Japan the Western-style satirical drawing, which soon came to be named *ponchi-e* or *tôba-e*. Two different kinds of Japanese illustrated magazines soon developed. On the one hand, *nishiki-e shimbun* (colored woodblock-print news sheets) rejuvenated the Edo period's kibyôshi genre in the form of tabloidlike magazines filled with illustrated stories of gruesome murders and vengeful ghosts; the most famous was the Tokyo-based *Nichinichi Shinbun*. On the other hand, satirical magazines in the vein of *Punch*, with strong political overtones, directed jibes at the authorities and establishment, and were harassed by censorship like the *Marumaru Chimbun*,[7] founded in 1877 by Nomura Fumio (1836–1998), a reformist expelled from the civil service who became a founding member of the progressive Kaishintô Party in 1882. These magazines — both the political and the popular ones — employed illustrators who came from the ukiyo-e industry and used brushes and black ink for drawing.

In the middle of the 1890s, American newspapers started weekly supplements featuring cartoons using balloons and frames, which soon came to be copied in Japan. The archipelago was experiencing a period of political change, rapid industrialization and social turmoil. The whole country braced itself to modernize. Democratic-minded reformists confronted the authoritarian conservative mainstream as the first national election was held in 1889, followed by years of tumultuous confrontation between the reformist parties, which had a majority in the lower house of the Diet, and the imperial government. In 1897, the *Marumaru Chimbun* published a series suggesting that the newspaper's political cartoons had been influential in the victory of the presidential candidate William McKinley in the U.S. election the preceding year. In 1900, the leading reformist Fukuzawa Yukichi (1835–1901) added to his newspaper *Jiji Shinpô* a weekly supplement titled *Jiji Manga*.

It was the first appearance of the word *manga* in the title of a publication. Reformists deemed both tôba-e and ponchi-e inappropriate terms for naming the new illustrated medium, because of ancientness or foreign origin. A lively debate ensued, lasting until the beginning of the Taisho period (1912–1923), with the reformists pushing *manga* as replacement (Asian Manga Summit 2002, 13). Although ukiyo-e master Hokusai Katsushika (1760–1849) is commonly credited for inventing this term in 1814, the world had been in use since the end of the eighteenth century.[8] *Manga* means "sketches made for fun or out of a sudden inspiration," and is often translated as "derisory pictures"; however, the connotation of "free" was probably as important as "derisory" for the journalists of the *Jiji Shimpô*, exposed to censorship as they were.

It was in the *Jiji Manga* that the first weekly comic strips appeared. Illustrator Kitazawa Rakuten (a pen name for Kitazawa Yasuji, 1876–1955) created *Tagosaku to Mokube no Tokyo kenbutsu* (Tagosaku and Mokube Sightseeing in Tokyo), a six-frame series about two country bumpkins who discover the modern world, running water, and gas lamps. Three years later, Kitazawa launched the full-color satirical monthly *Tokyo Puck* (1905–15), where many *mangaka* (manga artists) earned their spurs. Perhaps the first star mangaka, Kitazawa was awarded the Légion d'Honneur by the French government. He is the first mangaka to whom a museum — the Saitama City Manga Museum — has been dedicated.

During the Taisho era (1912–26), manga was already recognized as a genre worthy of learned criticism and academic analysis, as shown by the publication in 1924 of Hosokibara Seiki's *Nihon manga-shi*, the first history of the genre (Asian Manga Summit 2002, 13). Besides the daily newspapers, sophisticated cultural and news magazines like *Asahi Gurafu* (1923–2000) published manga side by side with pictures, illustrations, and reporting. As the labor movement and political Left strengthened in the wake of rapid industrialization, manga was still used as a tool for political expression by Kitazawa, Okamoto Ippei (1886–1948); the star mangaka of the famous daily *Asahi*, and the members of the League of Proletarian Mangaka (*Nihon Mangaka Renmei*) who drew *nômin manga* (people's manga) and *rôdô manga* (workers' manga). At the same time, manga developed as mass entertainment. Magazines for youngsters — sometimes of two hundred pages or more — published literary texts, reporting, and manga series, the most popular of which were published afterward in paperback book form. Unlike France and the United States, where BD and comics were mostly the domain of small or middle-sized specialized publishers, the large mainstream Japanese publishing powerhouses entered the manga business from the beginning. The largest one, Kodansha, launched the manga magazine for teenage boys, *Shônen Kurabu*, in 1914, and then *Shôjo Kurabu* (1923) for teenage girls and *Yônen Kurabu* for younger children (1926).

In effect, mainstream Japanese publishers turned manga into a mass industry. In 1931, according to Schodt (1983, 51, 49), Kodansha printed as many as 950,000 copies of *Yônen Kurabu*; it also reissued more than 100 paperback versions of *Dango Kushisuke man'yuki* (The Travels of Dango Kushisuke), a samurai series by Miyao Shigeo, between 1924 and 1934. After World War II this industry support would become key to the profitability and worldwide expansion of manga and manga by-products. Successful manga series soon morphed into movies and radio serials — for example, the Japanese remake of George McManus's *Bringing Up Father* — and numerous marketing items were made from popular characters like the black dog Norakuro, the hero of the eponymous series drawn by Tagawa Suihô.

Japanese mangaka largely drew their inspiration from American comics and cartoons, and the graphics were overwhelmingly Disneylike. However, mangaka developed original themes and characters that were to reappear and prosper in postwar manga: young samurais endowed with supernatural powers (*Dango Kushisuke man'yuki*), children battling international conspiracies (*Supîdî Tarô* [Speedy Tarô], by Sakô Shishido 1930) or traveling through outer space (*Kasei tanken* [Voyage to Mars], by Ôshiro Noboru and Asahi Tarô 1940). The overarching themes of these manga somewhat reflected Japan's efforts, as a newcomer not quite accepted by the Western powers, to locate itself within the international world order at that time. Another specific Japanese genre that flourished in the rather liberal context of the Taisho era is the *ero-guro-nansensu*. This "erotic-grotesque nonsense" was a distant heir of absurd zenga painting, shunga, and the ghosts-and-blood Kabuki tradition melded to Western imports such as surrealism, fantasy literature (à la Edgar Allan Poe) and German sexology books like Richard von Krafft-Ebing's *Psychopathia Sexualis* (1886). In the 1920s, no fewer than ten journals focused upon "perverse" sexuality (McLelland 2006), and the public interest in the genre was further aroused by the famous Abe Sada "murder plus penis-cutting" case in 1936.[9]

After the assassination of Prime Minister Hamaguchi Ôsachi (1930) and the invasion of Manchuria (1931) came a militarist regime, renewed censorship, and fifteen years of war. Manga was enlisted in the war effort. In *Shônen Kurabu*, Norakuro the dog, a not-so-exemplary soldier when he debuted in 1931, now bravely routed the Chinese (depicted as cowardly pigs), and spawned imitations like the faithful dog Hachikô.[10] Between 1933 and 1939, the young hero of *Bôken Dankichi* (Dankichi the Adventurer), a series by Shimada Keizô in *Shônen Kurabu*, won the hearts and minds of the natives of a Pacific Island, converted them to Shintô, and taught them how to battle victoriously the white foreigners who tried to subjugate them. The various mangakas' associations were fused together into an official one whose monthly publication *Manga* was the only one to continue during the war despite the scarcity of paper (Schodt 1983, 55–56).

In summary, prewar Japan appropriated the imported art of comics and melded it with its own culture's diversified tradition of graphic narration. This marriage enlisted the new phenomenon of manga as both a media for political and social debate and a mass market for teenage entertainment organized by mainstream publishers. However, prewar Japanese comics were still a far cry from the art that was to become known worldwide as manga and that now floods the global market for imaginary universes. For such a transformation to happen, it took the conjunction of the enduring national trauma suffered by the Japanese collective consciousness as a result of its defeat in the war, seven years of U.S. occupation of Japan, and an increasingly sophisticated marketing effort by the publishing industry.

THE LEGACY OF WAR AND DEFEAT

What the world now knows as manga — and the Japanese know as *kindai manga* (modern manga) — first appeared in April 1947, with the publication of *Shin takarajima* (The New Treasure Island), by Tezuka Osamu (1921–89), which reportedly sold 400,000 copies in a few months.[11] Nicknamed "the God of Manga," Tezuka was subsequently credited with the chief innovations that have made contemporary manga what it is — notably, graphic techniques in imitation of cinema and "story manga" with long, complex plot lines.

Many of the first generation of mangaka, Tezuka included, had been teenagers during the war. Too young to fight, they were nevertheless mature enough to feel the trauma of defeat very deeply. This trauma brought manga four elements that gave it a complexity and dramatic intensity unlike anything found in American and Franco-Belgian comics. The first was an underlying scenario involving adult failure, the destruction of the world, and the survival of a group of young people bound together by friendship and optimism, which recurs in countless series into the twenty-first century. The second was the *mecha* genre, in which combat robots piloted by teenagers save Japan (or the world) from attack by another race — a clear illustration of the frustration felt by sons who dreamed of winning a war lost by their fathers. The third was the *kagaku bôken* (scientific adventure) genre, reflecting the almost sacred status accorded to science in the immediate postwar period by the Japanese, whom it had brought to its knees. The fourth was the fruit of the enforcement of new ideals imported by U.S. occupation (freedom, democracy) upon a nation whose traditional values had failed but not disappeared. This uneasy juxtaposition resulted in a combination of regrets, protest, and a passion for progress, which inspired the mangaka — as well as writers like Tanizaki Junichirô and Mishima Yukio — to offer far more complex lessons in life than those available to American and French comics readers, as well as a more dramatic tone. Such complexity lies at the heart of Tezuka's famous *Tetsuwan Atomu* (translated either as *Mighty Atom* or *Astroboy*) series, started in 1951 and arguably the best-selling and best-known manga in history;[12] although *Tetsuwan Atomu* is intended for children under age twelve, many people die brutal deaths as the young robot-hero battles for tolerance, democracy, the peaceful use of science, and against racism — while offering a rather bleak picture of the United States to its young Japanese audience. Not every artistic genre has the "luck" to rise out of the fires of the atomic bomb and the painful birth of a new society.

In the postwar period manga took two main forms. On the one hand were the series for children, published by major Tokyo publishers in monthly magazines, whose very short episodes still displayed an unmistakable Disney-like style. On the other were the cheap "red books" (*akabon*) from small publishers largely located in the Osaka area. Intended mostly for adult readers,[13] these books were primarily distributed by rental libraries — there were as many as 5,000 of them in the early 1960s — but were also sold in general stores and peddled aboard trains and boats (Nagano 2004, II-2). The akabon dealt with social dramas and the most inadmissible and shameful human passions, including incest and necrophilia, in the tradition of the illustrated popular novels of Edo. In tune with the spirit of the times, happy endings were exceptional, the graphic style was dark and the tone "hard" (*dogitsui*). In 1957 the term *gekiga* (dramatic images) was coined for this genre.

Also worth mentioning is the *kamishibai* ("paper theater"), a street performance in which a storyteller entertained the audience using a set of illustrated boards to accompany the narration. In the second half of the 1940s, up to 10,000 storytellers earned their living in that way, and some future stars of the manga world — including the *jidai mono* (historical manga) master Shirato Sampei and the horror master Mizuki Shigeru, whose famous character Gegege no Kitarô was first created for the paper theater — started their career by drawing boards for kamishibai.

Manga succeeded because of its combination of gekiga and series for children. Manga matured alongside a baby boom audience who thus developed a lifelong dedication to the format. As boomers near retirement today, they continue to patronize the manga of their youth and wait the advent of "silver manga" to brighten up their senior years.

FROM SCHOOLBOY SERIES TO A NATION OF MANGA READERS: 1959–90

In 1959, the first baby boomers reached age twelve and moved to high school — an age at which Japanese parents felt that children should stop reading manga. Publishers successfully challenged this expectation by launching the first weekly magazines — *Shônen Magazine* (Kodansha) and *Shônen Sunday* (Shogakukan), and Japanese teenagers now had enough pocket money to buy their own magazines and defy parental wishes. The slackening parental control opened the door to series whose young heroes' escapades aroused the (vain) fury of teachers against "vulgar manga" (*geihin na manga*; Nagano 2004, I-5). In this same period, prosperity and television led readers of gekiga away from the rental libraries, most of which thus folded.

When the baby boomers entered university their passage to adulthood proved tempestuous. The student movement that began in 1968 was long-lasting and brutal, and manga mirrored its readership's rebellious spirit. The major magazines hired comics artists from the gekiga, supplanting those who had cut their teeth on schoolchildren's series, with the notable exception of Tezuka, who successfully developed dramatic and historical series and some that dealt with sex. These iconoclasts broke taboo after taboo. For example, Nagai Gô, creator of Grendizer,[14] who, from 1968 to 1972, had enormous success with his "indecent school" (*Harenchi gakuen*). In Nagai's high school the main occupation of the boys and teachers — when they aren't boozing, defecating in the corridors, or exposing themselves — is lifting the skirts of the girls, some of whom seldom complain. The series, included by major publisher Shueisha in its flagship weekly *Shônen Jump*, ignored protests from outraged parents and teachers' associations until Nagai finished it with an attack on the school mounted by the parents that culminated in a general massacre. The rebelling students also loved series like *Hikarukaze* (1970), by Yamagami Tatsuhiko, which denounces a possible comeback of the militarism, and *Ashita no Jô*, by Chiba Tetsuya, the story of a reformatory school escapee who breaks free from the oppression of society to become a world boxing champion.

Around the same time, manga was consolidating its readership of grown-up girls, whom the American and French comics industry had never managed to engage. At the very beginning of the 1970s, *shôjo manga* (girls' manga), largely the provenance of male cartoonists, was taken over by the *Hana 24-nen gumi*, a generation of women comic artists in their early twenties. They invented a completely new aesthetics for the genre, offered a feminine vision of love and sex and dealt with problems such as pregnancy and rape. In macho Japanese society, teenage girls were unable to figure themselves out in a love relationship with a boy on an equal footing. To dissipate the anxiety of their readers and permit them to identify with the characters, the female cartoonists used tricks that remain today a distinctive trademark of manga: the transvestite heroine — like Oscar in the famous *Berusaru no bara* by Ikeda Riyoko — and the so-called *shônen-ai* genre of love stories among pretty, effeminate young boys (*bishônen*), whose best first examples are *Juichigatsu no gimunajiumu* (A High School in November; 1971) and *Tôma no Shinzô* (The Heart of Thomas; 1974) by Hagio Moto, and Takemiya Keiko's *Kaze to ki no uta* (The Songs of Trees and Winds; 1976).

Having successfully accompanied the baby boomers, both male and female, through their coming of age, the manga industry further pursued the market segmentation by age group. It created *seinen manga* (young men's manga), which combines love and sex with social problems of contemporary relevance. The period around 1975, when the baby boomers were settling down, saw the arrival of "salaryman manga" and "office ladies' manga," featuring plots set in the business world. The most famous character of salaryman manga — the young *buchô* (section chief) Shima Kôsaku, born in 1983 and working in a commercial company in Hirokane Kenshi's *Kachô Shima Kôsaku* series — had a career parallel to that of its most successful readers and was still doing well in 2007 as *senmu* (vice president or senior executive director). As for women, since the "office ladies" married and became thirty-something mothers and housewives in the early 1980s, their manga offered series of an often risqué nature building upon the shôjo-ai genre of their shôjo time.

These were not the only manga genres, and publishers continued to increase the variety of genre manga, including series dealing with sports or martial arts, a proliferation of science fiction manga and mecha, historical series (*jidai mono*), hard-boiled and detective stories, manga dealing with social problems (*shakai manga*), fantasy, horror, gag manga, *gurume manga* (gourmet manga; series on cooking), and series about any conceivable hobbies (from mah-jong to fishing, golf, and pachinko),[15] not to mention a large output of pornography to suit every possible taste.

MASS MEDIA, MASS INDUSTRY, AND OFFICIAL RECOGNITION

The start of manga's profitable association with television came in 1963 with the launch of the series based on Tezuka's *Tetsuwan Atomu* and sponsored by major chocolate makers Meiji. Since then, in association with a broad range of sponsors that soon encompassed much more than toys and the food-and-drink industry, publishers have continued to develop the art of the media mix, with weekly comics, the reissue of successful series in paperback volumes, TV and OVA series,[16] animated films, live action films, music (from TV shows and movies) and musicals, advertising featuring popular characters, and merchandising products by the thousands. Since the 1990s, the mix also includes video games, short stories or novels, and even fashion magazines like *Nana*, which takes as its title the name of the principal characters from Yazawa Aï's very successful manga series of the same name. This multiplicity of media has enabled manga to create imaginary worlds that are rich enough to offer a refuge to many young people feeling alienated from society. The culture of the so-called *otaku* developed among the post–baby boom generation[17] — a culture that, discouraged from protest by the failure of its elders in 1968, has instead opted for mild escape from society. In the 1980s, the high level of affluence attained in Japanese society permitted the otaku to pursue this way of life, and in the 1990s the advent of Internet technology enabled them to build communities via the World Wide Web.

The combination of maturation strategy, market segmentation, and media mix has turned manga into a mass industry with no equivalent in the world. In 1967, manga magazines numbered less than 50 and sold about 78 million copies; at their height in 1994, they numbered 260 and sold 1,890 million copies, plus around 700 million softcover books, for a sales figure of about ¥520 billion (Nagano, 2003).[18] Although the volume of production has diminished by more than 33% since 1995 — down to 1,260 millions in 2006 [JETRO, 2008] — due to combination of demographics, economic crisis, and social and cultural changes — the Japanese manga industry still produces 10 copies of magazines and books per year for every Japanese, as opposed to fewer than 40 million copies for French comics and 110 million for American comics (one for three Americans). More than 100 million copies of some manga series have been sold and, at its height in 1995, *Shônen Jump*, the top-selling weekly for teenagers, had a circulation of 6 million and was read by about 20 percent of the population (Stumpf, 2003).

An important change in the social status and impact of manga occurred in 1986, when the major business daily *Nihon Keizai* commissioned mangaka Ishinomori Shotarô to create *Manga Nihon Keizai nyûmon* (Japan Inc: Introduction to Japanese Economy). In 1989 Chûô Kôron, flagship publisher of the Japanese intelligentsia, commissioned Shotarô and a team of fifty academics to create a history of Japan (*Manga Nihon no rekishi*) approved by the Ministry of Education for use in the schools. Since then manga has become a fully-fledged communication medium used by authorities, business, politicians, and even the European Community delegation in Tokyo. During the 1990s, some series touching political or social subjects — among them *Black Jack ni yoroshiku* (Say Hello to Black Jack) by Satô Syuho, *Zipang* by Kawaguchi Kaiji and the whole work of the provocative revisionist cartoonist Kobayashi Yoshinori — sparked national, and even international, debates.

Manga owes its influence to its ability to keep pace with new developments in society and attitudes, as illustrated by three changes in the genres inherited from the defeat and nuclear traumas: the post-apocalyptic, the *mecha* and the so-called "scientific adventure". From the 1970s to the end of the twentieth century, the original postapocalyptic scenario moved from the unshakable optimism of Nakazawa's *Hadashi no Gen* (1972) to complete uncertainty about the future in Ôtomo Katsuhiro's *Akira* (1984–93). From Grendizer (1975) to *Neon Genesis Evangelion* (1994), mecha's simplistic clashes between big machines gave way to an exploration of the existentialist worries of their young controllers, including girls, who now have leading roles — just as they do in *Akira*. Since the 1990s the bright scientific future of which Tezuka once dreamed has turned dark, with gods and/or nature cruelly punishing humankind for polluting the earth (Hokazono Masaya's *Inugami*; 1996–2002), deviant genetic manipulations (Sôryo Fuyumi's *Eternal Sabbath*; 2001–4) and deadly viruses manufactured by evil organizations (Urasawa Naoki's *20th Century Boys*; 1999–2006), while the passion for tolerance has sometimes been replaced by strident neonationalism in the work of successful authors like Kobayashi Yoshinori.

Now, near the end of the first decade of the twenty-first century, Japan has become the world's second largest exporter of cultural products. The media mixes that manga is a part of are among the "content industries" that have officially become a pillar of the restructured Japanese economy since the crisis of the 1990s. They generate ever-expanding sales figures: since its debut in 1996, *Pokemon* has earned more than US$152 billion, and the total exports of "J-Pop" goods reached 1,500 trillion yen in 2002 alone (Sugiura 2003). The otaku generation, whose rejection of a society felt to be too constraining has been embraced by most Japanese during the 1990s, have found their place within the nation. Tezuka has been elevated to the rank of national treasure, and manga is taught in many universities.

Yet, since the middle of the 1990s, the manga industry has been having some problems. The circulation of magazines — but not the sales of tankôbon — steadily declines because of a shrinking base of new readers resulting from a declining birth rate, the competition from video games in the young cohort of readers, and the difficulty of retaining the interest of aging baby boomers. Because of this phenomenon, some experts prophesize "the death of the magazines" and their replacement by digital manga diffused on mobile phones and computers. However, manga remains a crucial component of popular culture in present-day Japan, and there is no doubt that the mammoth publishers that turned Japanese comics into a mass product with worldwide appeal will be able to adapt to the new trends of the market.

Notes

1. In this chapter, Japanese peoples' names are presented in the traditional Japanese way — that is, surname first.
2. *Toiretto Hakase* is a series by Torii Kazuo, started in 1970; its main character is a "philosopher" whose preferred topic for meditation is human excrement (Schodt 1993, 122).
3. Most noticeable in France is the work of Tardi, especially *Rumeurs sur le Rouergue* and the *Adèle Blanc Sec* series.
4. *Yaoi* is short for *yama nashi ochi nashi imi nashi* (no climax, no plot, no sense), but today's fans use it mostly to refer to love stories between boys.
5. Hergé is the pen name of Georges Remi (1907–83), author of the *Tintin* series.
6. *Marumaru Chimbun*'s name alludes to the "circles" (*maru*) that the censors used to mark the part to be deleted.
7. Suzuki Kankei, in *Mankaku zuihitsu* (1771); Santô Kyôden, a *kibyôshi* writer and illustrator, in *Shiji no yukikai* (1798); and Aikawa Minwa, in *Manga hyaku onna* (1814), all predated Hokusai, according to Wikipedia (http://fr.wikipedia.org/wiki/Manga).
8. Sada Abe (1905–87) erotically asphyxiated her lover Ishida Kichizo, then cut off his genitals and carried them around in her handbag until she was arrested two days later. This case became a national sensation and was given mythic overtones in many subsequent books and movies.
9. *Chûken Hachikô* (The Faithful Dog Hachikô), by Ôshiro Noboru and others (see Akiyama 1998).
10. This commonly found assertion can be doubted, especially if one considers the rarity — and ensuing exorbitant price — of the surviving copies.
11. See the "Manga les plus célèbres (Most Cited Manga) section at Manga Network (France), http://www.ceri-sciences-po.org/themes/manga/index.php.
12. However, Tezuka's *Shin takarajima* and many of his earlier works for children appeared in this form because Tezuka lived near Osaka.
13. The character is also known as Goldorak (in France) or Goldrake (in Italy). During the 1970s this character was hugely successful in Europe as an TV animated series.

At the beginning of the 1990s, those who had watched these series as children became the first generation of Western manga fans.
14. For a nearly complete review of the genres, see Schodt 1983.
15. OVA (original animation video) are series made to be released on home video formats, and not intended for showing on TV or theaters.
16. *Otaku* ("your home," meaning "you") is the most possibly neutral way — devoid of hierarchical connotation — of addressing other people. It started to be used mainly among hardcore sci-fi animation fans around the mid-1970s.
17. This was equivalent to about $US5.5 billion at that time.

References

Akiyama Masami, ed. (1998). *Maboroshi no sensô manga no sekai* [The illusory world of war manga]. Tokyo: Natsume shobô.

Asian Manga Summit, Japan Executive Committee (2002). *A Guide to Books on Japanese Manga*. Tokyo: AMSJEC

Cohn, Neil (2007). "Japanese Visual Language: The Structure of Manga." Unpublished manuscript.

Groensteen, Thierry (1991). *L'univers des mangas* [The universe of mangas]. Tournai, Belgium: Casterman.

Itasaki Gen (1975). *Chôninbunka no kaika* [The blossoming of townspeople's culture] Tokyo, Kodansha International.

JETRO (Japan external Trade Organization) (2008), A Research for Information and Media Society, Tokyo, Diamond sha.

Koyama-Richard, Brigitte (2007). *1000 ans de manga* [1000 years of manga]. Paris: Flammarion.

Krafft-Ebing, Richard von (1886). *Psychopathia Sexualis*. Stuttgart: Ferdinand Enke. Reprinted by Arcade Publishing, New York, 1999.

Kure Tomofusa (1997). *Gendai manga no zentazô* [A global vision of contemporary manga], Tokyo, Futabasha.

Lehmann, Jean-Pierre (1982). *The Roots of Modern Japan*. New York: St. Martin's Press.

McCloud, Scott (1993). *Understanding Comics*. London: Harper Perennial.

McLelland, Mark (2006). "A Short History of 'Hentai.'" *Intersections: Gender, History and Culture in the Asian Context* 12, http://intersections.anu.edu.au/ issue12/mclelland. html.

Nagano Haruyuki (2004). *Manga sangyô ron* [The theory of manga industry], Tokyo, Shikuma shobô.

Natsume Fusanosuke (2003). *Manga wa naze omoshiroi no ka?* [Why is manga interesting?], Tokyo, NHK Library.

Pons, Philippe (1988). *D'Edo à Tokyo: Mémoires et Modernités* (From Edo to Tokyo: Memories and Modernities). Paris: Gallimard.

"Sada Abe" (n.d.). Wikipedia, http://en.wikipedia.org/wiki/Sada_Abe.

Schodt, Frederik L. (1983). *Manga! Manga! The World of Japanese Comics*.Tokyo: Kodansha International.

Seidensticker, Edward (1983). *High City, Low City: how the shogun's ancient capital became a great modern city, 1867–1923*, New York: Alfred A. Knopf.

Stumpf, Sophie (2003). *Le Potentiel de la BD Française au Japon*, Paris: RJC Marketing Research.

Sugiura Tsutomu (2003). "Hi wa mata noboru: Pokemon kokokuron." *Bungei Shunju*, October, 186–93.

Yokoi Kiyoshi (1975). *Chûseiminshu no seikaku bunka* [Life in the Middle Ages], Tokyo, Tokyo daigaku shuppankai.

Suggested Manga Reading

Aki Katsu (1977–). *Futari H*, published in *Young Animal*. Tokyo: Hakusensha.

Chiba Tetsuya (1968–73). *Ashita no Jô*, published in *Shûkan Shônen Magazine*. Tokyo: Kodansha International.

Hagio Moto (1971). *Juichigatsu no gimunajiumu*, published in *Bessatsu Shôjo Comic*. Tokyo: Shogakukan.

—— (1974). *Tôma no Shinzô*, published in *Shôjo Comics*. Tokyo: Shogakukan.

Hirokane Kenshi (1983–92). *Kachô Shima Kôsaku*, published in *Morning*. Tokyo: Kodansha International.

Hokazono Masaya (1996–2002). *Inugami*, published in *Gekkan Afternoon*. Tokyo: Kodansha International.

Ikeda Riyoko (1972–73). *Berusaiyu no bara*, published in *Shûkan Marguerite*. Tokyo: Shûeisha.

Ishinomori Shotarô (1986–88). *Manga Nihon keizai nyûmon*, 4 vols. Tokyo: Nihon keizai shinbun sha.

Ishinomori, Shotarô (1989–93). *Manga Nihon no rekishi*. 48 vols. Tokyo: Chuô kôron sha.

Kawaguchi Kaiji (2000–). *Zipang*, published in *Morning*. Tokyo: Kodansha International.

Kitazawa Rakuten [Yasuji] (1902). *Tagosaku to Mokube no Tôkyô kenbutsu*, published in *Jiji Shimpo*.

Miyao Shigeo (1922). *Dango Kushisuke man'yuki*, published in *Tôkyô Maiyu Shinbun*.

Mizuki Shigeru (1992). *NonNonBa*. Tokyo: Kodansha International.

Nagai Gô (1968–72). *Harenchi gakuen*, published in *Shûkan shônen Jump*. Tokyo, Shûeisha 1968–72.

Nakazawa Keiji (1973–85). *Hadashi no Gen*, published in *Shûkan Shônen Jump* (Shûeisha, 1973–74), *Shimin* (1975–76), Bunka Hyôro (Shin Nihon shuppan sha, 1977–80) and *Kyoiku hyôron* (1982–85).

Okano Reiko (1993–2005). *Onmyôji*, published in *Comic Burger* (Gentô sha) and *Gekkan Melody* (Hakusen sha).

Ôshiro Noboru and Asahi Tarô (1940). *Kasei tanken*. Tokyo: Nakamura shoten.

Ôshiro Noboru, *Chûken Hachikô*.

Ôtomo Katsuhiro (1984–93). *Akira*, published in *Young Magazine*. Tokyo: Kodansha International.

Sadamoto Yoshiyuki (1995–). *Neon Genesis Evangelion*, published in *Gekkan Shônen Ace*. Tokyo: Kadokawa shôten.

Satô Syuho (2002–6). *Black Jack ni yoroshiku*, published in *Morning*. Tokyo: Kodansha International.

Sawai, Toshio, *Bobobo-Bo Bo-Bobo*, published in *Shûkan Shônen Jump*, Tôkyô, Shûeisha, 2001–7.

Shimada Keizô (1933–39). *Bôken Dankichi*, published in *Shônen Kurabu*. Tokyo: Kodansha International.

Sôryo Fuyumi (2001–4). *Eternal Sabbath*, published in *Morning*. Tokyo: Kodansha International.

Tagawa Suihô (1931–41). *Norakuro*, published in *Shônen Kurabu*. Tokyo: Kodansha International.

Takemiya Keiko (1976, 1982–84). *Kaze to ki no uta*, published in *Shûkan Shôjo Comic* (1976) and in *Petit Flower* (1982–84). Tokyo: Shogakukan.

Torii Kazuo (1970–77). *Toiretto hakase*, published in *Shûkan Shônen Jump*. Tokyo: Shûeisha.

Tezuka Osamu (1947). *Shin takarajima*. Osaka, Ikuei shupan, 1947.

—— (1952–68). *Tetsuwan Atomu*, published in *Shônen*. Tokyo: Kobunsha.

Toriyama Akira (1984–95). *Dragon Ball*, published in *Shûkan Shônen Jump*. Tokyo: Shûeisha.

Ueda Hajime (2000). *FuliCuli,* published in *Gekkan Magazine Z.* Tokyo: Kodansha International.

Urasawa Naoki (1999–2006). *20th Century Boys,* published in *Shûkan Big Comic Spirits.* Tokyo: Shogakukan.

Yamagami Tatsuhiko (1970). *Hikarukaze,* published in *Shônen Magazine.* Tokyo: Kodansha International.

—— (1974–81). *Gakideka,* published in *Shûkan Shônen Champion.* Tokyo: Akita shoten.

Yazawa Aï (1999–). *Nana,* published in *Cookie.* Tokyo: Shûeisha.

2
An Overview of Manga Genres

Mio Bryce and Jason Davis

Any attempt at providing an overview of the variety of genres in manga, even limiting the scope to just commercially available English translations, runs the risk of appearing selective in its coverage, and our effort is no exception. The genre headings used in this chapter are by no means a comprehensive listing of the staggering array that is published in any year in Japan or republished as translations elsewhere. The listings used here reflect both the filtering of manga through the availability of English translations as well as the accretion of attention that particular genres have garnered through English-language scholarship. In a more direct sense, then, the overview provided here seeks to foreground the *depth* of genre hybridity — how elements or characteristics particular to one genre are often recombined with others as creative reworkings that drive readership appeal as well as plot and character development. Moreover, we have also included examples of *mangaka*, or manga artists who have worked in different genres. There is, of course, the overarching imperative to map manga cursorily introduced here against the readership categories that now inform Western popular media accounts of the phenomenal publishing success of translated works as well as coverage of the online communities consuming and circulating manga in electronic formats, such as "scanlations." The headings used in this chapter therefore seek to mention a series within a genre that are *shōjo* or *shōnen* in their orientation — that is, targeting female or male teenagers as their core readership. There are also *josei* subgenres targeting young adult women as well as *seinen* works that strongly appeal to young adult males. Other genres were selected for their ability to showcase the variety in use of layout and publishing formats. Where possible we have indicated the year when an individual series commenced and ended publication in Japan in manga magazines, and as a quick pointer to how devoted the following of a series can become by virtue of its longevity, we have indicated such a series as ongoing via the use of an open-ended dash: –. To indicate the availability of English translations of a manga series, the italicized English title has been used and a second date has been provided, while manga titles that are not translated have been indicated with an asterisk (*).

FANTASY, THE MYTHOLOGICAL, AND THE SURREALISM OF THE EVERYDAY

The salient feature characterizing fantasy and legend manga are the rich milieus they (re-)create through adaptations of mythological, folkloric, and literary sources. Chinese legends and settings are recurring textual sources, such as the ancient Chinese literary legend of the Buddhist pilgrimage *Saiyūki* (Journey to the West), also known as *The Adventures of the Monkey God*. Character-based retellings of this legend, such as Katsuya Terada's *The Monkey King* (1995–/2005–), Kazuya Minekura's *Saiyūki* (1997–2002/2004–5) series and Akira Toriyama's immensely popular quest series *Dragon Ball* (1984–95/1998–2004) are as diverse in their interpretations as the visual techniques used to illustrate them. Ancient Greek myths have also been the basis for a single manga series such as Yoshikazu Yasuhiko's *Arion* (1979–85*), while individual Greek gods such as Athena and Deimos appear in contemporary settings, as in Koge-Tonbo's *Kamichama Karin* (2002–5/2005–7) and Etsuko Ikeda and Yūho Ashibe's *Bride of Deimos* (1975–83/2002–4). Norse deities also feature as central characters, as in Sakura Kinoshita's *The Mythical Detective Loki Ragnorak* (2002–5/2004–5) and Kōsuke Fujishima's *Oh My Goddess!* (1988–/1994–), the latter having the Norse goddess Belldandy living with a techno-geek student. Wakako Mizuki's *Itihāsa* (1986–97*) envisions an ancient Japan inhabited by a pantheon of deities locked in a cosmological struggle over good and evil, with humans in between. The fantasy genre also evidences the envelopment of the reader in worlds of strikingly imaginative originality. Hiroshi Masumura's *Atagooru Tamatebako* (1984–94*) depicts an alternative fairy-tale reality whose denizens are cats sharing a language with humans, a linguistic feature Masumura enhanced by creating his own dialect for the characters to speak.

Fantasy manga can also combine elements of quest-based adventure with magical or mythical sources, with very strong shōjo or shōnen and seinen orientations. The shōjo manga by the group of authors known as CLAMP epitomize such genre hybridity, with series, such as *RG Veda* (1989–96/2005–6), which draws on Hindu mythology; *Cardcaptor Sakura* (1996–2000/1999–2003), a retelling of the Sleeping Beauty fairy tale; and the sword-and-sorcery kingdom of *Magic Knight Rayearth* (1993–96/1999–2001). Similarly, Yū Watase's *Ceres: Celestial Legend* (1996–2000/2001–6) and Reiko Shimizu's *Kaguya-hime* (1994–2005) offer richly detailed portrayals of contemporary Japan combined with folkloric narratives involving celestial maidens. Japanese fairy tales, or *dōwa*, have also been adapted for shōjo manga, as in CLAMP's 1992 treatment of the Snow Goddess (*Shirahime-Syo: Snow Goddess Tales*, 1992/2004), while Junko Mizuno gives European fairy tales Gothic and creepily cute reworkings for the twenty-first century (Junko Mizuno's *Cinderalla* [*sic*], 2000/2002; *Hansel and Gretel*, 2000/2003; and *Princess Mermaid*, 2002/2004). Shōjo series featuring girls or women gifted with magical abilities who undergo personae transformation as central characters are now a genre by themselves ("magical girls' manga," or *mahō shōjo* manga), and they include Naoko Takeuchi's *Sailor Moon* (1992–97/1997–2001), Arina Tanemura's *Full Moon O Sagashite* (2002–4/2005–6), and Chiho Saitō and Be-Papas's *Revolutionary Girl Utena* (1996–98/2000–2004). Shōnen and seinen examples include Kazushi Hagiwara's hypermasculine heroic fantasy *BASTARD!!* (1988–/2001–), which created a standard-setting sensation among fantasy fans in the late 1980s with anime-like character designs and detailed fantasy-settings; Eiichirō Oda's immensely popular gag-filled, pirate-based *One Piece* (1997–/2002–), Makoto Inoue's *Fullmetal Alchemist* (2002–/2005–), set in an alternate early twentieth century where alchemy is widely practiced; Kentarō Miura's darkly violent medieval-based *Berserk* (1989–/2003–), and Masashi Kishimoto's feudalistic ninja adventure fantasy *Naruto* (1999–/2002–).

Juxtaposing, even colliding, the mundane against the improbable, surrealistic manga works suspend storytelling conventions for unsettling arrangements, or outright derangement, of the reader's expectations through affective or psychological states, images, and visual styles. The mangaka most prominently identified as exemplars of this visual approach include Yoshiharu Tsuge, Usamaru Furuya, and Yūko Tsuno. Tsuge garnered a cult following with *Neji-shiki* (Screw Style) (1967/2003) a twenty-three-page exercise in disquietude that guides the reader through eerily detailed settings, tracking a lone and nameless wanderer (Gravett 2004, 132, 138). Furuya's manga, such as his ground-breaking *Palepoli* (1996*), expands on this visual mixing of techniques within a work as well as across a range of titles by aiming at the immersion of readers in the darkly humorous and arrestment of their attention with the jarringly bizarre. *Palepoli* draws on the four-panel tradition of manga and incorporates a range of visual references from Western art influences and manga styles and genres (Lehmann 2005, 67–69). While more subdued in her story-based arrangements of the mundane with the dreamlike, Yūko Tsuno's manga, such as *Runpunyaku* (Powdered Fish Scale Medicine*; 2000) recasts some of the key motifs characteristic of the shōjo genre by subtly interleaving the reality world of her characters with their dreams as well as places and people from their memories (Lehmann 2005, 206–11).

HISTORICAL REPRESENTATIONS

Manga's capacity for graphic (re-)creation of traditional visual styles and the adaptation and retelling of traditional sources underscores how it is a medium not only for extending, but also engaging with, the historical imaginary central to contemporary Japanese identity. History in manga can include period settings as backgrounds to story lines, such as the Edo period *Sakuran* (2001–3*), created by the female mangaka Moyoco Anno, which follows the life of a courtesan in a red light district; the samurai dramas *Lone Wolf and Cub* (1970–76/2000–2002) written by Kazuo Koike and cocreated with artist Goseki Kojima; Sanpei Shirato's *The Legend of Kamui* (1965–71*), and Hiroshi Hirata's bushido drama *Satsuma Gishiden* (1977–83/2006–7). Renowned for their frenzied depiction of the dueling movements of sword fights, rendered with flowing ink-brush strokes, and the unfolding portrayal of human drama, feudal-period manga epitomizes the *gekiga* style of realism emblematic of the visual storytelling challenge that gekiga artists presented to manga consumers in the 1950s and '60s. Feudal-era Japan has also been the setting for more recently published fantasy-based manga, such as the demon-plagued world of Rumiko Takahashi's popular *Inu Yasha* (1996–/1997–), while the 1878 setting of Nobuhiro Watsuki's *Rurōuni Kenshin* (1994–99/2003–6) combines steam-powered locomotives with samurai weapons and dojos with business suits. European historical settings also figure prominently in manga, especially series based on historical figures, such as Riyoko Ikeda's *Eikou no Napoleon — Eroika* (The Glorious Napoleon*; 1986–95) and Jirō Taniguchi and Sekigawa's *Botchan no Jidai* (In the Time of Botchan*; 1987–96), based on the life of the Japanese intellectual and writer Natsume Sōseki. Even a European country can be the subject of historical treatment, as in Riyoko Ikeda's *Ten no Hate Made: Poland Hishi* (To the End of the Sky, the Secret History of Poland*; 1999). Historical representations in manga can also be so steeped in historical detail that they visually convey period-specific information to their readers. Captivating examples of this approach are Yōko Iwasaki's *Ōto ayakashi kitan* (1990–2002*) and Reiko Okano's *Onmyō-ji* (1994–2004*), a re-creation of the life of Abe no Seimei, a Heian period (tenth century) imperial astrologer. First published in 1993, Okano's work, based on the novel of the same name by Baku Yumemakura, exquisitely expresses meticulous attention to period specific-detail, such as costumes and rituals through tones and layers of visual patterns (Lehmann 2004, 142–50). Manga is also widely used as an educational aid as part of the learning of Japanese history, as in the case of Shōtarō Ishinomori's forty-eight-volume work *Manga Nihon no rekishi* (The Manga History of Japan*; 1989–93), which was endorsed by the Japanese Ministry of Education and Culture (Kinsella 2000, 73).

In the four decades since the first historical gekiga manga were published, the visual documentation of historical pasts in manga have been stylistically developed and refined by some of the most prominent manga artists working today. In the 1970s and '80s Kazuichi Hanawa expanded on the offerings of samurai drama with Edo, Meiji and Heian period stories that demonstrate attention to traditions and historical events as well as folkloric elements of the strange. Takehiko Inoue, the mangaka responsible for the immensely popular *Slam Dunk* series, has created *Vagabond* (1998–/2001–), a manga adaptation of Eiji Yoshikawa's *Musashi*, a biographical account of the seventeenth-century warrior Miyamoto Musashi. Tatsuya Egawa, the mangaka who created the popular school dramas *Be Free!* and *Tokyo Daigaku Monogatari* (Tokyo University Story) has also produced history-based manga, such as *Nichirosensō Monogatari* (The Russo-Japanese War Story*; 2001–) and fictional works with historical settings, such as *Genji Monogatari* (The Tale of Genji*; 2001–). Taken together these works evidence an extraordinary range of visual styles — from highly expressive use of form to denote speed to visual immersion of the reader in subjective points of view, as well as exacting attention to historical authenticity, even including calligraphic rendering of archaic Japanese — that are used to communicate the visual dimensions shaping or mediating Japanese experience and understanding of the historical.

HORROR AND THE SUPERNATURAL

Manga exploring horror and supernatural themes are perhaps the postwar genres most readily evidencing intertextual traces of elements from different forms of Japanese storytelling, including folkloric and literary sources, religious traditions, the paranormal and urban myths as well as influences from other visual media such as magazines, film, and fashion. Folkloric and paranormal influences can range from characters and settings that are incarnations of the phantom world of *yōkai*, or spirit-monster legends, to depictions of the reach of paranormal entities into the everyday world of humans (Foster 2008). The most famous character-based incarnations of yōkai are those inhabiting the pages of Shigeru Mizuki's 1959 creation *Ge Ge Ge no Kitarō* (Kitaro the Spooky) (1959–69/2002) which follows the titular boy hero, an outcast and the last of a family line of yōkai, and his continual intervention in conflicts between the communities of ghost-goblins and humans. More recent incorporations of yōkai influences include CLAMP's highly stylistic *xxxHolic* (2003–/2004–), which follows the fated efforts of a high school student to escape the spirits haunting him, and Akihisa Ikeda's series *Rosario + Vampire* (2004–7, 2007–) which is set in a school for yōkai who are disguised as humans. Christian iconography and a range of Gothic influences from Western literary works and filmic imagery are also visual elements that are drawn on for setting and character design, as in CLAMP's apocalyptic saga *X/1999* (1992–2003/1996–2005), Gō Nagai's *Devilman* (1972–73/2002–3) and *Devilman Lady* (1997–2000*); Kōta Hirano's *Hellsing* (1998–/2003–) series and Bisco Hatori's shōjo manga *Millennium Snow* (2001–2/2007).

Young characters possessing psychic abilities or supernatural powers causing the death of others are also recurring story lines. Examples include Katsu Aki's *Psychic Academy* (1999–2003/2004–6), a series about a school-age boy undergoing self-discovery through development of his psychic powers; Tite Kubo's monster-fighting *Bleach* (2001–/2004–), a supernatural mixture of occult spiritualism and samurai sword prowess involving a teenager who can see ghosts; *Zombie-Loan* (2003–*), a series created by the mangaka duo known as Peach Pit, which depicts the ability of a young girl to psychically "see" those who will soon die; Tsugami Ohba and Takeshi Obata's *Death Note* (2004–6/2005–7), which involves the ability of a notebook to induce the death of whoever has his name written in it; and *Alive: The Final Evolution* (2003–/2007–), Tadashi Kawashima and Toka Adachi's unraveling of the relationship between a high school boy and mass suicides throughout the world.

The genre also displays the sliding of horror toward the darkly psychological and the surrealistic. Junji Itō's *Uzumaki: Spiral into Horror* (1998–99/2001–2) depicts the inhabitants of a small Japanese town and their obsessive behavior toward — and eventual bodily infestation with — spirals. Hitoshi Iwaaki's *Parasyte* (1990–95/2007–) transforms the faces and limbs of parasite-infected humans into rapaciously murderous nonhuman creatures. Shōu Tajima and Eiji Otsuka's series *MPD-Psycho* (1997–2006/2007–) unfolds its story line through a number of disjointed narratives to capture the multiple personalities of an exceptional criminal profiler of serial killers.

For horror manga works that are singularly nightmarish invocations of cruel and gruesome compositions of sadism and violence, the creations of Hideshi Hino and Suehiro Maruo remain unsurpassed. With works such as *Hatsuka nezumi* (White Mouse*; 1995), *Hell Baby* (1986), *Panorama of Hell* (1989), and the *Hino Horror* volumes that were published in English in 2004, Hino has created a grotesquery populated with adults, children, deformed babies, and animals transmogrified into bloody, mutilated corpses or nonhuman creatures, their faces rendered with his signature abstraction of their isolating disfigurement — bulging, lidless, vacantly staring eyes atop an agape mouth. Contrasting stylistically with Hino's manga, Suehiro Maruo's works, such as *Yume Q-Saku* (Q-Saku Dream*; 1982), *Mr. Arashi's Amazing Freak Show* (1992), *Ultra-Gash Inferno* (2001) and *Maruo jigoku* (Maruohell*; 1995) merge the erotic with the grotesque into friezelike studies of perversion and violence that are horrific showcases of detailed draftsmanship. As strongly visual works that draw associations to as well as direct references from a range of visual sources — medieval picture scrolls depicting horror, death, and bodily disintegration, atrocity *ukiyo-e* or Japanese woodblock prints, Japanese and German visual culture of the 1920s and '30s (Berndt 2006; Hand 2004; Maruo 2007; Pandey 2000, 2001; Stephanides 2005, 28) — the manga of Hino and Maruo exemplify how horror manga is continuous with a number of visual traditions as well as popular visual culture.

HUMOR

Appearing in Japanese newspapers as well as manga magazines and anthologies, humor in manga encompasses an astonishing range of styles or expressions such as satire, gaglike punch lines, surrealistic absurdities, parody, comedy, caricature, and outright nonsense. The subject matter of humorous manga can extend from the very sophisticated, such as Kentarō Takekuma and Kōji Aihara's *Even a Monkey Can Draw Manga* (1989–1990/2002), a biting, satirical examination of mass-market trends and themes in the manga industry, to situation-based white collar work-place humor exemplified by Kotobuki Shiriagari's *Hige no OL Sasako Yabuuchi* (Sasako Yabuuchi, the Moustached Office Lady*; 1996–2000); Risu Akizuki's *Survival in the Office: The Evolution of Japanese Working Women* (1989–/1999–2000); and Yoshikazu Ebisu's *Sarariiman* (Salaryman*) series, described as "black-humour survival guides to working in the neurotic hierarchy of Japanese company organizations" (Schodt 2002, 149). There are also gag-related revelings in body humor for boys, such as Kazuo Umezu's "perpetually snot-nosed urchin" *Makoto-chan* (1976–81*; Thompson 2007, 54), Akira Toriyama's *Dr. Slump* (1980–85/2005–8), Kazuyoshi Torii's *Toiretto Hakase* (Professor Toilet*; 1970–77), and Shinbo Nomura's *Babū Akachin* (1994*). Humor in manga can also be wordless and bereft of humans, as in Masashi Tanaka's *Gon* (1991–2002/2007–), a series depicting the escalating trouble a little dinosaur becomes ensnared in as a result of his own harmless actions. Moreover, humor is also invested with the capacity to reflect the world-defining experiences of a particular age group, such as Minoru Furuya's shōnen-oriented depiction of the "closed-off world of young teenagers" (Amano 2004, 444) in his gag manga *Ike! Ina-chū Takkyūbu* (Go! Ina-chu Middle School Ping-Pong Club*; 1993–96). Humor is also used for reaching across age groups by virtue of reader identification and nostalgic appeal, as with the gentle humor of Momoko Sakura's *Chibi Maruko-chan* (1986–96*) series, which draws on Sakura's own childhood experiences of the 1970s and is enjoyed by children and adults alike.

Another distinctive characteristic of the genre is the range of publication formats. Humorous manga ranges from one-frame and four-frame gag manga to short episodes and ongoing story-based manga magazine serializations and as *tankōbon* volumes (Japanese comic books that comprise a collection of manga episodes that have previously appeared in magazines). Given the different formats for manga publishing, there is surprisingly no prescription for a particular type of humor being more inherently suited to one format over another. Nor is one format more of a preserve for social reflection on, or insightful indicators of, contemporary Japanese society. Kiyohiko Azuma's popular *Azumanga Daioh* (1999–2002/2003–4) began as a four-frame gag manga that focuses on the highly subjective experiences characterizing the everyday lives of a group of Japanese high school girls, while Ken Akamatsu's shōnen-oriented series *Love Hina* (1998–2002/2002–3), a love/comedy about a luckless twenty-year-old man and his humiliating existence living in a women's dormitory inhabited mostly by teenagers unresponsive to his urges, provides its male readers with a vicarious haremlike existence that is a telling reflection of the social scripts shaping gender identity. Similarly, Yoshito Usui's *Crayon Shin-chan* (1990–/2002–4), a gag strip focusing on the young Shin-chan and his troublemaking, sometimes vulgar, disruptions of his 1990s nuclear family, invests the humorous escapades of the title character with "an uncanny penchant for exposing the foibles and pretensions of his vain and materialistic parents and other adults" (Lee 2000, 200). The internationally popular children's manga series *Doraemon* (1970–96/2002–5), which follows the adventures of Doraemon, a blue, earless robot cat from the future and his human friend Nobita Nobi, has for decades provided its young fans with gently humored reading experiences combined with optimistic reassurance. Created in 1970 by Fujio Fujiko (a mangaka pen name for the duo of Hiroshi Fujimoto and Motoo Abiko), the series is imbued with optimistic attitudes toward technology (Shiraishi, 1997), but the continual guardianship and wish fulfillment it also provides is deeply reflective of the psychological needs of children (Bryce 2004; Shilling 1993; Schodt 1996, 219).

POLITICS AND REPRESENTATIONS OF THE POLITICAL

As a medium that aims for both entertainment and education, manga can depict political events, both national and international, in startlingly different ways. This includes adopting current events in the world as international settings or backdrops to character-driven story lines, as does Takao Saito's

Golgo 13 (1969–/2006–8), which follows the international assignments of a contract killer. There are also political thrillers with contemporary backdrops, such as *Sanctuary* (1990–95/1993–98), written by Shō Fumimura and drawn by Ryōichi Ikegami, which dramatically intertwines character development with the machinations underpinning the worlds of Japanese organized crime and the parliamentary system of the National Diet. Aspects of the Japanese political imaginary are also dramatically personified, such as the deeply symbolic investment in American-style presidential authority of a Japanese-born political hero-figure. Kaji Kawaguchi's *Eagle: The Making of An Asian-American President* (1997–2001/2000–2002) and *The First President of Japan* (1998–99/2002–3), written by Ryūji Tsugihara and drawn by Yoshiki Hidaka, are two political fantasies that are in a sense working through the historical legacy of the United States and its relationship to Japanese identity. *Eagle* follows the 2000 political campaign of the Japanese-American senator Kenneth Yamaoka for the U.S. presidency, and so invokes interracial as well as historical issues for Japanese and Japanese Americans relating to U.S. citizenship as well as providing insights into U.S. political primaries. *The First President of Japan*, the story of the first Japanese prime minister to possess U.S. presidential-style executive powers that are tested by the international climate of escalating tensions between nations, adopts and invokes the very form of political power and constitutional authority that the United States denied postwar Japan.

The realities of Japan's political culture and international relations are also the subject of manga treatments, becoming popular vehicles for disseminating popular discourses for public attention. In terms of reflecting on Japanese politics, political gag manga provides forms of popular commentary, while Yoshinori Kobayashi's *Gōmanizumu sengen* (The Declaration of Arrogance*), which began serialization in 1991, exemplifies the essayistic possibilities of manga for fervent social and political critiques and anti-establishment views. Other examples include works exploring Stalinist North Korea, such as *Introduction to Kim Jong Il: The Truth about the North Korean General** and *The Shogun's Nightmare**, both of which reached combined sales of over 700,000 copies in 2004 (Voice of America 2004). In the same year, *Manga Akushon* (Manga Action) magazine published *Megumi*, a nine-part series based on the abduction of Megumi Yokota, a thirteen-year-old girl kidnapped by North Korean agents in 1977. Social protest against the Japanese government's refusal to formally acknowledge and redress the Imperial Army's sexual enslavement of thousands of women and girls during World War II has also appeared in manga form, as in Jae-Cheol Park's *Even If I Have to Do It on My Own* (1992), which is based on Song Shiin-Do's account of her forced sexual enslavement by the Japanese military (Berndt 1997, 180–85). The Japanese government has resorted to accompanying the release of its policy papers with manga adaptations, such as the Defense Ministry's 2005 white paper explaining the geostrategic role of the Japanese Self Defense Forces as part of the international contingent supporting the U.S.-led invasion and occupation of Iraq. Similarly, the Japanese Defense Agency has adopted the manga-inspired characters Prince Prickles and Miss Parsley as mascots for the Self Defense Agency's public relations promotion and image management of the Japanese military (Frühstück 2007, 128–37). Manga is also a means for fomenting conservative and nationalistic beliefs, as in the case of Kobayashi's *Sensō ron* (The War Revisited*; 1998) and *Taiwan ron* (The Taiwan Question*; 2000) as well as racist and xenophobic attitudes, as in the case of George Akiyama and Huang Wen-hsiung's *Chūgoku Nyūmon: Yakkai-na rinjin no kenyu* (Introduction to China: A Difficult Neighbor*; 2005), and Sharin Yamano's *Kenkanryū* (Hating "the Korean Boom"*; 2005). Such works not only bolster nationalistic calls for the historical revision of Japan's war past as a brutal colonial aggressor and ruler, but also openly promote anti-Chinese and anti-South Korean sentiments (Marukawa, 2003; Marukawa and Bhowmik 2004; Miller, 2004; Sasada 2006, 118–19). Although representing a somewhat selective snapshot of the Japanese political imaginary manifesting in a medium competing with and reacting to other media sources, the above examples do evidence the scope of the contribution of manga to Japan's political culture.

RELIGION AND SPIRITUALITY

The representation of religion and spirituality in manga in Japan has for over fifty years been a rich visual source for thematic expression of religious and spiritual belief systems and practices. The most immediate association of manga with religion is the adoption of the medium for proselytizing religious teachings and doctrines, an approach to manga every religious and spiritual organization or sect in Japan has undertaken (MacWilliams 2000, 113; 2002, 177; Tesshū 2003, 173; Thompson 2007, 247–49). A spectacular contrast to this conventional approach can be found in Osamu Tezuka's *Buddha* (1972–83/2002–5). First serialized in 1972, *Buddha* is Tezuka's highly unique interpretation of the story of Prince Siddartha that eschews both a direct retelling of Buddha's life and transcription of Buddhist doctrine. Creating strong visual resonances of the iconographic, such as the devotional imagery of Buddha, Tezuka infuses the ancient setting for the series with contemporary references, action sequences, visual humor and linguistic puns, meditations on the divine inspiration of the natural world, and additional historical actors for greater drama and momentum for character development. Moreover, Tezuka invests the episodic, meditative layers of *Buddha*'s storytelling with a capacity for moralistic and psychological reflections on the existential dilemmas of human life, such as suffering, death, and loss (MacWilliams 2000).

Although no mangaka has since approached the epic scale of Tezuka's religious storytelling, the representation of religions in fictional manga continues to assume a variety of different forms (Thompson 2007, 247–49). Treatments of Christianity range from *Jesus* (1997/2000), Yoshikazu Yasuhiko's portrayal of the biblical life of the savior, to the use of Catholic and occult ritual and imagery in *Cross* (1997–2001/2004–6), Sumiko Amakawa's series about a young Catholic priest dedicated to performing exorcisms. The historical establishment of Buddhism in Japan forms the background for Ryōko Yamagishi's series *Hi Izuru tokoro no Tenshi* (Heaven's Child in the Land of the Rising Sun*; 1980–84), an exquisite adaptation of the life story of Prince Shōtoku (574–622), regent and politician of the imperial court. Portrayed as sexually ambiguous and imbued with folkloric psychic powers, the manga recounts Shōtoku's promotion of Buddhism in Japan. Reiko Okano's shōjo-oriented *Fancy Dance* (1984–90), authentically re-creates the monastic commitments of Tokyo teenagers as Zen monks dedicating themselves to the ritual-laden world of a Soto-sect Zen temple (Lehmann 2005, 140–41).

In *Hi no Tori*, or *The Phoenix* (2003–7) Tezuka targets contemporary Japanese understandings of spiritual identity. First published in 1954, with storytelling installments continuing until Tezuka's death in 1989, *The Phoenix* is an epic work. Described as "a mix of speculative fiction, sci-fi phantasmagoria and historical re-imagining" (Brophy 2006, 129), *The Phoenix*'s storytelling alternates the time period for each of its successive episodes, with the story line oscillating between the distant past and the distant future. What threads this time leaping is the recurring appearance of a mythical, immortal phoenix, which not only induces in the characters ruinous quests for immortality but also serves as a motif for the spiritual questioning and critical thinking Tezuka urges his readers to undertake. This questioning includes acceptance of mythical transcendence of science over religion, the historical legacy of the religiosity of the imperial system as foundational myths of Japanese national identity, and the exclusion of the everyday from the realm of religious experience and spiritual affirmation (MacWilliams 2002).

SCIENCE FICTION IN MANGA

As a genre mostly associated — and even regarded by U.S. audiences as visually synonymous with — Japanese animation, manga works of science fiction encompass a greater variety of iconographic embodiments of the genre: the nonhuman, the otherworldly, and the technological promises of the future(s) to come. The postwar publishing phenomenon of Osamu Tezuka's *Tetsuwan Atomu* (Mighty Atom, or Astro Boy; 1952–68, 2002–

4) expanded on the popular appeal of science fiction as a form of visual storytelling. Translating the national scale of postwar reconstruction and sociotechnological changes facing Japan by focusing on the interaction of humans with nonhuman characters (Kashiwagi 2006, 47–56; Schodt 2007, 98–118) — in this case, an atomic-powered robot boy with immense powers — Tezuka's *Mighty Atom* series prefigured other fantasy robot creations, humanoid fighting warrior machines that dwarf their human pilots, such as Mitsuteru Yokoyama's *Tesujin 28 gō* (Iron Man No. 28*; 1956–66) and Gō Nagai's *Mazinger Z* (1972–73*). In 2003, the influence of the *Mighty Atom* series returned in Naoki Urasawa's *Pluto* series, with the humanistic themes Tezuka explored in his portrayal of robots' cohabitation with humans philosophically expanded to encompass the global scale of the reach and consequences of human's social and psychological investment in robots.

Where science fiction manga of the 1950s and 1960s depicted the interfacings of human with machine as augmenting human powers from without, the science fiction manga of the 1980s and '90s can be typified by bio-technological fusions from within. Katsuhiro Ōtomo's groundbreaking *Akira* (1982–90/2000–2002) series dramatizes the fate of a twenty-first century Tokyo by intertwining the lives and actions of disparate characters from competing social groups — the military, religious cults, biker gangs, and revolutionaries — culminating in the psychic transmogrification of an adolescent male into a mutating biomass of rage. Yoshiki Takaya's series *Bio-Booster Armor Guyver* (1985–/1992–97) depicts the biotechnological fusion of humans with corporate-owned armor of alien origin. Cyborg characters commingle with robots in the futuristic corporate worlds of Yukito Kishiro's *Gunnm* (Gun Dream) (1990–95), released in the United States as *Battle Angel Alita* (1992–98), and Masamune Shirow's *Appleseed* (1985–89/1993–95). Shirow extended the futuristic social worlds and corporate technoscapes cyborgs inhabit to include the cyberpunk domain of cyberspace with his famous *Ghost in the Shell* (1989–91/1995) series. Featuring heavily modified humanoid female creations or "gynoids" as the central characters, *Battle Angel Alita* and *Ghost in the Shell* represented a genre shift in character identification for male readers (Orbaugh 2003, 225–27). One of the more recent manga incarnations of gynoid characters competing for shōnen readership is Yū Aida's *Gunslinger Girl* (2002–/2003–5), which depicts technologically enhanced preadolescent girls psychologically controlled to perform acts of murder for their adult male handlers (Bryce, Barber, & Davis, 2008; Barber, Bryce & Davis 2010).

Storytelling in science fiction manga also evidences the influence of a range of mythical, literary, and folkloric sources, both Japanese and European. In the epic manga series *Nausicaä of the Valley of Wind* (1982–94/1988–2004) Hayao Miyazaki's postapocalyptic exploration of ecological themes focuses on the shōjo character of Nausicaä as a youthful intermediary between the war-driven human societies and the insect-dominated natural world; a role drawing on both the mythical Nausicaä from *The Odyssey* as well as the insect loving Mushi-mezuru Princess from the twelfth century Japanese tale *Tsutsumi-chūnagon Monogatari*. Similarly, premodern intertextual associations can be found in the hi-tech world of the *Chobits* (2000–2/2002–3) series by the mangaka group CLAMP. Although *Chobits* serves more "to reassert a pattern of heterosexual bonding grounded in love, nature and monogamy" through its naturalisation of gender roles (Stephens and Bryce 2004, 44), its depiction of male self-discovery through deep, transformative romantic love with an artificial female or gynoid mass produced for companionship resonates with Japanese folkloric traditions of heavenly, nonhuman brides and their male human husbands (Davis and Bryce 2007). More speculative and challenging treatments of sexuality and gender identity as well as racial identity can be found in Moto Hagio's *Maajinaru* (Marginal*) and Tatsuya Egawa's *Yapoo, the Human Cattle*. First appearing in 1985, Hagio's series reexamines the social meanings of maternity in a futuristic male-only society (Ebihara 2002), while Egawa's *Yapoo, the Human Cattle*, an adaptation first published in volume form in 2003, of Shōzō Numa's infamous novel of the same name (Lehmann 2005, 60; Tatsumi 2006, 54–59), is a disturbingly perverse projection of racial self-hatred through colonialist and imperialist fantasies that envision the masochistic transmogrification of Japanese people into biologically engineered furniture and sexual appliances for white people.

SHŌJO AND JOSEI ROMANCE AND (HOMO/HETERO) SEXUALITIES IN MANGA

To include within a single grouping consideration of a number of genres of manga whose targeted readerships can safely be generalized as demographically different, even mutually exclusive, may appear to be a counterintuitive way to highlight their respective characteristics. Yet such an approach serves to foreground how the categorizations of shōjo and josei encompass very different representations of the psychological, emotional and sexual dimensions layering the experiences of human relationships and gender identity. The interpersonal dynamics of being in a relationship as well as the pursuit of romantic love are portrayed not just from the point of view of female characters, but can also adopt a male viewpoint, as in Moyoco Anno's *Flowers & Bees* (2000–2003/2005). And while young women's dreams of married life with a perfect partner repeatedly drive female reader identification with romantic manga narratives and characters, exploring how a young woman falls in love with her husband *after* their marriage is a theme Mariko Iwadate develops by following her female character through an arranged marriage in *Angel* (1982*). Romance can also involve a "third party," as in Shinobu Nishimura's *Third Girl* (1984–93*), a series depicting a love triangle involving two university students and a junior high school student. Wataru Yoshizumi's *Marmalade Boy* (1992–95/2002–3) and Mitsuba Takanashi's *The Devil Does Exist* (1998–2002/2005–7) painfully demonstrate how parental relationships can also drastically complicate their children's romantic attachments, as these series depict two young lovers and their emotional dissolution at becoming half-sister and half-brother to each other. In Miki Aihara's *Hot Gimmick* (2000–2005/2003–6) the heroine's protection of her sister's pregnancy exposes her to blackmail-induced sexual abuse and victimisation. Romantic relationships are also explored in a range of social, cultural and institutional settings such as workplaces, high schools, sports clubs, universities, as well as different historical period settings. In terms of storytelling in romantic manga the social strictures of an historical period are used to intensify the complicated nature of relationships thereby heightening readers' identification with the situations. Osamu Tezuka's *Princess Knight* (1963–66/2001) and Riyoko Ikeda's *The Rose of Versailles* (1972–73/1981) build on this by portraying gender inversions of female characters through cross-dressing as a way of maintaining the patriarchal lineage of hereditary entitlements (Ogi 2001; Shamoon 2007).

Yet, there is another aspect to Ikeda's *The Rose of Versailles* that relates very strongly to how shōjo manga has expanded on the genre possibilities for depicting sexuality, namely the peculiar linking of sexual agency with, albeit ostensibly, same-sex partners which is a strong feature of shōjo. The significance of this motif relates to how shōjo manga mediates sexual identification for female Japanese readers. Male same-sex love stories, such as *shōnen'ai* manga, which depict romantic relationships between beautiful male youths (*bishōnen*) as androgynous or feminine partners, are created by women mangaka, and are extremely popular themes for teenage and young adult female readers (Thompson 2007, 413–17). As a genre depicting mutually engaging relationships between men that range from platonic expressions, to love affairs as well as sexual relationships, female readers' strong attraction to shōnen'ai has been linked to the lack of representations of heterosexual women's sexual agency in Japanese popular culture as well as the social pressures against Japanese women's experience of sexuality outside of the family (McLelland 2000a, 14–15; Orbaugh 2003, 211; Ogi 2001, 151–53). Examples of this storytelling style include Moto Hagio's *Thoma no Shinzō* (The Heart of Thomas*; 1974), Keiko Takemiya's *Kaze to Ki no Uta* (The song of the wind and the trees*; 1976–84), Ryōko Yamagishi's series *Hi Izuru tokoro no Tenshi* (Heaven's Child in the Land of the Rising Sun*; 1980–84), Wakuni Akisato's *TOMOI* (1987*), and Marimo Ragawa's *New York, New York* (1996–98*).

A further development of this formula has been the creation of forms of sexual manga referred to as *YAOI*, an acronym comprising the first letters of the Japanese words *yama nashi, ochinashi*, and *imi nashi* (no climax, no point, and no meaning). YAOI denotes boy-love stories involving male-male situations and encounters given over to sexual content at the expense of plot or character development (Cha 2005; McLelland, 2000b, 277).

As the predominant representation of homosexuality in Japanese visual culture, female created shōnen'ai and *YAOI* are at the same time marginal categories within the diverse expressions of sexuality and sexual agency in manga. The predominance of heterosexual male erotica or *ero-manga* covers the spectrum of male-oriented depictions representing the heterosexual imaginary, such as large breasts, rape fantasies, bondage and SM, sexual acts, violence and degradation involving human and nonhuman partners or attackers, such as aliens or monsters, perversities and fetishes, "Lolita Complex" erotica or *roricon*, as well as pornographic gag humor (Shigematsu 1999; Thompson 2007, 447–552). And while the range of sexual fantasies contrasts sharply with the content of sexual manga created for women, to simply affirm these works as male creations solely targeting heterosexual male desires is to elide over not only that women mangaka produce sexual manga for male audiences, but aspects of that sexual imaginary are also the object of women's ero-manga, such as SM and rape fantasies. Featuring in ladies manga, the visual pornography of rape fantasies overlaps aesthetically with shōjo manga, but it is distinctly different from shōnen'ai in that male bodies are generally an absent presence from inclusion in the sexual acts (Shamoon 2004, 83–86).

SPORT, HOBBIES AND COMPETITIVE GAMES IN MANGA

The number of manga devoted to portraying sports, martial arts and competitive games and the social worlds of their players are so extensive that an alphabetic list of the sports depicted is the best way to give immediate sense of the scope of titles on offer. The sports and games covered include: American football (*Eyeshield 21*), athletics (*Suzuka*), baseball (*Kyojin no hoshi* [Star of the Giants], *Boys of Summer, Touch, Kattobase Kiyohara-kun*), basketball (*Slam Dunk!, Dear Boys, Buzzer Beater, Harlem Beat*), billiards (*Break Shot*), boxing (*Ashita no Jō* [Tomorrow's Joe], *Surō Suteppu* [Slow Step], *Ringu ni kakero* [Put it all in the Ring], *One-Pound Gospel*), cycling (*ŌbāDoraivu* [Overdrive]), fishing (*Bass Master Ranmaru*), go (*Hikaru no Go*), golf (*Dan Doh!!, Ashita Tenki ni Nāre* [A Great Super Shot Boy]), judo (*Yawara!*), ice-skating (*Sugar Princess*), mah-jong (*Naki no Ryu*), martial arts (*Baki the Grappler, Tough*), ping pong (*Pītsū Rettsu Purei Pinpon* [P2!-Let's Play Ping Pong!]), rhythmic gymnastics (*Hikari no densetsu* [Legend of Light]), shōgi (*Sangatsu no Raion* [March Comes in Like a Lion]), soccer (*Captain Tsubasa, Whistle!*), street racing (*Initial D*), sumō wrestling (*Rikito Densetsu*), swimming (*Rafu* [Rough]), tennis (*Ace o Nerae!* [Aim for the Ace!], *The Prince of Tennis*), volleyball (*Sain wa V* [The Sign is V], *Crimson Hero*), wrestling (*Ultimate Muscle: The Kinnikuman Legacy, Tigermask*), and wheelchair basketball (*Riaru* [Real]). The above list covers over forty years of sports-based manga, a genre which by virtue of its sheer popularity has contributed to not only the introduction of some sports to Japanese audiences, but also maintained enough fervent interest in others to motivate young people to take up sports and develop their sporting abilities. For example, seeking to tap into national fervor following the gold medal success of Japan's women's volleyball team at the 1964 Tokyo Olympics, both the manga and *anime* versions of Mochizuki Akira and Jonbo Shirō's *Sain wa V* (The Sign is V*) and Chikako Urano's *Atakku nanbā wan* (Attack no. 1*; 1968–70) also served to stoke young women's interest in the sport in the late 1960s (Ōtomo 2007, p.122; Ito 2005, 470). Takehiko Inoue's *Slam Dunk* (1990–96/2002–4) series was singularly responsible for popularizing basketball in Japan in the 1990s (Lehmann 2005, 82), and Yōichi Takahashi's *Captain Tsubasa* (1981–88*) has been recognized by a number of soccer players in Japan's 2002 World Cup as an inspirational influence on them (Gravett 2004, p.54). The reasons for the immense popularity of this genre stem from the range of themes and values threaded through the story lines which readers, both male and female, strongly identify with, such as friendship, perseverance, sporting prowess, romance, teamwork, sportsmanship, personal bests, faithfulness, endurance, overcoming obstacles and limitations as well as self-sacrifice (Thompson 2007, 346–49), and what has been identified as "'supokon-kei' (or supōtsu-konjō-kei) which can be translated as the 'will power in-sports-genre'" (Otomo 2007, 122).

The other defining characteristic of sports manga is the incredibly striking use of visual layouts and paneling used to represent the action driven aspects comprising competitive events. Frenzied speed lines, cinematic framing that aims at multiple angles of a single action as well as inclusion of different shots of spectators; all of these are in a sense *remediations* or graphic reworkings of the visual effect of movement captured through video and televisual media and their techniques, such as slow motion. Inoue's *Slam Dunk* series pioneered the development of visual techniques in sports manga, and not just at a graphic and compositional level. The reduction of narrative flow to the density of suspenseful moments of play sequenced through a series of actions within a game permitted the breaking down of a four month high school basketball season into six years of weekly installments (Lehmann 2005, 84–87).

WAR

In the 1930s and 1940s war-related themes in Japanese comics served to propagandize Japan's military ascendancy as a colonial aggressor and imperial invader of South East Asia (Okamoto 2001). In the immediate postwar years Occupation censorship ensured war-related references did not surface in Japanese cultural works, but in 1957 war as a theme in manga returned, in particular in children's manga. Depicting Japanese pilots and planes in aerial battles, these manga works were collective acts of memorialization eliding the trauma of crushing national defeat through fixation on the technology of planes and the heroic bravery and sacrifice of their Japanese pilots (Eldad 2003; Penney 2007, 38–39). In the early 1970s Leji Matsumoto's science-fictional anime series *Uchū senkan Yamoto* (Space Battleship Yamoto) resurrected the sunken World War II battleship *Yamoto*, centuries after its sinking by U.S. forces, as the last defense for humans against the radioactive assault of the Earth by aliens. The resurrection of this deeply symbolic World War II artifact and its interstellar battle against overwhelming odds, led to wider questioning of identification with a distorted return of Japan's war past in an imagined future (Mitsuru 1979; Mizuno 2007; Napier 2005). Japan's military past and historical relationship to the United States resurfaces in Kaiji Kawaguchi's techno-thriller *Chinmoku no Kantai* (Silent Service*; 1988–1996). The series involves a joint U.S.–Japan developed, technologically advanced nuclear submarine and its mutinous takeover by a young Japanese officer and defection from Japan. Renamed the *Yamoto*, the submarine and its crew become embroiled in a tension-filled international political drama, while managing to stealthily evade and destroy most of the U.S. navy (Watanabe 2001, 135; Schodt 1996, 164–68). As a military fantasy that also imparts detailed technical information about the technology of war, Kawaguchi's *Chinmoku no Kantai* continues the manga tradition established by the Pacific air war manga of the 1960s which represented war as a form of technology focused entertainment (Penney 2007, 40). War fantasy manga can also have a counterfactual basis to their presentation of historical detail, as with the works simulating alternative events and outcomes of Japan's war with the United States, such as the stories depicted in *Nichibei Taiheiyō kessen* (Japan and America's Decisive Battle for the Pacific*; Kobayashi et al. 1995), which appeared in a 1995 special issue of the manga magazine *Konbatto Komikku* (Combat Comic) (Penney 2007, 45–46; Schodt 1996, 115–19; Seaton 2007, 167–68). In *Zipang* (2000–/2002) Kaiji Kawaguchi reworks the symbolic significance of contemporary Japanese naval technology by transporting an AEGIS missile cruiser back in time to the Battle of Midway. Post–World War II wars of colonization have also been the subject of manga, although with anthropomorphic changes, as in Motofumi Kobayashi's *Apocalypse Meow* (1991–2002/2004) which re-creates the Vietnam War with Americans as rabbits and Vietnamese as cats (Thompson 2007, 218).

Antiwar themes are also strongly evident in a number of manga works. In *Sōin Gyokusai Seyo!* (The Banzai Charge*), published in 1971, Shigeru Mizuki, creator of the manga horror series *Ge Ge Ge no Kitarō*, depicts his own brutal experiences under the leadership of the Imperial Army in World War II (Rosenbaum 2008a; Schodt 1996, 180–82). Leji Matsumoto's *99shiki no dengon* (The Message of the Type 99) first published in 1988, presented readers with an encounter between young military fanatics and elderly Japanese World War II army stragglers surviving on an unknown island (Penney 2007, 41). In *Planet of the Jap* (1996) Suehiro Maruo satirically attacks Japanese appetites for military fantasies by envisioning an alternative history in which the Japanese Imperial army devastates and occupies the United States. Yet the most hauntingly shocking indictment of war is Keiji Nakazawa's *Barefoot Gen* (1972–73/2004–). First serialized in *Shōnen Jump* in 1972, *Barefoot Gen* draws on Nakazawa's own childhood experiences of surviving a weapon of mass destruction — the U.S. atomic bombing of Hiroshima and the devastating effects of radiation on the survivors (Adams 2008; Itō and Omote 2006; Sabin 2006; Ōgi 2006; Rifas 2004).

CONCLUSION: MANGA WITHOUT BORDERS

In a *USA Today* story published online in late 2007, Paul Wiseman reported that sales of manga magazines "have tumbled from a peak of 1.34 billion copies in 1995" to 745 million in 2006, with the sales decline of 4 percent to ¥481 billion in 2006, marking "the fifth straight annual drop" (Wiseman 2007). Among the striking factors explaining this market trend in Japan, such as competing digital media (cellphones, video games, and the Internet), a decline in the consumption of print media, as well as a shrinking of "the potential pool of readers" age fourteen and younger, a result of Japan's plummeting birthrates, Wiseman highlighted a growing disinterest with existing manga story lines and characters. Yet, at the same time as the waning of manga magazine sales in Japan, more and more manga are being created, produced and distributed *outside* of Japan. Korean manga (or *manhwa*) as well as Chinese now compete for attention in the Japanese and U.S. markets. And the expanding international markets of manga in non-English countries in Europe supports and raises interest in French, German and Italian manga-inspired artists (Webb 2006), while the increasing international profile of work by original English manga artists, such as Australia's Queenie Chan and Madeline Rosca, the latter a runner-up in Japan's first International Manga Award in 2007 (Agence France-Presse 2007; Ridout 2007), foregrounds the need to expand on the scope of interest in manga story lines and genres that are developing and evolving as local creations with international readerships. Of course, the diffusion of manga outside of Japan has yet to register as an influence on either Japan's domestic manga market or Japanese manga artists and writers and their efforts to recapture shrinking readerships, but these international developments add further intercultural dimensions to understanding the reworkings, even reinvention of genre conventions.

References

Adams, Jeff (2008). "The Pedagogy of the Image Text: Nakazawa, Sebald and Spiegelman Recount Social Traumas." *Discourse: Studies in the Cultural Politics of Education* 29(1): 35–49.

Agence France-Presse (2007). "Aussie Wins Manga Runner-up Prize in Japan," June 29. ABC News, http://www.abc.net.au/news/stories/2007/06/29/1966302.htm?section=world

Barber, Christie, Mio Bryce and Jason Davis (2010). "The Making of Killer Cuties." In *Anime and Philosophy*, edited by Josef Steiff and Tristan D. Tamplin, 13–25. Chicago and La Salle: Open Court.

Berndt, Caroline M. (1997). "Popular Culture as Political Protest: Writing the Reality of Sexual Slavery." *Journal of Popular Culture* 31(2): 177–87.

Berndt, Jacqueline (2006). "'Adult' Manga: Maruo Suehiro's Historically Ambiguous Comics." In *Reading Manga: Local and Global Perceptions of Japanese Comics*, edited by Jacqueline Berndt and Steffi Richter, 107–26. Leipzig, Germany: Leipziger Universitätsverlag.

Brophy, Philip (2006). "Tezuka's *Gekiga*: Behind the Mask of *Manga*." In *Tezuka: the Marvel of Manga*, edited by Philip Brophy, 123–32. Melbourne: National Gallery of Victoria.

Bryce, Mio (2004). "'School' in Japanese Children's Lives as Depicted in Manga." Paper presented at the AARE International Education Research Conference, Melbourne, November 29–December 2, 2004.

Bryce, Mio, Christie Barber, and Jason Davis (2008). "Victimised Cyborgs: The Representation of Fragmented Self in *Gunslinger Girl*." Paper presented at the conference « Colloque International: Le Manga 60 ans après . . . » Paris, March 15–16, 2008.

Cha, Kai-Ming (2005). "Yaoi Manga: What Girls Like?" *Publisher's Weekly*, March 7, 45–47.

"Comic Books on N. Korean Leader a Big Hit in Japan" (2004). *Voice of America*, March 18.

Davis, Jason and Mio Bryce (2008). "I Love You as You Are: Marriages Between Different Kinds." *The International Journal of Diversity in Organisations, Communities and Nations* 7(6): 201–9.

Ebihara, Akiko (2002). "Japan's Feminist Fabulation: Reading Marginal with Unisex Reproduction as a Key Concept." *Genders* 36, http://www.genders.org/g36/g36_ebihara.html.

Foster, Michael Dylan (2008). *Pandemonium and Parade: Japanese Monsters and the Culture of Yōkai*. Berkeley, CA: University of California Press.

Frühstück, Sabine (2007). *Uneasy Warriors: Gender, Memory, and Popular Culture in the Japanese Army*. Berkeley and Los Angeles: University of California Press.

Gravett, Paul (2004). *Manga: 60 Years of Japanese Comics*. London: Laurence King.

Hand, Richard J (2004). "Dissecting the Gash: Sexual Horror in the 1980s and the Manga of Suehiro Maruo." *M/C Journal* 7(4), http://www.media-culture.org.au/0410/05_horror.php.

Inaga, Shigemi (1999). "Miyazaki Hayao's Epic Comic Series: *Nausicaä in the Valley of the Wind*: An Attempt at Interpretation." *Japan Review*, 11: 113–28.

Ito, Kinko (2005). "A History of Manga in the Context of Japanese Culture and Society." *Journal of Popular Culture* 38(3): 456–75.

Itō Yū and Omote Tomoyuki (2006). "*Barefoot Gen* in Japan: An Attempt at Media History." In *Reading Manga: Local and Global Perceptions of Japanese Comics*, edited by Jacqueline Berndt and Steffi Richter, 21–38. Leipzig, Germany: Leipziger Universitätsverlag.

Kinsella, Sharon (2000). *Adult Manga: Culture and Power in Contemporary Japanese Society*. Honolulu: University of Hawaii Press.

Kobayashi, Motofumi, Shinji Imura, Shin Ueda, Seihou Takizawa, Kazumi Kakizaki, Takeshi Kobayashi & Satoshi Kunishiro (1995) *Nichibei Taiheiyō kessen* [Japan and America's Decisive Battle for the Pacific]. Tokyo: Nippon Shuppansha.

Lee, William (2000). "From *Sazae-san* to *Crayon Shin-chan*: Family Anime, Social Change, and Nostalgia in Japan." In *Japan Pop! Inside the World of Japanese Popular Culture*, edited by William Lee and Timothy J. Craig, 186–203. Armonk, NY: M. E. Sharpe.

Lehmann, Timothy R. (2004). *Manga: Masters of the Art*. New York: Collins Design.

MacWilliams, Mark W. (2000). "Japanese Comics and Religion: Osamu Tezuka's Story of the Buddha." In *Japan Pop! Inside the World of Japanese Popular Culture*. Edited by Wiliiam Lee and Timothy J. Craig, 109–37. Armonk, NY: M. E. Sharpe.

—— (2002). "Revisioning Japanese Religiosity: Osamu Tezuka's *Hi no Tori* (*The Phoenix*)." In *Global Goes Local: Popular Culture in Asia*, edited by Timothy. J. Craig and Richard King, 177–207. Honolulu: University of Hawaii Press.

Marukawa, Tetsushi (2003). "Situating Yoshinori Kobayashi's *Taiwan ron* (The Taiwan question) in East Asia." *Postcolonial Studies* 6(2): 239–44.

Marukawa, Tetsushi, and Davinder L. Bhowmik (2004). "On Kobayashi Yoshinori's *On Taiwan*." *Positions: East Asia Cultures Critique* 12(1): 93–112.

Maruo, Suehiro (2007). *The Art of Hino Hideshi*. San Francisco: Last Gasp.

Masanao, Amano (2004). *Manga Design*. Cologne: Taschen.

McLelland, Mark. J. (2000a). "The Love between 'Beautiful Boys' in Japanese Women's Comics." *Journal of Gender Studies* 9(1): 13–25.

—— (2000b). "No Climax, No Point, No Meaning? Japanese Women's Boy-Love Sites on the Internet." *Journal of Communication Inquiry* 24(3): 274–91.

Miller, Jeffrey (2004). "A Response to Kobayashi Yoshinori's *On Taiwan*." *International Journal of Comic Art* 6(1): 266–80.

Mizuno, Hiromi (2007). "When Pacifist Japan Fights: Historicizing Desires in Japan." In *Mechademia: Networks of Desire*, edited by Frenchy Lunning, 104–23. Minneapolis: University of Minnesota Press.

Nakar, Eldad (2003). "Memories of Pilots and Planes: World War II in Japanese Manga, 1957–1967." *Social Science Japan Journal* 6(1): 57–76.

Napier, Susan J. (2005). "World War II as Trauma, Memory and Fantasy in Japanese Animation." Japan Focus, http://www.japanfocus.org/products/details/1972.

Ogi, Fusami (2001). "Beyond Shoujo, Blending Gender: Subverting the Homogendered World in Shoujo Manga (Japanese Comics for Girls)." *International Journal of Comic Art* 3(2): 151–61.

—— (2006). "Barefoot Gen and Maus: Performing the Masculine, Reconstructing the Mother." In *Reading Manga: Local and Global Perceptions of Japanese Comics*, edited by Jacqueline Berndt and Steffi Richter, 107–26. Leipzig, Germany: Leipziger Universitätsverlag.

Okamoto, Rei (2001). "Images of the Enemy in the Wartime Manga Magazine, 1941–1945." In *Illustrating Asia: Comics, Humor Magazines, and Picture Books*, edited by John A. Lent, 204–20. Honolulu: University of Hawaii Press.

Orbaugh, Sharalyn (2003). "Busty Battlin' Babes: The Evolution of the Shōjo in 1990s Visual Culture." In *Gender and Power in the Japanese Visual Field*, edited by Joshua

S. Mostow, Norman Bryson, and Maribeth Graybill, 201–27. Honolulu: University of Hawai'i Press.

Otomo, Rio (2007). "Narratives, the Body and the 1964 Tokyo Olympics." *Asian Studies Review* 31(2): 117–32.

Pandey, Rajyashree (2000). "The Medieval in Manga." *Postcolonial Studies* 3(1): 19–34.

—— (2001). "The Pre in the Postmodern: The Horror Manga of Hino Hideshi." *Japanese Studies* 21(3): 261–74.

Penney, Matthew (2007). "'War Fantasy' and Reality — 'War as Entertainment' and Counter-Narratives in Japanese Popular Culture." *Japanese Studies* 27(1): 35–52.

Ridout, Cefn (2007). "Manga without Borders." *Australian*, March 10, 2007.

Rifas, Leonard (2004). "Globalizing Comic Books from Below: How Manga Came to America." *International Journal of Comic Art* 6(2): 138–71.

Rosenbaum, Roman (2008a). "Mizuki Shigeru's Pacific War." *International Journal of Comic Art*, 10 (2): 354–379.

Sabin, Roger (2006). "Barefoot Gen in the US and UK: Activist Comic, Graphic Novel, Manga." In *Reading Manga: Local and Global Perceptions of Japanese Comics*, edited by Jacqueline Berndt and Steffi Richter, 39–58. Leipzig, Germany: Leipziger Universitätsverlag.

Sasada, Hinori (2006). "Youth and Nationalism in Japan." *SAIS Review* 26(2): 109–22.

Seaton, Philip A. (2007). *Japan's Contested War Memories: The "Memory Rifts" in Historical Consciousness of World War II.* New York: Routledge.

Schodt, Frederik L. (1996). *Dreamland Japan: Writings on Modern Manga.* Berkeley, CA: Stone Bridge Press.

—— (2007). *The Astro Boy Essays: Osamu Tezuka, Mighty Atom, and the Manga/Anime Revolution.* Berkeley, CA: Stone Bridge Press.

Shamoon, Deborah (2004). "Office Sluts and Rebel Flowers: The Pleasures of Japanese Pornographic Comics for Women." In *Porn Studies*, edited by Linda Williams, 77–103. Durham, NC: Duke University Press.

—— (2007). "Revolutionary Romance: The *Rose of Versailles* and the Transformation of Shojo Manga." In *Mechademia: Networks of Desire*, edited by Frenchy Lunning, 3–18. Minneapolis: University of Minnesota Press.

Shigematsu, Setsu (1999). "Dimensions of Desire: Sex, Fantasy, and Fetish in Japanese Comics." In *Themes and Issues in Asian Cartooning: Cute, Cheap, Mad, and Sexy*, edited by John A. Lent, 127–64. Bowling Green, OH: Bowling Green State University Popular Press.

Shilling, Mark (2003). "*Doraemon*: Making Dreams Come True." *Japan Quarterly* 40(4): 405–17.

Shiraishi, Saya S. (1997). "Japan's Soft Power: *Doraemon* Goes Overseas." In *Network Power: Japan and Asia*, edited by Peter. J. Katzenstein and Takashi Shiraishi, 234–72. Ithaca, NY: Cornell University Press.

Stephanides, Adam (2005). "Ero-Guru: The Erotic Grotesque of Suehiro Maruo." *Comics Journal* 5: 28–33.

Stephens, John, and Mio Bryce (2004). "'Nothing Dirty about Turning on a Machine': Loving Your Mechanoid in Contemporary Manga." *Papers: Explorations into Children's Literature* 14(2): 44–54.

Thompson, Jason (2007). *Manga: The Complete Guide.* New York: Ballantine Books.

Tatsumi, Takayuki (2006). *Full Metal Apache: Transactions between Cyberpunk Japan and Avant-Pop America.* Durham, NC: Duke University Press.

Tesshū, Shaku (2003). "Signs in Comics and Symbols in Religions." *Japanese Religions* 28(2): 167–76.

Watanabe, Morio (2001). "Imagery and War in Japan: 1995." In *Perilous Memories: The Asia-Pacific War(s)*, edited by Takashi Fujitani, Geoffrey M. White. and Lisa Yoneyama, 129–51. Durham, NC: Duke University Press.

Webb, Martin (2006). "*Manga* by Any Other Name Is . . . Do Japan's World-Conquering

Cartoons Have to Be Created by Japanese to Be the Real Deal?" *Japan Times Online*, May 28, http://search.japantimes.co.jp/cgi-bin/fl20060528x1.html.

Wiseman, Paul (2007). "Manga Comics Losing Longtime Hold on Japan." *USA Today*, October 18, http://www.usatoday.com/news/world/2007-10-18manga_N.htm.

Yoshida, Mitsuru (1979). "The 'Space Cruiser Yamato' Generation." *Japan Echo*, 6(1): 80–87.

A to Z of Manga in Japanese and English Referred to in This Chapter

The following is an alphabetical list of manga titles, followed by author name(s). Titles that have not been translated in English are indicated with an asterisk, while the publication information for translated manga series also includes details relating to the original Japanese serialization of the series.

"99shiki no dengon" [The message of the type 99*]/Leiji Matsumoto (1998) in *Za kokupitto* [The cockpit], vol. 8. Shōgakukan.

Ace o Nerae! [Aim for the ace!*]/Sumika Yamamoto (1973–80), serialized in *Margaret*, Shūeisha, 18 vols.

Akira/Katsuhiro Ōtomo (2000–2002), 6 vols., Dark Horse, serialized in *Young Magazine* (1982–90), Kodansha International, 6 vols.

Akisato, Wakuni (1987) *TOMOI**, Petit Flower, Shogakukan, 1 vol.

Alive: The Final Evolution/Tadashi Kawashima and Toka Adachi (2007–), 6+ vols., Del Rey, serialized in *Weekly Shōnen Magazine* (2003–), Kodansha International, 9+ vols.

Angel*/Mariko Iwadate (1982), serialized in *Margaret*, Shūeisha, 1 vol.

Appleseed/Masamune Shirow (1993–95), 4 vols., Dark Horse, published as 4 vols. (1985–89), Seishinsha.

Apocalypse Meow/Motofumi Kobayashi (2004), 3 vols., ADV, serialized in *Combat Magazine* (1991–2002), Softbank/World Photo Press, 3 vols.

Arion/Yoshikazu Yasuhiko (アリオン*; 1979–85), serialized in *Monthly Comic Ryū*, Tokuma Shoten/Chūō kōronsha, 4 vols., 1997.

Ashita no Jō [Tomorrow's Joe*]/Ikki Kajiwara and Tetsuya Chiba (1968–73), serialized in *Weekly Shōnen Magazine*, Kodansha International, 20 vols.

Ashita Tenki ni Nāre/(A great super shot boy*; 1981–91), serialized in *Weekly Shōnen Magazine*, Kodansha International, 58 vols.

Astro Boy/Osamu Tezuka (2002–4), 23 vols., Dark Horse, serialized in *Shōnen* (1952–68), Kōbunsha, 23 vols.

Atagooru Tamatebako*/Hiroshi Masumura (1984–94), *Moe*, Hakusensha, 9 vols .

Atakku nanbā wan (Attack no. 1*)/Chikako Urano (1968–70), serialized in *Margaret*, Shūeisha, 12 vols.

Azumanga Daioh/Kiyohiko Azuma (2003–4), 4 vols., ADV Manga, serialized in *Dengeki Daioh* (1999–2002), MediaWorks, Tokyo.

Babū Akachin*/Shinbō Nomura (1994), serialized in *CoroCoro*, Shōgakukan.

Baki the Grappler/Keisuke Itagaki (2002–4), Gutsoon! Entertainment, serialized in *Weekly Shōnen Champion*, Akita Shoten, 42 vols.

Barefoot Gen/Keiji Nakazawa (2004–), 4 vols., Last Gasp, serialized in *Weekly Shōnen Jump* (1972–73), Shūeisha, 10 vols.

Battle Angel Alita/Yukito Kishiro (1992–98), 9 vols., VIZ Media, serialized in *Business Jump* (1990–95), Shueisha, 9 vols.

Bass Master Ranmaru/Taiga Takahashi and Yoshiaki Shimojo (2001), ComicsOne, originally published in 1999, Sogotasho, 1 vol.

BASTARD!!!/Kazushi Hagiwara (2001–), 16+ vols., VIZ Media, *Weekly Shōnen Jump/*

Weekly Shōnen Jump Zōkan/Ultra Jump (1988–), Shueisha, 23 + vols.

Be Free!*/Egawa Tetsua (1984–88), serialized in *Morning*, Kodansha International, 12 vols.

Berserk/Kentarō Miura (2003–), 24+ vols., Dark Horse, serialized in *Young Animal* (1989–), Hakusensha, 31+ vols.

Bio-Booster Armor Guyver/Yoshiki Takaya (1992–97), 7 vols., VIZ Media, serialized in *Monthly Shōnen Captain/Monthly Ace Next/Monthly Shōnen Ace* (1985–), Tōkuma Shōten/Kadōkawa, 7 vols.

Bleach/Tite Kubo (2004–), 23+ vols., VIZ Media, serialized in *Weekly Shōnen Jump* (2001–), Shueisha, 27+ vols.

Botchan no Jidai (In the Time of Botchan*)/Taniguchi Jirō and Sekigawa (1987–96), serialized in *Manga Action*, Futabasha, 5 vols.

Boys of Summer/Chuck Austen and Hiroki Otsuka (2006–), 1 vol, Tokyopop.

Break Shot*/Takeshi Maekawa (1987–90), serialized in *Shōnen Magazine*, Kodansha International, 16 vols.

Bride of Deimos/Etsuko Ikeda and Yūho Ashibe (2002–4) 7 vols., ComicsOne, serialized in *Princess Comics* (1975–83), Akita Shōten.

Buddha/Osamu Tezuka (2003–5), 8 vols., Vertical, serialized in *Kibō no Tomo/Shōnen World/Comic Tom* (1972–83), Ushio Shuppan, 7 vols.

Buzzer Beater*/Takehiko Inoue (1997–), serialized in *Weekly Shōnen Jump*, Shūeisha, 4 vols.

Captain Tsubasa*/Yōichi Takahashi (1981–88), serialized in *Weekly Shōnen Jump*, Shūeisha, 37 vols.

Cardcaptor Sakura/CLAMP (1999–2003), 6 vols., Tokyopop, serialized in *Nakayoshi* (1996–200), Kodansha International.

Ceres: Celestial Legend/ Yū Watase (2001–6), 14 vols., VIZ Media, serialized in *Shōjo Comic* (1996–2000), Shōgakukan, 14 vols.

Chibi Maruko-chan*/Momoko Sakura (1986–96), serialized in *Ribon*, Shūeisha.

Chinmoku no Kantai [Silent service*]/Kaiji Kawaguchi (1988–96), serialized in *Weekly Morning*, Kodansha International, 32 vols.

Chobits/CLAMP (2002–3), 8 vols., Tokyopop, serialized in *Weekly Young Magazine* (2000–2002), Kodansha International, 16+ vols.

Chūgoku Nyūmon: Yakkai-na rinjin no kenyu (Introduction to China: A difficult neighbor*)/George Akiyama and Huang Wen-hsiung (2005), Tokyo: Asuka Shinsho.

Crayon Shin-chan/Yoshito Usui (2002–4), ComicsOne/CMX, serialized in *Weekly Manga Action/Manga Town* (1990–), Futabasha, 45+ vols.

Crimson Hero/Mitsuba Takanashi (2005–), 8+ vols., VIZ Media, serialized in *Bessatsu Margaret* (2002–), Shūeisha.

Cross/Sumiko Amakawa (2004–6), 5 vols., Tokyopop, serialized in *Asuka* (1997–2001), Kodawa Shoten, 5 vols .

Dan Doh!!*/Nobuhiro Sakata and Daichi Banjou (1995–2000), serialized in *Shōnen Sunday* (1987–2007), Shōgakukan, 29 vols.

Dear Boys*/Hiroki Yagami (1989–97), serialized in *Weekly Shōnen Magazine*, Kodansha International, 23+ vols.

The Devil Does Exist/Mitsuba Takanashi (2005–7), 11 vols., CMX, serialized in *Bessatsu Margaret* (1998–2002), Shūeisha, 11 vols.

Devilman//Gō Nagai (2002–3), 5 vols., Kodansha International, serialized in *Weekly Shōnen Magazine* (1972–73), Kodansha International, 5 vols.

Devilman Lady*/Gō Nagai (1997–2000), serialized in *Weekly Morning*, Kodansha International, 17 vols.

Doraemon/ Fujiko Fujio (2002–5), Shōgakukan English Comics, serialized in various magazines (1970–96), Shōgakukan, 45 vols .

Dragon Ball/Akira Toriyama (1998–2004), 16 vols., VIZ Media, serialized in *Weekly Shōnen Jump* (1984–1995), Shūeisha, 16 vols.

Dr. Slump/Akira Toriyama (2005–8), 15+ vols., VIZ Media, serialized in *Weekly Shōnen Jump* (1980–86), Shūeisha, 18 vols.

Eagle: The Making of An Asian-American President/Kaji Kawaguchi (2000–2002), 5 vols., VIZ Media, serialized in *Big Comic*, Shōgakukan, 5 vols.

Eikou no Napoleon — Eroika [The glorious Napoleon*]/Riyoko Ikeda (1986–95), Chuoukouronsha, 14 vols.

Even a Monkey Can Draw Manga/Kentarō Takekuma and Kōji Aihara (2002), 1 vol., VIZ Media. serialized in *Big Comic Spirits* (1989–1990), Shōgakukan, 1 vol.

Eyeshield 21/Riichiro Inagaki (2005–), 20+ vols., VIZ Media, serialized in *Weekly Shōnen* (2002–), Shūeisha, 24+ vols.

*Fancy Pants**/Reiko Okano (1984–90), serialized in *Petit Flower*, Shōgakukan, 9 vols.

The First President of Japan/Ryuji Tsugihara and Yoshiki Hidaka (2002–3), 4 vols., Gutsoon! Entertainment, serialized in *BART* (1998–99), Shūeisha, 4 vols.

Flowers & Bees/Moyoco Anno (2005), 6 vols., VIZ Media, serialized in *Young Magazine* (2002–3), Kodansha International, 7 vols.

Fullmetal Alchemist/Makoto Inoue (2005–), 16+ vols., VIZ Media, serialized in *Monthly Shōnen Gangan* (2002–), Square Enix, 16+ vols.

Full Moon O Sagashite/Arina Tanemura (2005–6), 7 vols., VIZ Media, serialized in *Ribon* (2002–4), Shūeisha, 7 vols.

Ge Ge Ge no Kitarō [Kitaro the spooky]/Shigeru Mizuki (2002), Kodansha International, 3 vols., serialized in *Weekly Shōnen Magazine* (1959–69), Kodansha International, 9 vols.

Genji Monogatari [The tale of Genji*]/Tatsuya Egawa (2001–5), Shūeisha, 7 vols.

Ghost in the Shell/Masamune Shirow (1995), 1 vol., Dark Horse, serialized in *Young Magazine Pirate Edition* (1989–91), Kodansha International, 1 vol.

Golgo 13/Takao Saito (2006–8), 13 vols., VIZ Media, Serialized in *Big Comic* (1969–), Shōgakukan, 140+ vols.

Gōmanizumu sengen [The declaration of arrogance*]/Yoshinori Kobayashi (1991–2003), serialized in *Spa/Sapio*.

Gon/Masashi Tanaka (2007–), 5+ vol, CMX, serialized in *Weekly Morning* (1991–2002), Kodansha International, 7 vols.

Gunslinger Girl/Yū Aida (2003–5), ADV Manga, 6 vols., serialized in *Dengeki Daioh* (2002–), MediaWorks, Tokyo.

Harlem Beat/Yuriko Nishiyama (1998–2007), 9 vols., Tokypop, serialized in *Weekly Shōnen Magazine*, Kodansha International, 29 vols.

Hell Baby/Hideshi Hino (1995), New York: Blast Books.

Hellsing/Kōta Hirano (2003–), 8+ vols., Dark Horse, serialized in *Young King Ours* (1998–), Shonen Gahosha, 8+ vols.

Hige no OL Sasako Yabuuchi [Sasako Yabuuchi, the moustached office lady*]/Kotobuki Shiriagari (1996–2000), Take Shobou, 2 vols.

Hi izuru Tokoro no Tenshi [Heaven's child in the land of the rising sun*]/Ryōko Yamagishi (1980–84), serialized in *LaLa/Hana to Yume*, Hakusensha, 11 vols.

Hikari no Densetsu [Legend of light*]/Izumi Asō (1985–88), serialized in *Margaret*, Shūeisha, 16 vols.

Hikaru no Go/Yumi Hotta, Takeshi Obata, and Yukari Umezawa (2003–), 12 vols., VIZ Media, serialized in *Weekly Shōnen Jump* (1998–2003), Shūeisha, 23 vols.

Hino Horror, vol. 1, *The Red Snake*/Hideshi Hino (2004), DH.

Hino Horror, vol. 2, *The Bug Boy*/Hideshi Hino (2004), DH.

Hino Horror, vols. 3–4, *Oninbo and the Bugs From Hell*/Hideshi Hino (2004), DH.

Hino Horror, vol. 5, *Living Corpse*/Hideshi Hino (2004), DH.

Hino Horror, vol. 6, *Black Cat*/Hideshi Hino (2004), DH.

Hino Horror, vols. 7–8, *The Collection*/Hideshi Hino (2004), DH.

Hino Horror, vol. 9, *Ghost School*/Hideshi Hino (2004), DH.

Hino Horror, vol. 10, *Death's Reflection*/Hideshi Hino (2004), DH.

Hino Horror, vol. 11, *Gallery of Horrors*/Hideshi Hino (2004), DH.

Hino Horror, vol. 12, *Mystique Mandala of Hell*/Hideshi Hino (2004), DH.

Hino Horror, vol. 13, *Zipangu*/Hideshi Hino (2004), DH.

Hino Horror, vol. 14, *Skin and Bone*/Hideshi Hino (2004), DH.

Hot Gimmick/Miki Aihara (2003–6), 12 vols., VIZ Media, serialized in *Betsucomi* (2000–2005), Shōgakukan.

Ike! Ina-chū Takkyūbu [Go! Ina-chu Middle School ping-pong club*]/Minoru Furuya (1993–96), serialized in *Young Magazine*, Kodansha International, 13 vols.

Initial D/Shuichi Shigeno (2002–), 30 vols., Tokyopop, serialized in *Weekly Young Magazine* (1995–5), Kodansha International, 32 vols.

Inu Yasha/Rumiko Takahashi (1997–), 33+ vols., VIZ Media, serialized in *Weekly Shōnen Sunday* (1996–), Shōgakukan, 49+ vols.

Itihāsa/Wakako Mizuki (1986–97), serialized in *Bouquet*, Shūeisha, 15 vols.

Jesus/Yashiko Yoshikazu (2000), 2 vols., ComicsOne, published as 2 vols. (1997), Japan Broadcast Publishing.

Junko Mizuno's Cinderalla/Junko Mizuno (2002), 1 vol., VIZ Media, originally published as *Mizuno Junko no Cinderalla-chan* (2000), Koushinsya, 1 vol.

Junko Mizuno's Hansel and Gretel/Junko Mizuno (2003), 1 vol., VIZ Media, originally published as *Mizuno Junko no Hansel & Gretel* (2000), Koushinsya, 1 vol.

Junko Mizuno's Princess Mermaid/Junko Mizuno (2004), 1 vol, VIZ Media, originally published as *Ningyohime Den* (2002), Bunkasha, 1 vol.

Kaguya-hime/Reiko Shimizu (1994–2005), serialized in *Hana to Yume, LaLa*, Hakusensha, 27 vols.

Kamichama Karin/Koge-Donbo (かみちゃまかりん) (2005–7), 7 vols., Tokyopop, serialized in *Nakayoshi* (2003–5), Kodansha International, 7 vols.

Katsuya Terada's The Monkey King/Katsuya Terada (2005–), Dark Horse, serialized in *Ultra Jump* (1995–), Shūeisha, 1+ vols.

Kattobase Kiyohara-kun/Junji Kawai (1987–94), 15 vols., Shōgakkan.

Kaze to Ki no Uta [The song of the wind and the trees*]/Keiko Takemiya (1976–84), serialized in *Shōjo Comic/Petit Flower*, Shōgakukan, 17 vols.

Kenkanryū (Hating "the Korean boom"*)/Sharin Yamano (2005), Tokyo: Shinyusha.

Kyojin no hoshi [Star of the giants*]/Ikki Kajiwara and Noboru Kawasaki (1966–), serialized in *Weekly Shōnen Magazine*, Kodansha International, 19 vols.

The Legend of Kamui/Sanpei Shirato (1965–71), serialized in *Garo* (1965–71), Shōgakukan, 21 vols.

Lone Wolf and Cub/Kazuo Koike and Goseki Kojima (2000–2002), 28 vols., Dark Horse, serialized in *Manga Action* (1970–76), Futabasha, 28 vols.

Love Hina/Ken Akamatsu (2002–3), 14 vols., Tokyopop, serialized in *Weekly Shōnen Magazine* (1998–2002), Kodansha International.

Makoto-chan/Kazuo Umezu (1976–81), serialized in *Shōnen Sunday*, Shōgakukan, 24 vols.

Manga Nihon no Rekishi/Shōtarō Ishinomori (1989–93), Chūōkōronsha, 48 vols.

Magic Knight Rayearth/CLAMP (1999–2001), 3 vols., Tokyopop, serialized in *Nakayoshi* (1993–96), Kodansha International.

Marmalade Boy/Wataru Yoshizumi (2002–3), 8 vols., Tokyopop, serialized in *Ribon* (1992–95), Shūeisha, 8 vols.

Maruo jigoku [Maruohell*]/Suehiro Marou (1995), 1 vol., Serindo.

Mazinger Z/Gō Nagai (1972–73), serialized in *Weekly Shōnen Jump*, Shūeisha, 5 vols.

Millennium Snow/Bisco Hatori (2007), VIZ Media, serialized in *LaLa* (2001–2), Hakusensha, 2 vols.

MPD Psycho/Sho-u Tajima and Eiji Otsuka (2007–), 5+ vols., Dark Horse, serialized in *Monthly Shōnen Ace* (1997–2006), Kadōkawa Shōten, 11 vols.

Mr. Arashi's Amazing Freak Show/Suehiro Maruo (1992), Blast Books.

The Mythical Detective Loki Ragnorak/Sakura Kinoshita (2004–5), 2 vols., ADV, serialized in *Comic Blade* (2002–5), Mag Garden, 5 vols.

Naki no Ryū*/Jun'ichi Nōjō (1986–91), serialized in *Bessatsu Kindai Mahjong*, Take Shobō, 9 vols.

Naruto/Masashi Kishimoto (2002–), 29+ vols., VIZ Media, serialized in *Weekly Shōnen Jump* (1999–), Shūeisha, 37+ vols.

Nausicaä of the Valley of Wind/Hayao Miyazaki (1988–2004), 7 vols., VIZ Media, serialized in *Animage* (1982–94), Tokuma Shōten.

Neji-shiki [Screw style]/Yoshiharu Tsuge (2003), *Comics Journal* 250 (February), 135–57, originally published in *Garo* (1968).

New York, New York*/Marimo Ragawa (1996–98), serialized in *Hana to Yume*, Hakusensha.

Nichibei Taiheiyō kessen [Japan and America's decisive battle for the Pacific*]/ Kobayashi Motofumi et al. (1995), in *Konbatto Komikku* [Combat Comic], Nippon Shuppansha.

Nichirosensō Monogatari [The Russo-Japanese war story*]/Tatsuya Egawa (2001–6), serialized in *Big Comic Spirits*, Shōgakukan, 22 vols.

ŌbāDoraivu (Overdrive*)/Yasuda Tsuyoshi (2005–), serialized in *Weekly Shōnen Magazine*, Kodansha International, 15 vols.

Oh My Goddess!/Kōsuke Fujishima (1994–), 30+ vols., Dark Horse, serialized in *Afternoon* (1988–), Kodansha International, 34+ vols.

One Piece/Eiichirō Oda (2002–), 18+ vols., VIZ Media, serialized in *Weekly Shōnen Jump* (1997–), Shūeisha, 44+ vols.

One Pound Gospel/Rumiko Takahashi (1994–96), 3 vols., VIZ Media, serialized in *Young Sunday* (1987–2007), Shōgakukan, 4 vols.

Onmyō-ji*/Reiko Okano (1994–2004), Hakusensha, 11 vols.

Ōto Ayakashi Kitan*/Yōko Iwasaki (1990–2002), serialized in *Princess Gold*, Akita Shoten, 12 vols.

Parasyte/Hitoshi Iwaaki (2007–), 5+ vols., Del Rey, serialized in *Morning/Afternoon* (1990–95), Kodansha International, 12 vols.

Phoenix/Osamu Tezuka (2003–7), 12 vols., VIZ Media, serialized in various magazines (1956–89), 12 vols.

Palepoli*/Usamaru Furuya (1996), Serindo.

Pītsū Rettsu Purei Pinpon [P2! — Let's play ping-pong!*]/Tatsumi Ejiri (2006–7), serialized in *Weekly Shōnen Jump*, Shūeisha, 5 vols.

"Planet of the Jap"/Suehiro Maruo (1996), in *Comics Underground Japan*, edited by Kevin Quigley (ed.), New York: Blast Books, 98–114. Originally published as *Nihonjin no wakusei* in *Ginsei kurabu*, vol. 5 (1985).

Pluto*/Naoki Urasawa (2003–), serialized in *Big Comic Original*, Shōgakukan, 5 vols.

The Prince of Tennis/Takeshi Konomi (2004–), 25+, VIZ Media, serialized in *Weekly Shōnen Jump* (1999–) Shūeisha, 37+ vols.

Princess Knight/Osamu Tezuka (2001), 1 vol., Kodansha International, serialized in *Nakayoshi* (1963–66), Kodansha International, 6 vols.

Psychic Academy/Katsu Aki (2004–6), 11 vols., Tokyopop, serialized in *Magazine Z* (1999–2003), Kodansha International, 11 vols.

Rafu [Rough*]/Mitsuru Adachi (1987–89), serialized in *Weekly Shōnen Sunday*, Shōgakukan, 12 vols.

Revolutionary Girl Utena/Chiho Saitō and Be-Papas (2000–2004), 5 vols., VIZ Media, serialized in *Ciao* (1996–98), Shōgakukan, 5 vols.

RG Veda/CLAMP (2005–6), 10 vols., Tokyopop, originally published as *Seiden RG Veda*, serialized in *Wings* (1989–96), Shinshōkan.

Riaru (Real*)/Takehiko Inoue (1999–), serialized in *Young Jump*, Shuiesha, 6 vols.

Rikito Densetsu*/Takeshi Obata and Masaru Miyazaki (1992–93), serialized in *Weekly Shōnen Jump*, Shūeisha.

Ringu ni kakero [Put it all in the ring*]/Masami Kurumada (1977–83), serialized in
   Shōnen Jump, Shūeisha, 25 vols.
Rosario + Vampire*/Akihisa Ikeda (2004–7, 2007–), serialized in *Monthly Shōnen Jump/
   Weekly Shōnen Jump/Jump Square*, Shūeisha.
The Rose of Versailles/Riyoko Ikeda (1981), 1 vol., Sanyusha, serialized in *Margaret*
   (1972–73), Shūeisha, 2 vols.
Runpunyaku [Powdered fish scale medicine*]/Yūko Tsuno (2000), Seirindo, 1 vol.
Rurōuni Kenshin*/Nobuhiro Watsuki (2003–6), 28 vols., VIZ Media, serialized in
   Weekly Shōnen Jump (1994–99), Shūiesha.
Sailor Moon/Naoko Takeuchi (1997–2001), 18 vols., Tokyopop, serialized in *Nakayoshi*
   (1992–97), Kodansha International, 18 vols.
Sain wa V [The sign is V*]/Mochizuki Akira and Jonbo Shirō (1968–70), serialized in
   Shōjo Friend, Kodansha International, 10 vols.
Saiyūki/Kazuya Minekura (2004–5), 9+ vols., TokyoPop, serialized in *Monthly
   G-Fantasy* (1997–2002), Enix, 16+ vols.
Sakuran*/Moyoco Anno (2001–3), serialized in *Evening*, Kodansha International,
   1 vol.
Sanctuary/Shō Fumimura and Ryōichi Ikegami (1993–98), VIZ Media, 9 vols., serialized
   in *Big Comic Superior* (1990–95), Shōgakukan, 9 vols.
Sangatsu no Raion [March comes in like a lion*]/Chika Umino (2007–), serialized in
   Young Animal, Hakusensha, vol 1.
Satsuma Gishiden: The Legend of the Satsuma Samurai/Hiroshi Hirata (2006–7), 3 vols.,
   Dark Horse, serialized in *Zokan Young Comic/Weekly Manga Goraku* (1977–82),
   Shonen Gahosha/Nihon Bungeisha, 5 vols.
Sensō ron [The war revisited*]/Yoshinori Kobayashi (1998), Tokyo: Gentosha.
Shirahime-Syo: Snow Goddess Tales/CLAMP (2004), Tokyopop, originally published as
   Shirahime-shō (1992), Kobunsha, 1 vol.
Slam Dunk!/Takehiko Inoue (2002–4), 5 vols. Gutsoon! Entertainment, serialized in
   Weekly Shōnen Jump, Shūeisha, 31 vols.
Sugar Princess*/Hisaya Nakajo (2005–6), serialized in *Hana to Yume*, Hakusensha, 2
   vols.
Surō Suteppu [Slow step*]/Mitsuru Adachi (1986–91), serialized in *Ciao*, Shōgakukan,
   7 vols.
Survival in the Office: The Evolution of Japanese Working Women/Risu Akizuki (1999–
   2000), Kodansha International, 5 vols., serialized in *Morning* (1989–), Kodansha
   International, 26+ vols.
Suzuka/Kouji Seo (2006–), 10+ vols., Del Rey, serialized in *Weekly Shōnen Magazine*
   (2004–), Kodansha International, 15+ vols.
Taiwan ron [On Taiwan*]/Yoshinori Kobayashi (2000), Tokyo: Shōgakkan.
Ten no Hate Made: Poland Hishi [To the end of the sky: The secret history of Poland*]/
   Riyoko Ikeda (1999), Chūōkoron-shisha, 2 vols.
Tetsujin 28 gō [Iron man no. 28*]/Mitsuteru Yokoyama (1956–66), serialized in *Shōnen*,
   Kōbusha, 21 vols.
Third Girl*/Shinobu Nishimura (1984–93), serialized in *Comic Gekiga Sonjuku*, Koike
   Shoin, 8 vols.
Thoma no Shinzō [The heart of Thomas*]/Moto Hagio (1972–73), *Shōjo Comic*,
   Shōgakukan.
Tiger Mask*/Ikki Kajiwara and Naoki Tsuji (1968–71), serialized in *Weekly Shōnen
   Magazine*, Kodansha International.
Toiretto Hakase [Professor Toilet*]/Kazuyoshi Torii (1970–77), serialized in *Weekly
   Shōnen Jump*, Shūeisha.
Tokyo Daigaku Monogatari [Tokyo University story*]/Tatsuya Egawa (1993–2000),
   serialized in *Big Comic Spirits*, Shōgakukan, 34 vols.
TOMOI* Wakuni Akisato (1987), serialized in *Petit Flower*, Shōgakukan, 1 vol.

Touch*/Mitsuru Adachi (1981–86), serialized in *Shōnen Sunday*, Shōgakukan, 26 vols.

Tough*/Tetsuya Saruwatari (2004–6), 6 vols., VIZ Media, serialized in *Young Jump* (1993–2003), Shūeisha, 42 vols.

Ultimate Muscle: The Kinnikuman Legacy/Yudetamango (2004–), 19+ vols., VIZ Media, serialized in *Weekly Playboy* (1998–2005), Shūeisha, 29 vols.

Ultra-Gash Inferno/Suehiro Maruo (2001), Creation Books.

Uzumaki: Spiral into Horror/Junji Itō (2001–2), 3 vols., VIZ Media, serialized in *Big Comic Spirits* (1998–99), Shōgakukan, 3 vols.

Vagabond/Takehiko Inoue (2001–), 27+ vols., VIZ Media, serialized in *Morning* (1998–), Kodansha International, 25+ vols .

Whistle!/Daisuke Higuchi (2005–8), 19 vols., VIZ Media, serialized in *Weekly Shōnen Jump* (1998–2003), Shūeisha, 39 vols.

X/1999/CLAMP (1996–2005), 10 vols., VIZ Media, serialized in *Asuka* (1992–2003), Kodawa Shōten, 14 vols.

xxxHolic/CLAMP (2004–), 12+ vols., Del Rey, serialized in *Weekly Young Magazine* (2003–), Kodansha International, 13+ vols.

Yapoo, the Human Cattle*/Tatsuya Egawa (2003–), Gentosha, 3+ vols.

Yawara! Naoki Urasawa (1986–93), serialized in *Big Comic Spirits*, Shōgakukan, 29 vols.

Yume Q-Saku [Q-Saku dream*]/Suehiro Maruo (1982), Serindo.

Zipang/Kaiji Kawaguchi (2002), 4 vols., Kodansha International, serialized in *Morning* (2000–), Kodansha International, 28+ vols.

Zombie-Loan/Peach-Pit (2003–), serialized in *GFantasy*, Enix, 9+ vols.

3

What Boys Will Be: A Study of Shōnen Manga

Angela Drummond-Mathews

The largest segment of manga publishing is *shōnen* or young boys' manga. Read by boys, men, girls, and women alike, these stories reflect the fantasies and social history of an evolving Japan. Despite being initially aimed at boys, elements such as expanded story lines and universal themes make boys' manga appealing to nearly everyone. Manga is so popular in Japan in general that at least three times as many people read manga than circulation figures would indicate (Kinsella 2000, 54). Of the many manga magazines that make up those circulation figures, the most popular is *Weekly Shōnen Jump*, which has been said to be one of the highest selling magazines in the world, having sold as many as six million copies per week (Scodt 1996, 68). On its heels follow *Shōnen Magazine* and *Shōnen Sunday*, both strong competitors in the weekly race to provide boys' manga to a hungry readership. Over 40 percent of manga produced in Japan during the 1990s was aimed at boys (Kinsella 2000, 45), a testament of the power and importance of this genre. Even as book sales decline due to the influence of video games and television, manga readership remains steady (Allen & Ingulsrud 2003, 674).

HISTORY

Japanese comic art has long been growing as a tradition, from as early as the twelfth century when a Buddhist priest named Toba created satirical drawings of animals dressed as clergymen called Chojugiga, or "Animal Scrolls" (Schodt 1983, 28). The form continued its growth into the twentieth century with a focus on satire, politics, and current events. Manga for children, however, only became popular in the 1950s (Ito 2005, 466). Following a post-

World War II boom in magazines such as *Manga Club*, *Manga Shōnen*, and *Tokyo Pakku*, *mangaka* such as Osamu Tezuka and others began to sell children's-oriented manga magazines by the hundreds of thousands (Ito 2005, 467). Japan was moving into a period of social and economic stability. A Japanese government economic white paper released in 1956 pronounced Japan officially free from the postwar stage. This news spurred a period of economic and cultural growth (Ito 2005, 468). Tezuka's manga became a leading influence during this time. Seeking to create stronger narratives, he pioneered the use of cinematic techniques inspired by Walt Disney and Max Fleischer to produce long "story manga" in which the manga covers an entire story line as opposed to consisting only of short humorous pieces (Schodt 1997, 63). Tezuka's influence spread throughout the manga world. Dramatic manga featuring serious story lines and realistic depictions that appealed to older children and young adults began to appear by 1957 (Ito 2005, 467), and by 1959, manga weekly magazines for boys first debuted. *Shōnen Magazine* and *Shōnen Sunday* began a heated rivalry when they released their first issues on the same day, March 17, 1959. During the 1960s, more weeklies followed. Titles such as *Champion*, *King*, and *Ace* sprang up as demand for boys' manga rose (Gravett 2004, 56). Manga began to deal with more serious issues, and even the young boys' manga carried series dealing with politics, history, or protest (Kinsella 2004, 32).

As themes in boy's manga broadened, so did the desire to take risks with taboo forms of expression. For example, in 1968 *Shōnen Jump* began to allow nudity and vulgarity, much to the dismay of parents and teachers (Ito 2005, 469), but it only grew in popularity, privileging concepts of friendship, perseverance, and success in the stories it serialized (Schodt 1996, 89–90). These daring strides began in children's manga with humor or gag manga. Early gag manga for children was similar to the fare common in American comics, but in the 1960s comedies in shonen manga began breaking taboos by adding scatological humor, sexual situations, and graphic violence (Schodt 1997, 120). While American comics artists were struggling against the industry self-censorship of the Comics Code Authority, which prevented them from including anything that would "injure the sensibilities of the reader" (quoted in Wolk 2007, 38). Japanese mangaka were veering in the opposite direction. Fujio Akatsuka spearheaded this trend with manga such as *Tensai Bakabon* in 1967, which featured parody, wordplay, and sight gags inspired by American movies such as those of Abbott and Costello (Schodt 1997, 122). A former assistant of Akatsuka, Kazuyoshi Torii, released his own offering, *Toiretto Hakase*, in 1970 that featured a research scientist whose specialty is scatology and who works from a lab shaped like a toilet (Schodt 1997, 121). Other mangaka also pushed this trend. Gō Nagai's *Harenchi Gakuen* challenged the rigid order of the Japanese school system with students who played games and drank sake in class while conspiring to catch one another naked (Schodt 1997, 122). *Gaki Deka*, by Tatsuhiko Yamagami, was a very popular taboo-busting manga running in *Shōnen Champion* from 1974 to 1981. It featured an irreverent child/policeman who always wore a police hat and polka-dotted tie and who never hesitate to doff his clothes to show off his buttocks and testicles (Schodt 1997, 123). This kind of humor has permeated manga since that time. *Crayon Shin-chan*, by Yoshito Usui, is one obvious heir to this trend. Much like the protagonist in *Gaki Deka*, six-year-old Shin-chan says inappropriate things, removes his clothes, moons people, and even urinates in public, much to the horror of his parents and other adults. Such comic antics simultaneously provide wild hilarity and social commentary.

In manga meant for children, violence was similarly tame prior to the 1960s, rarely showing blood (Schodt 1983, 124). More daring fare was typically found in manga aimed at adults, easily obtained at pay-libraries or *kashibon'ya* (Schodt 1983, 66). These book-lenders functioned in much the same way as video rental stores do today. However, by the 1960s, the market had changed. The economy had improved, and people could afford to buy manga as opposed to borrowing it; thus the pay-libraries began to fail (Schodt 1983, 67). Artists who had previously worked for the more adult orientated pay-library manga outlets began to move to the weekly and monthly magazine market, bringing their more realistic and violent style with them.

GENRES

Since then, the manga industry has continued to grow and boys' manga has continued to dominate. Sports manga is one of the more popular genres (Schodt 1997, 79). Manga about sports proliferated in the 1950s, motivating children to engage in games (Gravett 2004, 54), and it substituted for war manga during the postwar period, when expressing warlike sentiments became "politically incorrect" (Schodt 1997, 79). In 1952, Eiichi Fukui's *Igaguri-kun* appeared in *Boken'o* magazine, and its main character Igaguri was a judo expert. The popularity of this title led to even more sports manga featuring nearly every imaginable sport. (Schodt 1997, 80)

Takehiko Inoue's *Slam Dunk* is a perfect example. This thirty-one-volume series tells the story of the unlikely sportsman Hanamichi Sakuragi, a student at Shohoku High School. Hanamichi is not popular with girls, and eventually resorts to baseless bragging to get the attention of a girl, Haruko. In order to prove his claims, he joins the basketball team, even though he has never played. Natural ability, however, allows him to succeed despite odds against him. The manga progresses as Hanamichi strives to become better at basketball, for himself, for Haruko, and for the sake of the team.

Another sports manga, *The Prince of Tennis*, by Takeshi Konomi, also exceeds thirty volumes. Its hero, Ryoma Echizen, is a highly talented player who works toward becoming the ultimate tennis champion. While navigating high school pressures, he learns struggles to perfect highly complex tennis moves and to make good friends along the way.

Eyeshield 21, Riichiro Inagaki's American football manga, centers on a young boy, Sena Kobayakawa, who has a remarkable ability to run and dodge despite his otherwise unassuming appearance. He is recruited by an American football team at his high school, but fearing that he might be stolen by a rival team, the coach forces Sena to play wearing a green eyeshield to hide his true identity, and he is otherwise known as the team's secretary. Sena and his teammates struggle to overcome their poor record and win a chance at a bowl game.

Daisuke Higuchi's *Whistle!* is a soccer manga about a boy named Sho Kazamatsuri who, despite being a poor player, mistakenly ends up on his new school's soccer team; however, he has the spirit to persevere. His optimism and never-say-die attitude propel him as he endeavors to overcome his deficiencies and become a successful player.

Sports manga are not only limited to typical sports such as football or basketball; combat sports are also covered and are a favorite of many readers. The martial arts manga *Baki the Grappler*, by Keisuke Itagaki, relates how Baki Hanma, a young martial artist, labors to become the best at his fighting style, and the famous *Ashita no Jō*, by Tetsuya Chiba, became the symbol of a struggling 1970s underclass as the title character, Joe Yobuki, climbs his way from the orphanage to the heights of boxing fame. But combat is not limited to hand-to-hand battle. Shinji Saijyo's *Iron Wok Jan* turns cooking into battle, pitting its hero Jan Akiyama against other chefs in a quest to become the greatest in the world, while *Hikaru no Go*, by Yumi Hotta and Takeshi Obata, popularized the traditional go board game as young Hikaru Shindo, aided by the spirit of a Heian period go master, Fujiwara-no-Sai, moves from merely cursory interest in go to becoming a professional level competitor.

Action/adventure manga are nearly as popular as sports manga. These often contain fantasy or science fiction elements paired with combat and a quest. One of the most popular of this genre has been Akira Toriyama's *Dragon Ball*. The main character, SonGoku, is based on the story of the Monkey King from *Journey to the West* (Wu 2003). He begins a quest to find the legendary "dragon balls" that will enable the holder to ask the great dragon Shenlong to grant a wish. At the same time, he trains as a martial artist and competes in tournaments to be the best in the land. Along the way he battles fantastical beings who threaten to destroy the world — or at least their little portion of it. Goku and his friends confront fierce monsters and comical demons from the earliest chapters on, and each tale is laced with the humor that is the legacy of gag manga. For instance, Goku saves a village from the terror of a shape-shifting demon, Oolong, who turns out to be in reality a rather tiny pig. Goku's friend and training partner Kuririn battles the quite offensive Bactrian in the Tenkaichi Budokai, whose primary weapon is that he has never bathed in his entire life; Bactrian's weapons include rancid breath and flatulence! Kuririn wins the battle when Goku reminds him that, not having a nose, he is actually impervious to Bactrian's attacks. Kuririn retaliates with his own gaseous attack and defeats Bactrian, amazing all around that anyone so smelly could actually be affected by other people's odors. *Dragon Ball* becomes more serious in its later volumes when Goku becomes an adult (marked in the American publications by the title *Dragon Ball Z*). Fantasy explanations are enhanced by science fiction rationalizations, and the fights become more violent and the stakes become higher, but the series never completely abandons humor, such as Kame-Sennin's lecherous attitude.

Martial arts manga, like *Fist of the North Star*, created by Tetsuo Hara and Buronson, blend fantasy, sport, and action. *Fist* takes the reader to a postapocalyptic world in which people have resorted to violence in order to survive. Kenshiro is a young man who possesses the knowledge of a deadly martial art known as Hokuto Shinken that allows him to kill by striking an opponent's acupressure points. He travels the land on a quest for his lost fiancée Yuria, battling gangs who oppress the weak.

War manga made a comeback in the late 1950s and early 1960s (Nakar 2003, 57). In the postwar period, American occupation discouraged warlike sentiments (Schodt 1997, 79). Fearing the return of the propaganda-heavy war manga of the 1930s and '40s, the government banned such topics, particularly in children's media (Nakar 2003, 71). After U.S. occupation, poetry, narratives and other art forms served to express Japan's memories of war (Nakar 2003, 70). However, by the late 1950s a different picture of war began to take shape, and new narratives emerged. Many of these new stories focused on the positive aspects of war: heroism and bravery against insurmountable odds and often impossible circumstances. Naoki Tsuji's *Zero-sen Hayato* tells the story of a young fighter pilot named Hayato who is a member of a team that flies a new type of plane known as Zero and whose bravery and skill saves his team (Nakar 2003, 60). Other war related manga depicted the hardships and struggles of both soldiers and civilians trying to survive in a war-torn country (Nakar 2003, 74). *Barefoot Gen*, by Keiji Nakazawa and Art Spiegelman, is based on Nakazawa's own experiences with the atomic bombing of Hiroshima. The title character, Gen, is a child living in Hiroshima. He survives the bombing, witnessing the horrors of the explosion, the fires, the maimed civilians, and countless deaths. The manga recounts his and others' struggle for survival.

Other action manga take a completely different path. *Trigun*, by Yasuhiro Nightow, is an unlikely blend of the American West with science fiction. *Trigun*'s main character, Vash the Stampede, is an outlaw gunman on the planet Gunsmoke with a hyperbolic talent for getting into trouble. Chased by bounty hunters and followed by two insurance agents — Meryl Stryfe and Milly Thompson of Bernardelli Insurance, who try to minimize his damage — he roams the countryside upholding a vow never to kill regardless of his superhuman marksmanship. A multifaceted tale, *Trigun* explores themes as complex as pacifism, exploitation, identity, and genocide while still making room for gag humor and puns. Meryl Stryfe (in constant strife chasing Vash) and Vash's antagonistic brother Knives both have names symbolic of their characters. A healthy fascination for guns and gun culture is evident from the names Thompson and Bernardelli, both names of gun manufacturers.

Of course, action-oriented manga are not always fantastical. Some take the average (or not-so-average) high school as their topic. *Great Teacher Onizuka*, by Tōru Fujisawa, follows former gang member Eikichi Onizuka as he leaves the streets and works to become the best (and probably the most unorthodox) teacher in Japan. On the other side of the desk, Eiji Nonaka's *Cromartie High School* details the efforts of a plucky student, Takashi Kamiyama, to better his high school, which is notorious for housing the worst juvenile delinquents.

School is not always fun and games, however, and nowhere is this more true than in Japan. The rigorous curriculum, strict discipline, and pressure to excel may sometimes seem like a nightmare to Japanese students. That nightmare comes alive in the horror-themed *Drifting Classroom*, by Kazuo Umezu. Originally serialized in *Weekly Shōnen Sunday* between 1972 and 1974 (Thompson 2007, 90), the story transports an elementary school with its staff and students to a veritable hell on earth, a strange deserted wasteland in which they must all fight to survive. *Drifting Classroom* sports violent images and situations that most Americans would not abide in a comic meant for children. In fact, the American publication of it is marked with a label warning that it contains explicit content.

Horror has become a popular theme in shōnen manga. One example, *Death Note*, by Tsugumi Ōba, has caused an international stir. *Death Note* tells the story of a young man named Light Yagami. Light finds a strange notebook with the words "Death Note" written on it. Inside he finds instructions explaining that anyone whose name is written in the notebook will die. He tests the instructions and finds out that the book is indeed what it claims to be. Soon, Light meets with the *shinigami*, or death god, who owned the book and decides to create a new world by doing away with people he deems to be evil or destructive. This results in a series of mysterious deaths, which the police are anxious to solve. A detective known only as "L" leads the investigation to find this mysterious killer, called "Kira" by the public. Filled with thrills, suspense, and creepy otherworld characters, *Death Note*, the manga and its live-action, novel, and anime incarnations, has become popular worldwide, particularly with teens. So taken are they with the story that some have apparently taken to acting out the ideas in the manga. Some schools in China banned *Death Note* and other horror manga after students threatened and teased each other and their teachers by creating their own "death notes" and writing in the names of people they didn't like (Death Note Stirs Controversy in China 2005"; Virginian Teen Suspended over Names in 'Death Note.'" 2007). In Belgium, a body was found with a note that read "Watashi wa Kira dess" (with a Romanized misspelling of the verb *desu*), or "I am Kira" ("Police Reach Dead End in Belgian 'Manga Murder' Case," 2007). Schools in the United States have also had to discipline students for writing names of other students in so-called death notes ("Virginian Teen," 2007).

Historical manga tend to fall within the action/adventure category. Many of them focus on samurai. Samurai represent Japan the way cowboys represent America, and samurai became role models in boys' manga (Schodt 1997, 68–69). Since Japan was no longer a military nation, postwar samurai manga focused on humor and sportsmanship (Schodt 1997, 70). Recent samurai manga, however, have returned to concepts of good versus evil. *Rurōuni Kenshin*, by Nobuhiro Watsuki, tells the story of a Meiji-era swordsman and erstwhile wartime assassin. Regretting the life he has led he vows never to kill again, but is repeatedly confronted by past enemies. Though this manga has a serious theme, it also has a great deal of humor and romance.

No discussion of shōnen manga (or of anime, for that matter) would be complete without giant robots. The first giant robot manga was *Tetsujin 28 Gō*, also known as *Gigantor*, by Mitsuteru Yokoyama, the story of a boy who controls a huge robot. With a good versus evil story line, it became the prototype for the genre (Gravett 2004, 57). Later, *Mazinger Z*, by Gō Nagai, would provide the inspiration for later robot manga and anime like *Voltron*, *Transformers*, the *Gundam* series, and others (Gravett 2004, 57). The title character Mazinger Z is a superrobot made from a special alloy that can only be manufactured in Japan. He is Professor Juzo Kabuto's secret weapon against evil. The giant robot manga and the anime they inspire let readers indulge in the fantasy of war machinery while emphasizing peacekeeping and relationships.

It is useful to note that even though boys' manga is read by someone in nearly every demographic group, as time passes and boys grow into men they may be interested in the same themes, but their tastes may change to some degree. To appeal to these more experienced readers, there are men's manga, or seinen manga. These are characterized by mature story lines and by more graphic depictions of violence, sex, or nudity. For example, *Trigun* began as a boys' manga, but in its second incarnation, *Trigun Maximum*, it became a seinen manga, featuring darker story lines and more realistically depicted violence.

Lone Wolf and Cub, Monster, and *Welcome to the N.H.K.* are also examples of seinen manga. *Lone Wolf and Cub,* by Kazuo Koike and Goseki Kojima, is the saga of Ogami Itto. Having been unjustly forced from his position as the Shogun's executioner, he wanders on a quest to take revenge on the Yagyu clan, carrying with him his young son. This series has enjoyed immense popularity in Japan and has inspired many other artists since its initial run, which began in 1970. Naoki Urasawa's *Monster* is a dark tale of a young doctor, Kenzo Tenma, who becomes unwittingly involved in a series of murders. Tenma is a talented young surgeon working in a German hospital. He defies hospital policy in order to save a child patient rather than interrupting that operation to work on a prominent government official as hospital administrators have demanded. He saves the child, but the politician dies. As a result Tenma's social status is ruined. Subsequently several murders occur, and Tenma becomes a suspect; he cannot be tied to the murders, however, so he is never charged. However, the child he saved and the boy's mysterious sister have disappeared. Years later, Tenma becomes the head of his department, a convenient result of the earlier deaths. A series of circumstances lead him to reencounter the young boy he saved, now a young man and a sociopathic killer. Though Tenma attempts to stop his former patient, now known as Johan, he ends up being blamed for the murders for which he continually arrives just too late to thwart. Chased by police and a dogged investigator named Runge, he travels across Europe in an attempt to clear his name and to find the true killer, Johan. *Monster* explores complex ethical themes. Should Tenma have saved the child or the politician? Is it better to follow policy or to adhere to personal convictions? Runge, too, is confronted by these issues as he sacrifices personal and professional concerns for his obsession with capturing Tenma.

In a lighter vein, Tatsuhiko Takimoto's *Welcome to the N.H.K.* is a humorously bittersweet story of a young man, Tatsuhiro Satō, who fails to live up to society's standards and becomes a nearly agoraphobic shut-in known in Japan as a *hikikomori*. He develops an odd relationship with a girl about whom he knows little but who claims to be able to cure him of his reclusiveness. This manga explores the hikikomori phenomenon as well as other social trends such as suicide and Internet porn addictions.

Another favorite of seinin manga is the harem manga. In it, a young man is surrounded by beautiful women in an awkward living arrangement that results in numerous awkward sexual or romantic situations. *Love Hina*, by Ken Akamatsu, is a popular example. The main character, Keitaro Urashima, becomes the manager of an all-girl dormitory. While he tries to study for college entrance exams, he clumsily attempts to perform his duties managing the dorm — as well as his turbulent relationships with the women who live there.

As is true with *shōnen manga*, seinen manga has a great deal of crossover readership, even extending to the more precocious boys and girls. *Fist of the North Star* is technically a seinen title, but it is read by many younger readers. *Tenchi Muyō!* (No Need for Tenchi!), by Hiroshi Negishi, is a shōnen anime that became a harem manga series, but it is popular with all ages.

NARRATIVE STRUCTURE

Shōnen manga typically follow the pattern of the heroic journey. The hero cycle, described by Joseph Campbell in *The Hero with a Thousand Faces*, is analogous to the rites of passage or coming of age, separation, initiation, and return. The hero leaves a place of familiarity to cross a threshold or barrier into a world of unfamiliarity. She must suffer trials, usually with assistance from a helper figure or a shaman. The hero will likely suffer some kind of nadir and atonement that will be followed by gaining a boon, wisdom, power, or a magical item that can be brought back upon the return to benefit the world (Campbell 1973). The cycle begins with the call to adventure.

The Call to Adventure

The hero is living in the world when something happens to disrupt the normal or usual flow of things. In *Dragon Ball*, SonGoku is living in the forest when a young woman named Bulma engages him on a quest to find dragon balls. Ichigo Kurosaki, in Tite Kubo's *Bleach*, receives his call when Rukia Kuchiki, a soul reaper, interrupts his nearly normal high school life and enlists him in her task of reaping souls and destroying demons. Nobuyuki Anzai's Recca Hanabishi, in *Flame of Recca*, begins his quest after discovering his latent power to control fire and his heretofore hidden heritage.

Refusal of the Call

Sometimes the hero refuses the call. Of course, there would be no story if the hero succeeded in refusing this call. Usually the hero who has refused is forced to change his mind whether by irresistible forces or by being literally thrown into the unknown. *Bleach's* Ichigo is not willing to go with Rukia initially, but must be convinced of impending dangers that he cannot otherwise avoid. Kenshin often refuses the call, having promised never to kill and fearing that to begin a journey is to return to his past as an assassin.

Crossing the Threshold

The threshold is the barrier between the known world and the unknown world. For Ichigo, this is the barrier between the living and the dead. Manta, in *Shaman King*, enters into the world of spirits when he begins to associate with Yoh Asakura. *Dragon Ball's* Goku crosses many barriers along his journeys. He leaves his forest home to seek dragon balls throughout the world, and each time he ventures into a new land he crosses into a new unknown. Eventually this extends to other planets and even to the land of the dead.

Initiation

Once the hero has crossed from the known world into the unknown world, she faces many trials and tests. These can be physical or spiritual in nature. In *Dragon Ball* this is often a period of training or meeting and fighting lesser enemies on the way to the primary nemesis. In *Fullmetal Alchemist*, by Hiromu Arakawa, Alphonse and Edward learn new things, travel, seek, and fail as they journey toward their goal of finding the philosopher's stone. Typically, the initiation period reaches a very low point at which the hero is in as much danger as can be imagined. This point is the moment of apparent death or defeat. In *Dragon Ball* and other manga in which there is a focus on combat, this moment is often a death or a near-death experience in battle.

The Return

The hero who overcomes the initiation phase has learned skills and achieved some boon that he uses to revitalize the world. This boon could be magical power (like Recca's flame), a special weapon (like Kenshin's reverse-blade sword), or unique knowledge or insight into one's own powers (like Goku's transformative powers). The return phase is often characterized by flight or a chase, and is often the last stand for the nemesis. Once this last battle has been won, the world has been saved, or the crisis has been averted, the hero returns to living in the world in preparation for the next journey. Of course, the world of manga is not the world of Hollywood and is therefore not bound to provide a happy ending. If the hero loses that last battle, he might return to the world in tragedy, but he will still prepare for the next journey.

DRAGON BALL AND RAISING THE STAKES

When a manga runs for multiple volumes, it is not unusual for the characters to repeat the hero's journey cycle multiple times. *Dragon Ball* is a prime example of this phenomenon. Akira Toriyama's globally popular manga ran for eleven years in the popular magazine *Shōnen Jump*. It had a hero's journey plot structure and carried its saga over more than forty volumes without much loss of suspense. In *Dragon Ball*, as in most hero stories and in many manga and anime, suspense is created by a combination of increased danger and the addition of obstacles to the hero reaching his goal. In *Dragon Ball*, whenever the stakes were raised for a character or group of characters, Toriyama chose each plot point in such a way that it stood directly in the path of both internal and external goals for more than one character. It was the very thing that might be described not as the worst thing that could *ever* happen but as the worst thing that could happen for those characters *at that moment*. Their goals were clearly defined and the trials or obstacles referred directly to them. This is also simply illustrated in video games that are based on the hero cycle, such as Nintendo's *Legend of Zelda* series. The trial the character undergoes bears a direct relation to the goal he must accomplish.

Following the hero's cycle, the protagonist must embark upon or be thrust into a journey that will involve the achievement of some goal, even if that goal is to return home, as in Homer's *Odyssey*, or to protect one's home and family, as in Toriyama's *Dragon Ball*. In order for the story not to appear trivial by only having external goals, the characters must also have internal goals. In *Dragon Ball*'s "Cell Saga," the character Gohan must undergo a coming-of-age transformation in addition to accomplishing the external goal of saving the world from the nemesis. These trials and/or obstacles affect both internal and external goals. Each obstacle is greater than the next, but they build on each other in a stepwise fashion instead of randomly — which is to say that each is related to the other, proceeds from characters' attempts to achieve their goals, and relates directly, not tangentially, to the characters' goals. The plot or path of conflict can be seen as very like the logical syllogism. Imagine that the primary conflict or goal is the conclusion. The events in the story have to point directly at the primary conflict, as if the unfolding plot points are the premises that lead necessarily to the conclusion. To achieve this linking of character, goals, conflicts, and actions, the characters in manga must be considerably more developed than the average character in an American comic book.

DISTINGUISHING FACTORS

Manga aimed at boys enjoys popularity not only in Japan but worldwide, and the United States market is continuing its rapid growth. To the contrary, American comics have not become as popular in Japan (Gravett 2004, 56). American comic book superheroes are a reflection (and a construction) of the audiences who read them, an audience that gravitates toward a conservative aesthetic that privileges the preservation of the status quo over the creation of a new order (Wolf-Meyer 2003). In this respect, manga are not dissimilar to American comics. Both reflect and inform their readers and the culture from which they spring; however, because manga is a nearly ubiquitous medium in Japan, that audience does not exert the same kinds of pressures on the manga industry as do American comic book fans on American artists and editors. Matthew Wolf-Meyer asserts that American comic book fandom is a "subculture predicated on a language of difference" (2003, 3), and in its unique differences engages in discourses with writers and artists that invariably shape what American comics have become. Japan's manga fandom, on the other hand, is not subculture, but mainstream. Manga producers must appeal to everyone from children to grandparents, housekeepers to salarymen — hence the wide variance of manga genres and styles. For that very reason, the Japanese manga hero must differ from the superheroes of American comic book fame. Japan has never been attracted to the American style costumed superhero. Typical Japanese superheroes derive from samurai. They exhibit stoicism and reticence, and they usually have some kind of affiliation with a group, though they can also be depicted as loners (Schodt 1997, 58).

A distinguishing factor of shōnen manga that separates it from American-style heroic comics is its reliance on the initiation phase of the hero's journey. Unlike American comic heroes, shōnen manga heroes spend the bulk of their narrative time in the initiation phase of the hero's journey, while American heroes spend most of their narrative time in the return phase of the journey. In a Superman comic, for example, the reader does not participate in the hero's initiation. American heroes are often self-made; they are heroes not because they learned and grew and overcame difficulty. They are either born heroes or, at least, the reader's first encounter with them is as the heroes they are. Their development is static. While they may undergo a difficulty in achieving the goal in a particular episode, this difficulty is rarely a life changing event. The American reader is not reading for that kind of development. As Jeffrey Lang and Patrick Trimble explain, "The American monomyth secularizes Judeo-Christian ideals by combining the selfless individual who sacrifices himself for others and the zealous crusader who destroys evil. This supersavior replaces the Christ figures whose credibility has been eroded by scientific rationalism, but at the same time reflects a hope of divinity and redemption. . ." (Lang & Trimble 1988, 2). The reader seeks to see fulfilled the prophecy inherent in the hero as he is. Thus the main idea of a Superman or Batman comic is to see the hero defeat the villain, verifying for the reader the prowess, skill, or power predicted by the name of the hero. At the end of the comic, the hero is the same person he was at the beginning of the comic, with only a few exceptions.

In manga, however, character takes center stage. Once the character crosses the threshold, she will stay in the initiation phase for a long period of time, often for the entire series, until the culmination in which she may or may not succeed in defeating her enemy, but she will definitely be changed.

The manga hero will have grown, matured, and learned something that not only enriches herself but also the world around her. It is for that reason that the manga hero has such an enduring and expansive popularity. Readers do not spend the bulk of their lives in the redemptive phase of the journey. Real life is spent predominantly in the initiation, learning, growing, and having struggles and trying to overcome them. The shōnen manga hero provides a mirror of the reader's life. The heroic act is in the example set for the reader by the hero's struggle. Campbell's theories affirm this concept: "The influence of a vital person vitalizes, there's no doubt about it. . . . People have the notion of saving the world by shifting things around, changing the rules and who's on top, and so forth. No! Any world is a valid world if it's alive. The thing to do is bring life to it, and the only way to do that is to find where the life is and become alive yourself. . ." (quoted in Myers 1998). The shōnen manga hero vitalizes not by becoming a deus ex machina to rescue the helpless but by reaffirming the value of the struggles we all share.

WORLDWIDE SHŌNEN

Shōnen manga has grown from propagandistic tales during World War II, to tame light humor in the immediate postwar period, to craft-centered stories in the 1950s, to an explosion of daring expressiveness in the 1960s and 1970s. Since then it has only gained in popularity, readership, and diversity. The latter part of the twentieth century and the start of the twenty-first saw a marked increase in female readership in what was supposedly a masculine genre ("Oricon: #1 Manga Mag for Japanese Girls Is . . . Shonen Jump," 2007). Female readers became so influential to boys' manga that they began to shape the content in the weekly magazines. Content that was previously geared toward fighting and adventure began to include some romance (Schodt 1996). Female characters began to take stronger roles, and in some cases they were main characters, fighting and striving just as hard alongside male characters (Schodt 1997, 75). The years have also seen boys' manga, and manga in general, spread worldwide. The United States joined the party relatively late, but is now a wholehearted consumer of Japanese culture. American fandom has experienced rapid and exciting growth in recent years. Manga sales in the United States were nearly $60 million in 2002 and over $100 million in 2003 (Gustines 2004). As Frederik Schodt posits of aspects of Japanese popular culture, "superficially, they are extremely similar to what is available in America. But they are also a little different. The similarities make them understandable to Americans and also nonthreatening . . . but the differences also make them very appealing" (quoted in Kelts 2006, 181–82). The trend, however, has not been a one-way street. As Americans absorb and become influenced by manga and anime, the Japanese are influenced by American culture. Fred Gallagher and Rodney Caston's *Megatokyo* is clearly a manga-inspired comic that even pokes fun at manga and anime fandom. On the other side of the spectrum, Santa Inoue's *Tokyo Tribes* features Japanese gang members who are wrapped up in hip-hop culture. Shōnen manga has hit upon a formula that appeals to just about everyone. As *Shōnen Jump* editor Hiroki Goto described manga's goals in 1991, "if you work hard, you can accomplish anything. That's what our stories are saying. And that philosophy appeals to both children and adults" (quoted in Gravett 2004, 59) Shōnen manga is a combination of universal truths and culture absorbed, adopted, and re-created. It started its journey speaking only to its own war-torn youth; today it continues to grow and takes on its future hand in hand with the rest of the world.

References

Allen, Kate, and John E. Ingulsrud (2003). "Manga Literacy: Popular Culture and the Reading Habits of Japanese College Students." *Journal of Adolescent and Adult Literacy* 46: 674–83.

"Beijing Bans Scary Stories to Protect Young." Reuters, http://www.reuters.com/article/lifestyleMolt/idUSPEK30969020070515.

Campbell, Joseph (1973). *The Hero with a Thousand Faces.* Princeton, NJ: Princeton University Press.

"Death Note Stirs Controversy in China." Anime News Network, http://www.animenewsnetwork.com/news/2005-02-06/death-note-stirs-controversy-in-china.

Gravett, Paul (2004). *Manga: 60 Years of Japanese Comics.* New York: Collins Design.

Gustines, George Gene (2004). "Girl Power Fuels Manga Boom in U.S." *New York Times*, December 28.

Ito, Kinko (2005). "A History of Manga in the Context of Japanese Culture and Society." *Journal of Popular Culture* 38(3): 456–75.

Kelts, Roland (2006). *Japanamerica: How Japanese Pop Culture Has Invaded the U.S.* New York: Palgrave Macmillan.

Kinsella, Sharon (2000). *Adult Manga: Culture and Power in Contemporary Japanese Society.* Consumasian Book Series. Honolulu: University of Hawaii Press.

Lang, Jeffrey, and Patrick Trimble (1988). "Whatever Happened to the Man of Tomorrow? An Examination of the American Monomyth and the Comic Book Superhero." *Journal of Popular Culture* 22: 157–73.

Moyers, Bill (1998). "Joseph Campbell and the Power of Myth." Montauk, NY: Mystic Fire Video.

Nakar, Eldad (2003). "Memories of Pilots and Planes: World War II in Japanese Manga, 1957–1967." *Social Science Japan Journal* 6(1): 57–76.

"Oricon: #1 Manga Mag for Japanese Girls Is . . . Shonen Jump" (2007). Anime News Network, http://www.animenewsnetwork.com/news/2007-04-10/oricon-no.1-manga-mag-for-japanese-girls-is-cite-shonen-jump/cite.

"Police Reach Dead End in Belgian 'Manga Murder' Case" (2007). Anime News Network, http://www.animenewsnetwork.com/news/2007-11-27/police-reach-dead-end-in-belgian-manga-murder-case.

Schodt, Frederik L. (1996). *Dreamland Japan: Writings on Modern Manga.* Berkeley, CA: Stone Bridge Press.

—— (1983). *Manga! Manga! The World of Japanese Comics.* New York: Kodansha International.

Thompson, Jason (2007). *Manga: The Complete Guide.* New York: Del Rey.

"Virginian Teen Suspended over Names in 'Death Note'" (2007). Anime News Network, http://www.animenewsnetwork.com/news/2007-11-22/virginian-teen-suspended-over-names-in-death-note.

Wolf-Meyer, Matthew (2003). "The World Ozymandias Made: Utopias in the Superhero Comic, Subculture, and the Conservation of Difference." *Journal of Popular Culture* 36: 497–517.

Wolk, Douglas (2007). *Reading Comics: How Graphic Novels Work and What They Mean.* Cambridge, MA: Da Capo Press.

Wu, Cheng'En (2003). *Journey to the West.* 4 vols. Peking: Foreign Languages Press.

Suggested Manga Reading

Akamatsu, Ken (2002). *Love Hina,* vol. 1. New York: Tokyopop.

Anzai, Nobuyuki (2003). *Flame of Recca,* vol. 1. San Francisco: VIZ Media.

Arakawa, Hiromu (2005). *Fullmetal Alchemist,* vol. 1. San Francisco: VIZ Media.

Buronson, and Hara Tetsuo (2003). *Fist of the North Star.* Master ed., vol. 1. Los Angeles: Gutsoon! Entertainment.

Chiba, Tatsuya (2000). *Ashita no Jō* [Tomorrow's Joe]. Tokyo: Kodansha International.

Gallagher, Fred, and Rodney Caston (2004). *Megatokyo,* vol. 1. Milwaukie, OR: Dark Horse.

Higuchi, Daisuke (2004). *Whistle!* vol. 1. San Francisco: VIZ Media.

Hotta, Yumi (2004). *Hikaru No Go* [Hikaru's Game of Go], vol. 1. San Francisco: VIZ Media.

Inagaki, Riichiro (2005). *Eyeshield 21,* vol. 1. San Francisco: VIZ Media.

Inoue, Santa (2005). *Tokyo Tribes,* vol. 1. New York: Tokyopop.

Inoue, Takehiko, (2003). *Slam Dunk,* vol. 1. Los Angeles: Gutsoon! Entertainment.

Keisuke, Itagaki (2003). *Baki the Grappler,* vol. 2. Los Angeles: Gutsoon! Entertainment.

Koike, Kazuo, and Goseki Kojima (2000). *Lone Wolf and Cub,* vol. 1, *The Assassin's Road.* Milwaukie, OR: Dark Horse.

Konomi, Takeshi (2004). *The Prince of Tennis,* vol. 1. San Francisco: VIZ Media.

Kubo, Tite (2004). *Bleach,* vol. 1. San Francisco: VIZ Media.

Nagai, Gō. *Devilman,* vol. 1. Los Angeles: Verotic, 1995.

Nakazawa, Keiji, and Art Spiegelman (2004). *Barefoot Gen,* vol. 1: *A Cartoon Story of Hiroshima.* San Francisco: Last Gasp, 2004.

Nightow, Yasuhiro (2003). *Trigun,* vol. 1. Milwaukie, OR: Dark Horse.

—— (2004). *Trigun Maximum,* vol. 1, *The Hero Returns.* Milwaukie, OR: Dark Horse/ Digital Manga.

Nonaka, Eiji (2005). *Cromartie High School,* vol. 1. London: ADV Manga.

Ōba, Tsugumi (2005). *Death Note,* vol. 1. San Francisco: Viz Media.

Oiwa, Kenji, and Tatsuhiko Takimoto (2006). *Welcome to the N.H.K.,* vol. 1. New York: Tokyopop.

Okuda, Hitoshi (1997). *No Need for Tenchi!* vol. 1. San Francisco: VIZ Media.

Saijyo, Shinji (2002). *Iron Wok Jan vol. 1.* Fremont, CA: ComicsOne.

Takei, Hiroyuki (2003). *Shaman King,* vol. 1, *A Shaman in Tokyo.* San Francisco: VIZ Media.

Toriyama, Akira (2003). *Dragon Ball,* vol. 1. San Francisco: VIZ Media.

Umezu, Kazuo (2007). *Drifting Classroom,* vol. 1. San Francisco: Viz Media.

Urasawa, Naoki (2006). *Naoki Urasawa's Monster,* vol. 1. San Francisco: VIZ Media.

Usui, Yoshito (2002). *Crayon Shin-Chan,* vol. 1. Fremont, CA: ComicsOne.

Watsuki, Nobuhiro (2003). *Rurōuni Kenshin* [Wandering Swordsman Kenshin], vol. 1. San Francisco: VIZ Media.

4

The "Beautiful Boy" in Japanese Girls' Manga

Mark McLelland

INTRODUCTION

It comes as a surprise to many people that the most extensive representations of male homosexuality in Japan (outside the pages of the gay press) exist in comics directed at girls and young women (*shōjo* manga). Representations of gay men (and less so lesbian women) are also quite common in other Japanese media, where they are frequently pictured as gender deviant, transgressing over to the feminine in both appearance and sensibility. In mainstream Japanese media gay men are generally understood to be *okama* — literally, a "pot," which is a slang term for the buttocks and thereby a reference to a passive anal sex partner (Long 1996). Okama are thus considered funny, but ultimately sad, women manqué. In media directed at women, however, the representation of gay men as feminine is more positively received and depictions of gay men as *bishōnen* (beautiful boys) are common.

Young Japanese women's interest in male homosexuality is not confined to comics, however; in the 1990s it spilled over into movies and television dramas that represented gay men as best friends and even ideal partners for women (McLelland 1999). These representations tended to stress gay men's perceived intersexual status, presenting them as uniting the best features of both sexes; this has resulted in some gay magazines carrying "marriage corners" where women can advertise for gay partners whom they assume resemble the gay characters they read about in comics and see onscreen (Lunsing 1995; McLelland 1999). However, most representations of gay men in specifically gay magazines reject this "feminine" image and instead portray gay men as hypermasculine figures, moving in a strictly homosocial world from which women and their concerns have been banished (McLelland 2000). This chapter looks at the characteristic images of predominantly male homosexuality found in Japanese girls' comics in the closing decades of the last century and suggests reasons why women's depictions of love between men should have differed so radically from those representations created by gay and straight men.[1]

REPRESENTATIONS OF WOMEN'S SEXUALITY IN POPULAR CULTURE

It is only possible to comprehend the attraction same-sex love stories hold for Japanese women in the context of the variety of discourses positioning women's sexuality in contemporary Japan. Until recently, Japanese society maintained a strict double standard regarding the sexual expression of men and women. A vast sex industry that employs large numbers of both native and foreign female sex workers exists to fulfill the fantasies of Japanese men (Constantine 1993), and yet the only sanctioned expression of female sexuality has traditionally been within marriage (Buckley 1993, 130). The difficulty in gaining access to reliable contraceptive methods has made sex an anxious experience for many women: despite twenty years of debate, the low-dosage contraceptive pill was not made available by prescription until 1999. This resulted in overreliance on abortion as the contraceptive measure of last resort (Hardacre 1997).

Traditionally, Japanese women experienced intense pressure to get married "on schedule" and start producing children while still in their twenties. Many women marry, as anthropologist Jennifer Robertson comments, "neither for love nor as an expression of their sexuality, but, as is common knowledge, to survive economically" (1998, 145). As a result many Japanese women tend to value such factors as financial stability and good career prospects in a prospective spouse over more affective elements, and *omiai*, or "introduction-marriages" where suitably matched partners are brought together by an intermediary, remain common — especially among women from more elite families (Iwao 1993). Once married, it is expected that wives will give up their jobs and get down to the serious woman's work of producing and caring for children. Women who resist this pressure to get married in order to pursue a career or remain unmarried past their twenties for some other reason are often regarded as odd. Women who work in the sex industry face particular stigma and find it difficult to even rent property, being forced to reside in specific areas of town (Mock 1996).

Helen Hardacre, in her study of discourses stigmatizing women who have had abortions, argues that there has been a marked rise in media interest in women's sexuality since the 1970s. This was a time when women, having won greater economic and social rights, were beginning to insist on their right to sexual self-expression outside of marriage. Hardacre argues that the media reacted negatively to women's perceived increased sexual license and its negative consequences (disease, unwanted pregnancy, abortion) and they created the figure of the "menacing fetus" that lay in wait for women who expressed themselves sexually outside of marriage. She "examines the development in tabloids of a symptomology and discourse of *mizuko kuyō* [religious rites for aborted fetuses], which since the mid-1970s has stigmatized — even demonized — the nonreproductive sexuality of young women" (1997, 14). Hardacre argues that from this time on, the tabloid press has been full of images that picture "women's degradation as a result of sex, a consequence from which men are immune, and of which women can never be free" (1997, 85). Richard McGregor also supports this point, arguing that "promiscuous" Japanese women are penalized by the media in a way that men never are, citing a TV documentary that used staged footage to prove the supposedly loose morals of Japanese female office workers on holiday in Hawaii (1996, 243). Karen Ma also points to sensationalized reports in the Japanese press of how Japanese women who sleep with foreign men were introducing AIDS to Japan, although the extensive sex tourism of Japanese men throughout Southeast Asia "went unmentioned" (1996, 64).

Women who want sex outside of marriage "get what they deserve" — they are used as sexual objects on the terms dictated by their male partners. McGregor points out that "the two lines used most by AV (adult video) actresses are *yamate* [sic; *yamete*] (stop it) and *itai* (it hurts)" (1996, 245). Donald Richie also comments that Japanese pornographic movies "are about something other than the joys of sexual union . . . [they are] about the denigration of women" (1991, 161). Richie notes that in many pornographic representations "women are evil . . . sex is their instrument . . . and men are their prey" (1991, 168). Women's sexuality, a site of considerable anxiety for men, may be connected with the fact that women's menses, traditionally known as the "red pollution" (*akafujō*; Namihara 1987, 68), have associated them with uncleanliness and taboo. This stigma has not been entirely overcome, even today. Hardacre (1997) points out that effective contraception is severely compromised in Japan because of women's unwillingness to talk about their menses and the workings of their sexual organs with their partners, or even to handle them (tampons have been unpopular in Japan for this reason).

SEX AND VIOLENCE IN MEN'S COMICS

Manga is a very popular form of entertainment in Japan, read by a wide variety of different social groups and both men and women. The social attitudes structuring and limiting women's sexuality in Japan are given graphic representation in comics directed at a male audience where depictions of sex

— especially violent and intrusive sex — have become common. As Anne Allison (1996) comments, "sexuality is heavily imbricated with violence in Japanese comics" (1996, 71). Masculinity in men's comics is variously represented, but there are few figures who approximate the beautiful boys (bishōnen) of women's writing. Men in men's comics are usually hypermasculine figures who are highly competitive and aggressive. Allison describes them as being "drawn with harsh features — few smiles, gruff expressions, meanness around their eyes" (1996, 64). These men who "both look and act like brutes" (1996, 64) have short hair and exaggerated muscles, quite the opposite of the bishōnen, who usually have long hair, slender limbs, and few muscles. Of course, straight men are sexually active and sexually aggressive: Allison notes that "the sexual aims that are dominant in *ero manga* [erotic comics] and dominantly male are seeing, possessing, penetrating and hurting" (1996, 64).

Censorship requires that the penis cannot be drawn, so it is instead symbolized by phallic objects such as baseball bats, beer bottles, swords, knives, and even trains! Because graphic representations of genitalia must be avoided, interest is generated in other ways, most typically through extreme violence. Men in general are presented as obsessed with sex, constantly on the lookout for it, and physically endangered if they don't get it. Allison remarks that "male behavior is brutish and narcissistic, driven by extreme emotions that find expression in acts of violence . . . almost everything about males is jagged. Their faces are chiseled and nasty; their bodies are laden (and interfused with) machinery and object parts; their language is sparse and incomplete. And most important, they attack, expressing their desires through aggression" (1996, 73). Women are represented as compliant with men's sexual needs and as inviting sexual domination; "sex, typically, is something that is done to them" (1996, 62).

For example, in Yanagisawa Kimio's (1997) *Iro otoko iro onna* (Randy Man, Randy Woman) a man in the midst of sex says, "For the first time, I've stopped being a man and become a male animal" (*Watashi wa iya ore wa hajimete otoko de naku osu ni natta*). His language here is interesting, shifting from the polite gender-neutral first-person pronoun *watashi* to the vulgar, exclusively male first-person pronoun *ore*; he first refers to himself as a "man" (*otoko*), then corrects himself, using the term *osu*, usually applied only to male animals. In Hatanaka Jun's (1997) comic serial about a high school boy, *Ryōta*, a woman teacher is shown being persistently spied on and sexually harassed during a school trip to a hot spring. However, she actually enjoys the harassment, at one point saying, "I want to be annoyed, treated violently, and insulted by men" before drinking from a bottle of beer that she has inserted between the thighs of a male student in a simulation of fellatio. He quickly substitutes his penis and after he has come in her mouth, she says "you shafted your teacher's throat, you'll be expelled for this you bastard!" Fortunately for the student, next morning she seems to have forgotten about the expulsion, commenting "I slept so well. I was drunk last night and I can't remember anything that happened."

When not depicted as sexually aggressive, men are shown to be rather sad and pathetic creatures who need their egos taken care of by women who do this through providing sex, as in Aogi Yuji's (1996) *Naniwa kin'yūdō* (The Osaka Money Trade) in which the sad little salaryman who has just masturbated to a pornographic magazine in his small, messy room says "I need a wife" and Yamamoto Yasuhito's (1995) *Iron Man*, where the husband, Teruo, asks his wife to suckle him from her breast as she does the children. The latter comic is significant in its conflation of the figures of wife and mother; Teruo stands in a similar relation of dependence to his wife as his children do to their mother. She is always there for him and is a much sought-after refuge from the hardships of everyday life as a salaryman. Although never sexually aggressive or precocious herself, the wife is always sexually available to Teruo, and sex is her gift to him, a means to lessen his tension. The artist focuses upon her huge breasts which are large not because they are the sexually fetishized breasts of the prostitute or pinup girl but because they are overflowing with mother's milk.

Heterosexual sex is rarely presented as an equitable exchange in men's comics, mainly because the men are either aggressive superheroes or miserable failures. In the first case sex is a commodity men take from women, and in the latter case it is a commodity women bestow on men. Rarely is there the sense of mutual exchange that is common in the boy-love (*shōnen-ai*) stories featured in women's comics. Heterosexual sex rarely takes place in the context of a relationship, nor does it lead to a relationship; Allison comments that "sex acts are momentary and superficial, engaged as much (if not more) to break someone down than to achieve orgasmic release, and they rarely result in enduring unions" (1996, 72). Gay men's pornographic comics share many of the features common in men's comics in general, as Wim Lunsing comments, gay magazines tend to present gay men as "sex maniacs" (1995, 71). The same constraints about the depiction of genitalia apply to all pornographic representations, gay or straight, and so gay men's comics also tend to rely upon scenes of violence, bondage, sadomasochism (SM), and a rapid change in partners in order to maintain reader interest. This is very different from many of the sexual relationships between bishōnen, the beautiful boys depicted in some girls' manga, which are represented as both caring and enduring, based on love, not sex.

THE HISTORY OF "BOYS' LOVE" COMICS

Romantic stories about male-male love (*nanshoku*) have a long tradition in Japan, usually focusing on the attraction between a priest or samurai lover (*nenja*) and his acolyte (*chigo*) or page (*wakashu*; Leupp 1995; McLelland 2005; Watanabe & Iwata 1989). Indeed, "erotic relations between males (but not between females) carried a certain amount of cultural prestige" and were "interpreted as a sign of masculine rectitude or an admirably refined sensibility" (Reichert 2006, 6). During the Edo period (1603–1857), the apogee of samurai culture, male-male love was genuinely regarded as a heroic virtue. However, with the onset of modernity in Japan, male-male love was written out of the Japanese canon (although it has continued to exist at the margins). By the 1960s, contrary to the earlier tradition where male love was the providence of male authors, Japanese women writers had begun to interest themselves in stories concerning beautiful boys. One of the first was Mori Mari, who wrote a series of novellas throughout the 1960s dealing with older men's infatuation with beautiful younger men. The early 1970s saw a significant increase in tales about male-male love when girls' manga began to deal with male homosexuality, particularly the love between beautiful boys in a genre which came to be known as "boys love," or shōnen'ai.

What kind of stories and situations did this genre contain? In particular, it was characterized by antirealism. The stories were usually set in an ill-defined "other" place (often Europe or America), in another historical period (more often the past but sometimes the future) and often dealt with boys who were also somehow "other," being aristocrats, historical figures, vampires, angels, or even aliens. All the boys did, however, have something in common: they were always beautiful, depicted with the big eyes and flowing hair that often characterizes female figures in both men's and girls' comics. In fact, the boys were very androgynous, and it could be difficult for someone not familiar with the illustrative tropes of the genre to work out the gender of the figures depicted.

Indeed, gender fluidity is a characteristic of girls' manga (and popular culture directed at girls in general). For instance, the wildly popular *Rose of Versailles* by Ikeda Riyoko (1972–74) is a story of cross-dressing and mistaken identity, a common trope in Japanese culture dating back at least to the Heian period (794–1185) story of transgenderism *Torikaebaya monogatari* (If Only They Could Be Switched). Sandra Buckley states that the *Rose of Versailles* "plays endlessly with gender identity and the relationship between that identity and sexuality, disrupting the myth of biology as destiny. Gender is mobile, not fixed in this story" (1993, 172).

Significantly, the story was taken up by the all-woman drama troupe, the Takarazuka, and was "a phenomenal success . . . the most popular girl's comic ever staged by the Takarazuka" (Buruma 1984, 118). In the stage play, the heroine is a girl who passes as a boy so that she can serve as a general in the army. She plays a significant part in the French Revolution, finally being killed by a cannonball while storming the Bastille. She is then taken up to heaven on a chariot surrounded by clouds of dry ice as the chorus sings. Ian Buruma refers to the sense of *akogare*, or "yearning," that many Takarazuka fans say they feel with regard to the cross-dressed actresses on the stage. He notes that "it is used for people, places and ideals that seem impossibly far away" (1984, 121). This is also emphasized in Jennifer Robertson's anlaysis of the Takarazuka theater's work, which she states was conceived as a "dream world" (*yume no sekai*) (1998, 71). The Takarazuka male-role specialist (*otokoyaku*) is thus an analogous figure to the bishōnen, who is neither man nor woman: "the player of men's roles can be seen as an exemplary female who can negotiate successfully both genders, and their attendant roles, without being constrained by either" (Robertson 1998, 82). In Japanese society, where gender roles have been rigidly fixed, popular culture aimed at women provides a safe space in which the normally nonnegotiable regimen of gender can be subverted and overturned. It is no surprise, then, that women, whose sexuality can be seriously restrained by its association in the popular imagination with either the sex trade or motherhood, should find these fantasies so attractive and be so involved in both their production and consumption.

There are a number of reasons why women's interest in love between boys should be greater than that of love between girls. One of the first writers to take up male homosexual themes in her work, Moto Hagio, said in an interview in 1981 that when considering a story about same-sex love, she was unsure whether to situate it in a boys' or a girls' school. She finally decided on a boys' school because "I found the plan about the girls' school to be gloomy and disgusting. . . . Take a kissing scene, for instance . . . as sticky as fermented soybeans" (Hagio, quoted in Aoyama 1988, 189). It is possible that Hagio made this decision in order to avoid homophobic reactions from her female readers who might have found the idea of girls kissing disgusting but would have found boys kissing somehow safer (just as some heterosexual men appreciate lesbian eroticism). However, manga that include representations of love and even sex between girls do exist, albeit fewer in number than those detailing love between boys. This is representative of the general invisibility of lesbianism in all Japanese media; as Buckley comments, "on the whole it remains true that tolerance of male homosexuality is greater than of lesbians" (1994, 174). First, most of these romances are situated in a non-Japanese fantasy setting and the use of men further removes same-sex attraction from the realm of experience of the female audience. Second, as argued above, representations of female sexuality that show women in control are often marginalized in Japanese media, lesbianism being no exception. This point was underlined when, in conversation with some women fans of the boy-love genre in a Tokyo coffee shop in 1998, it was suggested to me that an all-girl love scene would seem a little strange as it would be unclear who should "take the lead" (*riido wo shite*) in initiating a sexual encounter. It is not surprising then, that some women interpolate themselves in the ambiguously gendered figures of beautiful boys (see Welker 2006).

Although the sex scenes in shōnen'ai comics during the 1970s and early 1980s were somewhat candid and romantic in tone, more recent women's comics have included more graphic sex in their narratives. The early emphasis on boys' love gradually morphed into an interest in love between men in general, including "beautiful youths" (*biseinen*) and even "beautiful (adult) men" (*binan*) as, can be seen in the illustration from Akisato Wakuni's *Nemureru Mori no Binan* (The Handsome Man in the Sleeping Forest), part one of her manga novella *Tomoi* (see fig. 4.1).

Two popular manga anthologies in the 1990s, *June* and *B-Boy*, frequently represented explicit sexual interludes between a range of male figures. Yet, these males were still beautiful, slender, and often of ambiguous gender, depicted with the big eyes and long hair that characterizes female figures in men's comics. These boys and men were thus very different from the male figures depicted in men's comics, both gay and straight, just as they also differed from actual men. The plots were likewise rather fantastic: although the 1994 *B-Boy* anthology *Tenkōsei* (Students Who Changed School) takes place in the familiar realm of the high school, few Japanese boys celebrate graduation by French-kissing their peers as in "I Wanna Be Something" (*Dōnika naritai*; Uchida Kazuna, *B-boy*, December 1994); or have sex with their art and math teachers simultaneously, as in "I Want to Loosen Up in a Rude Kiss" (*Rūdona kissu wo rūzu ni shitai*; Fujisaki Takahiro, *B-Boy*, December 1994). Similarly, the characters in Tamaki Yuri's *Partners* (1993) are also hardly the boy-next-door type. This comic includes detailed descriptions of New York's SM scene including body piercing and fisting.

Other examples of this trend toward referencing actual environments, albeit with somewhat improbable plot lines, include Akisato Wakuni's (1987) *Tomoi* (see fig. 4.1), one of the first literary attempts in Japan to engage with the topic of AIDS. At the outset of the story the "beautiful youth" Tomoi starts work as an intern in a New York hospital, but becoming disillusioned with America, leaves for Afghanistan, where he helps the local insurgency against the Russian invaders. Sanami Matoh's (1994 [2003]) *Fake* (see fig. 4.2) is also set in the United States and details the growing love affair between two New York policemen. These latter examples do situate the sex as part of intimate, long-term relationships, and the sex scenes are, on the whole, aesthetically rendered and reciprocal. They differ markedly from depictions of

眠れる森の美男

FIGIURE 4.1: Tomoi, depicted both as a "beautiful youth" (biseinen) as he is at the beginning of the story and as a "handsome man" (binan) at the story's close. From by Akisato Wakuni, *Tomoi* © 1996 and reproduced courtesy of Shogakukan Inc.

sex marketed at both gay and straight men where the erotic potential of force and violence is commonly exploited.

That said, shōnen'ai fiction is not without depictions of aggressive sex. Tomoko Aoyama suggests that sex that takes place in "a violent context" becomes "an act of revenge" on the part of women readers who now "become a spectator rather than a prey" (1988, 196). Yet this reading depends upon a supposed polarity between the male characters and the female readership. Yet the bishōnen are not really men but androgynous figures, not simply in the way they look but in their sensibilities. When subjected to abuse they are portrayed as innocent victims, and when they instigate sex themselves they enjoy it in the way women are supposed to: as a reciprocal and emotional encounter. In these comics, young men are frequently portrayed as victims in

FIGIURE 4.2: Dee and Randy, two NYPD officers, experience their first kiss in Sanami Matoh's manga series *Fake*. © Sanami Matoh. Courtesy of Tokyopop.

sexual interactions which position them as "female." For example, in Ragawa Marimo's (1998) *New York, New York*, Mel is the beautiful twenty-two-year-old victim of childhood sexual abuse. He escapes from home, where he has been repeatedly humiliated and abused by his stepfather, only to become a street prostitute. He is saved from life on the street by a married client who later dumps him for fear that his wife will find out. Rejected, Mel attempts to commit suicide, but is rescued at the last minute and becomes the lover of a policeman, Kain. His life seems to be back on track until he is assaulted by a masked attacker (who turns out to be Kain's police partner who is himself secretly in love with Kain). Later in the series, Mel is abducted by a serial killer who holds him captive while subjecting him to violent and humiliating sexual abuse. All these situations of sexual subjugation are modeled upon roles traditionally fulfilled by female victims. The reader is clearly supposed to identify with the youth, who, as victim, is placed in a subordinate (read: feminine) position.

Violence is also a characteristic of a largely amateur genre of boys' love manga originally circulated by women fans at comic conventions throughout Japan and now widely available on the Internet, known as *yaoi*, an acronym for *yama nashi, ochi nashi, imi nashi* (no climax, no point, no meaning — a reference to the slender plot lines of these stories). It is interesting to recall that an alternate reading of the acronym yaoi sometimes offered is *yamete, oshiri ga itai!* (Stop, my ass hurts!). This playful derivation is not far off the mark for, as Akiko Mizoguchi points out, "in the 'boys' love' genre, virtually all the protagonists engage in anal intercourse" (2003, 65). Indeed, a main structuring device in yaoi narratives is the often tense relationship between two male leads termed *seme* (from *semeru*, "to attack") and *uke* (from *ukeru*, "to receive"). The seme (older, stronger, larger) character is in hot pursuit of sexual favors from his younger and weaker uke comrade and sometimes does not hesitate to use force, Mizoguchi noting that many yaoi stories feature "rape as an expression of love" (2003, 56). However, although the bishōnen are portrayed as feminine, and are often placed in roles normally associated with female characters, they still inhabit male bodies and are thus unencumbered with the burdens of reproduction.

SHŌNEN-AI COMICS AS SITES OF GENDER PLAY

It seems clear that women readers do not just vicariously participate in these homosexual love scenes but identify with the androgynous figures, not just as ideal lovers or partners but, in a sense, as their ideal selves. The boys are not only represented as feminine but are also inscribed in typically female situations because the primarily female readership sees itself depicted in these stories. Within patriarchy, which assigns very strict roles to women according to their supposed capacities, the androgynous youth is one way in which the female reader can picture herself as separate from the reproductive role assigned to her by the family system which ties female sexuality to child rearing. It is no surprise then, as Aoyama mentions, that in these stories female characters often "wish to be a male homosexual in order to love a beautiful boy" (1988, 191) because it is only a male who can love another male as an equal.

As discussed above, heterosexual sex in Japan has been structured in relation to two strong paradigms: the sex trade and the family. Feminist critic Chizuko Ueno points out that in Japan "men and women are not sleeping with the opposite sex, they are sleeping with a system" (1992, 140). However, it is women's sexuality that is more limited by this system because of the difficulty in Japan of utilizing effective contraception. Women's sexuality is always troubled by anxieties about pregnancy: if women were to love these beautiful youths as women, they would be liable to end up pregnant or loving them as wives, neither of which bear much romance in Japan. Only a boy who loves a boy (or a girl who loves a girl) is truly free in Japanese society to love beyond the constraining roles imposed by the marriage-and-family system. However, Buruma argues that Japanese girls do not want to be boys; what they really want is to be sexless "because they realize that becoming an adult woman means playing a subservient role in life" (1984, 118). This may explain why the heroes of shōnen'ai comics are so androgynous; they are of an *entirely* different order of being from the men presented in manga directed at both gay and straight men, making it easier for women to identify with them as idealized models. Buruma supports this reading when he contrasts the heroes in Japanese women's comics with those in Western comics: "although girls' comics in the West are full of impossibly beautiful young men . . . they are still unmistakably men. . . . In Japan . . . they are more ambivalent, and sometimes get each other" (1984, 124–25). He goes on to note that they are "a faraway romantic ideal. . . . *Bishōnen* are treated in a similar way to vampires or creatures from outer space. Outcasts all, they are the pure, eternally young victims of adult corruption" (1984, 127). The beautiful boys in women's fiction are not like real boys, nor are they like real gay men. These comics say nothing about how gender is, but much about how it ideally should be: negotiable, malleable, a site of play.

Shōnen-ai comics are predominantly written by and for women. However, the author's name is another site in which gender identity is destabilized. Many manga writers write under one or several pen names, and it is impossible to know whether a male-gendered name signifies a male writer or a female-gendered name a female writer. Many of the names chosen are not only deliberately obscure about gender identity but also contain coded references. Examples from the *B-Boy* special edition discussed above include Motoni Modoru (which could be read as "return to the origin"), and Maki Sayaka (made up of the characters "demon" *maki*, and "sand-night-flower," *sa-ya-ka*). The author of *New York New York*, discussed above, has the pen name of Ragawa Marimo. *Mari* is written with characters commonly found in women's names, but the *mo* character, when written separately, is pronounced Shigeru, which is always a man's name. By combining characters associated with both men's and women's names, the author makes it impossible for the reader to assign a gender. These writers do not attempt to provide sociorealist critiques of contemporary Japanese gender stratification; rather, the homosexual relationships they describe are simply a fantasy context for Japanese women to love without reference to reproduction. Buruma comments that "the young girl's dream is to go as far away as possible, sexually, emotionally, geographically, from everyday reality" (1984, 121). The girls' comic genre is characterized by everything that Japanese society is not: here gender is fluid, characterized by androgyny and mobility and, as Buckley notes, "normative or naturalizing narrative structures give way to narratives that follow a fantasy trajectory beyond the boundaries of dominant sexual identification and practice" (1993, 191). In Japan, male homosexuality has become a fantasy image both created and consumed by women.

CONCLUSION

It is ironic that in one of the most extensive romantic genres produced by women — that of the love of beautiful boys in manga fiction — women themselves are largely absent. This is not unusual in postwar Japanese popular culture, however, as Susan Napier has pointed out. In her book *The Fantastic in Modern Japanese Literature* (1990) she includes a chapter titled "Woman Lost: The Dead, Damaged, or Absent Female in Postwar Fantasy." In it she charts a paradigm shift in the treatment of women in Japanese literature that took place after World War II in which "women are no longer caretakers but objects of prey, only acceptable as victims upon which to enact male rage" (1990, 53). The male ego, rendered so fragile now that women have encroached upon all the areas of life that were once the sole domain of men — the realm of education, the workplace and even the sexual marketplace — sees itself as under attack. Napier comments that in literary portrayals, "male characters are shown as damaged and angry" (1990, 57) and women "are frequently seen as agents of entrapment or humiliation" (1990, 56), resulting in a situation where "women seem to have become increasingly Other, unreachable, even demonic" (1990, 57). She sees a profound feeling of separation and discontinuity as existing between the sexes, arguing, "In the works examined in this chapter, by male and female writers, all forms of love, from maternal to sexual, seem to become grotesque parodies of themselves, emphasizing the lack of connection between human beings" (1990, 59). Napier does not analyze manga fiction in the book. If she had, she would have found that many of the themes characterizing literary representations of the relationship between the sexes are also common in manga featuring stories about men and women. However, she would surely have noticed that the same-sex love affairs described in women's manga fiction manage to sidestep the many pitfalls that seem to be inherent in heterosexual relationships. In shōnen-ai fiction, homosocial love, what the popular psychologist Takeo Doi refers to as *dōseiai kanjō* (same-sex love feelings; 1985, 134), manages to circumvent the negative associations which are attached to heterosexual love stories. Shōnen-ai stories represent an ideal world of romance which is as much a utopia as the world of heterosexuality is a dystopia.

When Napier suggests that "the fantasies of both men and women can no longer envision any sort of connection or social community" (1990, 90) she is only right to the extent that she applies this statement to representations of relationships *between* the sexes. Same-sex love, however, manages to side-step all these difficulties and present a picture of love that is pure and unsullied by harsh reality. Ironically, it is a picture of romantic love from which women are largely excluded. If it is only in fantasy that Japanese women can live a sexual life outside of reproductive concerns and avoid the stigma of the sex trade, then, as Buckley questions "is it strange that schoolgirls are so attracted to a fantasy world of nonreproductive bodies, as remarkably non-Japanese as they are nongendered, moving across a backdrop of a nonspecific landscape that is nowhere, or more specifically, that is anywhere that is not Japan?" (1993, 179).

It would seem that in terms dictated by popular Japanese culture, women are trapped between a rock and a hard place. On one side, unreproductive sexual practice outside marriage is represented as dangerous, the results of which are damaged morals as well as damaged bodies. However, "licensed" sexuality that takes place within marriage leads to a wife becoming a mother, whereupon she is desexualized. Even when women, as wives and mothers, are represented as sexual, it is a sexuality which exists entirely in relation to their husbands. They exist to provide their husbands with sex just as they do food, as part of their general role as nurturers. Given these constraints on women's sexuality, it is then, perhaps no surprise that in comics written for women, the love that is celebrated is the love between young men. It is only in this context that love can be free of the "violence and harassment" that Buckley sees as "mechanisms for the containment and management of women's bodies and sexuality" (1994, 176). The comparative lack of homophobia among Japanese women and the long tradition of cross-dressing and transgenderism in Japanese theater have, however, enabled the development of an erotic fantasy genre that sidesteps the pervasive political divides involved in heterosexual representations by focusing upon love between beautiful young men. These "men" (or rather boys) are not really gendered as male but are shown as feminine both in sensibility and in the situations within which they are inscribed. It must therefore be questioned whether these representations have anything to do with Japanese gay men. More likely, they represent the concerns and fantasies of the women who avidly produce and consume them. This love among boys in Japanese women's comics therefore has more to say about the limitations of heterosexual relationships and the negative constraints on female sexuality in contemporary Japanese society. The "beautiful boy" embodies all the most attractive features of female gender, while able to move through the world unencumbered by the burdens of the female sex.

Notes

This is a revised version of an article first published in the *Journal of Gender Studies* 9(1), March 2000.

1. The original version of this article was written in 1999, at a time when Japan was in a period of rapid transformation. The Internet, which was to have a massive impact on girls' manga fandom (particularly aiding in its internationalization), was just beginning to take off. There were also unprecedented social transformations in Japanese work practices due to the by then decade-long recession, resulting in more flexible work practices for both women and men that have to some extent since undermined the "traditional" life paths for women described herein. "Boys' love" comics, however, maintain a huge audience in Japan and increasingly overseas.

References

Akisato Wakuni (1996) *Tomoi*. Tokyo: Shogakukan

Allison, Anne (1996). *Permitted and Prohibited Desires: Mothers, Comics, and Censorship in Japan*. Boulder, CO: Westview Press.

Aoyama, Tomoko (1988). "Male Homosexuality as Treated by Japanese Women Writers." In *The Japanese Trajectory: Modernization and Beyond*, edited by Gavan McCormac and Yoshio Sugimoto, 186–203. Cambridge: Cambridge University Press.

Buckley, Sandra (1993). "Penguin in Bondage: A Graphic Tale of Japanese Comic Books." In *Technoculture*, edited by Constance Penley and Andrew Ross, 168–95. Minneapolis: University of Minnesota Press.

—— (1994). "A Short History of the Feminist Movement in Japan." In *Women of Japan and Korea: Continuity and Change*, edited by Joyce Gelb, 150–87. Philadelphia: Temple University Press.

Buruma, Ian (1984). *Behind the Mask: On Sexual Demons, Sacred Mothers, Transvestites and other Japanese Cultural Heroes*. New York: Meridian.

Constantine, Peter (1993). *Japan's Sex Trade: A Journey through Japan's Erotic Subcultures*. Tokyo: Charles Tuttle.

Hardacre, Helen (1997). *Marketing the Menacing Fetus in Japan*. Berkeley and Los Angeles: University of California Press.

Iwao, Sumiko (1993). *The Japanese Woman: Traditional Image and Changing Reality*. New York: Free Press.

Long, Daniel (1996). "Formation Process of Some Japanese Gay Argot Terms." *American Speech* 71(2), 215–24.

Lunsing, Wim (1995). "Japanese Gay Magazines and Marriage Advertisements." In *Gays and Lesbians in Asia and the Pacific: Social and Human Services*, edited by Gerald Sullivan, 71–88. Binghamton, NY: Haworth Press.

Ma, Karen (1996). *The Modern Madame Butterfly: Fantasy and Reality in Japanese Cross-Cultural Relationships*. Tokyo: Charles Tuttle.

Matoh Sanami (2003). *Fake*, vol. 1. Los Angeles: TOKYOPOP.

McGregor, Richard (1996). *Japan Swings: Politics, Culture and Sex in the New Japan*. St. Leonards, New South Wales, Australia: Allen and Unwin.

McLelland, Mark (1999). "Gay Men as Women's Ideal Partners in Japanese Popular Culture: Are Gay Men Really A Girl's Best Friends?" *U.S.-Japan Women's Journal English Supplement* 17.

—— (2000). *Male Homosexuality in Modern Japan: Cultural Myths and Social Realities*. London: RoutledgeCurzon.

—— (2005) *Queer Japan from the Pacific War to the Internet Age*. Lanham, MD: Rowman and Littlefield.

Mizoguchi, Akiko (2003). "Male-Male Romance by and for Women in Japan: A History and the Subgenres of Yaoi Fictions," *U.S.-Japan Women's Journal* 25, 49–75.

Mock, John (1996). "Mother or Mama: The Political Economy of Bar Hostesses in Sapporo." In *Re-Imagining Japanese Women*, edited by Anne Imamura, 177–91. Berkeley and Los Angeles: University of California Press.

Namihara, Emiko (1987). "Pollution in the Folk Belief System," *Current Anthropology* 28(4) (supplement), S65–S74.

Napier, Susan (1990). *The Fantastic in Modern Japanese Literature: The Subversion of Modernity*. London: Routledge.

Reichert, Jim (2006). *In the Company of Men: Representations of Male-Male Sexuality in Meiji Literature*. Stanford, CA: Stanford University Press.

Richie, Donald (1991). *A Lateral View: Essays on Contemporary Japan*. Tokyo: Japan Times Ltd.

Robertson, Jennifer (1998). *Takarazuka: Sexual Politics and Popular Culture in Modern Japan*. Berkeley and Los Angeles: University of California Press.

Ueno, Chizuko (1993). *Sukāto No Shita No Gekijō* [Theater under the skirt]. Tokyo: Kawade Bunko.

Welker, James (2006). "Beautiful, Borrowed and Bent: 'Boys' Love' as Girls' Love in Shōjo Manga," *Signs* 31, 841–70.

Suggested Manga Reading

Akisato Wakuni (1996) *Tomoi*. Tokyo: Shogakukan

Hatanaka Jun (1996) *Ryōta*, vol. 1. Tokyo: Bungei Shunju.

Matoh Sanami (2003). *Fake*, vol. 1. Los Angeles: TOKYOPOP.

Ragawa Marimo (1998). *New York, New York*. Tokyo: Hakusensha.

Tamaki Yuri (1993). *Partners*. Tokyo: Bamboo Comics.

Yamamoto Yasuhito (1995). *The Iron Man*, vol. 9. Tokyo: Kodansha International.

Yanagisawa Kimio (1997). *Iro Otoko Iro Onna* [Randy man, randy woman], vol. 1. Tokyo: Bungei Shunju.

All Japanese names are written in Japanese order (surname first) except those Japanese authors whose cited works appear in English original or translation.

5

Shōjo Manga in Japan and Abroad

Jennifer Prough

INTRODUCTION

At the most basic level, *shōjo* manga is manga for girls. As I walked into the manga division of a major publishing house for the first of many interviews that would comprise much of my ethnographic research on the mainstream shōjo manga industry (2000–2002), I was struck by the extent to which gender pervaded the production of shōjo manga.[1] Gender is immediately palpable as the girls' section is rife with pastel and glitter on posters and flyers that embellish the walls and the magazines that line every aisle and bookshelf. The boys' section is also adorned, but the colors are primary and bold. As this simple organizational detail attests, gender is the principle publishing classification for manga.

In this chapter I discuss the genre of shōjo manga drawing attention to the difference that gender makes in its production at home and consumption overseas. Beginning with a discussion of the general themes and styles of the genre, I will examine the ways in which editors, artists, and scholars characterize manga for girls. Across the diversity of the genre, whether set in mythical lands or in a Japanese high school, shōjo manga are stories about human relations (*ningen kankei*). Furthermore, editors and artists characterize the creation of shōjo manga as a balancing of human relations; thus, I discuss how shōjo manga is produced with particular attention to the role that manga magazines play in the creation of the genre while highlighting the gendered aspects of magazine production. Shōjo manga magazines are gendered not only in content but in personnel — that is, artists are primarily female and editors are primarily male. Finally, I turn to an examination of the emergence of the shōjo manga market in the United States, focusing on the influence of and divergence from the original Japanese market. As there is not a comparably systematic genre of girls' comics outside of Japan, shōjo manga has had to forge new markets, drawing primarily from the anime fan base. Thus, in this chapter I will examine shōjo manga as a gendered genre, paying particular attention to how it is produced in Japan and how U.S. publishers negotiate the cultural differences embedded therein.

WHAT IS SHŌJO MANGA?

Shōjo manga is a broad genre that includes stories that run the gamut from those considered literary classics to your average pulp novel. As such, any attempt to characterize the genre dilutes the diversity (and will undoubtedly omit features of many people's favorite titles). However, shōjo manga has emerged over the past century as an identifiable genre, not only because it is manga published in shōjo manga magazines, but also particular narrative themes, aesthetic style, and techniques of representation have become regular features of shōjo style. In media theory, a genre is defined as a collection of texts grouped together by similarity of plot structure, setting, theme, emotional effect, and so on (Gledhill 1998, 351). Recent scholars have theorized genre as a pact between producers and consumers, a way to let the audience know what they will be getting (Valaskivi 2000, 309). In any genre a balance is required among standardization of themes, plot, setting, and differentiation, among other aspects; that is, genre texts need to be recognizable as such by their audience but also different enough from each other to be worth reading (Gledhill 1998, 355). Shōjo manga is a genre in this sense. It is governed by conventions that are understood by both its producers and consumers. And it is both the pleasure of recognition and the delight in the new that ensures the success of the genre.

In my conversations about what shōjo manga is with editors, artists, and scholars, most of them started with a comparison to boys' manga (*shōnen* manga). In part, this is because boys' manga has always comprised a bigger share of the overall manga market. Thus, many of those with whom I spoke began by delineating predictably gendered genres. The mantra, "boys manga is filled with more action — the drama and story are moved by action — whereas girls' manga is driven by human relations," was recounted time and again in my interviews. Accordingly, girls' manga tends to revolve around issues of love and friendship, and is filled with unrequited love, love triangles, friendships forged through the trials and tribulations of high school life, and the like. The content and form of shōjo manga reflects this general focus on human relations.[2]

In manga history, the late 1960s and early 1970s are considered the golden years of shōjo manga. In this period, Japan was well on the road to economic recovery and the publishing industry was flourishing; a generation of postwar children came of age, having grown up reading manga in magazines and rental books;[3] and women artists began to dominate the drawing/writing of shōjo manga. (Until this time almost all manga artists, including shōjo manga artists, had been men.[4]) These early women artists reinvigorated the genre as they sought to capture their protagonists' and readers' innermost feelings. Rather than the more action- and dialogue-based plot construction of the standard boys' genre of the time, these female artists began to experiment with how to express emotion, inner thoughts and feelings, memories, and musings. There was one loosely knit group of shōjo manga artists that has received substantial popular and scholarly attention: the *24 nengumi* (1949 cohort).[5] These renowned artists honed the genre through an expansion of content, a renovation of layout, and the enrichment of the characters. In this era what had been primarily a comedic medium took on a more dramatic and romantic quality. Whatever the genre (comedy or drama) and wherever the setting (Japanese school life, ancient China, or outer space), human relations and matters of the heart remain at the core of shōjo manga.

Not surprisingly, the protagonist in shōjo manga is almost always a young girl.[6] Typically the stories revolve around the heroine and her group of friends. While girlfriends are always an important part of these friend groups (*nakama*) a few male friends have become standard fare. Generally speaking, each of the main friends represents a different character type — the smart one, the stereotypically beautiful one, the comic one, and so on — with good and bad qualities. The plot relies in various ways on these friends working together to solve problems, whether personally or globally cataclysmic.

One extraordinary character type that has flourished in shōjo manga is the *bishōnen* (beautiful boy). The bishōnen can best be described as beautifully androgynous. To be sure, it is often hard for the uninitiated to identify these beautiful boys as male characters — their hair is typically long and flowing, their waists narrow, their legs long, and their eyes big in shōjo manga style. These pretty boys first appeared in the shōjo manga of the golden years and were some of the first male protagonists of the genre.[7] Today the bishōnen appears less frequently in mainstream manga, but when he does appear with his long hair, narrow waist, and gentle soul, he is identified consciously as a shōjo manga type.

Because shōjo manga is about human relations and romance, there are almost always love interests for the protagonist, her friends, or both. The women artists of the golden years set the stage for shōjo manga through their turn to drama and romance. In the shōjo manga of the 1950s and '60s, even kissing scenes were rare. Such proclivities were strictly taboo. However, in the golden age of the 1970s, the first kissing scenes and sex scenes were gradually introduced in the magazines aimed at older teens. By today's standards these scenes were extremely discrete, not depicting anything explicit. It is interesting to note that the earliest love scenes in shōjo manga were frequently between two bishōnen.[8] In the 1970s, stories of the twists and turns of tortured love between these "beautiful boys" became all the rage in shōjo manga, and this is where many of the 24 nengumi got their start. By using male characters (or gender-neutral characters) in these earliest representations of sexuality, the artists were not seen as proscribing sexual activity for their young readers, and yet it is precisely the visual femininity of these beautiful boys that allowed for identification on the part of readers (Fujimoto 1998, 45–62; Welker 2006, 852). By the 1980s, *shōnen-ai* (boys' love) had almost entirely moved out of the mainstream manga magazines and into specialty magazines. Today's mainstream shōjo manga is not as sexually explicit as its male counterpart, yet representations of sexuality have progressed since the genre's inception. It is uncommon to find any sex in shōjo manga aimed at the youngest readers, but the titles aimed at high school readers can be quite explicit. Today, the magazines *Shōjo Manga Cheese!* and *Be Love!* are marketed as having more sexual content. Nonetheless, no matter what the gender, sexual orientation, or age of the protagonists or readers, the drama of emotions, attachments, and inner feelings is always central to shōjo manga.

Shōjo manga protagonists and friends interact in a range of settings and scenarios, yet today they are more often than not ordinary girls in ordinary settings. Trends in setting have shifted throughout the past half century; most notably, in the late 1960s and early 1970s the most popular titles were set in exotic locales — from Europe to outer space and past, present, and future. Exotic and often imaginary settings allowed these artists to experiment with the genre and the themes in ways that an everyday setting during the early postwar years denied. However, in the consumer driven atmosphere that typified the 1980s, shōjo manga came to be set in the midst of everyday life in Japan. Love comedies, and particularly those set in a quintessential Japanese high school, called *gakuen rabu-kome* (school love comedies), became a mainstay of both boys' and girls' manga. *Ouran High School Host Club* by Hatori Bisco and *Hot Gimmick* by Aihara Miki are recent examples of the gakuen rabu-kome genre.[9] These everyday home and school dramas can still be found in many shōjo manga magazines and are known for their innocent schoolgirl characters, as well as for dramatic themes of human relations, unrequited love, family strengths and tensions, and the trials of friendship. They are quintessential contemporary *monogatari* (narrative stories) — in essence, bildungsromans — about growing up as a preteen or teenage girl in Japan today. In the words of one editor, "girls' manga has remained from the heart".

This is not to say that there is no adventure in shōjo manga; in fact, heroes and superheroes have populated the genre since the postwar period. Starting with *Ribon no Kishi* (Princess Knight) by Tezuka Osamu (circa 1953), the genre of female superheroes boasts some illustrious members, including *Cardcaptor Sakura* and *Sailor Moon*. However, superhero girl protagonists are frequently located (at least partially) in everyday Japanese life as they traverse both the ordinary and the extraordinary. Even as evil is vanquished and mysteries are solved in shōjo manga, the themes of human relations, romance, and friendship dominate the stories.

The focus on interiority during the golden years of shōjo manga initiated two important stylistic innovations — a montage style of panels, and big eyes. Manga differs from Western comics in its framing and this is, in part, thanks to the first group of women artists in the late 1960s. In a medium filled with square panels all lined up neatly and with word balloons to express speech, manga was originally driven by action and dialogue. But early women artists found this format restrictive and refashioned the page in order to better represent the more interior and emotional content of their manga. These artists experimented with the placement of panels, and the use of dialogue to really capture more aesthetics of feeling than had been previously possible in the genre. A montage panel format made it easier to track back and forth among characters' actions, dialogue, and thoughts. While this collage of panels is harder to read when first encountered, the protagonist's emotional state (mixed up, contemplative, angry, etc.) is nonetheless elicited at a glance beyond the images or text themselves. Furthermore, the use of montage to express interiority was enhanced by experimentation with different modes of expression. Most notably, artists used different shapes and textures for word bubbles to differentiate memory from speech, as well as including words floating across the page and outside of frames to indicate thoughts outside the main action and dialogue. Gradually, the montage style of shōjo manga has influenced shōnen manga as well, although generally speaking boys' manga is still primarily dialogue- or action- driven and has even come to characterize manga for international audiences (McCloud 1993).

A second dominant feature that stands out when comparing manga to other comic traditions is the use of extraordinarily big round eyes. While the use of big eyes dates back to Tezuka's early manga, inspired by Disney, shōjo manga pushed the use of this device to new levels. Increasing the size of eyes was another component of the experimentation with the representation of inner thoughts, feelings, and reminiscence in shōjo manga. The usefulness of eyes for expression is usually attributed to the fact that they are, as we say, the window to the soul. As several artists explained to me, with larger eyes a wider range of emotional states can be depicted. This use of anatomically impossible eyes develops the iconic nature of the comic book style to its utmost (McCloud 1993; Natsume 1999). Big doe-eyes have become a standard feature of shōjo manga, and one that has come to characterize manga more generally in the global field.

In a word, human relations (ningen kankei) can be used to sum up both the content and style of manga for girls. Shōjo manga has evolved as a genre that examines love and friendship though artistic style, the use of iconic images and frames, and dramatic stories about everyday life (real or imagined). As I have argued here, these features help producers and consumers alike to identify shōjo manga as manga specifically geared toward girls; and yet, montage frames, outrageously big eyes, and the focus on human relations that evolved within shōjo manga have also come to characterize manga internationally as a unique genre of comics.

PRODUCING SHŌJO MANGA MAGAZINES

Following the general overview of recurrent themes in shōjo manga, I turn now to an examination of how it is produced and the ways in which gender shapes that creation.

Both in Japan and the United States, research on comic books has treated manga primarily like novels — examining content, form, and particular artists.[10] Indeed, manga is a literary genre in Japan and to study it as such is apt. However, this approach leads to certain assumptions about coherency of narrative and authorial intention that are not necessarily born out in research on the production of manga. While we tend to think of manga stories as long narratives sometimes running into dozens of volumes, almost all manga first appear serialized in magazines. Thus, to understand shōjo manga we have to look at shōjo manga magazines, for it is in this context that artists and editors create manga stories in the nexus between business decisions and the creative process.

With few exceptions, all mainstream manga first appear as thirty- to forty-page serialized episodes in the plethora of monthly or weekly magazines that line the shelves of convenience stores, train station kiosks, and book stores. As of 2005 there were around three hundred different manga magazines (Shuppan Nenpō 2005, 241). Manga magazines themselves do not make any money; in fact, most run perpetually in the red. The magazines exist to try out manga storylines in order to evaluate what will be popular, what will sell more books, character goods, anime, etc. If a story proves popular, these serial stories are compiled into books (tankōbon) and become the novelized manga most of us are familiar with. Thus, while manga is still the main product — where the money is made, how artists become famous, and what publishers are known for — its format and story is shaped month by month by the magazine system. What is important about this is the way in which the arc of any given story is affected by the whims of market as well as the rhythms of the magazine production industry.

In her book on adult manga, Sharon Kinsella highlights the contentious relationship between editors and artists in the production of manga in her chapter titled "Creative Editors and Unusable Artists" (Kinsella 2000, 162–201). While the tenor of her account of editors and artists in the men's manga division at the publisher Kodansha is stronger than the characterization of this relationship related to me by shōjo manga editors and artists, that the relationship is precarious was clear. Everyone admitted that this relationship is at once the crux and the crucible of manga production. Even though editors work primarily behind the scenes and rarely enter the limelight, their managing role is notorious. Tales of heavy-handed editors "raising artists" by sequestering them in tiny apartments for days on end in order to meet a deadline, chastising the artistic skills of even veteran artists, and generally dominating their creative counterparts abound.

The job of an editor can be misleading to a Western audience; as one veteran editor explained it, "Unlike our Western counterparts, Japanese editors do not simply proofread texts, but coordinate putting things together, actually working with the artists to make the stories and then the magazine. Thus, the editors who work on a given magazine have a great deal of influence over its style and content". The main job of an editor is working with artists to create interesting manga — manga that will sell — on time in order to meet the monthly deadlines. At every stage of the process editors weigh in on the content, tenor, and artistic quality of the manga story, from coming up with story lines and characters to approving the final draft. In the original planning of a story, the editor's role may range from approving an artist's prototype and helping the artist flesh it out to telling the artist it is not an interesting idea and she needs to come up with something else. At the most extreme, editors even develop a story line and then search for an artist who can draw/write the story for them (Naoko Takeuchi's *Sailor Moon* is a successful example of this process). Similarly, after the artist has sketched the *nēmu* (the rough draft of an episode) the editor has a great deal of input as to whether or not the story, characters, and pacing work. In the meetings at which I was present, the editor's copy of the draft was covered in red pencil marks and the editor walked the artist through necessary changes, many of which involved everything from rearranging and resizing boxes to better directing the flow and punch of the story. An episode may go through only one edit before moving on to the *genkō* (the final draft of the manuscript), or may go through several. In each of these stages the editor and artist meet to solidify the creation of manga.

Because manga editors play such a strong role in the creative process, the making of manga is generally understood — for better or worse — as negotiation between artists and editors. Several editors likened their job to that of a sporting team's coach or a movie director — that is, someone who works behind the scenes yet is an integral part of the process. One young editor provided insight into this process, noting, "So much of the job has to do with human relations: understanding readers, working with other editors, interacting with artists, and designers, you are the intermediary. All artists work slightly differently, their communication styles, work pace, and needs are different and you have to change and adapt to each in a way. So listening, adapting, and communication are crucial to the job of editors — human relations."

Thus, here too human relations dominate as editors and artists work together to create manga balancing creativity, perceived readers' needs, and profit margins. Of course, the extent of collaboration depends on the levels of experience of both the artist and the editor, but most accounts I was given held with this general description. While artists receive credit and sometimes even fame for the stories they create, the process of producing manga is a combination of the push and pull of creativity and what will sell, as determined by the editors in charge.

There is another level at which gender influences the creation of manga, and that is in the makeup of publishing house personnel. Not only is shōjo manga a fundamentally gendered genre, but there is a gendered division of labor in its production — that is, roughly 75 percent of shōjo manga editors are men, while 99 percent of the artists are women (mostly in their teens to late twenties). To some extent, the business practices of the company managerial system shape this division of labor: the postwar "economic miracle" was predicated on the tripartite social system of work, home, and school. The company employment system provided a living wage and pension as part of the social contract that advocated that women (as wives and mothers) take care of the household and children. The mainstream publishing industry is part and parcel of this system (even as it declines). Editors are traditionally corporate men (salarymen); full-time employees on the career track thus tend to be men. However, with the passage of the Equal Employment Opportunity Clause in 1986, women began to join the ranks of salarymen everywhere and publishing was no exception. Today, of the new employees hired by the main publishing houses each year, between 30 and 40 percent are women. Yet, in the shōjo manga divisions where I conducted my research the proportion of women editors was closer to 20 percent and almost all were still in their twenties.

As noted above, in the prewar and early postwar era all manga artists were men, but by the late 1960s most of the artists writing for shōjo manga were women. As one veteran editor recalls, "When women artists started — you know, Ueda Toshiko, Hasegawa Machiko, Maki Miyako, etcetera — it was clear right away that girls were really drawn to the manga of women writers. Looking at the texts themselves I couldn't tell how it was different, but something was transmitted. By the time I left [in the early 1960s] most of the male authors were doing boys' stuff and almost all artists for shōjo manga were women. That's still true today". This notion that women make the best artists for shōjo manga is something that infused many of the conversations that I was a part of or privy to. As this editor's statement alludes, there is a feeling that women artists are closer to understanding the hearts and minds of female readers. After all, who better to know what girls will like than a girl?[11] Thus, the very industry itself — not just the texts — is shaped by gender. Mostly male editors and young women artists work together within the constraints of gender relations and publication deadlines to create manga for girls.

In this section I have argued that manga stories are shaped, at least in part, by the dynamics of their production. The elaborate marketing structure of the magazine system, with its relentless competition and pace, influence the flow of a given story while giving editors a stronger hand in the construction of manga than literary analysis might reveal. Furthermore, gender is a component of the creation of manga for girls not only in its content but also in the composition of the industry itself as young women artists are recruited for their similarity to readers to work with older male editors in the publishing business. Ultimately it is the dynamic between these various players that creates shōjo manga.

SHŌJO MANGA AT LARGE

During the tenure of my research, Japanese popular culture had become a global force to be reckoned with, and manga had emerged from the nooks and crannies of fan culture to line the shelves at Barnes and Nobles, Borders, Virgin Megastores, and other retail venues throughout the United States, Europe, and Australia. Nevertheless, despite the sizable increase in exported manga in recent years, exports are still a minor portion of the industry totals. Furthermore, in spite of the countless books and articles that have appeared in Japan recounting and theorizing Japanese popular culture's recent global popularity,[12] the major publishing houses still consider foreign markets an afterthought. In interviews with artists and editors I found a level of curiosity about foreign markets, yet time and again I was told that it is great to have foreign readers but ultimately the audience they are writing for is Japanese girls. While the largest publishing houses — Kodansha, Shogakukan, Shueisha, and Kadokawa — have well-established markets throughout Asia, and markets in Europe, the United States, and Australia that are growing, most exports are still initiated by outside interest rather than internal motivation.

In the years since my fieldwork, this attitude toward foreign markets has begun to change. The number of manga titles on bookstore and library shelves across the world is increasing exponentially. The Japanese publishing industry is beginning to embrace these new markets, following in the footsteps of toy companies that have been flooding international markets for the past decade with Pokémon and Yu-gi-oh goods to the delight of children all over the world. Accordingly, in the past few years each of the mainstream Japanese publishing houses covered in my research has made significant structural inroads into the American market. VIZ, located in San Francisco, has been one of the main translators and publishers of manga in English since 1987, when it was founded by Shogakukan. In 2005 VIZ merged with ShoPro to become VIZ Media, a joint venture owned by Shogakukan and Shueisha (VIZ Media 2005). Thus, VIZ publishes manga primarily from Shogakukan, Shueisha, and Hakusensha. Similarly, in 2005 Kodansha began a joint venture with Random House, starting the Del Rey manga line, which publishes Kodansha's most popular titles (Del Rey Manga 2005). Both of these new mergers represents a foothold in the U.S. market, a change from simply fielding requests for the right to translate titles to active involvement with a U.S. publishing house to sell manga in English. Furthermore, U.S. publishing houses' exclusive connections with Japanese publishing houses represents an extension of the Japanese industry structure overseas.

These Japanese publishing houses have not only taken a bigger interest in selling manga books overseas; in the past few years they have begun to try their hand at selling manga magazines abroad. In 2002, the first English language issue of *Shōnen Jump*, the foremost boys' manga magazine, was released by VIZ Media, and in 2005 the first issue of *Shōjo Beat*, a girls' manga magazine, premiered. Both magazines have exceeded initial expectations and fueled manga markets in the English-speaking world. Thus, despite the reticence about a Western manga market that I encountered in my fieldwork, in the intervening years the publishing industry has begun to test this market, if not cater to it.

As can be seen in the example of manga magazines in the United States, Japanese publishers are beginning to market manga abroad in ways similar to those used to market it at home. In part this is possible because the market for manga overseas has been driven almost exclusively by fan interest. It is the demand for more manga by the fans of anime communing at conventions and then on the Internet that TokyoPop, VIZ Media, and Del Rey are now tapping into. One of the interesting dynamics of this fan-driven industry is a desire for texts as close to the original as possible. Thus, unlike earlier manga and anime imports, manga today emphasizes its Japanese roots. For decades most Japanese popular culture that entered the U.S. marketplace was localized, erasing all hints of its Japanese origin in order to appeal to Americans.[13] This is no longer necessary; in fact, Japanese origin has become a badge of honor. When you open a cover of a manga title in English, most likely the first thing you will see is a warning that you are reading the last page. Japanese books are read right to left, and many manga in English today follow suit. Even *Shōjo Beat*, which is trying to reach out to new audiences, plays up its Japanese origin by including articles about Japanese culture, Tokyo fashion, and the latest Japanese teen trends. This particular dynamic allows its Japanese producers to remain focused on the Japanese market and still make extra profit selling to the international market.

Nonetheless, shōjo manga has been slow to enter the international market, driven as it is by fan interest and anime, which is dominated by shōnen titles. In several of my discussions with editors and scholars about the potential for a shōjo manga market in the United States, the lack of comics for girls was always the first point raised. Time and again I was asked why girls in the United States didn't like comics. Of course, there are girls/women who read comics in the United States, and there are some comics that explicitly cater to them, but for the most part there is no comparable tradition of a female comic genre. Thus, it was only on the tail of the growing popularity of shōnen anime, shōnen manga, and shōjo anime that shōjo manga was formally introduced. VIZ Media's early attempt at introducing shōjo manga provided the following definition for its American audience inside the front covers of its manga books:

> shô•jo (sho'jo) *n.* 1. Manga appealing to both female and male readers.
> 2. Exciting stories with true-to-life characters and the thrill of exotic locales.
> 3. Connecting the heart and mind through real human relationships.

Here we see the quintessential focus on human relations and intimacy for girls, discussed throughout this chapter, but marketed to both male and female readers. Manga for girls is promoted as a subgenre, though not just for girls despite its name. Here again we see a trait that exemplifies shōjo manga as one of the features that distinguishes manga from other comic traditions. Abroad, the gendered aspects of shōjo manga titles themselves become articulations of human relations and distinguish manga from indigenous media traditions.

CONCLUSION

Throughout this chapter I have outlined the general contours of shōjo manga while focusing on the difference gender makes in the production of the genre as well as the ways these contours begin to shift in transnational context. As I began this chapter, shōjo manga is manga for girls, as the glittery pastel magazine covers and the focus on human relations and romance in the stories attest. Yet shōjo manga is not just filled with gendered content, rather the genre is produced within a nexus of human relations wherein the editor/artist dynamic as well as editor/audience dynamic are shaped by relations of gender. Furthermore, the innovations of creative women artists have developed stylistic techniques such as montage frames and large eyes that highlight interiority and emotion; and these very features have shaped modes of expression in manga more generally. Furthermore, as the essays in this volume attest, manga is becoming a global style, yet one that remains inherently linked to Japan. Even though shōjo manga is a relatively small subgenre, the aesthetics of form and content cultivated within its pages have become signature features of manga, both at home in Japan and abroad.

Notes

1. This chapter is based on two years of research on the mainstream shōjo manga industry in Tokyo, 2000–2002. Manga is predominantly produced in Japan's largest publishing houses and I interviewed extensively throughout the shōjo manga divisions of the top four shōjo manga publishers: Kodansha, Shogakukan, Shueisha, and Hakusensha. Thus, this chapter focuses on mainstream shōjo manga.
2. For a succinct account of the history of shōjo manga in English, see Masami, 2007.
3. Rental books (*kashibon*) flourished in the early postwar years as a cheap entertainment genre for children. For only about 10 yen, manga and illustrated stories could be rented from small book rental stalls and shops which peppered the streets of cities and towns in the 1950s.
4. Ueda Toshiko, Imamura Yōko, and Hasegawa Machiko are notable examples of earlier women artists.
5. The name *24 nengumi* refers to the year in which most of these artists were born, Shōwa 24 (1949). The 24 nengumi is generally thought to include Hagio Moto, Takemiya Keiko, Ikeda Riyoko, Ōshima Yumiko, Yamato Waki, Kihara Toshie, and Yamagishi Ryoko, among others.
6. There are notable counterexamples, including Hagio Moto's *Thoma No Shinzō* (Thomas's Heart); Sasaki Noriko's *Dobutsu No Oishasan* (Animal Doctor); and Maki Yoko's *Aishiteruze Baby* (I Love the Baby).
7. The work of Hagio Moto, Ikeda Riyoko, and Takemiya Keiko is most widely cited for starting the bishōnen genre.
8. Much has been written in English on shōnen-ai and its contemporary counterpart *yaoi*; see especially Mark McLelland's "The 'Beautiful Boy' in Japanese Girls' Manga," chapter 4 in the present volume; see also McLelland, 2000; Midori, 1993; Mizoguchi, 2003; and Welker, 2006.
9. Note that the style used in this chapter is: family name, given name.
10. Sharon Kinsella's research on men's manga is the exception. See, for example, Kinsella, 2000.
11. This gendered division of labor is further generalized as female artists have remained primarily ensconced within the genre of shōjo manga. Takahashi Rumiko and the artistic group CLAMP are among the select few women writing manga for boys' and men's magazines.
12. See, for example, Hosogaya, 2002; Iwabuchi, 2001; Natsume, 2001; and Ōtsuka, 1998.
13. For more on the localization of Japanese popular culture, see Allison, 2006.

References

Allison, Anne (2006). *Millennial Monsters: Japanese Toys in the Global Imagination.* Berkeley and Los Angeles: University of California Press.

Del Rey Manga (2005). "Manga: About Us." Random House, http://www.randomhouse. com/delrey/manga/about.html.

Fujimoto, Yukari (1998). *Watashi no ibasyo wa doko ni aru no?* [Where is my place?] Tokyo: Gakuyō Shobō.

Gledhill, Christine (1998). "Genre and Gender: The Case of the Soap Opera." In *Representations: Cultural Representations and Signifying Practices,* edited by Stuart Hall, 337–86. London: Sage.

Hosogaya, Atsushi, ed. (2002). *Manga Guidebook.* Yokohama, Japan: Kawasaki City Museum.

Iwabuchi, Koichi (2001). *Toransunashonaru Japan: Ajia wo tsunagu popuraa bunka* [Transnational Japan: Connecting to Asia through Popular Culture]. Tokyo: Iwanami Shoten.

Kinsella, Sharon (2000). *Adult Manga: Culture and Power in Contemporary Japanese Society.* Honolulu: University of Hawaii Press.

Matsui, Midori (1993). "Little Girls Were Little Boys: Displaced Femininity in the Representation of Homosexuality in Japanese Girls' Comics." In *Feminism and the Politics of Difference,* edited by Sneja Marina Gunew and Anna Yeatman, 117–96. Boulder, CO: Westview Press.

McCloud, Scott (1994). *Understanding Comics.* New York: HarperPerennial.

McLelland, Mark J. (2000). *Male Homosexuality in Modern Japan: Cultural Myths and Social Realities.* Richmond, England: Curzon.

Ministry of Foreign Affairs, Japan (2007, October 27). "Creative Japan"; http://www. creativejapan.net/index.html.

Mizoguchi, Akiko. 2003. "Male-Male Romance by and for Women in Japan: A History and the Subgenres of Yaoi Fictions." *U.S.-Japan Women's Journal* (25): 49–75.

Natsume, Fusanosuke (1999). *Manga no chikara* [The power of manga]. Tokyo: Akira Bunsha.

——, ed. (2001). *Manga Sekai Senryaku* [Manga's world strategy]. Tokyo: Shogakukan.

Ōtsuka, Eiji (1998, May). 'Sekai ni kantaru "otakubunka"' [One of the world's greatest otaku cultures]. *Voice,* 174–83.

Shuppan Nenpō, ed. (2005). *Shuppan shihyō nenpō: 2005-nenban* [Annual indexes of publishing: The 2005 edition]. Tokyo: Shuppan Kagaku Kenkyū Senta.

Toku, Masami (2007). "Shojo Manga! Girls Comics! A Mirror of Girls' Dreams." In *Networks of Desire: Mechademia vol. 2,* edited by Frenchy Lunning, 19–32. Minneapolis: University of Minnesota Press.

Valaskivi, Katja (2000). "Being a Part of the family? Genre, Gender and Production in a Japanese TV drama." *Media, Culture and Society* 22(3): 309–25.

VIZ Media (2005). "Merger between Two Japanese Entertainment Giants Complete: Announcing VIZ Media!" VIZ Media, http://www.viz.com/news/ newsroom/2005/04_vizmedia.php.

Welker, James (2006). "Beautiful, Borrowed, and Bent: 'Boys' Love' as Girls' Love in Shojo Manga." *Signs* 31(3): 841–70.

Suggested Manga Reading

Aihara, Miki (2003). *Hot Gimmick.* San Francisco: VIZ Media.

CLAMP (2002). *Cardcaptor Sakura.* Los Angeles, CA: Tokyopop.

Hagio, Moto. 1972–74. *Thoma No Shinzō* [Thomas's heart]. Tokyo: Shogakukan.

Hatori, Bisco (2005). *Ouran High School Host Club.* San Francisco: VIZ Media.
Maki, Yoko. (2002–4). *Aishiteruze Baby* [I love the baby]. Tokyo: Shueisha.
Nakajo, Hisaya (2004). *Hana-Kimi: For You in Full Blossom.* San Francisco: VIZ Media.
Sasaki, Noriko (1988–94). *Dobutsu No Oishasan* [Animal doctor]. Tokyo: Hakusensha.
Takaya, Natsuki (2004). *Fruits Basket.* Los Angeles: Tokyopop.
Takeuchi, Naoko (1998). *Sailor Moon.* Los Angeles: Mixx Entertainment.
Tezuka, Osamu (1953). *Ribon No Kishi* [Princess Knight]. Tokyo: Kodansha International.
Yazawa, Aï. 2005. *Nana.* San Francisco: VIZ Media.

Manga
in Depth

6

Oishinbo's Adventures in Eating: Food, Communication, and Culture in Japanese Comics

Lorie Brau

Going by its television programming, Japan seems practically obsessed with food. Of course, you can watch people cook on TV in the United States, too — on PBS, the morning talk shows, and the Food Network, for example. But in Japan, programs about food are everyday fare, scheduled in prime time on the major networks. In addition to the well-known *Iron Chef*, which is no longer broadcast in Japan, Japanese viewers have enjoyed everything from food travelogues (where to find the best ramen noodles) to celebrity cooking segments (*Bistro SMAP*) on evening variety shows and even a children's cartoon, broadcast in 2002–3 in the United States as *Fighting Foodons*, featuring monster-fighting plates of fried rice.

If food may seem an unusual subject for prime time television, let alone a cartoon, so is the idea of a "gourmet" comic book. But just about anything will do as a subject for manga. As in the United States, there are Japanese comics about superheroes, but there are also manga about sports, school, gangs, telephone sex, corporate life, and samurai. Some manga interpret the Japanese literary classics. Adventure, romance, mystery, science fiction, horror, and humor — every popular genre is represented. History, how-to manuals, political analysis, and parody have all been published in manga form, and millions of Japanese, including adults, read it. In fact, by the 1990s the domestic manga market produced three times the revenue of the domestic film industry (Kinsella 2001, 41). Most manga stories appear serially in thick comic magazines printed on recycled paper. The more popular series are then reissued in *tankôbon*, paperback volumes of eight to ten stories, which are collected by fans.

Frederik Schodt, one of manga's best-known Western scholars, claims that "manga have as much to say about life as novels or films" (Schodt 1983, 16). Manga certainly have much to say about food and, as I shall demonstrate in my brief sampling of a few of the many current and past titles in the gourmet genre, elaborate an assortment of themes. I focus, however, on a few episodes of *Oishinbo* (The Gourmet), one of the most successful food manga series, to explore how food figures as a vehicle of communication in comics. How does food in this best selling manga forge and mediate relationships and construct cultural identity?

INTRODUCING GOURMET COMICS

Comics about food are called *gurume* (gourmet) or *ryôri* (cooking, cuisine) manga in Japanese. When I marveled to a Japanese friend about how many of these titles I had discovered, she, too, expressed some puzzlement. How can they be popular when so many young Japanese don't cook? she wondered. Perhaps it is because people cook less these days that they enjoy the experience of cooking and eating vicariously in comic book form.

Japan's gourmet boom of the 1980s likely provided the biggest push to the proliferation of gurume manga. *Oishinbo*, the most popular "gurume manga," began publication in 1983. The manga's title combines the word for delicious, *oishii*, and the word for someone who loves to eat, *kuishinbo*. Written by Kariya Tetsu and illustrated by Hanasaki Akira,[1] *Oishinbo* appears in *Big Comic Spirits*, a thick biweekly comic magazine with a target audience of male college students and white-collar workers under thirty. The first episode of *Oishinbo* sold over a million copies and launched its fame. From the mid-1980s to the mid-1990s it was publisher Shogakukan's second-biggest-selling manga series (Kinsella 2000, 82). To date, 103 tankôbon volumes have been published. The series ended its twenty-five-year run in the May 26, 2008 issue of *Big Comic Spirits*. *Oishinbo*'s popularity spawned a weekly half-hour animated television show from 1988 to 1992, a live-action feature film, a computer game, and fan websites that index the many recipes embedded within the text.[2]

Oishinbo may have the greatest circulation among gurume manga, but it is not the first to concern itself with food: manga have made allusions to food for decades. In the difficult postwar years, a number of manga featured characters named after foods. For example, Sazae-san, the eponymous housewife heroine of one of Japan's most popular and long-lived manga (and animated television show) was named after the turban shell, a kind of conch. Members of Sazae's family also bore names of marine foodstuffs: her brother was Katsuo, which means "bonito" (a type of fish) and her baby sister was Wakame, a kind of seaweed.

In the 1970s, food and cooking came into greater prominence in manga, when stories recounting the trials of apprentices or athletes in their quest for mastery became a popular subject. One of the first manga to focus on the ordeals of culinary training was *Hôchônin no Ajihei* (Ajihei the Knifeman), serialized from 1973 to 1977. The reader followed Ajihei's initiation into the secrets of the trade — the best way to peel an onion, for example. *Tekka No Makihei*, a pun on the tuna sushi roll, *tekkamaki*, featured competitions that judged the apprentice sushi chef's techniques and aesthetics (Schodt 1983, 111). A more recent sushi series, titled *Shôta No Sushi* (Shota's Sushi), also follows the struggles of a young apprentice sushi chef whose sincerity and effort win him favor over his more experienced elders. Sometimes the heroes of these manga about work or professions are "lone wolf" types, such as the wandering chef of *Za Shefu* (The Chef), who recalls the hero of *Black Jack*, Tezuka Osamu's famous manga about a wandering surgeon.[2]

The age and interests of the protagonists of food manga indicate that some of them are written for teenagers, but many appear to be directed toward an adult audience. Most seem to have been written by and intended for men. As in the West, while women are responsible for feeding the family, men usually rule the professional kitchen. The traditional association of men with the outside, the social world of work, and women with the inside, the home, has brought men into contact with professional cooking to a greater extent than women.[3] The connoisseurship championed in gurume manga also tends to be a male activity. Nevertheless, *Oishinbo* author Kariya Tetsu, who has described himself as a kuishinbo, denied being a connoisseur in an interview conducted in 1986, asserting that his manga is not aimed at specialists and admitted to being embarrassed when food professionals glanced at it (Kariya 1986, 343). In an information-obsessed culture like Japan, however, food savvy is a desirable attribute, a means toward asserting one's sophistication. Additionally, though it appears that the preponderance of gurume manga's readers are men, women also read and even write them. *Yume iro kukkingu* (Dream-Colored Cooking), a gurume manga that fits into the category of *shôjo*, or girls', manga, features love stories and recipes for confections and other foods favored by teenage girls.

Gurume manga not only appeals to a variety of readers, but also introduces those readers to a variety of cuisines. *Cuisinier's* chefs produce French classical cuisine and compete in *Iron Chef*–like contests. The heroes of *Aji ichimonme* (A Pinch of Flavor; a pun on *hana ichimonme*, a Japanese game similar to "Red Rover") work at a small, traditional Japanese restaurant, or

FIGURE 6.1: Yamaoka Shirô and Kurita Yûko in the foreground on the cover of "The Great Controversy on How to Cook Rice". © 1997 *Oishinbo*, Kariya Tetsu and Hanasaki Akira, Vol. 64; Shogakukan. Used by permission.

koryôriya. There is even *Raamen hakkenden* (Legend of the Discovery of Ramen), a manga about a young white-collar worker who operates a ramen noodle stand at night. Yoichi, in *Misutaa Ajikko* (Mr. Flavorchild) is a young culinary genius who cooks at his mother's restaurant, a homey, low-priced establishment serving a number of Western/Japanese comfort foods like spaghetti and *tonkatsu*, breaded fried pork cutlet. *Kareinaru shokutaku* (The Splendid Curry Table) features a group of teenagers who run a restaurant specializing in Japanese style curry rice. *Chûka ichiban* (The Best Chinese Food) introduces readers to Chinese dishes.[4] The heroes of some gurume manga are amateur cooks, such as the cooking papa (and mama) of *Kukkingu Papa* (Cooking Papa), who adopt a less formal approach to cooking than that of professional chefs. In one episode, the mother mixes last night's leftover curry sauce with the breakfast *nattô*, fermented soybeans.[5]

The word *aji* that appears in many of these characters' names and titles — Ajihei, Ajikko, and *Aji ichimonme*, for example — means "flavor" in Japanese. Another "flavorful" manga, *Ajimantei* (House of Full Flavor) departs from the extended narrative manga format and parodies contemporary Japanese obsession with food in four-panel strips.[6] Reflecting a Japan where eaters and cooks come in all sizes and perversions, *Ajimantei* turns the rules of eating on their head. Mismatch Yokozuna, a sumo champion, makes rice sandwiches on white bread. Full Course Dandy takes apart a convenience store rice ball wrapped in nori seaweed and stuffed with an *umeboshi* (salty, pickled plum) and eats it in courses; the seaweed is his salad, the rice his main course, and the plum his dessert.[7] Kamaboko [Fishcake] Man manages the transformation into super-hero, but as a log of fish cake stuck on a piece of wood he lacks the mobility to catch the crooks.[8] Diet Girl — dieting being a fairly recent concept in Japan — decides that it is psychologically unhealthy to suppress her desires. Just one ice cream, she pleads, as she takes out a huge container from the freezer.[9] Searching for originality in their sushi making, two sushi chefs come up with the towering "Big Mac Sushi" and another creation popular with the ladies, "Strawberry Short Sushi." The red of the strawberry looks lovely set off by the pale green of the wasabi-flavored whipped cream, remarks the chef.[10]

CUISINE AS COMIC BOOK

Gurume manga artists work in the cinematically inspired tradition of visual representation that has become standard in manga stories. They draw their images from a variety of angles, in wide shots and close-ups. Scenes of food preparation display a strong sense of movement: in one, a chef dynamically prepares fried rice; in another, a live fish flops wildly under a chef's steady grasp. The act of cooking takes on the drama of a sword fight.

As in other comic books, both Japanese and non-Japanese, sound effects are inscribed into the drawings of gurume manga. But here the sound effects record the sizzle of a steak more frequently than the impact of a punch. The Japanese language boasts a prodigious onomatopoeic and mimetic vocabulary (*giseigo* and *gitaigo*, respectively) to express sensual experiences. *Oishinbo* employs this vocabulary extensively, both as illustrated sound effects and as part of the characters' utterances, to evoke the sounds of preparing and eating food: the *ton ton ton* of a knife chopping, the *gu gu* or *gura gura* of a stew simmering, the *juu* sizzle of hot broth poured over fried rice, the *saku saku* sound made when a character crunches into something crisp. Even the temperature and textures of the food are identified with their own mimetic effects. The word *hoko* is superimposed on a picture of a hot sweet potato (*hoka hoka* means hot; *hoku hoku* suggests the softness of a starchy food); when a sound effect is written into such an illustration, it almost seems as if the food is speaking for itself.

As might be expected, *Oishinbo* features many scenes of people eating, with morsels of food suspended midair between chopsticks. When raw and prepared foods appear alone in a panel, as they frequently do, they tend to be illustrated in a different style from that of the characters. In the comic book technique called "masking," a story's characters are drawn in outline, in a simplified cartoon style, while backgrounds are rendered in a more detailed style, similar to a commercial illustration. This allows readers to "mask themselves in a character and safely enter a sensually stimulating world" (McCloud 1994, 43). *Oishinbo* and some other gurume manga use masking, but the technique produces different effects. Rendering the food illustrations in crosshatched, photographic detail often makes them more prominent. Portrayed in close-ups, food becomes as large as or larger than the characters animating the surrounding panels. These drawings emphasize the difference between food as fact and the story as fiction. Like the manga's many scientific explanations of why food tastes as it does, they bring the narrative to a halt with their graphic realism and temporarily stop the flow of fantasy.

OISHINBO: AN "ULTIMATE MENU" OF INFORMATION AND ENTERTAINMENT

The variety of drawing styles employed in *Oishinbo* and other gurume manga underscores the multiple aims and pleasures of these manga: to entertain with a story and to educate with recipes and other "real life" information about food and cooking. This interweaving of culinary information and story is particularly evident in *Oishinbo*. The first episode begins with a taste test. Three glasses of water and three blocks of tofu are set before the apprehensive employees of the *Tôzai Shinbun* (*East-West News*). Now tell me, their boss the publisher asks, which of these glasses contains city water, which local well water, and which mountain spring water? Which of these chunks of tofu come from a supermarket, which from a famous tofu shop in Tokyo, and which from a famous shop in Kyoto?

Only the young new female employee Kurita Yûko and her male colleague Yamaoka Shirô can discern the variations among and identify the sources of the samples of tofu and water, substances that are generally considered tasteless, so the publisher chooses this unlikely pair to develop a menu, an "ultimate menu" comprised of culinary masterpieces. This *kyûkyoku no menyû*, as it is called in Japanese, will not only commemorate the newspaper's history; it will also serve as a "cultural treasure to bequeath to the future."[11] Kurita's and Yamaoka's ongoing assignment engenders the umbrella narrative of the manga, the frame within which it introduces a variety of dishes, both Japanese and foreign.

Like the chef in *Za Shefu*, Kurita and Yamaoka use food to rescue people from various types of distress. Though he has certainly mellowed over the twenty years since the manga's inception, Yamaoka's outspoken nature and lack of concern about others' opinions set him apart, earning him the reputation of being a problem employee. He is often described as *guutara* — lazy, good for nothing. But he becomes a hero when he patches up broken relationships or speaks out against the dissemblers in the food business who pass off inferior products on an unsuspecting public.

"Tofu and Water," the first episode of *Oishinbo*, sets out an ideology for the manga based on the idea that "human culture is food culture" and on the fact that "today Japan imports food from every country. Japan is the first country to have access to so many food cultures."[12] This message also signals a concern: in the face of all this variety, how does one choose what to eat? *Oishinbo* assumes the role of guide, steering its readers through a dizzying array of culinary possibilities in a time of rapid change.

When *Oishinbo* was first serialized in 1983, Japanese were storming Gucci stores all over the world on the strength of the yen. It was a time of plenty before the bursting of the bubble and subsequent recession. One can afford to become fussy about food when there is a great variety and abundance to choose from, and Tokyo does indeed offer such a variety. While *Oishinbo* introduces foreign, exotic, and sometimes costly foods, it has tended to assume a conservative stance, advocating loyalty to Japanese tastes. Readers learn about Thai, Vietnamese, French, Italian, and even Australian aborigine food, but most of the stories teach such lessons as the proper way to steam Japanese rice, what makes good miso, or how to slice fish for sashimi. Even when the focus is on foreign cuisines, however, *Oishinbo* tends to celebrate simple, traditional foods.

Oishinbo traces a number of plot lines through its recurring characters. The most significant threads are the father-son conflict between hero Yamaoka and his gastronome father, Kaibara Yûzan, and the relationship between Yamaoka and Kurita, which eventually results in a marriage and twins. In addition to the overarching story lines, most episodes focus on people and their problems. These human-interest stories not only propound a moral code but also present detailed and often scientific culinary information.

Not all of the culinary information is dry, however. *Oishinbo*'s characters communicate their *subjective* experiences of food. In one episode, for example, Yamaoka praises a dish that the cook introduces with the phrase *Nihonjin ni umarete yokatta* — "I'm glad I was born Japanese" (in order to be able to appreciate and enjoy this very "Japanese" dish, in other words). He describes "the crisp bite of well-toasted fried bean curd, the plumpness of steamed whitebait on the tongue! What a pleasant combination! The rich sweetness of the fired bean curd, the light sweetness of the whitebait, all pulled together with the refreshing flavor of grated daikon radish!"[13] Lacking the luscious visual images of food that stimulate the salivary glands on such Japanese television programs as *Dotchi no Ryôri* (Which Dish?), readers of *gurume* manga rely on this kind of language to engage in vicarious eating. In the absence of color, sound, and smell, they recall their own eating experiences in order to interpret the illustrations, sound effects, and characters' verbal description of food.

Like *Hôchônin no Ajihei* and a number of other ryôri manga, *Oishinbo* falls into the subgenre of manga about work. However, while we visit many kitchens in the manga, the primary workplace in *Oishinbo* is a newsroom. The manga's heroes are journalists who gather and disseminate information and interpret it for the public. That the heroes should be journalists is significant: as in the United States, information is a hot commodity in contemporary Japan. *Oishinbo*'s didacticism responds to the demand among many of its readers for knowledge about food. The quest to know the "ultimate" that shapes the entire series of *Oishinbo* may not only be a reaction to this demand but may itself feed the food obsession that I have alluded to in the opening to this chapter. Indeed, the term *kyûkyoku*, applied to the "ultimate menu" that Kurita and Yamaoka are responsible for creating, has come into general slang usage.

FIGURE 6.2: Yamaoka Shirô and Kaibara Yûzan face off in 'The Spirit of Hospitality' © 1986. *Oishinbo* Vol. 5: 173; Kariya Tetsu and Hanasaki Akira; Shogakukan. Used by permission.

THE CONTEST AND THE WAY OF CUISINE

While hunger for information dominates at times in *Oishinbo*, more dramatic elements such as competition engage readers' attention. Competition not only plays a significant role in dramatizing the subject of food on Japanese television in *Which Dish?* or *Iron Chef*; it also appears frequently in gurume manga. Perhaps the popularity of competitions in a manga genre about an art created with knives has some connection to Japan's tradition of popular samurai tales, in which problems are solved through sword fights. Not all the competitions involve knife skills, though. As we have seen, *Oishinbo* begins with a taste test to find the most refined palate. As the series develops, Yamaoka's newspaper, the *Tōzai News*, pits its "ultimate" kyûkyoku no menyû against the rival *Teitô News* (*Capital News*) shikô no menyû ("supreme menu") to establish a hierarchy of dishes as well as a ranking of the chefs and gourmets who produce or discover them.

Yamaoka frequently resorts to the culinary challenge to settle arguments about which chef or which dish is the best. One such cook-off early in the series involves that most Japanese of dishes, sushi. In the episode titled "Sushi no kokoro" (Spirit of Sushi) a sushi chef scolds a customer for his clumsy grasp of a morsel of sushi. "Don't you know my sushi is a work of art?"[14] When Yamaoka rebukes the chef for his rudeness to the customer, the chef lunges at him with a knife. He accepts Yamaoka's challenge to match his skill against that of an acquaintance of Yamaoka, a seasoned old chef who works out of a tiny restaurant on a backstreet in an out-of-the-way Tokyo neighborhood. Yamaoka and several other employees of the newspaper perform a blind taste test. Of course the old man's sushi wins, which outrages the arrogant chef. As he does in numerous episodes, Yamaoka turns to the persuasive power of science to explain why the old master chef makes a better piece of *nigiri* sushi. He sends the sushi samples to a university hospital for a CT scan, which reveals that the grains of rice in the older chef's sushi are regular and, as they should, have some space between them. Yamaoka remarks, "Do you see now? You were so busy bragging about your sushi that you weren't paying attention. You smashed the grains together too much. Sushi made without feeling is just a clump of rice grains — it's not sushi."[15] The conceited chef made his sushi too hastily; he lacked Zen-like attention and care. Science provides the evidence, but ultimately the problem is one of spirit.

Sushi has become a connoisseur's food, an insider's food. Esoteric knowledge of this cuisine offers a pleasurable opportunity to both chef and customers to show off and distinguish themselves. But exclusivity can be taken too far and a sushi chef can become too inflated with power. Yamaoka and the elder sushi chef proclaim the true value of a sushi experience: feeling is the important thing. The elderly chef puts it this way: "I'm just trying to run an honest, friendly business for my regulars, without pretensions, as I did in the old days."[16] The intimacy created between chef and customer means more than showing off one's knowledge but, as the story implies, this intimacy seems to be disappearing in Japan today.

Perhaps the most important competition in *Oishinbo* sets Yamaoka against Kaibara Yûzan, the gastronome father from whom he is estranged. Kaibara is modeled after the real life potter, artist, writer, gastronome and restaurateur Kitaoji Rosanjin, himself introduced in one of *Oishinbo*'s episodes. Kaibara's imposing, kimono-clad figure casts an ominous shadow over the narrative as he blasts Yamaoka for his inadequacies or fires a cook who smokes. While Kaibara clearly has no tolerance for others' foibles, his knowledge and palate are unparalleled and indeed enthusiastically trumpeted by everyone except his rebellious son. Yamaoka left home at an early age, alleging that his father's imperiousness drove his mother to her death. Although later in the series their relationship seems to soften a bit when Yamaoka marries Kurita and they have children, Yamaoka generally expresses only contempt for his father. Nor does Kaibara show any love for Yamaoka. But through his harshness one perceives his true purpose: to train his son in the "way of cuisine."

Kaibara elaborates this "way" early on in a story called "Motenashi no kokoro" (The Spirit of Hospitality).[17] In this episode Yamaoka faces off against his father's former servant in a contest to prepare the basics of many a Japanese meal: rice and miso soup. As exquisite as Yamaoka's entries are they cannot hold a candle to those presented by the servant, a reprise of a meal that he had prepared for his boss years before. This was a simple repast of miso soup and rice, but, of course, no ordinary soup and no ordinary rice. The servant sorted through his rice grain by grain, to make sure that each was the same size and that the rice would cook evenly. He pounded fermented soybeans to make his own miso paste, using a pestle that he had carved from a branch of prickly ash that was still green. The pestle imparted a subtle flavor to the miso and clam broth.

It is not his former employee's culinary performance alone, but also the heart behind them that Kaibara praises. He claims that the only condition that raises epicureanism to the level of art is the stirring of a person's spirit. And the only thing that can move a person's spirit is another person's spirit. Ingredients and skill alone do not suffice; cooking is an act of communication between souls.[18]

"Heibon no hibon" (The Ordinary Extraordinary) also enacts the principle of consideration for one's guest, care, and kindness, or *omoiyari* in Japanese.[19] To win the support of a millionaire named Kyôgoku, who has promised to lend a Renoir painting for the *Tôzai News* art exhibition, Yamaoka's bosses wine and dine him at a restaurant alleged to be the best in Tokyo, if not in all of Japan. A gourmet, Kyôgoku flies into a rage when he is served foods out of season, taboo in Japan's culinary aesthetic. Yamaoka performs some damage control by inviting Kyôgoku to another dinner. His research on his guest reveals that Kyôgoku once worked in the rice trade and knows his rice. Yamaoka thus instructs the chef to prepare the best quality rice the old fashioned way, over a wood fire. Yamaoka appeals to the millionaire's affection for his hometown by serving a type of sardine common in his home province of Tosa. The humble fish awakens in Kyôgoku a profound nostalgia. In addition to beguiling his palate, the meal offers him an opportunity to display his knowledge of rice and its preparation and impress the rest of the company. Pleased with the meal, he decides to lend the Renoir.

One Japanese writer on food culture blamed what he saw as a loss of omoiyari in social relations on the loss of these feelings in the preparation and consumption of food (Hirano 1978, 12). As much as he plays the heartless connoisseur who values quality above human sentiment, even Kaibara Yûzan promotes omoiyari. Yamaoka has clearly absorbed this lesson from his father, as time and again throughout the series he emphasizes it, as in this quote from one episode: "The idea behind cooking is to bring joy to the person who is eating your cooking. If that's the case, you would naturally prepare and season the food to the tastes of the person whom you wish to make happy, wouldn't you?"[20]

The "extraordinary ordinary" and the "spirit of hospitality" also propound the idea that one need not be from a higher class or have pricey ingredients at one's disposal to be a gourmet or a good host. When planning his dinner for Kyôgoku, Yamaoka consults a homeless man he knows to learn where to find the best food in the Ginza. Working for leftovers, the homeless are back-door restaurant critics, a theme also elaborated on in Itami Jûzô's 1985 film *Tampopo*. While Yamaoka's colleagues are aghast at the simple meal set before them and their honored guest, the happy result proves that simple food can be just as good as, if not better than, "gourmet" food, especially if it is offered with consideration of the person for whom it is prepared.

In *Oishinbo*, not only does one not need to be rich to be a gourmet, one does not even need to be Japanese. An episode titled "Hôchô no kihon" (The Fundamentals of the Knife) advances the idea that even foreigners can be sensitive to the principles of the way of Japanese cuisine.[21] The episode also contests the emphasis on presentation and performance at some Japanese restaurants. Americans certainly enjoy the knife-juggling displays at such popular *teppanyaki* chains as Benihana. But are these displays what Japanese food is really about? An American named Jeff Larson has asked Yamaoka's boss Tanimura to find him a place to train as a chef. Tanimura takes Jeff, Yamaoka, and Kurita to West Coast, a snazzy restaurant with a branch in Los Angeles, thinking that Jeff will be able to find employment there on his return to the United States. Jeff observes that the restaurant looks like a boutique on Rodeo Drive. The chef there uses a showy technique to slice sashimi; the Americans love it, the owner brags. Conforming to the Japanese stereotype of Americans as outspoken, Jeff frowns and comments that the sashimi doesn't taste good. The hot-tempered chef flashes his knife. Once again, Yamaoka suggests a competition to settle the conflict.

One week later, Jeff and the chef of West Coast will each prepare a dish of *koi no arai*, carp sashimi on shaved ice. Of course, Yamaoka has a plan for Jeff. He takes him to a cantankerous old master chef from Kyoto for a crash course in how to cut, perhaps the most important technique of Japanese cooking. Jeff demonstrates the Japanese traditional value of persistence, practicing day and night with a cleaver until he can peel a daikon radish into a wide, paper-thin ribbon at least three meters long. In the contest, Jeff triumphs. All the judges, including the restaurant owner, declare his sashimi the tastier. Yamaoka turns to science to explain why. The chef's ostentatious knife techniques were rough on the carp flesh, breaking down the cells so that they absorbed more of the melting ice, making the slices taste watery. Sashimi must be sliced carefully. Even the restaurant owner revises his notion that it's all about presentation. The episode teaches that being a chef is about training hard, understanding the basics, and respecting the food.

RICE AND THE EXPRESSION OF JAPANESE IDENTITY

It may be no accident that it is a foreigner whose presence gives rise to discourse about the essence of Japanese food. It is against the backdrop of international culinary abundance that Japanese food identity emerges: *Oishinbo* often defines the Japanese culinary self in relation to a non-Japanese other. Perhaps the most charged food in *Oishinbo*'s treatment of international relations is rice. *Oishinbo*'s emphasis on rice reflects the centrality of this symbol of Japan. Although a very small percentage of Japanese make their living as farmers, and although white rice has not been a staple food for the average Japanese since ancient times, it remains a central, sacred symbol for "we Japanese" as opposed to "you foreigners."

The proper preparation of rice is the subject of numerous episodes in *Oishinbo*, as in "Gohan no takikata ronsô" (An Argument about How to Cook Rice).[22] Another story, "Tai mai no aji" (The Flavor of Thai Rice),[23] responded to a real-life crisis: a poor rice harvest in 1994 necessitated the importing of rice from abroad, despite the protests from farmers and citizens. A visiting Thai journalist defends her nation's rice from the criticism that it looks and smells bad, and that it is not sticky enough. "Thai farmers sweat to produce this rice," she reminds the Japanese.[24] Yamaoka suggests which Japanese foods go best with this fragrant, fluffy rice. Of course, sautéed dishes marry well with the rice, and even grilled, salted salmon works. Nevertheless, some of the characters suffer a "culture shock" when they learn that the traditional way to cook Thai rice is to first boil it in a large quantity of water as one would boil noodles and then throw away the cooking water that produces the glutinous quality that Japanese prefer. *Oishinbo* tackles head on Japan's culinary xenophobia when it comes to rice.

Oishinbo addressed the issue of the rice import liberalization problems of the early 1990s in a story titled "Nichibei Kome Sensô" (Japanese-American Rice War).[25] The anti-rice import faction's argument centers on the importance of rice to Japanese identity. Their leader argues that in ancient times Japan was called Mizuhonokuni ("land of vigorous rice plants"), and in the Edo period a samurai's income was measured in quantities of rice. The leader points to Japanese fall festivals, which primarily celebrate the rice harvest, as the "soul of the Japanese." If rice production were to cease, he explains, the Japanese people would lose the foundation of their spirit.[26]

In these episodes, Yamaoka's opponent is American congressman Dan Foster, who is visiting Tokyo for trade talks. Foster believes that the Japanese consumer would gladly buy high-quality California rice for one-fifth the price of the domestic product. He refuses to buy into what he regards as Japanese mystification of the issue.

Yamaoka speaks through the medium of food to convince Foster of the importance of rice to the Japanese. He serves a meal of *funazushi*, a fermented fish preserved in rice, a salad of seaweed and red clam made with rice vinegar, and fine sake; no rice is served, but all the foods are rice-based. Yamaoka even appeals to Foster through his interest in Japanese ceramics. The meal is served on Bizen ware, made from clay that originated in rice paddies. In the last segment of the story, however, Yamaoka shifts the argument away from symbol and toward health. He reveals that Japanese object to the fact that the United States uses postharvest fungicides on rice for export. To be fair, Yamaoka notes that many Japanese farmers also use pesticides. In the end, it takes the shocking image of deformed Japanese macaques that have eaten cereals treated with pesticides to prove to Foster why many Japanese are so reluctant to import American rice.

FOOD AND MEMORY

While *Oishinbo*'s topicality and its debates on the politics of food may partly account for its popularity, it is the cooking techniques, descriptions of food, and food-centered, sentimental stories about human relationships that dominate the series. The theme of food and memory figures prominently in these stories and even links some of the personal problems with the social problems critiqued in *Oishinbo*. The manga notes, for example, that such changes in the food industry as rationalization and commercialization usually yield a less healthful, less flavorful dish than the one remembered from one's younger days.

The discourse of nostalgia found in the story of the millionaire who savors the taste of his hometown Tosa sardine pervades *Oishinbo* and underscores the manga's notion of memory as a taste enhancer. In "Haha naru ringo" (Mother Apple), nostalgia takes the form of a man's quest for his mother's love.[27] Apple pie and apple tea evoke Aosawa's childhood memories of mother. Perhaps American mythology suggested this idea to writer Kariya, as apple pie is not a dish in the average Japanese homemaker's repertoire. In fact, the mother in the story, who was forced by the courts to relinquish custody of her eldest son to his father when she divorced, lost contact with him when she remarried and went to the United States. Her son, Aosawa, cannot forgive her and feels abandoned and bitter. As a result of his past he has trouble committing to a relationship; he has lost faith in family and does not want to start one of his own. And he is a bit obsessive about what he orders at coffee shops.

Yamaoka intuits from the fact that Aosawa only orders apple pie and apple tea every time he goes to a café that these must have been his mother's specialties. The pie in the coffee shops never satisfies him. Made with frozen apples, it always tastes artificial. Of course, the apples are not the real problem.

Though his mother now lives in Japan and has tried to reestablish contact with her son, Aosawa is still so angry that he has refused to meet with her. Yamaoka contacts her with the hope that maybe Aosawa will eat her pie, and asks her to bake it at a certain café where he has invited Aosawa to tea.

The pie and tea stir Aosawa's heart. He savors the tea: "Ah this natural rich fragrance! It invigorates me to my depths. It was for this that I burned with passion!" Biting into the pie, he exclaims, "the fragrance and freshness of the apples . . . their natural tenderness, gentle aroma; such a rich flavor, a balance of tart and sweet! This was the taste that I was looking for! This was the flavor that I tasted in my dreams!"[28] He recognizes the woman leaving the café kitchen as his mother and runs out in pursuit. The two hug in a tearful reunion. Lest readers despair that they cannot reproduce the tastes of Aosawa's mother's pie, Yamaoka supplies a rational explanation for their superior taste. She used tart baking apples, not the sweet eating apples popular in Japan. And she infused her tea with apple peels, the natural way.

In the fantasy world conjured up in *Oishinbo*, food functions as a kind of symbolic code. When people have trouble communicating, Yamaoka and Kurita devise ways to allow food to speak for them. In the story "Ai aru chôshoku" (A Breakfast with Love), Yamaoka himself learns how food communicates what words may not succeed in conveying.[29] In this episode, the "ultimate" versus "supreme" menu competition centers on breakfast. The purpose of the competition is to call attention to the fact that an increasing number of students and commuters are skipping breakfast, which allegedly results in lower grades, decreased productivity, and poorer health. The story's human-interest angle concerns the main characters, Yamaoka and Kurita.

Her heart set on Yamaoka, Kurita has been resisting the proposals of two other admirers, a software millionaire and a famous photographer. These suitors recognize Yamaoka as a rival and individually approach him about their intentions. Yamaoka, oblivious to his own feelings, gives each one his blessing with Kurita, with the caveat that they have other competition. Meanwhile, he becomes despondent and starts drinking heavily. Concerned about Yamaoka's health and frustrated by his inaction with regard to Kurita, Ochô — a faithful servant who served in Yamaoka's household during his childhood and continues to work for his father, Kaibara Yûzan — schemes to bring them together. Discouraged by his parents' turbulent married life, Yamaoka insists that he will never marry. He holds fast to the belief that his father bullied his mother to death. Ochô points out to Kurita that since Yamaoka left home during high school, he failed to understand a good deal about his parents' relationship; he did not know the real story.

As part of her plan, Ochô teaches Kurita a number of breakfast dishes that Yamaoka's mother used to prepare in the days after the teenage Yamaoka had left home. One Saturday morning, the two knock on Yamaoka's door. They have come to fix him rice porridge topped with a thickened broth containing tofu, spring onion, and thinly sliced Chinese fried cruller. Because of his hangover, Yamaoka initially turns down the offer of breakfast, but its aroma invites him. He delights in the "fragrance and depth" that the cruller adds to the dish and comments, "The spring onion perks me up and revives my appetite!" When he learns that the porridge was his mother's recipe, he observes, "The dish seems simple but it isn't something that would occur to just anyone! What a brilliant idea!" Ochô replies, "Your mother thought up this dish for your father, you know. In those days he was overworked and had lost his appetite. Your mother racked her brains to come up with something that would give him energy and cheer him up."[30]

Kurita appeals to Yamaoka to allow her to handle the upcoming breakfast contest alone. Kaibara Yûzan, their opponent at the *Teitô News*, will undoubtedly have the advantage, influenced as he is by his late wife's magnificent cooking. Ochô reasons that even if she teaches the talented Yamaoka his mother's repertoire, his "mother complex" will prevent his winning.

Kurita's entry into the competition is a Japanese version of a Western breakfast. She begins with a glass of milk pasteurized at a low temperature, followed by a salad of seasonal vegetables dressed in a soy sauce-flavored sesame oil vinaigrette. She then offers Darjeeling tea or Columbian coffee to accompany homemade bread, homemade butter, and homemade marmalade. The judges initially express some disappointment at this ordinary fare until they get a whiff of the aroma and a taste of the freshly baked bread, with its crispy crust and moist, fluffy center (the Japanese preference). Their eyes widen when they taste the freshly churned butter. "It melts on the tongue like the finest sherbet!" one judge exclaims.[31] Kurita's final offering is a dish of homemade yogurt with strawberries, homemade strawberry jam, and Australian honey.

Kaibara Yûzan prefaces his presentation with his pessimistic views on why the contest will have no influence on whether or not people skip breakfast. He faults the Japanese lifestyle, which demands that students stay up late to study and that white-collar workers work themselves too hard. Few of these workers can find a decent place to live within a reasonable distance of their company and must commute long hours. They have neither the time nor appetite for breakfast so early in the morning. Yamaoka's boss adds, "If you boil it down, the fact that Japanese people don't have the leisure to eat breakfast is an indication of the impoverishment of Japanese society."[32]

While he feels that it is cruel to present his "supreme breakfast" in light of this situation, Kaibara Yûzan does so with the hope that Japan will create a

FIGURE 6.3: "Aosawa savors apple tea and apple pie prepared by his mother in 'Mother Apple'".
© 1988. *Oishinbo* Vol. 14: 101, Kariya Tetsu and Hanasaki Akira; Shogakukan. Used by permission.

society that can make time for this important meal. His entry begins with a glass of pure water, the most important substance to all living beings; a glass of clear, delicious water first thing in the morning regulates the digestive system and makes one feel serene, he explains.[33] Trays set before the judges are laden with the quintessential traditional Japanese breakfast. The meal includes *umi no sachi, yama no sachi* ("products of the sea and of the mountains"): miso soup with tofu; toasted nori seaweed; daikon radish pickled in rice bran; boiled spinach in soy sauce; grilled dried horse mackerel; the soft-cooked yolk of an egg served atop the finely chopped hard-cooked white; a salty pickled plum; and steamed rice — all of the finest quality. To the potential critique that his presentation is no more than the average breakfast eaten in eastern Japan, Kaibara responds that every region has its own "supreme" breakfast, based on what is traditionally eaten there. But he notes that in Japan today this traditional breakfast exists, for the most part, in form only. The quality of the ingredients has declined to such a degree that it has become difficult to prepare a "supreme" traditional breakfast, a sign of the ruin of the country. One judge notes, "What they say is certainly true: you can clearly see the condition of a society through its food."[34]

Although coffee and toast may not be as traditional as rice and miso soup, Kurita wins the day. The warmth and affection expressed in her freshly baked bread and freshly churned butter constitutes a response to the problems inherent in the trend to skip breakfast. One of the judges suggests that if a person whose life centered on making money — the kind of person who might skip breakfast — ate Kurita's breakfast he would be moved by both its flavor and the inner feelings of the cook who prepared it. Being so moved this person would probably think about changing his profit-seeking lifestyle.[35]

At the end of the contest Kurita apologizes to Kaibara for stealing his late wife's recipes, her *aijô o komotta aji* ("flavor full of tender feelings"). To this apology Kaibara responds that he remembers how his wife's fresh bread brought him back to himself when he was falling apart and helped him succeed in his work. Hearing his father's comment, Yamaoka thinks to himself, "This is the first time I heard that guy speak about my mother like that."[36] Is his hate toward Kaibara softening, perhaps? Kurita confesses to Kaibara that she was motivated in the contest by a desire to beat Yamaoka's mother. What she doesn't reveal is that she is competing for Yamaoka's affection. The surprised expression that Yamaoka registers when he hears Kurita confess to his father indicates that somehow he has understood. He proposes to her in the next volume of stories.

"Ai aru chôshoku" illustrates how a simple comic book story revolving around food not only informs its readers about food and gives them menu ideas, but critiques the economics and politics of food and even society as a whole. It also demonstrates that, at times, food can communicate feelings more effectively than language. Kurita's cooking enables Yamaoka to recognize the love between his mother and father, as well as the depth of the feelings that Kurita has for him.

The popularity of *Oishinbo* evidences Japanese awareness of the importance of food in social life. The manga appeals to readers' desire to know food cultures — their own and others'. *Oishinbo*'s sentimental stories even reinforce their cultural identity, reaffirming traditional values and at the same time offering cultural critiques.

It is important to remember, of course, that as much as it may reflect contemporary Japanese trends, to a great extent, the fantasy world conjured up in *Oishinbo* represents the vision of an individual writer, Kariya Tetsu. *Oishinbo* is an expression of his palate, his worldview and culinary knowledge. The fact that *Oishinbo* has been going strong for over twenty years, however, signifies that Kariya's food obsession strikes a chord in the minds and stomachs of many Japanese.

Notes

1. Names in the chapter text are presented in the traditional Japanese format, with family name first.
2. After a brief pause, Kariya and Hanasaki resumed production of *Oishinbo* for the comic magazine, *Big Comic Spirits* on February 23, 2009 (Anime News Network, http://www.animenewsnetwork.com/news/2009-02-16/oishinbo-cuisine-manga-to-resume-in-japan-next-week. Accessed November 24, 2009.) Additionally, in January 2009, Viz Media began publishing volumes of *Oishinbo* stories translated into English. As of November 2009 seven volumes of the English *Oishinbo* have come out, each one centering on a different theme, such as "Japanese cuisine" (Vol. 1), "Vegetables" (Vol. 5), and "Izakaya – Japanese pub food" (Vol. 7).
3. Ishiko Jun, "Za shefu" [The chef], in Ishiko 1988, 48.
4. This association may be changing as more women work outside the home.
5. This manga, written by Jôji Manabe, has drawn larger audiences, including American anime fans, through its animated series, broadcast on Fuji TV.
6. Ueyama Tochi, *Kukkingu papa* [Cooking papa], vol. 52, 3.
7. Ôno Shinjirô, *Ajimantei* [House of Full Flavor], 18.
8. Ibid., 38.
9. Ibid., 19.
10. Ibid., 36.
11. Ibid., 15.
12. Kariya Tetsu and Hanasaki Akira, *Oishinbo* [The gourmet], vol. 1, 28.
13. Ibid.
14. Kariya and Hanasaki, *Oishinbo*, vol. 61, 102. Following its title, *Yoku zo nihonjin ni umarekeri* [I'm sure glad I was born Japanese], volume 61 celebrates typically Japanese dishes that "only a Japanese person could truly understand."
15. Kariya and Hanasaki, *Oishinbo*, vol. 1, 63.
16. Ibid., 75.
17. Ibid., 77.
18. Kariya and Hanasaki, *Oishinbo*, vol. 5, no. 8
19. Kariya and Hanasaki, *Oishinbo*, vol. 5, 97.
20. Kariya and Hanasaki, *Oishinbo*, vol. 1, no. 4.

21. Kariya and Hanasaki, *Oishinbo*, vol. 51, 24.
22. Kariya and Hanasaki, *Oishinbo*, vol. 2, no. 5.
23. Kariya Tetsu and Hanasaki Akira, *Oishinbo*, vol. 64, no. 9.
24. Kariya and Hanasaki, *Oishinbo*, vol. 49, no. 1.
25. Ibid., 19.
26. Kariya and Hanasaki, *Oishinbo*, vol. 36, no. 5.
27. Ibid., 101.
28. Kariya and Hanasaki, *Oishinbo*, vol. 14, no. 5.
29. Ibid., 101.
30. Kariya and Hanasaki, *Oishinbo*, vol. 42, no. 4.
31. Ibid., 136.
32. Ibid., 154.
33. Ibid., 163.
34. Ibid., 165.
35. Ibid., 175.
36. Ibid., 177.
37. Ibid., 179.

References

Hirano, Masaaki (1978). *Shoku no bunka ko* [Treatise on the culture of food]. Tokyo: Shoseki.

Ishiko, Jun (1988). *Gendai manga no shujinkotachi* [The heroes of contemporary manga]. Tokyo: Kusa No Ne Shuppankai.

Kariya, Tetsu (1986). "'Oishinbo' sanbyakumanbu no himitsu" [The secret of *Oishinbo*'s audience of three million]. *Bungei Shunjû* 4: 340–44.

Kinsella, Sharon (2000). *Adult Manga: Culture and Power in Contemporary Japanese Society*. Honolulu: University of Hawaii Press.

McCloud, Scott (1994). *Understanding Comics: The Invisible Art*. New York: Harper Perennial.

Schodt, Frederik L. (1986). *Manga! Manga! The World of Japanese Comics*. Tokyo: Kodansha International.

Suggested Manga Reading

Abe, Zenta, and Yoshimi Kurata (1992). *Aji ichimonme* [A Pinch of Flavor], vol. 14. Tokyo: Shogakkan.

Funatsu, Kazuki (2002). *Kareinaru shokutaku* [The splendid curry table]: *Addicted to curry*, vol. 5. Tokyo: Shueisha.

Gyû, Jirô, and Biggu Jô (1995). *Hôchônin no Ajihei* [Ajihei the knifeman], vol. 1. Tokyo: Shueisha Bunkô.

Kariya, Tetsu, and Akira Hanasaki (1983–2003). *Oishinbo* [The gourmet]. 102 vols. Tokyo: Shogakkan.

Kube, Rokurô, and Tan Kawai (2000). *Raamen hakkenden* [Legend of the discovery of ramen], vol. 2. Tokyo: Shogakkan.

Kurita, Riku (1988). *Yume iro kukkingu* [Dream-colored cooking], vol. 1. Tokyo: Kodansha International.

Manabe, Jôji (1993–). *Chûka ichiban.* [The best Chinese food]. Tokyo: Kadokawa.

Nishimura, Mitsuru, and Masato Naka (2001). *Kyuijinie* [Cuisinier], vol. 4. Tokyo: Shueisha.

Ôno, Shinjirô (1997). *Ajimantei* [House of Full Flavor]. Tokyo: Kodansha International.

Terasawa, Daisuke (2001). *Misutaa ajikko* [Mister Ajikko], vol. 1. Tokyo: Kodansha Manga Bunkô.

—— (1992). *Shôta no sushi* [Shota's sushi], vol. 1. Tokyo: Kodansha International.

Ueyama, Tochi (1998). *Kukkingu papa* [Cooking papa], vol. 52. Tokyo: Kodansha International.

7

Osamu Tezuka's *Gekiga*: Behind the Mask of *Manga*

Philip Brophy

This work is a reprint from the original National Gallery of Victoria publication in 2006.

ICONICIZING THE MASK

The iconic visage of manga is the face of *kawaii* (cute). Bulbous-eyed and pencil-lipped, its facial glyph has become an international marker of a cuteness that is simultaneously endearing and unsettling. The specificity of the hyperkawaii face is deliberately flattened by manga inscription, appearing equally as it does in saccharine kiddie stories and extreme pornographic scenarios. Confusion understandably arises when one attempts to read faces in manga according to a Western semiotics of emotion. Japan's cute face has nothing to do with projecting cuteness — but everything to do with framing all it conceals.

Japan has long been perceived as a culture of masks. The kawaii face continues the tradition, taking place beside the making-up and mask-donning of children's festivals, geisha rituals, Kabuki attire and Noh gestures — not to mention the numerous forms of painting and illustration that further codify the face as an ideogram whose minimal marks instantly signify identifiable emotional states. Projecting through withholding connotes so much of Japan, and the role of masks is equally qualified by ancient mythological rituals and everyday social customs. Tezuka Osamu's earlier manga — from his first published children's work in the mid-1940s through to his capitalization of manga market trends by the mid-1960s — presents a veritable encyclopedia of the kawaii face. From central characters like Astro Boy in the work of the same name (*Tetsuwan Atomu*) and Leo in *Jungeru taitei* (Jungle Emperor), to the side character Chinku in *Ribon no kishi* (Princess Knight) and others like Michi from *Metoroporisu* (Metropolis) and Bokko in *Wanda suri* (Wonder 3) — all are distinctly Tezukian in stroke and acutely anthropomorphic in form.

Yet a considered reading of any of these manga will reveal an emotional range far in excess of the presumed signification these kawaii faces present. Cloying moments certainly abound, but remorse and revenge spike these titles. Their kawaii faces function as counterpoint; their simplistic, hypericonic design aggressively reduces emotional complexity into a glacial skin worn like a mask. Tezuka's characters in these early manga are consistently innocent yet abused, open-minded yet harshly judged, debilitated yet regenerative. The more their cuteness remains fixed, the more compressed their emotional composure. Read properly, any manifest cuteness more appropriately conceals a character's rounded connection to others. Their interactions are no mere affectations of sentimentality, as they exhibit compassion, resilience, and hopefulness. Astro, Leo, Bokko, Michi, and others yearn to comprehend humans yet remain destined to ponder their exclusion from the human domain.

From the outset of this earlier period, Tezuka's manga represented characters in high-theatrical modes inherited from the mannered gesticulation of Kabuki and the violent minimalism of Noh. He fully transposed their theatrical devices into the manga medium, using his pen to draw stylized faces just as the Kabuki and Noh actors donned makeup and masks, and inked pages in ways that recalled the graphic flatness of their stage scrims and backdrops. In this sense, Tezuka's pages are microstages whose calligraphic nature is laterally aligned to Japanese theater craft. Culturally contextualized, Tezuka's paragons of cuteness bear only the slightest resemblance to Walt Disney's beaming cherubs. While the latter stem from an idyllic prewar era, their assimilation by Tezuka into manga for a readership recovering from World War II is less a sign of Eurokitsch and more an anagram of Japanese inscrutability. The faces of Astro Boy and his counterparts embody a peculiar postwar traumatization akin to many depictions of doe-eyed waifs from the era, marking their character masks as distilled psychological hieroglyphs — reductive facial forms with broad expressive range.

SURFACING *GEKIGA*

If one cannot bypass the obvious cuteness of Astro Boy, it would be approaching illiteracy to miss the "scarred cuteness" in Tezuka's *gekiga* (drama pictures) manga. Gekiga is a more seriously toned, adult-oriented narrative form of manga that stresses realistic effect and emotional impact over the visual symbolism and high-keyed archetypes displayed in earlier mainstream manga. While *manga* ("comic pictures") is the umbrella term for all Japanese comics, gekiga has been viewed as a branch within manga, emanating from the late 1960s, when new styles and approaches to content were explored by a variety of manga artists. Originally associated with controversy, taboo-breaking, and radicalism, gekiga traits have since become subsumed into a wide range of manga, leaving the term *gegika* with more historical significance today than an overall descriptive function. While Tezuka's recognized identity as a master of the manga form predates the gekiga evolution, he did not let its mandate for politicized spleen and psychological acridity pass him by. According to some critics, he adopted the pose of gekiga; others register the slant he brought to the trend. Either way, some of Tezuka's gekiga works are more than mere examples of opportune synchronicity to a clichéd 1960s zeitgeist of social change.

If anything, it is Tezuka's transition into producing gekiga that best positions the divergence of his earlier hypericonic visages and his use of such characterization to portray the effect turbulent sociopolitical changes have on people. In this sense, the bulk of Tezuka's successful work produced in the immediate postwar period, while Japan was under American occupation (1945–52), did not directly address his surrounding conditions. Combining allegory, fable, and parable, he utilized a wide range of fantasy, comedy, and adventure genres to entertain his readers. Following the substantial success of his stories during this period, his work became speculative in purpose and serious in tone — to such a degree that characters in his postoccupation stories seem to symbolically enact traumas akin to those suffered by many Japanese immediately after the war, including bereavement, destitution, disillusionment, alienation, and the like. As his work became more closely aligned to the gekiga movement, parables of war, oppression, and subterfuge figure strongly, as if wartime conditions were recurring in his writing through karmic revisitation. Perceived in this philosophical light, Tezuka's gekiga characters are terse reconstitutions of the dramatis personae from his most famous earlier titles, now forced to endure the ravages born of dramatic situations to which they seem fated.

Directed as if they are stock actors in Tezuka's theater company, the archetypes of Astro Boy and Leo, as well as Sapphire from *Ribon no kishi* and Melmo from *Fushi ga no Merumo* (Marvelous Melmo), star in Tezuka's gekiga where they are "deiconicized." These once-cute character types are rebuilt from an emotional ground zero to explore how the Japanese psyche can contest and attend to the despoiling experiences their drama generates. Accordingly, their masks are recoded as signifiers of "postcute." Recalling the idea of Japan projecting through withholding, characters in manga like *Mu* (MW), *Apporo no uta* (Song of Apollo), *Kirihito sanka* (Eulogy to Kirihito), *Ningen konchu ki* (Human Metamorphosis), *Rudovihi B* (Ludwig B), *Buddha*, and *Hi no tori* (Phoenix) ordain that which is behind the mask as a formidable and foreboding presence. This is the psychological, and hence dramatic, crux of most of Tezuka's gekiga.

The face in Tezuka's gekiga highlights its surface sheen more than ever. If the earlier works invited identification with the cuddlesome, the gekiga works portend a harsh duality in their theatricalized two-facedness. Centered as so many of the stories are on the duplicitous and deceitful maneuvers of humans, the postcute effect of their visages serves to amplify the psychological mechanisms that motivate their actions. From portraits of self-disorienting quandaries of personal identity (*Rudovihi B*, *Apporo no uta*, and *Bomba!*) to investigations into self-destructive disregard for personal ethics (*Tsumi to batsu* [Crime and Punishment], *Mu*, *Ningen konchu ki*) to treatises on self-revelatory moments of personal enlightenment (*Kirihito sanka*, *Buddha*, *Hi no tori*), Tezuka's characters teeter on the brink of redefinition and reincarnation. Throughout these tales, the self is not mined in the quest of humanist aspiration, as we find in enlightened literature. Rather, it is excavated — abrasively hollowed out and clinically ground into a talcose selflessness that lines the interior of the manga mask. These faces appear graphically consistent and stable, yet the fixity of their iconic formation results from the massive force with which the self has been compacted.

Reductively, one could claim that Tezuka's gekiga concords with modernist journeys into existential inertia, romanticized nihilism, and world-weary despair. But the visceral, material outcomes of his manga escape the Eurocentric pull of such floundering and lock us into orbits of cosmological and transcendental explorations of the self as guided by Buddhist, Zen, and Shinto precepts. In this dizzying, phantasmal cosmos Tezuka performs as a theater director, his characters project through dramatic masks, and his manga pages operate as theatrical stages.

While Tezuka's narratives are mobilized by the graphic momentum he achieves through his visual-effects rendering, it is his sense of staging that shapes and controls the drama of his manga. Combining mergers of calligraphic ornamentation born of Japanese scroll paintings with a neobaroque framing inherited from European art history, his pages can perversely resemble gaudy Viennese appropriations of melodramatic Japanese theater productions. Never one to avoid such confounding cross-cultural blends — and proudly bearing the influence of the Takarazuka all-female theatrical musicals — Tezuka's manga heightens the artifice and hones the theatricality inherent to the medium. While this is standard artistry for the ocular sensibility of manga set in fantasy visions of European historical lore, Tezuka's extension of high-key detailing and florid visual arrangement into the realist contemporary settings typical of gekiga determines a disjunction between form and content — between puppet pantomime and psychological realism.

Viewed in this light, Tezuka's gekiga consciously stages human drama without resorting to realism, naturalism, or verisimilitude. As with most manga — gekiga or otherwise — the Western reading of its comic-book textuality tends to discount the maturity of their narrative formation. The power of Tezuka's gekiga lies in its refusal to conform to standards of either fictive plausibility or mimetic dramaturgy. *Ribon no kishi, Jungeru taitei, Tsumi to batsu,* and *Rudovihi B* offer cold comment on the human condition, yet not once do they refute their exaggerated Bavarian aesthetics through which characters suffer delirium, collapse from emotional exhaustion and faint at traumatic moments in disorienting, overwrought worlds imported from Disney's fantasy Euro-world. *Tetsuwan Atomu, Apporo no uta,* and *Hi no tori* calculate complex connections between the psyche and the cosmos, yet never do they renounce their futuristic settings pulped from American science fiction illustrations. Acknowledging how Tezuka's stagecraft and visual mise en scène govern his manga is the key to perceiving his transition into gekiga — where realism is evaporated and artifice is consolidated.

TRACING THE PSYCHE

The stage for the sprawling human drama of the *Hi no tori* saga is no mere setting; it is life itself. A mix of speculative fiction, sci-fi phantasmagoria and historical reimagining, the twelve chapters of *Hi no tori* ping-pong in sequence from a far future to the distance past. Tezuka's ultimate aim was to reduce the time gap between each vacillated chapter so that eventually the final chapter would occur in the present of his writing. While involving a formidable cast of characters, the key figure of the mythical phoenix appears in each installment, serving to guide characters to higher levels of consciousness. Most of them experience moments of intense illumination, wherein existence is encountered as an engulfing amoeba of consciousness guided by infinite interconnectivity. Freed from Judeo-Christian parameters of mortal finality and Godly directives, *Hi no tori* presents each character as a molecule of humanity: neither the essential human nor the universal everyman but an infinitesimal droplet of life's voluminous energy.

Tezuka's graphic sensibilities embolden what otherwise would appear as navel-gazing. *Hi no tori* is notable for stretches of pages where the human form and face become saturated with visual effects, reshaping characters into anthropomorphic globules and humanoid squiggles floating in vistas of pen and ink. Centered on the malleable interchangeability of cosmological scale, the borders between iconic characters and deiconicized psyches are blurred in fluid exchanges as characters are rendered in a flux of representational modes. Darkly cross-hatched panels flecked with white paint can be appreciated or read as symbolic chartings of stars and as dynamic passages of calligraphic marks of ink on paper. Like planetary dimensions revealed by microscopes, the resolutely abstracted graphics of *Hi no tori* provide a stage for its characters to disassemble and reassemble their selves. For key characters like Romy and Makimura (*Nostalgia*), Leona and Chihiro (*Resurrection*) and Tamami and Masato (*Future*), illuminating moments and disorienting points of transgression mark dimensional shifts in their consciousness. *Hi no tori* is Tezuka's most scintillating example of how his gekiga masks are powdered with the fine dust of selflessness meaning.

The drawn outlines of the characters in *Hi no tori* are not a matter of discernment, recognition, or identification. Rather, they are transmuted energies graphically encoded in the guise of humans. While actual humans are formularized as life forces, robots and aliens are calculated into indexes of human behavior. Collectively, these humans, robots, and aliens are connected by cosmic energies yet separated by their psyches. Robots will demonstrate compassion while humans will exhibit monstrousness — no definitive states apply. Their figuration symbolizes how humanity can deceptively shift and slip, the movement of which defines their status as characters.

Apporo no uta reconfigures *Hi no tori*'s irrigated network of spiritual reincarnation into the bubbling psychosexual confusion within the character Shogo — a serial sex offender interred in an experimental psychiatric clinic where he undergoes radical dream therapy. More than any other of Tezuka's gekiga, *Apporo no uta* is an uncompromising tale of how the self is a chaotic multiplication of chanced causes and unpredictable effects. Cited by Tezuka himself as his bleakest work in its extreme encapsulation of negativity, its study of Shogo's psychosis uncovers an angle on the societal malaise of sex offenders that in its causal analysis is surprisingly prescient for the time of its publication in 1973.

In place of *Hi no tori*'s karmic retribution with concatenated characters in fractal formation, *Apporo no uta* articulates cycles of abuse that imprint and control the mind of Shogo in a mix of hereditary and fateful narrative loops. Even though the bulk of the story takes place within his dream-altered mindscape, the story proposes this interiority to be the true matter behind his social mask. A nightmarish dimension unfolds, suffocating Shogo as he grapples with his asocial urges and psychosexual compulsions. His dream trips shuttle him through familiar war-torn zones (evoking though not labeling Japan's engagement in the Second World War) and unfamiliar sci-fi domains where cloning abounds in ways that decimate even Shogo's desultory summation of humanity.

Possibly the most salient difference that distinguishes Tezuka's gekiga from his earlier manga is the accent on sexuality; centralized in *Apporo no uta*, it manifests in depictions of erotic and violent schisms that fever Shogo's mind. Specifically, gender difference is capitulated across an unforgiving war zone in the battle of the sexes. Far from the fields of Eros, Shogo's rabid heterosexuality digs deep trenches in this terrain. His pathological violence underscores all that separates men from women. Tezuka employs manga's gender coding (jagged diagonals to express male violence; swirling curves to express female sensuality) to render Shogo and his lovers as tersely opposed yet fatefully conjoined. The result is an unflinching story of sexual attraction and romantic compulsion.

RENDERING EFFECTS

If *Apporo no uta* sensationalizes the darker side of man, *Ningen konchu ki* centralizes woman as a "black hole" in Japanese mythology (a particularly afeminist notion of woman). A portrait of Tomura, a woman who would do anything to get what she wants, the story trails her various exploits as she swims through a bottomless reservoir of amoral currents, seducing men and women alike in order to manipulate, blackmail, and crush them as she climbs to the top of her self-centred power domain. This depiction of woman as guileful manipulator partially replays standard misogynist tales of vixens in the modern world; however, such tales reverberate throughout Japanese cultural history and are portrayed by abused women who ply their sexuality with survivalist verve — from betrothed princesses to purchased geishas to abused "comfort women." *Ningen konchu ki* remains Tezuka's harshest assessment of the human condition by razing any maternal, sisterly, or romantic attributes from Tomura. Discounting such gendered prescription, Tezuka constructs a depressing yet realistic world devoid of chivalry, within which femininity is completely unshielded by the humanist collapse created by Tomura's implosive self-immolatory power.

Recalling the masks and makeup that crucially site manga's drama at face value and surface level, *Ningen konchu ki* typifies the onion-skin layering of what is presumed to be human. Yet in place of uncovering some primal or ultimate truth, Tezuka's operations of surfacing, tracing, and excavating are employed to remove the shell from human interiority and confront the nothingness attained through remorseless acts. Staged in a mix of hallucinogenic noir penumbra and lysergic glare, Tomura's being is pulped into arabesques of ink. Relating to the uniquely Japanese ideogramatic and contraillusionary sensibility that influences centuries of its graphic and painterly arts, Tomura's psychological makeup is poetically contoured through imaginative brushwork. From shadowed profiles to disembodied eyes to abstracted torsos, she is less fleshed out and more poured out and conjured as an emptied vessel.

While many of Tezuka's gekiga symbolize inner turmoil to the extent of diminishing stature and corporeal decomposition, *Kirihito sanka* reverses this tack and studies the psychological effects of bodily metamorphosis. Here Tezuka's interest in existential malleability and mutations of mind and form is realized through the main character, Dr. Kirihito Osanai, who contracts a rare disease after conducting research in a remote village. Afflicted with a bizarre mix of congenital and behavioral aberrations, he devolves into a bestial hybrid — hungry for raw meat, physiologically recast with canine features, yet all the while retaining human perception. Thus he becomes his other — not simply a mutated human, but a complete victim who he, as doctor, seeks to treat and cure.

Aligned with the arching cosmological template that dictates Tezuka's plot flows and situational flux, Kirihito's otherness is contained wholly within his being, while his malaise is revealed to be not simply within him but in the world around him. His physical, emotional, and social changes are ultimately moments of transition wherein he comes to understand himself through his relation to others — from accepting his affliction to comprehending people's fear of difference to realizing medicine's rejection of aberrant phenomena. With emotional and psychological metamorphosis at the thematic base of the story, Tezuka (himself a doctor of medicine) clinically directs Kirihito through a series of endurances, battles, and collapses that chart how a human is shaped — literally — by external forces. Inasmuch as the mask is a molding of the face — a cast of its surface form — Kirihito is a human reformed and remolded into the state of becoming a mask.

Tezuka's gekiga evidences the superior degree to which he conveys heightened states of subjectivity and graphic invention, pushing the language of manga to an abstract edge while always deriving these flourishes from dramatically motivated circumstance. Ultimately his gekiga is dedicated to surface effects — but in a way that redefines their purpose. While thematic discourse in the narrative arts tends to perceive "effects" as fluff of meager consequence to literate exposition, in manga they operate under self-reflexive cursive conditions. They refer equally to the illustrative techniques that dress manga's staging, and the cosmological impact characters have through their existence and actions. Most important, these two categories are dissolved into the one phenomenal, compound effect. Tezuka's characters are drawn on a flat surface — and that's where their depth resides. Pictograms of drama (possibly the most apt translation of gekiga), they are to be read through their caricatured physique, exaggerated stature, gross countenance, and grimacing masks. A mix of author, artist, director, and doctor, Tezuka similarly reads the rendered effects of people as symptoms of their interior psychological states and their social relations.

References: Selected Articles in English on Tezuka's Manga

Amano, Masanao (2004). "Osamu, Tezuka." In *Manga Design*, ed. Julius Wiedemann, 344–49. Translation by John McDonald and Tamami Sanbommatsu. Köln, Germany: Taschen.

Gravett, Paul (2004). "The Father Storyteller." In *Manga: Sixty Years of Japanese Comics*, 34–47. London: Laurence King/Harper Design International.

Ihara, Keiko. (1995, March 18). "A Prophet Spurned." *Japan Times Weekly*, 8–9.

Iwasaki, Yoshikazu (1990). "The Osamu Tezuka Exhibition within the Context of Museum Activity." In *Osamu Tezuka* (exhibition catalog), 10–13. Translated by Keiko Katsuya. Tokyo: National Museum of Modern Art.

Kazusa, Naomi (1995, March 18). "A Master Creator." *Japan Times Weekly*, 8.

Kinsella, Sharon (2000). *Adult Manga: Culture and Power in Contemporary Japanese Society*. Honolulu: University of Hawaii Press.

Kondo, Yukio (1990). "Astro Boy — Attempt in Understanding the Work." In *Osamu Tezuka* (exhibition catalog), 24–31. Translated by Keisuke Shimamoto. Tokyo: National Museum of Modern Art.

MacWilliams, Mark Wheeler (2000). "Japanese Comics and Religion: Osamu Tezuka's Story of the Buddha." In *Japan Pop! Inside the World of Japanese Popular Culture*, ed. Timothy J. Craig, 109–37. Armonk, NY: M. E. Sharpe.

Matsutani, Takayuki (2002). "Afterword." In Osamu Tezuka, *Phoenix: A Tale of the Future*, pp. 288–90. Translated by Akemi Wegmuller. San Francisco: VIZ Communications.

Motoe, Kunio (1990). "Osamu Tezuka — Une Dualité" [Osamu Tezuka — A duality]. In *Osamu Tezuka* (exhibition catalog), 14–23. Translated by Keiko Katsuya. Tokyo: National Museum of Modern Art.

Oniki, Yuji (1996). "Introduction: Tezuka's Twentieth Century." In Osamu Tezuka, *Adolf: An Exile in Japan*, 7–11. San Francisco: Cadence Books.

Randall, Bill (2005). "Behold Japan's God of Manga: An Introduction to the Work of Osamu Tezuka." *Comics Journal* 5: 46–57.

Schilling, Mark (1997). "Tezuka, Osamu." In *The Encyclopedia of Japanese Pop Culture*, 263–68. Trumbull, CT: Weatherhill.

Schodt, Frederik L. (1983). "Osamu Tezuka." In *Manga! Manga! The World of Japanese Comics*, pp. 64–66, 160. Tokyo: Kodansha International.

—— (1996). "Osamu Tezuka: A Tribute to the God of Comics." In *Dreamland Japan: Writings on Modern Manga*, 273–74. Berkeley, CA: Stone Bridge Press.

Thorn, Matt (1996). "Introduction: Tezuka's Modernism." In Osamu Tezuka, *Adolf: The Half-Aryan*, 7–11. San Francisco: Cadence Books.

Special Issue: "MangArt" (2004). *ART iT* 2(3): 32–90.

Further Reading

Brophy, Philip (2005). *100 Anime*. London: BFI.

——, ed. (2006). *Tezuka: The Marvel of Manga*. Melbourne: National Gallery of Victoria.

8

A Look at Hikawa Kyōko's *Kanata kara*

Mio Bryce

Manga, in particular *shōjo* (girls') manga, is characterized by strong narratives, fluid hybridity, and diverse depiction of otherness and inter-subjectivity. The imaginary arena created by the media functions to offer a liminal space wherein protagonists (and readers) explore their identity and subjective agency in relation to themselves and others through social interactions. Kath Woodward posits that identity is "always socially located" (2002, 2), and according to Robyn McCallum, the formation of subjectivity is dialogical, and thus always shaped by social ideologies. McCallum notes, "Conceptions of subjectivity are intrinsic to narratives of personal growth or maturation, to stories about relationship between the self and to others, and to explorations of relationships between individuals and the world, society or the past — that is, subjectivity is intrinsic to the major concerns of adolescent fiction" (1999, 3).

Love is the most intimate, individualistic, and ambivalent intersubjective interaction that can encourage or discourage personal maturation, largely with regard to gender issues. Romance is always an essential ingredient of shōjo manga, and now *shōnen* manga (boys' manga) as well, along with increasing genre crossing or hybridity (for more on this, see Davis and Bryce, this volume). Now myriad love stories are created and consumed either as the main or secondary themes in both genres. Romantic themes involving long-ing for true love between independent individuals are threaded throughout the protagonists' quests for their identities and individual values. The actual representation of romance in shōjo manga is diverse, from simple, child-like love in school to intricate love triangles in complicated science fiction fantasies such as Shimizu Reiko's *Kaguya-hime* (Princess Kaguya) to inces-tuous relationships, as in Yuki Kaori's *Tenshi Kinryōku* (Angel Sanctuary) and Kitagawa Miyuki's *Tsumi ni nureta futari* (The two who soaked in sin). However, they are "in essence, bildungsromans . . . about growing up as a preteen or teenage girl in Japan today" (Prough, this volume).[1]

This chapter will use Hikawa Kyōko's fantasy, *Kanata kara* as an exemplary case for looking at how perceptively romantic shōjo manga fantasies explore issues of identity, subjective agency, and ideal relationships, and thus how they provide encouragement to readers to live and love as they are (see Davis and Bryce, 2008). *Kanata kara* won the Seiun (Japanese science fiction) Award in 2004, despite it not including any typical devices of science fiction such as telecommunications or biotechnology (though it does portray human psychic powers, spirits, and other creatures, such as *chimo*, which help humans to teleport). The manga effectively employs literary and manga conventions, such as a nostalgic European fantasy setting, to imbue its subject matter with logic, clarity, sincerity, a sense of reality, and hope. This is in accordance with Rosemary Jackson's (1981) notion of fantasy being "a literature of desire." John Stephens posits that "fantasy is essentially a metaphoric mode" (1992, 7) that imbues themes with a more mythic dimension, characteristically linking it to the idea that a magical force inheres in material things and events that are apprehended "nakedly" (1992, 287).

Kanata kara is a touching fantasy of love, friendship, and adventure. It depicts the character Tachiki Noriko's unexpected journey in a parallel world, her relationship with the solitary warrior Izark and others of that world, and her subsequent maturation. Her affection toward Izark is genuine and straightforward; however, things are not as simple for Izark, because in his world Noriko is Mezame (The Awakener), who is prophesied to wake the monstrous power in Izark that will transform him into Tenjōki (lit., "heavenly demon"), an essential tool in evil's conquering of the world. In spite of his extraordinary physical strength Izark is shy, sympathetic, and reticent. Since childhood he has been tormented by people's fear of him as a monster. In order to escape from his fate to become Tenjōki, he initially plans to kill Mezame — only to find the hopeless, confused Noriko, whom he then rescues from a number of enemies. Noriko trusts Izark and attaches herself to him instantly upon their first encounter, unaware of her dangerous role as Mezame. Izark also grows fond of her, but for a long period he remains indecisive about how to deal with Noriko due to his fear of her influence on him. The narrative is set in a world where evil forces are growing rapidly and Izark and Noriko are hunted by many parties, especially the character Genkyo (the source of evil). It pivots around Izark's initially ambivalent, yet later devoted feelings toward Noriko and their concerted effort to fight the evil forces and establish Hiraki no sekai (the world of light) in which people are connected by mutual trust, respect, love, and interreliance. This forms the narrative underlying his journey of self-discovery, acceptance, and the revelation of his true power through the catalyst of his relationships with Noriko and others. Ultimately, the story reveals Noriko's true role as the awakener of Izark's ultimate inner strength, as embodied by his angel-like wings.

ROMANCE IN SHŌJO MANGA

Manga narratives are derived from Tezuka Osamu's innovative "story manga" from the 1950s, yet evolved differently through shōnen and shōjo manga in the 1970s. The clear storytelling boundary gradually became blurred and diffused through interactive border crossings, as exemplified by popular love comedies (Love-come) in the 1980s. This happened mainly through shōnen manga's assimilation of themes, styles, and techniques from shōjo manga, which had developed richer thematic, linguistic, and graphical forms of expression due to its exploration of a wide range of social, cultural, psychological, and ideological themes (e.g., gender issues) imposed upon girls, the intended readers. In turn, shōjo manga has learned from shōnen manga the strong comicalness and three key concepts exemplified in the manga story lines of *Shōnen Jump*: friendship, effort, and success (Saitō 1996). As Fujimoto Yukari (1998) argues, the core questions of shōjo manga are "Who am I?" and "Where is a place for me?" These later become shared questions with the male readers of shōnen manga, along with a general interest in "identity" in Japan from the mid-1980s on (Kayama 1999; Ueno 1992).

Shōjo manga's rich potential for complex representations of the human psyche in diverse sociocultural contexts was essentially constructed by Tezuka's androgynous character Sapphire in *Ribon no kishi* (Princess Knight) in 1953. With its visualization of masculinity and femininity within one body it was able to depict conflicting selves within one sexed body under pressure for social conformity, hence literally embodying the quest for identity and subjective agency (Fusami 2001; Orbaugh 2003; Schodt 1996; Shamon 2007; Thorn 2001; Toku 2007). From the outset of the 1970s, shōjo manga came to be associated with female artists who aggressively utilized androgynous, cross-dressing, half-human or nonhuman characters and created a full variety of stories of love and the longing for true love between independent individuals. These artists were young and close to the same generation as their targeted readers; they typically explored girls' pressing issues, making shōjo manga an effective tool for enlightenment and encouragement, and not just mere entertainment (Fujimoto 1991, 1998; Schodt 1983).

Taking a general view, there were originally two streams in shōjo manga: one with androgynous, masculine, or asexual protagonists searching for self and love, and another depicting more explicit romance involving an ordinary girl. These two elements were already conceived in Tezuka's Sapphire, as her androgyneity is not integrated like Ikeda Riyoko's character Oscar in

Versailles no bara (The Rose of Versailles; 1972–73) but is represented by two hearts of blue and pink; her oneness is thus only gained by giving up the blue heart. Sapphire was created intrinsically female, and when she behaves as a girl she is overtly feminine. She wears dresses, and sings and speaks in a girlish manner. It may be more accurate to depict her characterization as schizophrenic rather than androgynous. This schizophrenia is exemplified by a scene wherein Sapphire, wearing a dress, is happily weaving a garland of flowers for her mother but then at nine o'clock must become a "prince." Although at first softly lamenting her incomplete wreath, Sapphire in her prince attire — with a male facial expression and using male speech — takes her sword and destroys the wreath without hesitation.

The first stream of shōjo manga was developed by talented and ambitious female artists in the 1970s, beginning with Ikeda Riyoko, Hagio Moto, Takemiya Keiko, Ōshima Yumiko, and Yamagishi Ryōko, and can be characterized as having challenging themes and innovative methods of depiction. Their works are powerful, artistic, and individualistic and have enhanced the social status of shōjo manga dramatically. Their achievement involved developing further Tezuka's story manga — that is, a narrative evolution within the framework of shōnen manga (e.g., as eventful, realistic, historical), exemplified by Ikeda's *Versailles no bara*, which is underpinned by detailed historical knowledge of the French Revolution. These artists and their works are widely respected and frequently discussed in academia.

In comparison, the second stream of shōjo manga was quieter, sweeter, more conservative, and less individualistic, and was aesthetically/artistically represented by the adoption of pastel colors. It flourished and appealed to a wider, slightly younger, cohort of girls, in conjunction with consumerism (e.g., character goods) and *kawaii* (cute) culture (see Kinsella 1995; Shimamura 1991; Sōichi 1994; Yomota 2006). Although popular, this form of shōjo manga is less respected and less frequently discussed in academia. This stream focuses on the sensitive, inner world of an ordinary girl and her tender romance in everyday life, and is often called *otome-chikku* ("girlie") in a slightly condescending manner. According to Hashimoto Osamu (1984), these are typically stories of self-acceptance or the healing process of an everyday, shy girl with an inferiority complex over her appearance and/or ability. Her achievement is supported by her boyfriend's love and assurance of her intrinsic value ("I love you as you are"). Yoneyama Yoshihiro views such manga as a means for girl readers to "dream" (cited in Ohtsuka 1991). The leading artists in this genre include Mutsu Ako, Tabuchi Yumiko, and Tachikake Hideko from Shūeisha's *shōjo* manga magazine *Ribon* (Ribbon). Ohtsuka Eiji (1991) recognizes the group's contribution as the discovery of an ordinary girl's inner world — that is, the shōjo's selfhood.

The romantic stories are generally simple, domestic, and stereotypical, and — objectively speaking — uneventful. In short, what they embody is a girl's subjective inner world and her sentiments. The girl protagonists are focalized, and their monologues frame the discourses. The graphics are drawn in fine, delicate lines leaving substantial blank space to provide room for sentiment and contemplation. The characters are (modestly) cute with huge, starry eyes, disproportionately large heads, and thin, small bodies that stress their innocence, fragility, and submissiveness. The absence of explicit sexual depiction is rather formulaic in these works. The boyfriend's respect for the girl is commonly expressed in the absence of a physical relationship between the two. Hence, a story generally ends happily with the boy's acceptance of the protagonist as she is. With such stereotypical characters, scenarios, and gentle and slightly comical graphics, these romantic manga have been able to offer comfort to their readers for decades.

This second stream is closely related to the manga series focused on in this chapter, Hikawa Kyōko's *Kanata kara*. Hikawa's works are clearly identified as shōjo manga and were initially serialized in a typical shōjo manga magazine, *Lala*, and republished in *Hana to Yume Comics* (Flower and Dream Comics; fourteen volumes) and in *Hakuteisha Bunko* (pocketbook-sized comic books by Hakureisha, seven volumes). The front covers of *Hana to Yume Comics* feature only the characters Noriko and Izark, announcing to readers that it is a love story.

Hikawa frequently utilizes shōjo manga conventions, visually and linguistically stressing the contrasting qualities of masculinity and femininity in her male and female protagonists. Gender differences are classically embodied through clothing (girls are dressed in skirts) in *Kanata kara* as well as Hikawa's other works. Her stories have the appearance of a stereotypical and gender-oriented romance, in which a male's masculinity and girl's femininity are contrasted. A typical example is seen in her *Chizumi to Fujiomi-kun* series from 1979, in which Chizumi is small, sincere, sympathetic, friendly and humble yet often clumsy. In contrast, her slightly older boyfriend is tall, handsome, extraordinarily athletic, independent, reticent, reclusive, and often shunned by others. They are both caring, and their affection and understanding for one another are frequently signaled by their small gestures and limited yet meaningful speeches. Chizumi's ability to read the significance of Fujiomi's words and actions plays a key role in maintaining their bond and makes their dissimilarities serve to connect each other as indispensable, complementary partners.

Through the positioning of their protagonists with contrasting qualities horizontally, not hierarchically, Hikawa's stories are all about relationships, connectedness, and intersubjectivity — not only between lovers but also among their friends and enemies, as well as otherness within oneself and one's own sense of past and future.

Such complementary relationships are also found in a number of shōjo manga fantasies, such as Watase Yū's *Ayashi no Ceres — Tenkū Otogi-zōshi* (Ceres, Celestial Legend). Similarly, in *Tsuki no ko* (Moon Child), Shimizu Reiko depicts the androgynous Benjamin in an overtly feminine style, with long, abundant, curly hair; starry, tearful eyes; and a small physique in contrast to Art's manly physical and psychological disposition. In these narratives, the gender differences facilitate the protagonists' mutual maturation through development of their understanding of their differences and their respective selfhood.

VISUAL AND TEXTUAL DEPICTION

Manga narratives are essentially constructed with iconographic illustrations, frames, and speech (voiced and interior speeches, and limited narrations), as well as sound effects (e.g., onomatopoeia). They efficiently integrate these linguistic and visual texts to present lengthy and complex psychological stories which can be read quickly (Bryce and Davis 2006). The masterly manipulation of frames, the intensity of the drawing, and the literary and visual perspectives impart multiple voices and dimensions to Hikawa's works.

Hikawa's persuasive power as a manga artist lies in her ability to distinguish subtle emotional states and changes with carefully selected and combined gentle yet expressive visual effects, texts, and frames. Each of her techniques is rather conventional, yet the way in which she combines them is unique. Her works feature stylized graphics with refined lines, limited character speech and narration, flexible manipulation of perspectives, plenty of "white space," and frequent use of simple, angular panels. It is an incongruent yet eloquent combination of typical shōjo manga-style graphics with gentle, fine lines characterized by cuteness, and shōnen manga-style graphics with strong lines (e.g., in fight scenes), rigid frames, plentiful (and often handwritten) onomatopoetic descriptive injections and limited speech. Moreover, Hikawa also expressively utilizes narrative and graphic conventions, as exemplified by *Arano no tenshi-domo* (Angels in the wilderness; 1983–84), which employs clichéd expressions found in cowboy movies yet alters the framework by installing the tomboyish, clever girl Miriam as a chief protagonist (Kawamura 1997).

In manga, actual as well as mental events, their temporality, and special relationships to narrative information are largely constructed by frames, called *koma* (Natsume 1985; Yomota 1999), and the basic shape of these frames was generally square in earlier manga works. Since the 1970s, however — and in shōjo manga, in particular — the masterly manipulation of the shape and size of frames (e.g., quadrilateral) has dramatically increased, thereby bestowing psychological complexity — emotional ambience, intensity, the inducing of memories. This is exemplified by Ōshima Yumiko's *Tanjō!* (Birth! 1971) and Takemiya Keiko's *Kaze to ki no uta* (The Song of the Wind and the Tree; 1976–84; see Inuta 1999; Takemiya 2001).

Hikawa's use of frames is rather simple for shōjo manga, and it gives less emotional subtlety but adds clarity and speed to the visual action and narrative development in a manner similar to that of shōnen manga. Kawamura (1977) notes that Hikawa's combination of limited linguistic presentation and orderly frames tactically bestows a flow of time within a story,[2] driving the narrative's progress and a sense of speed to the action. *Kanata kara* opens with landscaped, square frames, and Hikawa continues to use them throughout the story, giving a sense of stability (Takeuchi 2005). With constant use of the same shape the frame becomes "invisible," thus highlighting any irregularly shaped frames that may appear in order to destabilize the mental landscape of the narrative. As the story progresses, in the scenes such as fight scenes, a number of irregularly shaped frames, often deformed triangles, impart a tenseness to the motion/emotion. Similar manipulations of frames are found in other shōjo manga, such as works by Shinohara Chie (e.g., *Ten wa akai kawa no hotori* [Red River], 1995–2002) and Akaishi Michiyo (e.g., *Towa kamo shirenai* [Perhaps Eternal], 1998–2000).

Hikawa's frequent use of blank (white) space, which is typical for romantic shōjo manga, gives lightness and softness in the story as a basic tone. When touching and/or philosophical matters are depicted fewer frames are used, thus providing mental space for appreciation and/or contemplation, similar to the effect of still pictures in anime, as can be seen in many of Tezuka's TV anime works and Anno Hideaki's *Shinseiki Evangerion* (Neon Genesis Evangelion) series. The frequent use of blank space is effective to project a limited number of dramatic scenes (e.g., fighting) with intense lines and irregular frames (Onoyama 1997).

Kanata kara is framed as mise en abyme, narrated and commented on by the character Noriko in her diary, which is later published by her father (himself an author of sci-fi works) as a book titled *Kanata kara*. Noriko's tone is genial, sincere, and clearly feminine, underpinning the stable ambience in the tale. The border separating her interior monologues from speeches addressed to the intended readers (including her family) is vague. The wording is mostly casual and intimate — sometimes as if a monologue, at other times as if softly speaking to Izark to seek his agreement in front of her friends, and at still other times addressing the readers to explain the situation in the manner of a travelogue. As in all good manga works, speeches — particularly Noriko's monologues — effectively capitalize on the nature of the Japanese language to demonstrate the diverse speech styles and vocabularies according to social position (gender, age, status, etc.), emotional states, and the psychological proximity of the speakers and those being spoken to.

In *Kanata kara*, story development is driven by actions that are compounded by limited linguistic texts, such as Noriko's narration, voiced and/or telepathic conversations, and interior monologues (generally of Noriko or Izark), all of which are clearly distinguished by the different shapes of speech bubbles ("balloons") or by the absence of them. Rigid squares are uniquely and frequently used for Noriko's interior monologues and some narrations, and are thus differentiated from other discourses, such as actual speech or someone's remembered speech. Through the employment of such, more voices and perspectives are added to the narrative. The placement of interior monologue outside of normal speech bubbles, with tails that are closely placed to the speaker, is one of the innovative methods of shōjo manga developed since the 1970s.

Izark's predestined bond with Noriko and his hesitation to get romantically involved with her are elaborated on the pages where Noriko falls into his world. One page is divided into three irregular rectangular panels so that in the first frame a relatively large, transparent image of Noriko is falling head first toward the forest. At the left corner of the panel one sees Izark's back as he gazes at the forest, but in the next two panels readers see only Izark — first his upper body from afar and then zooming in to focus on his head and shoulders. His upper face is consistently shadowed, to appear dark and ambiguous, in contrast to Noriko's peaceful face with closed eyes drawn in white. Izark's face is only revealed when Noriko has thrown her arms around him tightly and looks up at him, after being rescued by him from cannibalistic plants. His face is placid and slightly distant in contrast to Noriko's, who has instantly blushed upon realizing her bold action to a stranger. However, from then on, he spectacularly, and almost compulsively, continues to protect her, despite his original intention to kill her.

Noriko and Izark are visually contrasted in almost every possible way using typically shōjo manga graphics together with Hikawa's own style. Noriko is natural, tender, and perceptive and is depicted in soft, round, fine lines. She is cute and has a round face and vertically long, saucerlike eyes. Her eyes, countenance, and body are all expressive and constantly change to reflect her feelings. Typical comical depiction is frequently used for Noriko in which her body is shortened and her face slightly flattened. This comicality is an important element that generates a shift in ambience and emotional state, lifting any mood of seriousness or heaviness as well as ending any stalemate in a story. In this story, laughter is elicited mostly by Noriko's unintentional comicality, and her portrayal is therefore characterized by its softness and pliability. In other words, she is constantly captured in motion. In this way Noriko is bestowed with an engaging personality, lively mind, friendliness and ability to communicate, thus becoming the key to connecting herself and others to establish the sphere of light within the society.

In contrast, Izark's features are sharply defined in clear lines that express seriousness and hardness. He is handsome, tall and slender, like the typical male hero in shōjo manga. His face is thin and long; his chin is pointed; his eyes are long and slitted; his hair is long, straight, and black. His transmutation to Tenjōki is carefully observed by Noriko and described in detail, including his shape and color. His body becomes bluish-black, steellike and reptilian, and a short horn sprouts on his forehead. He has countless scales and sharp talons all over his body, as well as batlike wings, sharp fangs, and claws. His slitted eyes become narrower, sharper, and turn a piercing celestial blue. His hair becomes bluish silver. When he moves, his monstrous body makes a heavy noise (*gishi gishi*), like that of heavy armor or machinery. His quick recovery from injury also reminds readers of a reptile's ability to regenerate a damaged part of its body. Nevertheless, dystopian evil and any typical image of the abject (e.g., as dirty, shapeless, slimy — Julia Kristeva's formulation of abjection) are completely absent from Izark's depiction.

Hikawa's restricted linguistic discourses are fully compensated for by her emotional visualization. For example, shading is frequently employed to depict changes in the character's facial complexion. When Noriko blushes, her whole face or areas around the nose are often shadowed by fine, horizontal lines, whereas when she blanches her forehead is shadowed by fine, vertical lines. Her face thus demonstrates her spontaneous emotive expressions, thereby maintaining her dialogues with Izark and others as active and sincere.

Furthermore, handwritten onomatopoeia is heavily used, for the sounds themselves but also — more importantly — to augment the mental landscape. The frequent use of onomatopoeias is very common in shōnen manga but far less so in shōjo manga. A wide variety of onomatopoetic words constantly and colorfully appear in *Kanata kara*, exemplified by the sequence in which Izark teasingly fights with others. Colorful and slightly unusual onomatopoeia generate speed and comicality through actual sounds such as *bashi!* (the bang made by a strike of a heavy club) and *zuzaa!* (a thud when a heavy object is slammed onto the ground and slides and through mimesis such as *suka! suka!* Indicating the emptiness of missing a target (vol.4, 95–102). In addition, small *tsu* is frequently used to add dynamic feelings to the words.

Noriko's first encounter with Izark (vol. 1, 34) is depicted with various onomatopoetic words. When she runs to him and holds him, three *gachi* are scattered on her head, shoulder, and arm, showing that she is trembling and feels chilly. In contrast, the intensity of her tight hug is depicted as *gyuuu* in hiragana and in a curvy line over Izark's arm and hers (though they don't touch each other), indicating warmth and the considerable duration of this situation. This frame is followed by five frames in which *tokun*, Izark's light, constant heartbeats, are scattered in oval-shaped bubbles made of small, soft dots. Her inner speeches are written in squares in rather childish wording and show the intensity of her confusion: I'm lonely (*Kokorobosoi yō*), I feel worried (*Fuanda yō*) I don't like it (*Yada yō*).

A range of onomatopoetic words is constantly used for Noriko in conjunction with her facial expressions and gestures to confirm her mental states, such as *kaa!* when she blushes and *ha!* and *dokin!* when she realizes something. When Izark bangs the table and shouts at her to stop talking about their first encounter in order to avoid people's suspicion of their identities, her shock is depicted with her wide-open eyes almost completely white and only the outline of her eye and retina; her forehead is shadowed by vertical lines, and above it, on her hair, is written the onomatopoeia *biku!* in bold. The frame is small and oblique, and placed under the larger frame of Izark pounding the table.

OTHERNESS, COMMUNCIATIONS AND INTERSUBJECTIVITY

By integrating shōnen and shōjo manga-style graphics, conventions and narrative strategies, *Kanata kara* explores issues of otherness, communication, and coexistence. Facing the difference in others compels us to consider who we are and how we relate to those others. Since Tezuka's *Tetsuwan Atomu* (Astro Boy), manga/anime narratives have continued to visualize otherness by showing others with a strange body shape and/or occasional transformation to nonhuman beings, and depicting them as victims of "normal" humans rather than as predators. Such otherness generates confrontations, alienation, or connections. By sharing the other's experience and feelings as well as the majority's views, the reader is urged to contemplate the issues of identity, individuality, human rights, interpersonal relationships, and the like in a balanced way and to see every individual as an other; and finding that difference is an invaluable source of the communication, connection, mutual acceptance, and interreliance depicted in manga.

Otherness is a "relational" notion and only perceived against normativeness (Hijiya-Kirschnereit 2007). When one's unique individuality is seen as otherness it is likely to be subjected to discrimination and disdain. *Kanata kara* establishes both Noriko and Izark as the other for each other as well as for their surrounding world. Although Noriko is a stranger, as she has come from a parallel world, the pain of otherness is experienced not by her but by Izark, who is discriminated against by others in his own world due to his extraordinary physical strength and his prophesized future as Tenjōki. Noriko's sympathy toward Izark's pain and loneliness as the character made abject connects them profoundly, enabling them to develop their mutual bond as irreplaceable partners and to face the outside world as a pair.

Izark's suffering is from both external and internal factors as he fears himself and his other, Tenjōki. This is analogous to the girl Rinko who transforms into a vicious leopard in Shinohara Chie's *Yami no Purple Eye* (Purple Eye in Darkness). There is an abundance of similar examples in manga/anime, including Tezuka's *Vampire*,[3] in which Toppei, a boy, becomes a wolf upon viewing the full moon and is used by a cruel, ambitious boy named Rock. The majority of Tezuka's protagonists — Astro Boy, Leo, and Sapphire — represent strong otherness via their abnormal bodies (Ōno 2000).

Izark has been a loner and reluctant to associate with other people, with Gaya (a middle-aged female warrior) being the one notable exception. This is not because of his intrinsic personality but is due largely to his childhood trauma as a monster-to-be, as displayed by his recurring memory of his mother. Although having beneficial contact with the character Evil to help raise Izark, his mother comes to hate his otherness and abuses him; she even tries to kill him. When Izark has left home, their home is burned by Evil, instilling in Izark both hopelessness and a sense of guilt that tortures him. Izark's experience of hopelessness as a young and perplexed individual is depicted by rendering him as a small, white figure, abandoned in a vast darkness created by people's isolation of him, saying, "Don't be close to him!" (vol. 2, 42).[4]

Is Izark good or evil? His ambiguity baffles the seers, Zena and Gina, as they see only undistinguishable colors. Evil power is present in him and around him. His sinister potential is portrayed through dark shadow and/or a huge, frightening, black, sneering, male face that looms behind or above him. However, his innate kindness and aptitude toward goodness is also consistently confirmed in many episodes. His ambiguity is displayed through Zena's view: for the first encounter, she is strongly alarmed by his intense energy of darkness but upon seeing Izark and Noriko together, she percieves a ripple of light spreading and the sacred sound of a bell filling the air. Similarly, later, when the sadistic character Sid uses his powers of mimicry to copy Izark's abilities, the resulting visualization of a huge dragon signifying Izark's potential threat stuns not only other people but Izark himself. However, the tense atmosphere is broken by Noriko hugging him and also by Creagita's praise of Izark's ability to contain such an enormous force within himself. He also says that power itself is intrinsically neutral and the dragon image merely embodies Sid's malevolent inner self. All of the above denotes the pivotal significance of Noriko for Izark's power to be directed towards goodness, the world of the light.

Communication between Noriko and Izark from their very first encounter occurs not through linguistic dialogue but through actions of helping each other, and this shapes their bond accordingly. Their first encounter consists of a series of movements through several frames of different shapes and sizes that demonstrate Noriko's chaotic experience of having been transported to an unknown, parallel world. Realizing that she is not in a dream but in a completely unfamiliar and hostile place, Noriko cries like a child. When she is attacked by a gigantic carnivorous plant, Izark, who is observing her, spontaneously kills it. Shocked to see the dead plant, Noriko closes her eyes, dashes to Izark and throws her arms round him tightly. Hearing Izark's heart beats, she calms down. Her inner speeches (drawn in squares) accompany the series of her motions: "I can hear the sound of a heart . . . warm human body . . . ah . . . I am calming down . . . it was good that I could see someone . . . by the way, who is this person? . . . It's not the time to feel at ease! What have I done to someone I've never met before?" (vol. 1, 35).

This rather old-fashioned depiction of a heroine seeking solace in the arms of her savior is altered by Izark's freeing himself from her with a slightly perplexed facial expression after she has looked up at his face. Similarly, a little later, when Noriko thinks he is leaving her, she falls, unable to walk, and starts to cry like a child. He stays beside her until she falls asleep. These are not romantic scenes, but exhibit Izark's genuine care for her and Noriko's appreciation of that care. After these early encounters, Noriko frequently hugs Izark or clings to him without thinking. Similarly, Izark repeatedly rescues her, almost compulsively, though at the same time he tries to distance himself from her. At this stage they cannot understand each other's language and their dialogues are established through actions, visuals, and the acute reading of each others' thoughts. The development of their trust for each other is encouraged by Noriko's animated gestures such as her intimate, childlike hugs and her habit of falling into a deep sleep beside him when she is relieved after extreme tension.

An ability to initiate and nurture communication is intrinsic in Noriko. She does so generally through her spontaneous actions and gestures, particularly her joyful smile and childlike crying. When Noriko sees that Izark's serious stabbed wound has already almost healed, Izark turns his face slightly away as he expects her horrified response to his abnormal healing speed. But her response totally betrays his concerns: her smile beams to him her deep relief. It is portrayed via three frames: the first is the smallest and slightly overlaps the second, which depicts a larger picture of her full smile, followed by Izark's somewhat surprised face on the lower left-hand side of the page. After that, Noriko slowly collapses on the floor. The onomatopoetic text *heta heta heta* (a person's sudden loss of energy and subsequent fall in slow motion) in smaller, bold letters is written alongside her body and a single wavy line above her head (vol.1, 101). This scene follows her crying like a child, close to Izark's feet, then her sudden collapse into deep sleep. The spontaneity of her response to Izark's recovery confirms her genuine worry over his pain and well-being, which profoundly heals Izark's inner hurt.

Noriko's inner strength and positive attitude to life constitute the bedrock of the story. She is essentially a doer. Even in a hopeless situation, when she finds something to do, she regains hope and energy. It is exemplified by a comical sequence that depicts quick changes in her mental state inside Gaya's vandalized house — from being depressed, to telling Gaya to do something, to looking at the mess of the house and energetically cleaning it up. Similarly, Noriko's first conscious effort in the unknown world is her learning of language, as soon as she has recognized the need to help others. This happens when an injured man asks for water, and she cannot help as she cannot understand his words. This is symbolic and denotes her significance as a communicator in the story. Moreover, her speeches in this earlier period are childlike and comical (e.g., with wrong words or without particles), and this elicits a cheerful atmosphere between Noriko and the others.

Happiness and cheerful laughter are what Noriko brings to Izark's life. Natural laughter is a barometer of human happiness. After his full acceptance of Noriko as his love, Izark chuckles loudly, making Noriko blush with happiness, which further encourages him to enjoy humorous exchanges with her. Izark's initial inability to laugh has derived from his unhappy childhood and his constant fear of becoming a monster. In contrast, Noriko has been raised and loved as the youngest member of an affectionate and fun-loving family and has developed a basic sense of trust, mental stability, sensitivity, and intuition toward genuine warmth. Her personality and upbringing is expressed in her frequent and artless hugs and touching, particularly of Izark. With these attributes she is also able to see others' intrinsic qualities and establish genuine understanding and communication with them, beginning with Izark, Irk, the spirit of a tree called Asayuge ("morning mist") and Doros the abused (a breeder of chimo who betrays his abusive master Rachef and rescues Noriko, taking her to Izark via teleportation). Such reference to Noriko's background bestows a sense of probability into the narrative.

Noriko's gifts are her compassion and (telepathic) sensitivity, which play an important role in connecting people and easing tensions among them. She can envisage Irk and is able to help him and the souls of his people who are trapped in the forest by Evil. Moreover, in the forest, she can sense that the place has an evil influence over the travelers that is making them irritable. She tells Izark, who conveys this to the others, avoiding potential conflict.

Noriko and Izark's relationship is essentially reciprocal and is steadily strengthened through a number of experiences, becoming partners who accept and comfort each other when one or the other has to expose an extreme vulnerability. Their mutuality is extended to even physical acts, in spite of the apparent differences in their physical strength. The first time Noriko rescues Izark is when Izark is ill and they are attacked by bandits. Although Noriko is unable to understand his language, she notices Izark being unwell, and tries to protect him — and vice versa. At the end, in order to protect Noriko from enemies, Izark holds her and jumps from their room in an inn. Izark lies on the ground and urges Noriko to hide herself, but she successfully carries him with all her might to hide from the enemy. Noriko exhibits a strong desire to protect Izark, since she has witnessed his occasional collapses.

The profound and mutual acceptance between Noriko and Izark is portrayed with a fairy-tale convention — a princess's kiss for a cursed prince. It occurs at the time of Izark's first metamorphosis into a monster, when Noriko has been pinned down under rocks. His shock, resentment, and desperation release his violent power to transform him into the spectacular Tenjōki. He pleads with her not to look, writhing with shame and grief. In contrast to his apprehension of Noriko's fear and rejection, Noriko realizes that she is on the verge of losing him, grabs his hand, and begs him to stay with her: "No! Please don't go. Don't go, Please! I don't like it. I don't like to be apart from you anymore. Please stay with me. I love Izark. I love Izark. I don't mind what shape you are. I don't mind who you are. I love you, Izark" (vol.5, 142–45). She then kisses him, almost unconsciously, before fainting.

This pattern continues. Izark's second metamorphosis is again triggered by Noriko's kidnapping as a sacrifice to the wicked, bodiless creature Mokumen (lit., "silence face"). This time Izark's anger, desperation, and frustration over the endless fights he has to engage in to reach Noriko is so intense that Izark loses himself and nearly forgets what he is fighting for. Noriko senses his confusion and, as soon as she has a chance to escape, she dashes to hug him to calm him down. This sequence is cinematically depicted with Izark in almost complete darkness in the distance. His distressed figure gradually enlarges; Noriko's tiny, white, running figure appears in the centre of the page; and Izark's profile is positioned, in close up, on the bottom right of the page, as he looks back at her. The spatial progression captures the essence of their relationship and Izark's reliance on — and longing for — Noriko. He needs her in order to be himself, and she needs him for the same reason.

The more there is love, the more the fear of losing it intensifies. Along with developing their bond, both Izark and Noriko experience the fear of losing each other. They each suffer dreams in which they cannot find the other. With intense fear, Izark wonders if he has become stronger or weaker through his relationship with Noriko, something so precious and indispensable. Awakened by such a nightmare, he asks Noriko not to disappear. She blushes and utters a vow — "I will be with you as long as you wish. I will be with you, taking my life into my vow" (vol. 11, 100–01). Nevertheless, Izark's fear is actualized several times throughout the narrative, and on particular occasions his shock and helplessness is depicted by his inability to stop trembling, as, in one instance when Noriko is talking about her family and seems to disappear from his view, or when she is kidnapped by Rachef and confined in a room shielded from the outside world by magical stones and thus unable to communicate with Izark.

The story tells us that such deep emotions may be abused by evil, which is elusive, indefinable, and ubiquitous, embodied in amorphous black stains, dust, clouds, water, and a monster like a mass of hair in Irk's forest. Such nebulous illustrations stand out in Hikawa's clear drawing style, disturbing the generally stable ambience of the story. The elusiveness of darkness is also visually represented by their utterances, which are written in the combination of katakana and kanji (instead of hiragana and kanji); and by the unique, partially fragmented font as if written by brush. These metaphors signify evil's power as an ability to instigate, manipulate, and feed on people's negative emotions. The readers are reminded of Izark's monstrous metamorphosis being caused by fear, grief, and desperation over his anticipated loss of Noriko. Hikawa elucidates the structure of wickedness and warns of the danger of self-alienation, despair, and anxiety as a breeding ground from which manipulating evil grows (as embodied by the entity Genkyō with its ugly, terrifying face and teeth). This story depicts how sorrow and unhappiness make people cruel. There is no absolutely malicious character except Genkyō, a formidable oracle in the past, who had controlled the world over many reigns through the power of magical crystals. This character lost his body by failing to prolong his life and waited for a chance for his reembodiment in Izark's body. He spreads and amplifies evil, parasitically feeding on people's unhappiness, as in the events in Irk's forest. From trivial differences, once friendly people grow to display increasing hostility and end up killing each other. Even after their deaths, their souls are trapped and enslaved by the evil power.

Toward the end, the story reveals that reliance on power and threats are in fact symptomatic of individual weaknesses, self-deception, and lack of self esteem by exposing the frailty of Izark's most frightening enemy, the sadistic Kaymos. His monstrousness is augmented by the magic crystals in Genkyō's ruined shrine. Once defeated by Izark, Kaymos is obsessed with revenge. At his final defeat, his forcefully empowered body collapses, but he still begs Izark to continue the fight and not to ignore him. Izark comes to the realization that Kaymos has an inability to accept himself, as who he really is; he can only value himself through others' perceptions.

Similarly, Rachef eventually divulges his inner void. He is cruel and cunning, yet after all, he is Genkyō's effective tool. His kidnapping of Noriko and his demand of her to empower him with her love, and his intolerance for Noriko's refusal to do so, expose his desperation. He tells her that he has killed everyone in his way, including his own mother, but that his thirst only increases. His dream is hence to create a world in which everyone obeys him so that he no longer feels the void. As later Noriko realizes, Rachef's mad craving for dictatorship only intensifies his solipsism and his thirst.

YOU ARE YOU

Who am I? Is there any place for me? Is there anyone who loves me as I am? Is there anything I can do that genuinely reflects *me*? These are recurring questions throughout most manga narratives. In *Kanata kara*, the story develops along with Izark's struggle with his ambivalent sense of self until finally he discovers who he is in a most dramatic way. It comes at a most critical point — when he has been caught, severely injured, and nearly thrown to the bodiless Genkyō, while at the same time asking himself who he is. At that exact moment, Noriko rushes in. When he sees her falling toward him, he finds his answer — I am not Tenjōki. I am Me! Light bursts from him immediately. Noriko sees him opening his arms for her, while flapping his large, white feathery wings, which declares that his true strength has overcome his fate and his inherent, potentially dangerous aptitude.

Conversely, Noriko is mentally stable because of her awareness of her own limitations. Doing her best for others within her limited ability and situation is her way of self-acceptance and self-empowerment. This vocational desire is nurtured by her childhood memories of noticing and preventing a fire in her new neighborhood and her happiness when her mother thanked her as a younger girl for going shopping for her. Her trial comes in Irk's forest, when an illusionary Irk (evil) distracts her from the real Irk by tempting her with an offer to grant powers that she has always wished to have. This is an attractive thought, since she would no longer be a burden to others and would instead be able to help them. She eventually escapes from the trap, only by remembering the true Irk's words: "You can help others as you are." She thinks that if there is anything she can do as she is, then that is what she must do. She feels it is wrong if she has to give up what she now has in order to gain power.

Noriko's title as Mezame, The Awakener, is symbolic. It is near the closure of the entire story and during the final battle with the evils led by Rachef and Genkyo, when Noriko is depressed by her helplessness. Gaya encourages her, noting how significantly Noriko's expression of appreciation can empower others. This finally triggers Noriko's own awakening to open a door to the world of light.[5] She comtemplates how people can connect through expressions of gratitude, as her tiny power of gratitude is received and amplified by those who receive it, generating gracious interactions. She suddenly feels her consciousness being diffused and spread like a ripple of water to the wider world. Externally, an explosive light emits from her and violently pushes back the enemy goblins. This decides the victory of light against darkness. At the same time, Izark's body, injured as a result of his final battle with Kaymos, radiates white light that quickly heals his injuries. He then sees Noriko coming to reunite with him. She embraces him explaining that this is the world of the light they have been longing for. Rachef and his ruined shrine are soon destroyed.

This manga series delineates Izark and Noriko's physical and psychological journey toward their maturation as individuals and as a mutually involved pair by accepting who they are and strengthening what they have. Izark's development through outgrowing his solipsism is especially dramatized as a quest for his own place in society, through his relationship with Noriko. It is figuratively embodied by his metamorphoses into Tenjōki and then into an angelic being. This is essentially the same as Tōya's quest for himself in Watase Yū's *Ayashi no Ceres** (Bryce 2008). In this context, Izark and Tōya, more so than Noriko and Aya, embody the essential questions of shōjo manga: "Who am I?" and "Where is my place?"

These questions are also recurrently expressed in utterances by characters in the *Shinseiki Evangerion* (Neon Genesis Evangelion) TV series, for which the question "May I stay here?" was selected as a promotional quote by the director, Anno Hideaki. Hence, as Fujimoto (1998) argues, the girls' question of more than three decades — "Where is my place?" — is now being shared by boys. This signifies a new era, a move away from a time when a boys' place was secured in society by his acceptance of social roles and responsibilities and his struggle with the related problems while a girl's place was denoted through being loved by a boy.

CONCLUSION

Exemplifying what contemporary shōjo manga is, *Kanata kara* explores subjectivity and intersubjectivity: love, trust, sorrow, fear, hatred, light, and darkness. It imparts the importance of — and desire for — genuine, sympathetic communication as the essential basis for profound interactions. As the character Rachef would put it, a series of changes begins when a tiny stone called Noriko is thrown into the world and her presence progressively affects everything there, like a ripple, to eventually awaken Izark's monstrous Tenjōki. In fact, by being herself, Noriko becomes a catalyst for Izark and his inner self (embodied by his angelic wings of light), and for others around him, as well as the world within the sphere of light through which everyone is connected.

As evidenced by her ability to leave her body to join Izark of her own will, Noriko's sense of fusion of herself into the atmosphere is not experienced as

---

* — Tenkū Otogi-zōshi

a loss of self but as an embodiment of Mikhail Bakhtin's dialogism — individual subjectivity is intersubjective, and "a more positive view of the relationship between self and other, emphasizing the role of the other in completing the self" (McCallum 1999, 70–71).

Focusing on Hikawa Kyōko's *Kanata kara*, this chapter has tried to examine how romantic shōjo manga fantasies are able to investigate profound human issues in a way that readers can be not only entertained but also cheerfully encouraged — to be and live as they truly are in order to enjoy mutual love, affection, and friendship.

Notes

1. Personal names are presented in the traditional style, with family name first.
2. Rigid square frames are more frequently used in Hikawa's earlier works, such as *Arano no tenshi-domo* and its sequel *Jikan wo tomete matte-ite* (Please stop time and wait for me; 1985–87).
3. This work is incomplete, being first published in *Shōnen Sunday* between 1966 and 1967, and then in *Shōnen Book* between 1968 and 1969.
4. All translations from the Japanese are my own.
5. Furthermore, Fujimoto (1998) observes that since the late 1980s, shōjo manga has begun to depict less obvious and stereotypical emotions (e.g., love, resentment, friendship, sorrow, and jealousy), and to attempt to impart something more extremely subtle — namely, a form of communication — using sympathetic resonance as a key concept. This is exemplified by the character Arisu/Mokuren's ability to communicate with plants by tuning in her feelings in Hiwatari Saki's *Boku no chikyō wo mamotte* (Please Save My Earth).

References

Bryce, Mio (forthcoming). "*Ayashi no Ceres*: The Mythological Past and Present in Manga and Anime." *Journal of the Oriental Society of Australia*.

Bryce, Mio, and Jason Davis (2006). "Manga/Anime, Media Mix: Scholarship in a Post-Modern, Global Community." In *Proceedings of the CAESS Conference: Scholarship and Community*, ed. Michael Atherton, 1–10. Sydney, New South Wales, Australia: University of Western Sydney.

Davis, Jason, and Mio Bryce (2008). "I Love You as You Are: Marriages between Different Kinds." *International Journal of Diversity in Organisations, Communities and Nations* 7(6): 201–210.

Fujimoto Yukari (1991). "Onna to ren'ai: Shōjo Manga no Love Illusion" *New Feminism Review* 2: *Onna to hyōgen: Feminism hihyō no genzai*.

—— (1998). *Watashi no ibasho wa doko ni aru no? Shōjo manga ga utsusu kokoro no katachi*. Tokyo: Gakuyō shobō.

Fuse Hidero (2004). *Manga wo kaibō-suru*. Tokyo: Chikuma shobō.

Hashimoto Osamu (1984), "Yasashii Pornography: Mutsu Ako ron." In *Hana-saku otome-tachi no kinpira gobō*, vol. 2. Tokyo: Kawade shobō shinsha.

Hijiya-Kirschnereit, Irmela (2007). "Hermes and Hermès: Otherness in Modern Japanese Literature." In *Representing the Other in Modern Japanese Literature: A Critical Approach*, ed. Rachael Hutchinson and Mark Williams, 19–38. London: Routledge.

Jackson, Rosemary (1981). *Fantasy: The Literature of Subversion*. London: Methuen.
Kawamura Kyōko (1997). "Kaisetsu: Atarimae no yōde ite atarimae de nai monogatari."
    In *Jikan wo tomete matte-ite*, vol. 3, 234–39. Tokyo: Hakusensha.
Kayama Rika (1999). *Jibun wo aisuru to iu koto: watashi sagasi to jiko ai*. Tokyo:
    Kōdansha International.
Kinsella, Sharon (1995). "Cuties in Japan." In *Women, Media and Consumption in Japan*,
    ed. L. Skov and B. Moeran, 220–54. Honolulu: University of Hawaii Press.
Masubuchi Sōichi (1994). *Kawaii shōkōgun*. Tokyo: Nihon hōsō shuppan kyōkai.
Natsume Fusanosuke (1985). *Natsume Fusanosuke no manga-gaku*. Tokyo: Yamato
    Shobō.
Ogi Fusami (2001). "Beyond *Shoujo*, Blending Gender: Subverting the Homogendered
    World in *Shoujo Manga* (Japanese Comics for Girls)." *International Journal of Comic
    Art* 3(2): 151–61.
Ohtsuka Eiji (1991). *Tasogare-doki ni mitsuketa mono: Ribon no furoku to sono jidai*.
    Tokyo: Ōta shuppan.
Ōno, Akira (2000). *Tezuka Osamu: hen'yō to igyō*. Tokyo: Kanrin shobō.
Onoyama Rie (1997). "Kaisetsu" Hikawa manga — Hikari ni michita sekai." In Hikawa
    Kyōko, *Jikan wo tomete mate-ite*, vol. 2, 246–51. Tokyo: Hakuteisha.
Orbaugh, Sharalyn (2003). "'Busty Battlin' Babes: The Evolution of the Shojo in 1990s
    Visual Culture." In *Gender and Power in the Japanese Visual Field*, ed. J. S. Mostow,
    N. Bryson, and M. Graybill, 201–28. Honolulu: University of Hawaii Press.
Saitō Jirō (1996). '*Shōnen Jump' no jidai*. Tokyo: Iwanami shoten.
Schodt, Frederik. L. (1983). *Manga! Manga! The World of Japanese Comics*. New York:
    Kodansha International.
—— (1996). *Dreamland Japan: Writing on Modern Manga*. Berkeley, CA: Stone Bridge
    Press.
Shamon, Deborah (2007). "Revolutionary Romance: The *Rose of Versailles* and the
    Transformation of Shojo Manga." In *Mechademia: Networks of Desire*, ed. Frenchy
    Lunning, 3–18. Minneapolis: University of Minnesota Press.
Shimamura Mari (1991). *Fancy no kenkyū: 'kawaii' ga hito, mono, kane o shihai-suru*.
    Tokyo: Nesco.
Stephens, John (1992). *Language and Ideology in Children's Fiction*. London: Longman.
—— (2000). "Myth/Mythology and Fairy Tales." In *The Oxford Companion to Fairy
    Tales*, ed. Jack Zipes, 330–34. Oxford: Oxford University Press.
Takemiya Keiko (2001). *Takemiya Keiko no manga kyōshitsu*. Tokyo: Chikoma shobō.
Takeuchi Osamu (2005). *Manga hyōgen–gaku nyūmon*. Tokyo: Chikuma shobō.
Toku Masami (2007). "Shojo Manga! Girls' Comics! A Mirror of Girls' Dreams." In
    Mechademia: Networks of Desire, ed. Frenchy Lunning, 19–32. Minneapolis:
    University of Minnesota Press.
Thorn, Matt (2001). "Shojo Manga — Something for Girls," *Japan Quarterly* 48(3):
    3–50.
Ueno Chizuko (1992). *Watashi sagashi game: yokubō shimin shakai-ron*. Tokyo:
    Chikuma shobō.
Woodward, Kath (2002). *Understanding Identity*. London: Arnold.
Yomota Inuhiko (1999). *Manga genron*. Tokyo: Chikuma shobō.
—— (2006). *Kawaii ron*. Tokyo: Chikuma shobō.

Further Manga Reading

Akaishi Michiyo (1998–2003). *Towa kamo shirenai, Shō-Comi Cheese Flower Comics* (8
    vols. 1998–2000); Shōgaukan bunko (4 vols., 2003). Tokyo: Shōgakukan.
Hikawa Kyōko (1983–84). *Arano no tenshi-domo* in *Lala, Hana to Yume Comics*
    (3 vols.); Hakusensha bunko (2 vols. 1997).

—— (1986–97). *Jikan o tomete matte-ite* in *Lala, Hana to Yume Comics* (3 vols., 1986–88); Hakusensha bunko (3 vols., 1997).

—— (1991–2007). *Kanata kara* in *Lala, Hana to Yume Comics* (14 vols., 1992–2003); Hakusensha Bunko (7 vols., 2004–5); VIZ Media (14 vols., 2004–7) / *From Far Away* (14 vols. 2004–7) VIZ Media.

Hiwatari Saki (1987–98). *Boku no chikyū o mamotte* [Please save my Earth], in *Hana to Yume Comics* (21 vols., 1987–94), Hakuteisha bunko (12 vols., 1998), Tokyo: Hakusensha [*Please Save My Earth*] (21 vols., 2001–7), VIZ Media.

Ikeda Riyoko (1972–73). *Versailles no bara, Margaret Comics* (10 vols.), Shūeisha bunko (5 vols.), Tokyo: Shūeisha; *The Rose of Versailles* (1981), translated by Frederik L. Schodt, 2 vols. Tokyo: Sanyūsha.

Kitagawa Miyuki (1998–2007). *Tsumi ni nureta futari*, in *Shōjo Comics*; *Shō-Comi Cheese Flower Comics* (18 vols., 1999–2004); Shōgakukan bunko (9 vols., 2007), Tokyo: Shōgakukan.

Ōshima Yumiko (1970–86). *Tanjō!* in *Margaret*, Sun comics (1975); *Ōshima Yumiko senshū* vol. 1 (1986), Tokyo: Asahi Sonorama.

Shimizu Reiko (1988–). *Tsuki no ko* in *Lala, Hana to Yume Comics* (13 vols., 1989–), Hakusensha bunko (8 vols., 1998–99), Tokyo: Hakusensha.

—— (1988–). *Kaguya-hime* in *Lala, Hana to Yume Comics* (27 vols., 1994–2005), Hakusensha bunko (12 vols., 2007–), Tokyo: Hakusensha.

Shinohara Chie (1984–95). *Yami no Purple Eye* in *Shjo Comic*; *Shō-comi Flower Comics* (12 vols., 1984–87); Shōgakukan bunko (7 vols., 1995), Tokyo: Shōgakukan.

—— (1995–2007). *Sora wa akai kawa no hotori* in *Shjo Comic*; *Shō-comi Flower Comics* (28 vols., 1995–2002); Shōgakukan bunko (16 vols., 2006–7), Tokyo: Shōgakukan / *Red River* (28 vols., 2004–), VIZ Media.

Takemiya Keiko (1976–84). *Kaze to ki no uta* in *Shōjo Comic* (1976–82) and *Petit Comic* (1982–84); *Shō-comi Flower Comics* (17 vols., 1977–84), Tokyo: Shōgakukan; Hakusensha bunko (10 vols., 1995), Tokyo: Hakusensha.

Watase Yū (1996–2006). *Ayashi no Ceres — Tenkū Otogi-zōshi*, in *Shōjo Comic*; *Shō-comi Flower Comics* (14 vols., 1997–2000); Shōgakukan bunko (7 vols., 2005–6), Tokyo: Shōgakukan / *Ceres, Celestial Legend* (2003–6), VIZ Media.

Yuki Kaori (1994–2007). *Tenshi Kinryōku, Hana to Yume Comics* (20 vols., 1995–2001), Hakusensha bunko (10 vols., 2002–3), Tokyo: Hakusensha / *Angel Sanctuary* (20 vols., 2004–7), VIZ Media.

9

The Power of Truth: Gender and Sexuality in Manga

Tania Darlington and Sara Cooper

Sherrie Innes has posited that comic books are "at the cutting edge of exploring new definitions of gender because of their marginalization, which allows them to be what Ronald Schmitt [in 'Deconstructive Comics'] identifies as an 'important deconstructive and revolutionary medium in the 20th century' . . . . This deconstructive power is one of the reasons feminist theorists should be interested in comic books — texts that can create alternative worlds in which gender operates very differently than it does in our own real world" (Inness 1999, 141).

If comic books in general are indeed on a feminist cutting edge (and we would agree that they are), then the pages of some Japanese comics are slicing away at social norms one painful paper cut at a time. In marked contrast to mainstream United States comics, Japanese manga have repeatedly and openly dealt with a wide variety of gender expression as well as a range of manifestations of same-sex love. However firmly entrenched the expectations for actual Japanese young adults may be, depictions of the flouting of these expectations are in no way taboo in contemporary Japanese cultural production. We are interested in how certain manga challenge assumptions about gender and sexuality and critique gender-role expectations and compulsory heterosexuality even as they incorporate subtle elements that continue to support patriarchal and heteronormative hegemony, particularly in the context of male-to-female gender transitioning and same-sex relationships between women.[1] While the boys' love, or *shōnen-ai*, context in manga is well established, representations of female gender and sexuality are still evolving, albeit slowly, and mirror the slow change in values in Japanese society (Fujimoto 2005, 12–13). This study will look at male-to-female and female-to-male gender transitioning and same-sex female relationships (*yuri*) in the long-running *shōnen manga* (boys' manga) series *Ranma ½* and *A Cheeky Angel*; the classic and contemporary *shōjo manga* (girls' manga) offerings *Revolutionary Girl Utena*, *Sailor Moon*, and *Ouran High School Host Club*; and the *seinen manga* (men's manga) series *Kashimashi: Girl Meets Girl* to answer these principle questions: How are gender and sexuality represented? How are social reactions to gender and sexuality addressed in these manga? How do these manga address the issues of social reactions to gender and sexual nonconformity? How is the constant evolution of shōjo — that is, girlhood — reflected in manga depictions of sexuality? And finally, what may we surmise about the impact of these series on the reader and society at large?

Although manga in its modern form emerged in the mid-twentieth century, and the works presented in this study deal with issues that seem entirely contemporary, in actuality the concepts of gender performance and sexual ambiguity have been explored for centuries in Japan. Contrary to commonly held assumptions in the United States, Japan (like most cultures) has a history of gender performance, onstage and off, that mimics even as it undermines traditional divisions between male and female roles. For instance, one of the classical forms of theater in Japan is Kabuki, which has been performed since the 1600s. Although the first documented performances were played by an all-woman troupe, featured erotic dancing by a maiden named Okuni, and were consecrated to the shrine Izumo Taisha, soon the theatrical domain was usurped by men. Seen to be safer for the viewers and performers alike, more moral and less provocative, all-male Kabuki theater has been the norm for centuries (Yoshida 1971, 90–91).[2] Traditionally several male actors (*onnagata* or *oyama*) exclusively act in female roles, some retaining their gender performance offstage as well, and not surprisingly garnering the adoration of self-identified heterosexual men. Although some troupes now will use biologically female actors, and a few all-female troupes exist, some aficionados and critics claim that this is a failure, and that only onnagata can truly represent the essence of femininity in Kabuki ("Japan Fact Sheet: Kabuki," n.d.). It seems that the blurring and crossing of gender lines in manga has abundant precedence in Kabuki. Also worthy of note is the element of magic that permeates this theatrical genre, as well as most of the manga series under consideration here. This confluence of parallels surely owes at least partially to the association of gender change with "intense energy, with magic, with miracle, even with the supernatural" (Ramet 1996, xiii). Finally, one should consider the focus on spectacle and stylization that supercedes even the story line, another possible argument for Kabuki being a cultural influence on the manga discussed in this chapter.

When delving into the particulars of series such as *Utena* and *A Cheeky Angel*, it will be crucial to keep in mind the exact context of the creators and readers; both historical culture (i.e., Kabuki) and contemporary popular culture must figure into our interpretations of complex issues like gender. Notably, in Japan overt discussions of the very concepts of gender and biological sex are so foreign that feminist critics have resorted to "borrowing" the English words associated with gender studies and translating them into Japanese, as in *genda* (gender) and *sexu* (sex).[3] This does not mean that popular visual culture does not represent clashes with the norm, but rather that the direct commentary of the same has been constrained by certain limits of vocabulary and cultural perspective. Accordingly, Sabrina Petra Ramet cautions us that every society has a gender culture or, in other words, "a society's understanding of what is possible, proper, and perverse in gender-linked behavior, and more specifically, that set of values, mores, and assumptions which establishes which behaviors are to be seen as gender-linked, with which gender or genders they are to be seen as linked . . . and how many genders there are" (1996, 2). Challenges to this paradigm (what Ramet calls gender "reversals") always serve some function or another within the culture itself (1996, 4–14). Thus, we may go beyond describing the gender reversals that are found in Japanese manga and speculate as to the functions they play in Japanese society. Considering the original purpose of manga, to be "inexpensive entertainment for children, dreams that made it easier to live in the devastated postwar society in Japan," gender-fluid manga make it possible to live in contemporary Japanese (and global) society, where social constraints requiring us to repress and suppress so much can be equally emotionally devastating (Toku 2001a, 6). To some extent, the performance of gender bending and diverse sexual experimentation invokes the feminist pleasures discussed by Sue-Ellen Case (1990, 1–7). The consistence of transgression, the relative social acceptance of the other, and the romantic depiction of female sexual power offer pleasurable and exciting contrast to the rigid roles that tend to proliferate in both the mass media and real social interactions in Japan. In this case, manga like *Utena* and *Ouran High School Host Club* present alternative realities in which seemingly anything is possible, quite unlike the strict regimentation that maintains order in the midst of spatial and social crisis on the island. However, as will be discussed in terms of the six manga series under study, never is this performance of difference fully and completely accepted even by the characters in the series. The end result is the creation of a fantasy world that mimics a place of tolerance and justice, but that in actuality is unreal and therefore not considered to influence what is truly happening. Judith Butler notes that such loves and losses "[are] less than 'true' loves and 'true' losses. The derealization of this domain of human intimacy and sociality works by denying reality and truth to the relations at issue" (2004, 27).

As a brief aside that can provide some context for this discussion of girl-centered sexuality, same-sex attraction and gender fluidity appear in several subgenres within the shōjo manga genre. Particularly relevant to this discussion are the shōnen-ai, which focus on light romance and drama between young men, and the *yaoi*, which feature graphic sex between men. While the sexual content of yaoi can be shocking, and the same-sex focus of shōnen-ai is unexpected for the uninitiated, both forms are widely distributed and historically have been more accepted than yuri. This is no doubt due, in part, to the fact that the protagonists are men and boys, meaning that they are experienced as fairly traditional in terms of gender roles and expectations. However, even in the more conventional shōnen manga market transitional series that combine the more complicated elements of female-to-male gender fluidity with more adventure-oriented story lines can be found. *Ranma ½* (1987–96) illustrates fluidity of gender and its implications for sexuality. Ranma Saotome is a martial arts student whose original gender is male, but who was cursed (or blessed) when he fell into the Pool of the Drowned Girl, so that any contact with cold water temporarily turns him into a curvaceous young woman.[4] Subsequent dunking into hot water reverses his gender again, and s/he is transformed several times in each chapter. As Ranma deals with his feminine transitions, the heroic nature of the shōnen protagonist is complicated by the more shōjo-oriented questions of "love, family, responsibility, identity" (Davis 2000, 29). As Julie Davis explains, "love is, of course, perhaps the single most universal emotion, and *shōjo* focuses strongly on what to our modern sensibilities is perhaps the most important part of it — how your choice of who you love defines you" (2000, 29). Ranma is in love with the rebellious and strong Akane (always a girl), who as his best friend and love interest is attracted first by Ranma's feminine manifestation. It must be said that his female persona, unlike that of all the other male-living-as-female characters discussed here, is drawn as larger-boned and very muscled; this, however, seems to be merely a function of the artist's style. The fact that Akane loves Ranma both because of and in spite of his partial femininity suggests that true love must necessarily permit liaisons across gender lines. Ranma also is pursued by other young women, including "Shampoo, a girl from a tribe of martial artists somewhere in China, who at first finds herself pledged to marry male Ranma but kill female Ranma" (Decker 2003, 36). Readers may laugh out loud at the slapstick episodes of gender transition, but only those stubbornly wearing philosophical blinders can ignore the questions raised about culture, race, gender, and emotional object choice — in a word, *love*. Ranma may be embarrassed by his lack of control over his physical body, but in contrast to his readers he at least has the comfort of knowing that in either gender manifestation he will be a perfect specimen. He may also have to intermittently suffer the physical, social, and cultural restraints and challenges that are the domain of the female Japanese, but in essence these experiences allow him to grow as a person and understand his beloved on a level not permitted of most men. At the core of things he is still a boy (as the gendered definite articles of this paragraph attest), and any physical change is only temporary. The gender ambivalence here is partially for comic value, and partially to allow the main character a window into the soul and heart of his (one assumes) eventual life partner. The questions about gender and sexuality that the series poses only lightly critique social inequities and never ask the viewer to accept same-sex love as such. Nevertheless, *Ranma ½* challenges previously held U.S. conceptions of Asian culture, or Japanese culture specifically, and this series provides a fascinating exploration of how traditional gender expectations can exist simultaneously with representations of nontraditional characters.

Another comic and only nominally challenging shōnen manga series that highlights gender performativity and its impact on romantic relationships is *A Cheeky Angel* (1999–2003). Though the comedy borders on slapstick, with amply overexaggerated emotional faces and physical humor, the gender themes closely resemble those in *Ranma ½*. This series revolves around the exploits of Megumi Amatsuka, a physically alluring fifteen-year-old tomboy who was originally male. Like Ranma, her gender was switched by outside forces, though in Megumi's case the switch was permanent. When she was nine, Megumi saved a magician from being attacked by neighboring thugs. In return, he gave her a magical book that would grant her one wish. Megumi (then male) wished to be the manliest man in the world, but the genie in the book, claiming to have misheard, turned her into the womanliest woman in the world. When she returned home after the switch, no one but Megumi and her best friend Miki Hanakain remembered that she was ever anything but a girl. Despite the fact that Megumi's personality becomes increasingly girly as the series progresses, she never stops insisting that she is a boy and looking for the book that can turn her back.[5] Megumi exhibits many characteristics of male gender performance both prior and subsequent to her physical transformation. Early in the series, Miki alludes to the fact that Megumi had a bad reputation in junior high school because she was always beating people up. Though she does not routinely beat people up during the time frame of this series, she does fight often, and when her identity as a transformed male is questioned, she becomes belligerent. She engages more frequently in traditional "tough guy" actions, such as yelling, cursing, and picking fights; several times her friends remonstrate with her for "talking like a boy." Aside from her occasional masculine gender performances, however, she is so exceptionally feminine in appearance that her male fans continue to be attracted to her even when she confesses to them that she used to be a boy.

The dichotomy between Megumi's internal perception of herself and her outward appearance is particularly evident in a series of issues wherein Megumi inadvertently witnesses an attempted mob hit. Though she is able to defeat many of the mob members with her well-honed fighting skills, the female robber who got her involved in the situation still calls her a "dreamy girl" and muses, "This is my first time seeing such a girly girl." Megumi's toughness does little to interfere with her perceived femininity, manifest in the blond hair reaching almost to her knees, her gamine grace, and her refined and high-class features. On the other hand, her eyes are more almond-shaped, like those of the male lead Genzo Souga, and in the traditional conventions of manga drawing style this places her more in the sphere of masculinity in Japanese manga. (Note that the gender of a secondary male character who always wears glasses is called into question when his large round eyes are revealed!)

Megumi's relationship with Miki is particularly compelling, as Megumi clearly acts out both male and female gender roles with her. Miki constantly comments on how well Megumi is adopting female mannerisms, and she is thrilled to have Megumi as her female best friend, to the extent that she hopes Megumi always remains female. Indeed, the two seem to have a fairly typical schoolgirl friendship; however, underlying gender tensions are revealed when Miki comes of age and is obliged to drop out of school and carry out the terms of an arranged marriage. Determined not to lose Miki, Megumi invokes her masculine identity and says that, since she is a guy, she will marry Miki herself so they won't be split up. She envisions herself as a prince coming to Miki's rescue. For her part, Miki is so impressed by Megumi's displays of chivalry that she begins to realize that her playmate would make an ideal boyfriend and regrets her earlier wish that Megumi would always stay female. Though their romantic feelings are never acted on, Megumi and Miki's relationship clearly falls somewhere between friends and lovers. Much like real homosocial relationships, the line between feelings of friendship and feelings of love is blurred, and such blurring is depicted as both normal and acceptable.

Throughout the series the interplay of sexual ambivalence and gender complicates the relationships between Megumi and all of her friends and admirers. If Megumi is "really" male, then her heart throbs for Genzo and her interest in the "average guy" Fujiki are shōnen-ai. In contrast, from her own perspective her feelings for Miki are heterosexual, while Miki's feelings for her vacillate between yuri and heterosexual. All these sentiments and desires must be filtered through Megumi's initial reaction of disgust about any sort of physical intimacy, such as the thought of kissing or dating. She is repulsed and shocked when male classmates try to grab at her, wondering if all guys are like that, if she would be like that if she was changed back.

Megumi's experience of gender transformation is also temporarily mirrored when Genzo "wants to be a girl" in order to understand Megumi better. He dons a particularly plain dress, under which his large frame and bulging muscles call attention to his aberrant behavior, so that everyone who sees him stares, and many express their repugnance at his oddity. Experiencing the inequality of nontraditional gender roles and the helplessness that women often feel profoundly impacts him and adds a new level of understanding to his character that only deepens his respect and affection for Megumi.

What we see in *A Cheeky Angel* is that gender identity is not an unalterable fact or a choice between two poles but rather a flexible continuum. Megumi does not lose her masculine identity merely by being "changed" into a girl. Neither does she lose her feminine identity when she takes on the masculine roles of bully or protector. Nor does gender necessarily equate itself with appearance in this series. Megumi's merging of masculine and feminine identities reminds readers that their gender roles need not be determined by sex, a theme that becomes more pronounced in the shōjo and seinen manga to be discussed.

The shōjo manga surveyed for this chapter tend to portray more saliently the tensions between individual gender performance and social norms. These tensions tend to be played out through female homosocial/homosexual relationships and transgendered identities. In all three shōjo manga series the overt acceptance of nontraditional roles by social groups is set against subtle signals of disapproval of the portrayed lifestyle from the larger society.

Sharalyn Orbaugh defines shōjo as "a cultural construct, symbolizing a state of being that is socially unanchored, free of responsibility and self-absorbed — the opposite of the ideal Japanese adult" (2002, 458). In other words, shōjo represents a transitional period when the individual is free to experiment with nontraditional ways of being before settling in to the circumscribed roles expected of Japanese adults. It makes sense, then, that shōjo manga likewise experiments with nontraditional expressions of gender and sexuality while reinforcing the notion that such expressions are not traditionally accepted norms in adulthood. It is fair to say that depictions of shōnen-ai, yaoi, and yuri relationships and transgendered identities are well within the range of expected experimentation.

Shōjo manga often presents sexually ambiguous and gender-ambiguous characters, who are depicted respectfully and with great dignity as well as with occasional humor. Some of these characters are rebellious heroines who embody both feminine and masculine characteristics and who incite the adoration of admirers of both sexes. James Boren indicates that the 1953 manga *Ribon No Kishi* (Princess Knight) is the inspiration for these figures; in turn, *Ribon* creator Osamu Tezuka was inspired by the well-known Takarazuka theater group, composed entirely of women. The princess in question, Sapphire, is blessed with a double heart — that of a boy and of a girl; she is raised as a prince so as to conform to societal rules of inheritance, but she also roams her realm and has adventures in princess garb (Boren 2003, 29). A classic example of the gender-ambivalent and universally loved heroine-prince is manifest in the wildly successful *Revolutionary Girl Utena* (1996–97).

Utena Tenjou is a young lady who, for all intents and purposes, dresses and acts like a young gentleman. Utena has dedicated her life to rescuing damsels in distress and thinks of herself as a prince, hence her insistence on taking a modified male school uniform when she enters Ohtori Academy.[6] For the duration of the story line she is a student at this high-status educational institution, where as the result of numerous sword battles with the members of the Ohtori Academy Student Council she is "wedded" to the Rose Bride — a girl of her age named Anthy. Before Utena comes onto the scene, Anthy has been "won" and "wedded" by several male council members, who have had the right to demand any and every service from her; thus, the background story is an extreme manifestation of rigid gender roles in which a woman ultimately is subservient to male needs. Anthy's complete repression of any female and personal volition is symbolized by her behavior in a duel: she offers herself with open arms to the current champion, who then plunges a hand deep between her breasts in order to withdraw the magical sword (a delightfully phallic symbol), suggesting that she is no more than a tool or weapon for the victor's use. After the duel, she mutely and subserviently — with hands clasped and eyes downcast — waits for the current champion to take her where he will. Utena first decides to win and maintain control of Anthy in order to rescue her from male domination rather than to take the spoils of victory, showing a princely reserve and high principles. She continues to show other attributes that could be construed as masculine, such as a higher-than-usual sense of competitive spirit and the physical fortitude to win at any sort of endeavor, be it basketball or sword fighting. To complicate matters, however, the reader learns very early that Utena's original inspiration for her personal transformation was a visit from a nameless prince, who with the gift of a ring (engraved with a rose — a typical manga symbol for romantic feelings) assures her that he will return for her one day. Her choice to embody the male rather than become the idealized female is of course surprising both to the reader and to the other characters in the series. Nevertheless, her own gender nonconformity is balanced by an assumed underlying heterosexuality that will win out in the end.

Utena seems to be much more comfortable in the role of savior than in the position of beloved or lover. She apparently is horrified when Anthy suggests that she has performed intimate acts with other champions, and that she gladly would do the same with/for Utena. The protagonist shows discomfort and embarrassment at the frequent protestations of love from other class-mates. Nonetheless, as the series progresses, the reader is led to believe that her feelings for Anthy are increasing and becoming more complex, including the probability of romantic and sexual inclinations. Although Utena shows "proper" womanly restraint as well as consternation at the thought of becoming sexual, she is caught in increasingly compromising situations and must be understood to have moved past girlish innocence by the time of the "consummation" ceremony that she and Anthy must perform near the end of the series.

Utena and Anthy depict overtones of what has come to be called *yuri* — literally "lily," an all-inclusive word denoting female/female love, with or without sex; Yukari Fujimoto notes that depictions of lesbian love began to arise in the 1990s (2005, 15). Manifestations of girl-girl and woman-woman romance and love have become so abundant that the secondary term *shōjo-ai* (girl love) has been used more recently to indicate specifically romantic, nonsexual, love between girls (Doolan 2001). Japanese manga seems much more realistic than most United States comics for girls in that it simply portrays an inescapable reality — that in a gender-homogeneous environment the emergence of same-sex attractions is inevitable. In an atmosphere where excellence is pursued, such as the prestigious academic institutions that constitute the background for so many manga, the inescapability of one student becoming enamored of another is further exacerbated. In activities such as athletics, where perfections of the physical body are idealized, or academics, where intelligence and eloquence are prized, the select few who are seen as the epitome of success must be the object of envy and worship of their fellows. Although Ohtori Academy is coeducational, the social reality it portrays privileges friendships and social time within peer groups of the same sex, which is reflective of the majority of social interactions in such a traditional culture. During the vulnerable years of preadolescence and puberty, the added emphasis on corporeal changes and burgeoning sexuality brings into focus the desirability of any peer who stands out from the rest; the dividing line between what is desired as an asset that one may wish to possess and an attribute that one wishes to be close to is almost impossible to judge. This in conjunction with Alfred Kinsey's foundational research on human sexuality (subsequently affirmed by many other studies) — which indicates that humans exhibit a continuum of sexual and romantic attraction rather than the once assumed heterosexual/homosexual binary — simply underlines that both proximity and biological imperatives would contribute to exactly the phenomenon we see in *Revolutionary Girl Utena*. Indeed, a cultural sphere so firmly rooted in the expectations of a rigidly controlled adult behavior that includes heterosexual marriage and childbirth may see very real benefits in further romanticizing the already unpreventable female attachments at this age level. If Japanese society in no way admits the viability of homosexuality as an adult lifestyle choice (no matter the level of feelings or desire), and to a great extent does not consider advantageous or even possible the development of women as sexual beings, then love and romance between girls would be perceived as doubly safe. Of course, romantic affairs between girls offer the added perk of providing titillation for the male comic artist and consumer.

Another manga portrayal of same-sex attraction between girls, *Sailor Moon* (1983–97) targets a younger audience, that of grade school and early adolescent girls. The premise of *Sailor Moon* is that a group of best friends acquire special powers that allow them to transform into superheroes when the need arises to combat evil and injustice; the rest of the time they avoid homework, go shopping, and moon over boys. Although all of the series' heroines inspire the devotion of their classmates, even more interesting are sailors Uranus and Neptune of the *Sailor Moon S Series*, who are an excellent example of yuri characters. Haruka Tenou or Amara (Sailor Uranus) and Michiru Kaioh, or Michelle (Sailor Neptune), are clearly portrayed as a "butch-femme" couple. They have an ambiguous yet obviously intimate relationship (although U.S. readers are told they are cousins), and are initially mistaken by the younger characters in the series as "boyfriend and girlfriend." These younger girls exhibit adolescent crushes on Amara both before and after they discover this very butch character to be female. We can see then that while homosexuality as a lifestyle is not necessarily condoned in Japan, for some time now gender and sexual diversity, as well as spiritual and emotional love between same-sex partners, have been given a place of importance in manga genres. Equally important, the characters tend to be shown as whole people, with faults and defects as well as strong points and sometimes superhuman abilities. In these early examples, we as readers see images of romance and strength in diverse gender performances and sexual preferences without being asked to accept falsely perfect heroes. However, while sexuality and gender performance are merely significant subplots in *Sailor Moon*, they are the focal point of *Ouran High School Host Club* (2003–present).

The most recent work discussed in this essay, *Ouran* is intriguing for the way it magnifies and parodies the sexuality and gender issues dealt with in all of the aforementioned manga. However, while it revels in explorations of nontraditional conceptions of gender and sexuality, it may covertly do the most to enforce traditional expectations. At the center of *Ouran* is Haruhi Fujioka, a female scholarship student at Ouran High School, a private academy for the ultrawealthy. Haruhi, who claims her "consciousness for genders is lower than that of an average person," can't afford the school uniform and so dresses in a sweater, dress shirt, and slacks that give other students the impression that she is male. When she breaks an $80,000 vase she becomes beholden to its owners, the Host Club, a group of the richest and most popular *bishōnen* ("beautiful boys") in the school who meet every afternoon to offer entertainment and companionship to admiring school girls willing to pay for their services. Assuming Haruhi is male, they propose she act as a host in order to pay off her debt. When the other hosts discover that Haruhi is female, they keep her on and hide her gender from the rest of the student body, as she already has become very popular with clients. Haruhi is perhaps one of the best examples of the fluidity of both gender identity and desire. All of her fellow hosts harbor some level of romantic attraction to Haruhi the girl, attraction that seems to be enhanced, rather than lessened, by the knowledge that she routinely dresses as a man. Likewise, the male Haruhi is extremely popular with the women who attend the club, who like her for her gentle, down-to-earth personality but have no suspicion that she is actually a woman. All of Haruhi's suitors, both male and female, are nonetheless clearly fascinated by Haruhi's otherness, as her "commoner" heritage reveals a world of exotic attractions like fast food, instant coffee, and apartment living. Furthermore, since Haruhi's need to cross-dress for the Host Club is a direct result of her socioeconomic status, the hosts' fantasies of "rescuing" her from "poverty" are often intertwined with their desire to restore her femininity.

As is obvious from the above description, themes of homosexual attraction dominate *Ouran*. Because of its parodic nature, *Ouran* is free to engage these themes very overtly. To a great degree, all of Haruhi's relationships are based on some level of unwitting same-sex attraction. Though the hosts are attracted to the female Haruhi, most of their experience with her takes place in an environment where she is performing the male gender. Thus, their attraction to Haruhi as a woman is filtered through the lens of Haruhi as a man. At the other end of the spectrum, Haruhi's clients admire Haruhi in her male guise, yet it is Haruhi as female who bears the level head and gentle demeanor to which they are attracted. In fact, it is often stated that one of Haruhi's main attractions is her girlish appearance. These covert homosexual tensions are made overt in Haruhi's relationships with the minor character Benio Amakusa. Benio (more commonly known as Benibara) is the leader of the Zuka drama club at St. Lobelia Girls' Academy, a school of, by, and for girls. (Amusingly, the formal name of the Zuka Club is the White Lily Group — a play on the term *yuri*, perhaps?) Benibara, who is wildly popular with the women at her own school and believes that the purest form of love is love between two women, immediately recognizes Haruhi as a woman and is determined to remove her from the corrupting influence of the "garbage" of the Host Club. Haruhi admits that she finds Benibara's way of thinking "unique and interesting," but she elects to remain at Ouran. In a later chapter, hoping to steal her first kiss, Benibara kidnaps Haruhi and convinces her to play the heroine to her romantic lead in the latest Zuka Club production. Benibara represents overt longing for a homosexual relationship. She also represents the acceptability of same-sex attraction as, despite the fact that Haruhi does not accept her advances, virtually every girl at St. Lobelia Academy openly desires her. Although Benibara's audacity is framed as positive, these scenes are depicted in such a way to capitalize on the humorous and ridiculous elements, taking away somewhat from the serious nature of inquiry.

While *Ouran* seems to be particularly accepting in the way it deals with gender identity and same-sex desire, it is replete with instances that undermine this openness. When Benibara tries to remove Haruhi from the Host Club, citing the purity of love between women as her reason, Tamaki Suou, the Host Club king wonders what kind of productivity is there when women make love to each other. "Why did God create Adam and Eve?" While Tamaki is routinely the straight man and the butt of most jokes in *Ouran*, and it is clear this is a comedic moment, it is impossible to ignore how closely his question corresponds to longstanding mainstream arguments against homosexuality. Again, it is Tamaki who brings up typical social tensions when, frustrated with Haruhi because she gets hurt after standing up to a group of male thugs, he yells at her for not acting like a girl and refuses to speak to her until she apologizes for not conforming to the prescribed limitations of her own gender. More disturbing than Tamaki's reinforcement of traditional sexual and gender norms, however, is the role ascribed to Haruhi's father. A conventional argument of conservative culture against child rearing on the part of gay men and lesbians has been the mistaken assumption that if the parental role models are not heteronormative and gender conforming their children are bound to turn out the same way. Haruhi's variable gender identity is clearly depicted as just such a case. As her mother died when she was a young child, Haruhi has been raised by a single father who used to be bisexual, but became an *okama* (a gay male cross-dresser) after his wife's death. The implication seems to be that transgendered individuals are destined to pass gender confusion on to their children. Nevertheless, it is important to note that Haruhi's peer group from the Host Club do not show signs of discomfort around Haruhi's father, and on the contrary secretly conspire with him/her in what they believe to be the best interests of Haruhi. Like *Utena* and *Sailor Moon*, *Ouran* pushes the envelope in terms of acceptable levels of same-sex attraction and can perhaps push it farther because of its parodic nature. To a certain extent, however, parody undermines how seriously *Ouran*'s questioning of societal norms can be taken. Notably, though same-sex attraction has traditionally been the domain of shōjo, the most prominent and compassionate portrayal of yuri considered here is found in an altogether different genre.

As Fujimoto notes, shōnen-ai and yaoi have frequently been used in shōjo manga to help girls explore sexual identities and controversial issues without direct identification, without feeling threatened or exploited (2005, 15). Obviously, the same can't be said for yuri, where female readers can directly identify with both partners, simultaneously experiencing the role of both the lover and the beloved. Perhaps the emotional demand of this dual role-playing is one of the reasons yuri relationships have not been foregrounded in shōjo to the degree their yaoi and shōnen-ai counterparts have been. Nevertheless, yuri themes are becoming more prominent in manga and are the central focus of the only seinen manga discussed here.[7] *Kashimashi: Girl Meets Girl* (2004–7) revolves around a yuri triangle, as Tomari Kurusu and Yasuna Kamiizumi fight for the affections of Hazumu Osaragi. At the heart of this relationship, and indeed *Kashimashi* itself, are issues of gender performance. As it happens, Hazumu was a boy until high school, at which time she was run over by aliens who, in the process of resuscitating her, accidentally switched her sex. In the first chapter of this manga we see Hazumu the boy and quickly realize that he is timid and gentle and loves flowers — not at all the traditional shōnen character. In fact, in the first chapter we see the male Hazumu wishing on a "star" (actually a spaceship) for "a loving relationship," immediately following which he is changed into a woman, suggesting perhaps that the only hope for fulfillment of his wishes is a shift in gender identification. It is also worth noting that the male Hazumu is never shown without bangs completely covering his eyes, making him utterly devoid of any recognizable male identity. In later chapters we learn that even in childhood Hazumu performed a traditionally feminine role, crying when picked on and waiting for Tomari, his female best friend, to rescue him as well as proudly wearing dresses in contrast to Tomari's tomboy clothing. Indeed, Hazumu takes to the feminine role immediately and develops a more traditional gender identity than she ever had as boy. Tomari, on the other hand, takes on a sterotypically masculine role: she is on the track team, excels at sports, knows nothing about cooking, is physically violent and domineering, and punches men who make passes at her. Here we see the same acting out of traditional gendered roles within same-sex relationships that is apparent in boy-love manga. It is evident in Hazumu and Tomari that gender is less about biological sex (meaning genitalia, reproductive organs and secondary sex characteristics) than about performance. Given that, regardless of sex, Hazumu has always performed the traditional female role and Tomari the traditional male role, their love for each other is not affected by Hazumu's sex change.

The presence of Yasuna — another young female classmate — complicates the relationship between Hazumu and Tomari, being both deterrent and catalyst. Just hours before Hazumu was turned into a girl she confessed her love to Yasuna but was rejected. However, after Hazumu's transformation the normally quiet, introverted Yasuna becomes the instigator, actively exploring a relationship with Hazumu. It rapidly becomes apparent that Yasuna is not interested in pursuing relationships with men. In fact, as readers learn, Yasuna suffers from a unique "disorder" that causes her to see men as little more than gray blurs. One of the clearest indications that Hazumu has always been gendered (even if not "sexed") as female is that she was the only boy Yasuna could see. Despite the fact that *Kashimashi* is a seinen manga, Yasuna's "condition" corresponds to several of the overarching tensions of the shōjo genre — particularly the fear of sexualized relations with the opposite sex and the inwardness of the shōjo gaze. Yasuna's relationship with Hazumu is critical in formulating her sexual identity — an identity that can only be explored and formulated with another woman, since she can't "see" men. For Yasuna, as for many young girls, homosexual affection may not be an end, but a necessary step in the development and acceptance of her sexuality, as once her identity is awakened she is able to give up Hazumu, clearing the way for a long-term relationship between Hazumu and Tomari.

In the final issues of the series, the aliens responsible for Hazumu's transformation reveal that she only has thirty days to live. Unbeknownst to Hazumu, she can only live past that point if she loves one other person enough to share her fate with her. When Hazumu's time is at an end, a railing gives way and she plunges off a roof, presumably to her death. However, she "comes back to life" in the infirmary, discovering that in her last seconds she called out for Tomari. Hazumu and Tomari's acceptance of their love has saved her life. While *Kashimashi*'s ending may be overly sentimental, its emphasis on the liberating powers of gender fluidity and same-sex love is encouraging. It must be noted, though, that this emphasis is counterbalanced by its fantastic elements — the power to liberate its characters from prescribed gender and sexual roles lies, literally, in "alien" hands.

As must be abundantly clear by now, *Kashimashi* and the other five manga in this study seem to pose a number of questions: What is a man? What is a woman? How must men interact with men, and women with women? How should they interact when in contact with the "opposite gender"? How do national or cultural ideologies influence how we might answer these questions? What is tolerance, and who has the responsibility to show it? In the final frames of *Utena*, Anthy says of her relationship with Utena, "the world awaits the power of Dios [God], and it begins with us." Similarly, in the final volume of *Kashimashi*, Hazumu is saved from the clutches of death by the truth of her love for Tomari. Absolutely no mention is made of the fact that this love may transgress social boundaries; the power transcends harassment even when presented to the public gaze. Notably, the series correctly points out that here the actual power is that one human being (of whatever gender) escapes the selfishness and self-centeredness that plague our daily life in order to fully and completely pledge herself to the vulnerability required for someone to know her intimately. The power of *Utena* and *Kashimashi*, as well as the four other series discussed here, brings to mind Ramet's explanation of the function played by gender reversal in religion and spirituality. In religions of several cultures, including the Shinto religion of Japan, ritual cross-dressing and the assumption of cross-gender behavior actually brings one "closer to the Godhead" (1996, 5). "Associated with purification and with elevation to a higher state" (Ramet 1996, 5), gender reversal allows one to move past the inherent limitations of the physical and the social, to more fully feel one's spiritual essence, to more completely identify with God and the universal energy, which as the wellspring of all creation must include the entire continuum of gender within. Although *Ranma ½, Cheeky Angel, Utena, Sailor Moon, Ouran*, and *Kashimashi* clearly situate gender reversal and diversity of sexuality within a condemning social environment, which is a realistic depiction of cultural norms, the creators of the manga also link a more fluid gender and sexuality with the search for truth, the breakdown of illusion, and the achievement of true intimacy and love — in essence, with the only hope for the survival of humanity. If both the creators and the audience can make the intellectual and emotional leap and incorporate such a perspective outside of the boundaries of fantasy and the world of comics, then the ever-evolving medium of manga could prove a powerful force for social change.

Notes

1. We ruefully acknowledge the inherent problems of using the terms 'same-sex' and 'homosexual' when speaking of desire of or for individuals who transgress gender norms. Broad societal denial of a gender continuum in favor of both gender and sexuality binaries results in the lack of adequate language to express the complexities of the attractions seen in the manga studied here.
2. Female acting and dancing did not disappear, of course, but was relegated to the more specific milieu of the geisha. Here the link between performance and sexuality was not a threat to general society, as geisha was a privilege for the moneyed male gaze.
3. The lacunae of feminist terminology in the Japanese language emerged as a topic of discussion among participants of the symposium *The Power of Manga: What Can Comics Tell You?* at the University of California–Chico in November 2005, held in conjunction with the opening of the traveling exhibit *Shōjo Manga: Girl Power*. One of the participants, Tomoko Yamada, who is well known nationally and internationally as a researcher and writer of shōjo manga, was perhaps the most informed contributor to this discussion.
4. In exception to the rest of the volume, this chapter uses the English order of given name first, family name last to maintain coherence with the English translations of the manga under consideration.
5. Though the genie tells Megumi that the spell will only last for ten years, the characters seem to lose sight of this time limit after the first episode.
6. As Chiho Saita, the feminist manga artist who created *Utena*, comments, "'it isn't really a male uniform, is it? It's just the clothes that Utena likes. She's not bound by the same male/female conventions that previous characters may have been bound

by"' (quoted in Davis and Flanagan 2000, 6).
7. Significantly, seinen manga seems to be a site where yuri is largely accepted, as it has also been the demographic to which other recent yuri offerings such as *Strawberry Panic!* and *Simoun* have been targeted.

References

Boren, James (2003). "The Genesis of Shōjo." *Animerica Anime and Manga Monthly* 11(9): 29.

Butler, Judith (2004). *Undoing Gender.* New York: Routledge.

Case, Sue Ellen (1990). *Performing Feminisms: Feminist Critical Theory and Theatre.* Baltimore: Johns Hopkins University Press.

Davis, Julie (2003). "Girl Power." *Animerica Anime and Manga Monthly* 11(9): 28–29.

Davis, Julie, and Bill Flanagan (2000). "Chiho Saito and Kunihiko Ikuhara." Interview. *Animerica Anime and Manga Monthly* 8(12): 6–11.

Decker, Dwight (2003). "Ranma ½." *Animerica Anime and Manga Monthly* 11(12): 35–39.

Doolan, Andrea (n.d.). "About Yaoi." Moment, an Anime/Manga Page, http://www. touyaxyukito.com/yaoi.htm.

—— (n.d.). "About Yuri." Moment, an Anime/Manga Page, http://www.touyaxyukito. com/yuri.htm.

"Japan Fact Sheet: Kabuki" (n.d.). Web Japan, Japanese Ministry of Foreign Affairs, http://web-japan.org/factsheet/pdf/30kabuki.pdf.

Fujimoto, Yukari (2005). "A Life-Size Mirror: Women's Self-Representation in Girls' Comics." In *Shōjo Manga: Girl Power*, ed. Masami Toku, 12–15. Chico, CA: Flume.

Inness, Sherrie A. (1999). *Tough Girls, Women Warriors and Wonder Women in Popular Culture: Feminist Cultural Studies, the Media and Political Culture.* Philadelphia: University of Pennsylvania Press.

Orbaugh, Sharalyn (2002). "Shojo." In *Encyclopedia of Contemporary Japanese Culture*, ed. Sandra Buckley, 458–9. London and New York: Routledge.

Ramet, Sabrina Petra (1996). *Gender Reversals and Gender Culture.* New York: Routledge.

Toku, Masami (2001a). "What is Manga? The Influence of Pop Culture in Adolescent Art." *Art Education*, March, 11–17.

—— (2001b, October 10). "Gender in Japanese Manga." Lecture delivered at California State University–Chico.

——, ed. (2005a). *Shōjo Manga: Girl Power.* Chico, CA: Flume.

—— (2005b). "What Is Shōjo Manga?" In *Shōjo Manga: Girl Power*, ed. Masami Toku, 5–8. Chico, CA: Flume.

Yoshida, Chiaki. *Kabuki.* Tokyo: Japan Times, 1971.

Suggested Manga Reading

Akahori, Satoru. *Kashimashi: Girl Meets Girl.* Translated by Adrienne Beck. 5 vols. Los Angeles: Seven Seas Entertainment, 2006–8.

Hatori, Bisco. *Ouran High School Host Club.* Translated by Kenichiro Yagi. 11 vols. San Francisco: VIZ Media, 2005–.

Nishimori, Hiroyuki. *A Cheeky Angel.* Translated by Joe Yamazaki. 20 vols. San Francisco: VIZ Media, 2004–8.

Saito, Chiho. *Revolutionary Girl Utena.* Translated by Lillian Olsen. 5 vols. San Francisco: VIZ Media, 2003.

Takahashi, Rumiko. *Ranma ½.* Translated by Gerard Jones and Matt Thorn. 36 vols. San Francisco: VIZ Media, 1993–2006.

Takeuchi, Naoko. *Sailor Moon.* Translated by Mixx Entertainment. 18 vols. Los Angeles: Tokyopop, 1998–2001.

10

The Reluctant Messiah: Miyazaki Hayao's *Nausicaä of the Valley of the Wind* Manga

Marc Hairston

Miyazaki Hayao is not a name that comes to mind when making a list of modern manga creators. Far better known as the animator of films such as *Tonari no Totoro* (My Neighbor Totoro), *Mononoke Hime* (Princess Mononoke), and the Academy Award winner *Sen to Chihiro no Kamikakushi* (Spirited Away), Miyazaki is a cultural icon in his native Japan and considered a "god" by both Japanese and American animators.[1] But he owes his success as an animator to his lesser-known manga work. His epic twelve-year manga series *Kaze no Tani no Naushika* (Nausicaä of the Valley of the Wind) was the catalyst for establishing his Studio Ghibli and ultimately the creation of his animated masterpieces.

Like many Japanese children in the postwar generation, Miyazaki grew up devouring the manga of Tezuka Osamu, along with that of Fukushima Tetsuji and Shirato Sanpei, and dreaming of someday becoming a manga artist (McCarthy 1999, 27). In college he worked to develop his own original style while struggling with "'how best to peel away the Tezuka influences buried deep within me'" (quoted in McCarthy 1999, 28). His career plans changed when, as a high school senior in 1958, he saw Japan's first feature-length color animated film, *Hakujaden* (Legend of the White Serpent; 1958). Referring to the goddess Bai-Niang in the film he later wrote, "I fell in love with the heroine of a cartoon movie. My soul was moved . . . it's easy to analyze and dismiss it, but meeting with *Hakujaden* left a strong impression on me" (Miyazaki 1998). Smitten with both the heroine and the medium of animation, he decided to become an animator instead of a manga art-ist. Attending Gakushuin University in Tokyo he studied economics and political science, but more importantly he spent time in an extracurricular "study circle" that focused on children's literature from around the world. After graduating in 1963 he went to work at the Toei Doga animation studio where he started at the entry level job, an "in-betweener" doing the drudge work of drawing the series of frames between the poses in key frames done by a "key animator." There he met Takahata Isao, five years his senior, who started as his mentor but later became his animation partner. Through the 1960s he made his way up the ladder at Toei Doga working on numerous TV shows, theatrical shorts, and, most notably, as an assistant to Takahata on his feature film *Taiyou no Ouji Horusu no Daibouken* (The Adventures of Hols, Prince of the Sun; 1968). In the 1970s Miyazaki and Takahata left Toei Doga to work on various other projects. Together they worked on the short feature *Panda Kopanda* (Panda! Go Panda! 1973) and the *Lupin III* TV show. On his own Miyazaki directed the TV series *Mirai Shounen Konan* (Future Boy Conan; 1978) for NHK and was finally able to direct a feature film of his own, *Lupin III — Castle of Cagliostro* (1979).

After the release of *Cagliostro* the *Nausicaä* manga was born as a result of the timely midwifery of Suzuki Toshio. As the editor of *Animage*, a highly popular monthly magazine devoted to anime, Suzuki had become friends with Miyazaki. Tokuma Yasuyoshi, the president of Tokuma Shoten (the pub-lishing company behind *Animage*), was interested in producing anime films, so Suzuki arranged for Miyazaki to pitch feature films ideas to the board. Unfortunately, all of Miyazaki's proposals were based on original stories of his own.[3] Then (as now) most anime films and series were based on preexisting manga series to ensure a built-in audience for the anime, so the board declined to fund an original film. Afterward Suzuki offered Miyazaki the chance to do a monthly manga in *Animage*, and a later TV documentary on the history of Studio Ghibli suggested that Suzuki was already thinking of using this manga as the basis of a future anime (Studio Ghibli 1997b). If Suzuki was thinking along these lines, Miyazaki certainly was not. In an interview after the end of the series Miyazaki denied starting *Nausicaä* with any intention of converting it into an anime: "I did not . . . even remotely think that the comic would ever become a movie. If I draw a comic, I draw something not meant to be ani-mated. Although there are lots of comics like that, they are inferior products. A comic book is a comic book. It's different from a movie" (Miyazaki 1995).

Kaze no Tani no Naushika (Nausicaä of the Valley of the Wind) debuted in the February 1982 issue of *Animage*, ultimately running for fifty-nine install-ments (usually sixteen pages each) through March 1993.[4] The length and complexity of the entire *Nausicaä* manga would require a book to explore fully, so only a brief summary touching on the key points can be presented here.[5] The story takes place in a postapocalyptic world a thousand years after the "Seven Days of Fire," an event when giant manmade cyborgs called God-Warriors destroyed the technological world as punishment for humans polluting and destroying nature. In the aftermath a strange ecosystem called the "Sea of Corruption" (*fukai*) appeared consisting of thick forests of plants and fungi giving off poisonous gases (the miasma) and inhabited by giant mutant insects. At the top of this ecosystem are the Ohmu, whale-sized pillbug-like creatures with a psychic group mind whose role is to protect the forest. A greatly diminished human population clings to the small regions on the edges of the forest where the air is breathable and the land can still be cultivated. The Valley of the Wind is a small fiefdom by the sea where the sea winds keep the miasma at bay. Influenced by his earlier Marxist political views, Miyazaki envisioned this fiefdom as an idealized cooperative agrarian society (though still ruled by a lord). Although the level of technology appears to be approximately that of the late European feudal period, salvaged bits of ancient technology appear as anachronistic elements. Thus, people in the valley live in castles and huts, use windmills for power, farm using only hand tools, but, paradoxically, also have a jet fighter for defense. In addition, most of the animals are unfamiliar descendents of genetic mutants — such as the horseclaws, large birds that serve as horses.

Nausicaä, the princess of the valley, is first introduced as she explores the Sea of Corruption using a small jet-powered glider (called a *mehve*) and wearing a gas mask. She explores to find materials for the Valley's use but also as part of her own quest to understand the nature and purpose of the forest. Immediately this establishes her not as a standard passive Disney cartoon princess but as an active explorer involved with her world. She has an empathic link with the insects of the forest and is psychically able to communicate with and gain knowledge from the group mind of the Ohmu. Miyazaki based her on two literary characters: the courageous Phaeacian princess Nausicaä from Homer's *Odyssey* who rescued the injured Odysseus, and an eccentric heroine from classical Japanese literature known as "the princess that loved insects," a young woman who shunned court life to explore nature (Miyazaki 2004).

The valley's peaceful existence is shattered when war erupts between the two remaining great powers, the Torumekian Kingdom and the Dorok Empire. The Torumekians have discovered a buried and unused God-Warrior from before the Seven Days of Fire and are preparing to use it as the ultimate weapon against the Doroks. The Valley of the Wind is aligned with the Torumekian Kingdom, but because her father, Lord Jhil, is too ill to fight, Nausicaä goes in his place. While flying with the Torumekians to the battle, she crashes into the heart of the forest. There, at its center, she discovers its true secret: that the trees function as biological filters, drawing the poisons and pollutants out of the soil to turn them into inert sand, thus healing the natural world from the damage inflicted by the ancient humans. The poison forests of the Sea of Corruption are not the enemy of humanity, but the ultimate salvation of the planet.

With her new epiphany she escapes the forest with Asbel, a boy from the neighboring kingdom of Pejitei, but both are captured by a fleet of airships containing Dorok refugees. The Dorok Empire is a theocracy made up of a loose confederation of tribes ruled by priests and overseen by the Holy Emperor, Miralupa. On board the refugee ship Nausicaä meets the tribe's priest, referred to only as the Holy One, who recognizes Nausicaä as a peacemaker. She thwarts a Dorok plan to use an injured baby Ohmu as bait that would cause an Ohmu stampede and destroy the Torumekian encampment. After rescuing the baby, the Ohmu lift her up on their golden tentacles and miraculously heal her injuries. The Holy One recognizes this event as the fulfillment of prophecy: "and one shall come to you, garbed in raiment of blue, descending upon a field of gold to forge anew our ties with the lost land" (2:121). He is the first to recognize Nausicaä as both peacemaker and savior, thus establishing her role as a messiah figure. Afterward Nausicaä begins her own odyssey to the various groups in her world in an attempt to stop the war and reconcile humanity with nature.

While *Nausicaä of the Valley of the Wind* is obviously based on traditional conventions drawn from many science fiction and fantasy narratives, Andrew Osmond points out that Miyazaki has specifically referred to three English-language novels as influences (Osmond 1998). The first is Frank Herbert's eco-epic novel *Dune*, which centers on a messianic figure and giant sandworms that are the key to the planet's environment. Miyazaki said the name for the giant insect Ohmu was taken from the Japanese name for Herbert's sandworms, *sando uomu*. Next is Brian Aldiss's novel *The Long Afternoon of Earth* (British title, *Hothouse*), which describes a future Earth taken over by exotic plants and the adventures of a young boy who becomes infected with a sentient fungus that teaches him about the true nature of his world. Last is Ursula Le Guin's fanstasy novel *The Farthest Shore*, the third book in her *Earthsea* series, which follows the archmage Ged and the young Prince Arren on a spiritual quest to the edge of the world where they discover the secrets of life and death. Miyazaki credited Le Guin's term "windkey" (a mage who can see and control the winds in *Earthsea)* with his creation of the concept and term "windrider" for Nausicaä's talent in reading the winds while flying (Miyazaki 2007). It was also during this early period of work on *Nausicaä* that Miyazaki and Suzuki contacted Le Guin in an unsuccessful bid to make an anime feature based on her *Earthsea* trilogy (Le Guin, 2006).[6]

By early 1983 it was clear that *Nausicaä* was a hit with *Animage's* readers, so Tokuma Shoten asked Miyazaki to make a feature anime based on it. Miyazaki agreed, taking a thirteen-month hiatus from the manga in order to direct the film with Takahata as the producer and using a hired animation studio named Topcraft. Now he faced several challenges. First, as part of his belief that manga should be different from anime, he had deliberately drawn *Nausicaä* to make it difficult to animate. Unlike most manga where the artwork has relatively few lines and simple backgrounds, *Nausicaä* had been made so detailed and dense that the artwork looked more like an engraving. Second, the movie must have an ending, but the manga had not yet reached a resolution and was still ongoing. In fact, he had annoyed his readers by stopping at a cliffhanger when Nausicaä had just been swallowed by a giant insect (3:36). To fit the manga's plot into a movie he simplified the story line, reducing the number of characters and players in the conflict. In the film the Doroks are removed and the conflict is between Torumekia and the city-state of Pejitei over possession of the God-Warrior that the Torumekians had brought to the Valley of the Wind. He restaged the Ohmu stampede so that now the Pejitei forces directed it toward the Valley in order to destroy the captured God-Warrior. The film climaxes with Nausicaä sacrificing her life to stop the stampede, then being resurrected by the Ohmu holding her aloft on their golden tentacles. The elder matriarch of the Valley recognizes Nausicaä's resurrection as the fulfillment of prophecy and proclaims it at the end of the film. Since both sides witnessed this miracle (and the God-Warrior was destroyed in the process), the conflict ends and both sides leave the valley in peace during the final credits. Miyazaki was unhappy with the forced deus ex machina ending he created and personally gave the film a grade of only 65 out of 100 points.[7]

Released in March 1984, *Nausicaä* was a box office success, prompting Tokuma Shoten to back the formation of Miyazaki's own animation production company, Studio Ghibli. Since its founding, Studio Ghibli has produced a series of increasingly successful animated films directed by Miyazaki and others. But this production schedule prevented Miyazaki from returning to the *Nausicaä* manga full-time. Instead he worked on it during breaks between films. There were a total of four breaks in the publication of the serial, the longest being thirty-four months between June 1987 and April 1990. But this was not necessarily a bad thing; as Miyazaki pointed out, "I made movies partly because I wanted to escape from [doing] *Nausicaä*. I didn't intend to do the light stuff because I was doing the heavy stuff here, but if I hadn't been writing *Nausicaä*, I think I would have struggled trying to put a bit heavier stuff into the movies" (Miyazaki 1994). It is probable that Miyazaki and Ghilbi's early box office success with family films such as *Tenkuu no Shiro Rapyuta* (Laputa: Castle in the Sky; 1986), *Tonari no Totoro* (My Neighbor Totoro; 1988), *Majo no Takkyuubin* (Kiki's Delivery Service; 1989), and *Kurenai no Buta* (Porco Rosso; 1992) would not have been as great had they included darker themes. Tellingly, Miyazaki's first film after finishing the *Nausicaä* manga was *Mononoke Hime*, which examined many of the themes from the manga and is arguably the darkest film in his career.

The many changes in theme and direction the manga takes over the course of the story makes any concise analysis difficult. Part of the manga's complexity results from the fact that Miyazaki himself did not have an overall plan for the story when he started, and during most of the writing he had no idea how it would end. "I didn't have any big plot," he said in an interview after the end of the manga. "The writing process was such that 'it looks that way, so let's go that way.' . . . I continued working, telling myself such lies as 'it'll work out eventually. The magazine will go out of business before that.' . . . From the beginning to the end, I ended up writing a whole lot of things I couldn't understand" (Miyazaki 1994). In addition, there was the change in Miyazaki's politics and philosophy during this period. The fall of the Soviet Union, and particularly the descent of Yugoslavia into warring ethnic factions, forced him to reassess the Marxist ideals he had held since his youth (Miyazaki 1994), so a happy ending where Nausicaä would be able to create a perfectly just and ideal society out of this conflict was now impossible for him to write. Nausicaä's journey through her world became a reflection of Miyazaki's own personal exploration of various philosophical and spiritual questions.

Within the manga, Nausicaä inhabits multiple roles of leader, warrior, peacemaker, advisor, nurturing mother/big sister, scientist, and finally and most powerfully, a messianic figure. Even before her revelation in the forest she had been looking at the bigger picture, trying to find a means of reconciliation between humans and a natural world that appeared to be hostile. After stopping the Ohmu stampede, Nausicaä prepared to rejoin the Torumekian forces to fulfill her political obligations. By then she had already passed beyond her sectarian and ethnic identity and taken on an inclusive worldview. "A girl from the Valley of the Wind puts on Dorok dress dyed for her by the Ohmu [blood], and prepares to depart in a Torumekian warship," she tells Mito, one of the valley men. "I can hear a voice in my heart, all the time. Go forward, it tells me. . . . Isn't it strange? I can't help but feel that I'm not alone. It's as if all these people are watching over me . . . " (2:88–89). The role of messiah is not one of her own choosing, but one that events force upon her. By the end of the story she meets every single major player in her world and, one by one, she converts almost all of them to her understanding, ultimately redeeming most of them.

The spiritual turn of the story is reflected in the key events from the middle section of the story: Nausicaä's meeting of the characters of Chikuku and Selm and later a dream quest she takes within herself. Chikuku is a young boy being raised in a monastery as a future religious leader who will oppose the theocratic rule of the Dorok Emperor. He identifies Nausicaä on her mehve as an angel descending from heaven and attaches himself to her as a disciple. Selm is a young man, slightly older than Nausicaä, who is one of the Forest People, a group who has shunned the world and returned to live with nature in the toxic forests. After witnessing a *daikaisho*, a stampede where the Ohmu destroy the human-inhabited land to spread the spores that grow into a new section of the toxic forest, the depressed Nausicaä attempts to die with the Ohmu. But she is swallowed by one of them and encased in a serum gel that protects her and puts her into a coma. From there she takes a dream journey into the depths of the forest. There she psychically meets Selm, who serves as her guide on this spiritual quest, revealing some of the deeper secrets and meaning of the forest to her. In the dream journey she also meets the soul of the recently deceased Dorok Emperor, Miralupa. Earlier in the story he had tried to kill her and once more he tries to overwhelm her with his evil nature. Nausicaä destroys his outer self, leaving only the crippled and repulsive figure of his true soul. Showing compassion, she asks if he wishes to travel with her (a scene later repeated in the film *Spirited Away* when Chihiro asks the loathsome No-Face if he wishes to go with her on the train to Zeniba). The three of them travel deep into the forest to find a place where it has completed its work so the land and air have been restored to their original pure state. Miyazaki leaves it ambiguous whether this is an actual location deep within the physical forest or just a symbolic spiritual place within Nausicaä's psyche. Miralupa's spirit moves happily onto the afterlife, but Nausicaä decides to return to the physical world. "We mustn't contaminate this one," she says (6:87).

Returning to the strife, Nausicaä flies on her mehve to the middle of the Dorok refugee camp. Using Chikuku's power to provide a psychic link, she gives a literal "sermon on the mount" to the tens of thousands of refugees there. She warns them of the new Emperor's plans to conquer Torumekian lands with the God-Warrior he has captured from Torumekia. "That path leads only to hatred and an endless cycle of revenge," she preaches. "Hatred and revenge give birth to nothing. . . . Move to the edge of the Sea of Corruption and make a new life there. . . . Choose love over hatred" (6:131). Hearing her speech the new Dorok Emperor, Namulith (Miralupa's brother), taunts Nausicaä by activating the God-Warrior and then giving it to her. "Go ahead and take [it] to the 'pure land' or wherever you damned well please . . . crawl around with the whole bloody lot on your shoulders, and then see if you can save the world!" (6:148). Like a baby duck, the giant God-Warrior imprints on the first person it sees. Gently picking Nausicaä up, it calls her "Mama."

This cliffhanger is where Miyazaki stopped the manga for the fourth and final break of two years. Nausicaä, the messiah of peace and understanding, the leader who had rejected worldly power, suddenly finds herself in control of her world's most horrific ultimate weapon. And it thinks she is its mother. Although his *Animage* editor was willing to let the series run indefinitely,

Miyazaki decided that he had to end it, but felt he had painted himself into a corner. As he said in an interview with *Comic Box*, "Continuing *Nausicaä* for that last year was really hard, . . . I guess the problem was that I HAD TO WRITE WHAT I DIDN'T KNOW . . . I had to go so far as to think about the very meaning of life. I didn't know [the meaning of life], so it was very difficult" (Miyazaki 1995). In her travels Nausicaä has learned that the Dorok technology comes from the mysterious Crypt in the holy city of Shuwa. Naming the God-Warrior "Ohma," which means "peace," she decides to use it to destroy the Crypt, thus preventing the poisons of its technology from disrupting the world any further, but she faces one final temptation.

Outside of the city of Shuwa, Nausicaä and Ohma discover a beautiful garden sanctuary tended by one of the servants of the Crypt. This "caretaker" attempts to persuade Nausicaä to give up her quest, telling her the final secret of her world and the Crypt: the forest, the animals, and the humans now alive were all genetically engineered by the pre-Seven Days of Fire humans to survive in the polluted world and, in fact, can *only* survive in the polluted world. There is no natural world left; *everything* is artificial. The "eggs" of the pre-Seven Days of Fire humans are stored at the Crypt so that when the forests finish purifying the world and the current genetically altered humans die out, the descendents of the ancient humans will be reborn to retake their rightful place as rulers of the world. Nausicaä is forced to make a monstrous decision: to side with the current humans and their "artificial" natural world even though their days are numbered, or to side with the original humans and original natural world even though that means turning everything over to the very people who precipitated the disaster in the first place.

In the end she chooses the former, ordering Ohma to destroy the Crypt, its technology, and its precious cargo of eggs. "I shudder at the depth of my sin," Nausicaä says of her decision (7:211). Her decision is presented in counterpoint to the earlier choice of the original Holy Dorok Emperor. Back in the garden the "caretaker" told Nausicaä that the father of Namulith and Miralupa started out years before as an idealist like her who wished to be a compassionate philosopher king. He chose to use some of the technology from Shuwa in the hopes of improving the lives of his people. But disgusted by the behavior of his subjects and seduced by the power he acquired, he became a corrupt and cynical ruler. In a messiahlike decision, Nausicaä rejects the offered power outright. She destroys the Crypt and its technology (just as Frodo destroys the One Ring in J. R. R. Tolkien's *The Lord of the Rings*) in order to remove the temptation of such power from the human grasp forever. Nausicaä's final choice proved very controversial with the fans, and even Miyazaki was not satisfied with it, commenting, "I still wondered if this was the right conclusion for *Nausicaä*, but I didn't know. Even now I'm not sure" (Miyazaki 1995).

Miyazaki's ending here seems inconsistent. At first he appears to be siding with technology, as Nausicaä chooses an artificial world over the true natural world. But what she is really choosing is a world unguided by humans and their technology no matter in what form its "nature" started. "An ecosystem with a goal. Its very existence runs contrary to the laws of Nature," Nausicaä realizes during her discussion with the "caretaker." "According to the plan, we should have been well along the path to rebirth, but in reality, foolishness has continued, and nihilism and despair have only spread" (7:133). Miyazaki explained Nausicaä's choice by commenting, "I didn't want to have Nausicaä just denounce the people who made the world what it was as foolish. The fact is that they were very intelligent people, and it's not so easy just to call them liars and fools. But no matter how pure and logical the plan was, no matter how right, 'dirt' was bound to stick to it in the actual implementation, . . . and things started to go wrong" (Miyazaki 1995).

Such ideas may seem pessimistic, but they accurately reflect Miyazaki's personal outlook. In 2004 he told a journalist that he hoped for the day when "'developers go bankrupt, Japan gets poorer, and wild grasses take over'" (quoted in Talbot 2005, 67). Later he also commented, "I'm hoping I'll live another thirty years. I want to see the sea rise over Tokyo and the NTV tower become an island. I'd like to see Manhattan underwater . . . I'm excited about that. Money and desire — all that is going to collapse, and wild green grasses are going to take over" (quoted in Talbot 2005, 75).

But this is not an entirely hopeless viewpoint. Nausicaä has come to realize that she must "let nature take its course," but even a blind, almost nihilistic nature, one that may mean the ultimate extinction of humanity, is still a source of hope for her. There is still the chance that this unguided ecosystem may yet allow humanity to continue after the forests complete their work. As Nausicaä defiantly tells the Crypt keeper in Shuwa, a holographic projection of an ancient human, "If such a morning is to come, then we shall live to face that morning! We are birds who, though we may spit up blood, will go on flying beyond that morning, on and on. To live is to change . . . the Ohmu, the mold, the grasses and trees, we human beings . . . we will go on changing, and the sea of corruption will live on with us. But you cannot change. You have only the plan that was built into you. Because you deny death" (7:198). Andrew Osmond (1998) points out that this is a clear echo of the climax of Le Guin's *The Farthest Shore* as the archmage Ged confronts the wizard Cob, who believes he has gained immortality. Ged tells him, "'All who have ever died, live; they are reborn, and have no end, nor will there be an end. All save you. For you would not have death. You lost death, you lost life, in order to save yourself. . . . You have given everything for nothing'" (LeGuin 1972, 180). It is fitting then that the final line of the manga is Nausicaä saying, "We must live" (7:223).

Miyazaki was often asked if he would make an anime sequel to the film version of *Nausicaä*, but his reply was always no. Still, his next feature after completing the *Nausicaä* manga was *Mononoke Hime* (1997), a film that drew heavily from themes in the final part of *Nausicaä*. Set in the Muromachi era of Japan (1392–1573), it depicted the beginnings of the modern world with the struggle between nature, in the form of the gods of the forest, and humans, in the form of workers at an early iron smelter cutting down the forest for fuel. Miyazaki split the character of Nausicaä into two: the rational Prince Ashitaka, an outsider under a curse who attempts vainly to reconcile the two sides, and San, the "Princess Mononoke," a feral girl reared by a wolf-god who is in touch with the natural world and determined to destroy all other humans to save the forest. Miyazaki ended the film *Nausicaä* on a positive note with Nausicaä healing the rift between humans and nature, but he ended *Mononoke* more darkly with a standoff similar to the ending of the *Nausicaä* manga. San and Ashitaka realize that neither side can win, there can only be an uneasy truce, but even in this standoff there is the chance for happiness. As Miyazaki stated in his proposal for the film, "there can be no happy ending to the war between the rampaging forest gods and humanity. But even in the midst of hatred and slaughter, there is still much to live for. Wonderful encounters or beautiful things still exist."[8] This is a clear echo of his earlier statement in a 1991 interview: "In my movies for children, I want to express before anything else the themes: 'The world is profound, manifold and beautiful,' and 'You children are fortunate to have been born into this world. . . . Although the world's beset with lots of seemingly intractable problems, . . . it's nevertheless a wonderful thing to live'" (Miyazaki 1991).

But Miyazaki's final word on *Nausicaä* may have actually come before *Mononoke*. His first animation project after completing the manga was a music video for the Japanese music duo Chage and Aska's song *On Your Mark*. Deliberately working against the song's lyrics he created a six-minute minimovie set in near future where nuclear accidents, ozone depletion, and pollution have driven the remaining humans into subterranean cities. There two police officers (drawn to resemble the two singers) rescue an angel, a young girl with wings, from her captivity by a religious cult, then turn her over to scientists for study (à la *E.T. — The Extraterrestrial*). Whether the angel is truly supernatural or just a mutant caused by radiation is never made clear. Realizing they have simply transferred the angel from one form of captivity (by religion) to another (by science), they stage a daring rescue and take her to the dangerously contaminated outside world. There they find a "coffined" nuclear reactor with the natural world reclaiming the area around it, an image Miyazaki based on news reports of the area around the Chernobyl nuclear reactor reverting to nature after the area's people were evacuated. Outside the policemen release the angel, allowing her to fly free back into a perfect blue sky filled with clouds. What fans noticed immediately was the resemblance between the angel and Nausicaä, and Miyazaki himself referred to the angel as *tori no hito* ("bird girl"), a nickname he often used for Nausicaä (Miyazaki 1996). Thus, *On Your Mark* can be read as Miyazaki's "freeing" of Nausicaä. Perhaps, like William Shakespeare releasing his characters through the persona of Prospero freeing Ariel at the end of *The Tempest*, Miyazaki created the policemen and the angel in the music video in order to symbolically free Nausicaä. Having literally put her through the hell of her extended odyssey through war, suffering, and even the underworld, he was finally able to release the beautiful young and innocent girl into that perfect blue world where she always truly belonged.

Notes

I wish to thank Pamela Gossin, Andrew Osmond, and Watanabe Yuki for their assistance with this chapter.

1. See the comments from various animators (e.g. John Lasseter), filmmakers (e.g. Akira Kurosawa), and comic artists (e.g. Möbius) at http://www.nausicaa.net/ miyazaki/miyazaki/impact.html.
2. Unless otherwise noted all background information comes from the extensive websites about Miyazaki and his works, http://www.nausicaa.net/miyazaki/ and http://www.nausicaa.net/wiki/Main_Page. The author is one of the creators and maintainers of these sites.
3. Samples of the artwork from these rejected film proposals can be found in Miyazaki 2007, 154–75.
4. A complete listing of the installments and their publication date is given in Miyazaki 2007, 206, and also at http://www.nausicaa.net/miyazaki/manga/ chapter_guide.html.
5. All quotes and references to this work manga are taken from the most recent edition of the English language version, published in seven volumes by VIZ Media in 2004; volume amd page numners will hereafter be cited parenthetically in the text. VIZ first published *Nausicaä* as twenty-seven individual comic books (running from 1988 to 1996), then in two compiled collections, one in seven volumes (1990–97) and a second "Perfect Collection" in four volumes (1995–97). The 2004 edition is notable as the first time the English version was published with the pages and artwork reading from right to left as in the original Japanese. All the earlier editions from VIZ flipped the artwork to read left to right. Also the 2004 edition is the largest in size (10 1/8" x 7 1/8"), almost as large as the original *Animage* artwork (11.8" x 8.3").
6. While Le Guin turned down the unknown animator in the early 1980s, in 2005 she agreed to Studio Ghibli making a film based on her books *The Farthest Shore* and *Tehanu*. Entitled *Gedo Senki (Tales of Earthsea)*, it was directed by Miyazaki's son, Goro, and released in 2006.
7. Miyazaki quoted in *Mainichi Shimbun* newspaper (April 22, 1984); reprinted in Studio Ghibli, 1996, *Sutajio Jiburi Sakuhin Kanren Shiryou-shuu 1* (Archives of Studio Ghibli 1), Tokyo, Tokuma Shoten.
8. Project proposal, reprinted in Studio Ghibli 1997a, 20.

References

Le Guin, Ursula K. (1972). *The Farthest Shore*. New York: Bantam Books.
—— (2006). "*Gedo Senki*, A First Response." Ursula K. LeGuin personal website, http://www.ursulakleguin.com/GedoSenkiResponse.html.
McCarthy, Helen (1999). *Hayao Miyazaki: Master of Japanese Animation*. Berkeley, CA: Stonebridge Press.
Miyazaki, Hayao (1988, January 28). "About Japanese Animation." *Course Japanese Movies* 7; English translation by Ryoko Toyama. Hayao Miyazaki Web, http://www.nausicaa.net/miyazaki/interviews/aboutanime.html.
—— (1991, January). "Money Can't Buy Creativity." *Pacific Friend* 18(9): 7–8. Hayao Miyazaki Web, http://www.nausicaa.net/miyazaki/interviews/creativity.html.
—— (1994, June). "Now, after Nausicaä Has Finished." Interview, *Yom* magazine. English translation by Ryoko Toyama. Hayao Miyazaki Web, http://www.nausicaa.net/miyazaki/interviews/afternausicaa.html.
—— (1995, January). "I Understand Nausicaä a Bit More Than I Did a Little While Ago." Interview. *Comic Box* magazine, http://www.comicbox.co.jp/e-nau/e-nau.html.
—— (1996, November). "*On Your Mark*." Interview in *Animage*. English translation by Ryoko Toyama. Hayao Miyazaki Web, http://www.nausicaa.net/miyazaki/interviews/m_on_oym.html.
—— (2004). "On Nausicaä." In *Nausicaä of the Valley of the Wind*, vol. 1, 135, San Francisco: VIZ Media.
—— (2007). *The Art of Nausicaä: Watercolor Impressions*. San Francisco: VIZ Media. First published in Japanese by Tokuma Shoten, 1996.
Osmond, Andrew (1998). "Nausicaä and the Fantasy of Hayao Miyazaki." *Foundation* 72: 57–81. Revised and updated version. Hayao Miyazaki Web, http://www.nausicaa.net/miyazaki/nausicaa/article_ao_foundation.txt.
Studio Ghibli (1996). *Sutajio Jiburi Sakuhin Kanren Shiryou-shuu* [Archives of Studio Ghibli], vol. 1. Tokyo: Tokuma Shoten, 1996.
—— (1997a). *Princess Mononoke*. New York: Hyperion, 1999. Originally published Tokyo: Tokuma Shoten, 1997, as *The Art of The Princess Mononoke*.
—— (1997b). *This Is How Ghibli Was Born*. NTV special. An updated and subtitled version was included on the English-language DVD of *Nausicaä of the Valley of the Wind*, released in 2005 by Buena Vista Home Video.
Talbot, Margaret (2005, January 17). "The Auteur of Anime." *New Yorker*, 64–75.

Further Reading: Miyazaki's *Nausicaä of the Valley of the Wind*

Miyazaki, Hayao (2004). *Nausicaä of the Valley of the Wind*, 7 vols. San Francisco: VIZ Media. Vol. 1 first published in English in 1990; first published in Japanese in 1982. Vol. 2 first published in English in 1990; first published in Japanese in 1983. Vol. 3 first published in English in 1990; first published in Japanese in 1984. Vol. 4 first published in English in 1990; first published in Japanese in 1987. Vol. 5 first published in English in 1993; first published in Japanese in 1991. Vol. 6 first published in English in 1995; first published in Japanese in 1993. Vol. 7 first published in English in 1997; first published in Japanese in 1995.

Reading Manga

11

Japanese Visual Language: The Structure of Manga

Neil Cohn

Many authors have intuitively associated the "comics" medium with language, and the same analogy holds with manga. The celebrated "God of Manga" Osamu Tezuka has commented on his process by stating, "'I don't consider them pictures . . . in reality I'm not drawing, I'm writing a story with a unique type of symbol'" (quoted in Schodt 1983, 25). One of the first Americans to write about manga, Frederik Schodt, reiterates this, commenting that "manga are merely another 'language,' and the panels and pages are but another type of 'words' adhering to a unique grammar" (1996, 26).

Schodt's remarks are perhaps more than just an eloquent metaphor, as recent theories have proposed that the visual expression of concepts, when put into discrete sequences, is literally a form of language (see Cohn 2003, 2005). Like sequential units of sound in speech or bodily motions in sign languages, sequential drawings ordered by a rule system — a grammar — literally comprise a visual language (VL). Culturally, this visual language combines with written language in comics, manga, *bande desinée*, and the like, uniting their readers and authors in a common (visual) linguistic community. Following this, unique cultural styles of drawing simply become different visual languages, the same way that verbal (and signed) languages differ throughout the world.

Bearing this in mind, the word *manga* has come to have two meanings outside Japan. Some use it to designate Japanese "comics," the sociocultural objects, and often the industry and community surrounding them. However, others use "manga" to name this visual language itself — loosely conceived of as an "aesthetic style" (see Rommens 2000). Since the conflation of these ideas can be confusing and inappropriate, in this chapter the term *manga* will be used in the first sense — to designate a sociocultural artifact — while referring to the system of graphic expression as Japanese Visual Language, or JVL. While JVL is the graphic system of communication, manga is the sociocultural context in which it appears most.

This chapter will focus on the structural properties of JVL — what is known about how it works and functions — especially in contrast to the visual languages found in other cultures. Many readers are probably familiar with the well-known elements of manga. For instance, that manga pages are read from right to left and that human faces are often drawn with large eyes and pointy chins. While somewhat superficial in the scope of the totality of JVL, at the very least these features can point toward many deeper insights into the rich structure of Japanese Visual Language.

STANDARD JVL

Conceiving of visual creation as a language might seem odd, since the signs are often *iconic* — they resemble what they mean — leading to almost universal intelligibility. A drawing of a person means "person" because it looks like a person. Iconic signs differ from two other types of signs: those that are *indexical* and those that are *symbolic* (see Peirce 1931). Indexical signs express meaning by an indicative or causative relation, such as the index finger when pointing. In contrast, symbolic signs convey meaning through cultural agreement alone, such as most words. These characteristics are not rigid categories either — a *mixed sign*, like a weathervane, might be iconic to a rooster, yet indexical to the wind in the direction it points. Symbols are not the only conventional sign though,[1] since icons and indexes can also appear systematically throughout a culture. For instance, all smiley faces (☺) are iconic to the human face, yet they occur in a specific schematic pattern that pervades our culture. In contrast, the faces that are created through life drawing are not conventional at all, since they mimic ever-changing perception of the real world.

Traditional thinking about language has held that it only uses symbols (see, e.g., Hockett 1977; for a dissenting view, see Clark 1997), which would exclude iconic representations like drawings. The iconicity of images gives the illusion that all drawings are universal and easy to understand, since they can mimic the character of objects in our daily perception. Despite this, the ways "visual speakers" draw people remain just *patterns in the minds of "artists."* This is particularly evident in JVL, since people are commonly drawn in a recognizable pattern — the stereotypical big eyes, big hair, small mouth, and pointed chins of characters in manga.[2] This "style" is so schematized that often characters' faces cannot be distinguished from each other, leading to authors' use of other features to allow readers to differentiate them (Natsume 1998; Rommens 2000), such as wildly varying hair color (Levi 1996, 12).

This predominant manga "style" maintains both conventionality and iconicity, and represents patterns no less cognitive than any other linguistic form. The iconicity makes it accessible and easily decodable to individuals across the globe, while its conventionality reflects that its patterns are shared by many "visual speakers." Some individuals use this visual vocabulary, while others have drawn from the perceived world as a template. Others have been inspired by alternative visual styles, like *Akira* creator Katsuhiro Ōtomo, who was influenced greatly by French artists (Schodt 1996, 242). Indeed, many manga are drawn in diverse and varying styles, especially in the "artistic," or *garo*, genre. While diversity clearly exists across all genres of manga and warrants interesting discussion, this piece will focus on the conventionalized manner of drawing.

A "language" begins as a cognitive system in an individual's brain — a collection of mental patterns organizing the expression of concepts for expression in some sensorial modality. This system transforms into a "language" culturally, through the mutual intelligibility of various individuals' cognitive patterns. Speakers of the Tokyo and Kyoto vernaculars remain intelligible enough that the broader patterns are labeled as "Japanese," while the differences are thought of only as unique aspects of "dialects." Like the way that Tokyo-ben is considered the "standard" dialect of spoken Japanese, this stereotypical "manga style" can be considered the "standard" dialect of Japanese Visual Language since it uses a common model for drawing people shared by a broad range of "visual speakers." This overarching schema in JVL is commonly attributed to Osamu Tezuka — himself greatly influenced by the drawing styles of Walt Disney and Western comics (Gravett 2004). So, just like most other languages in the world, JVL's graphic vocabulary did not appear out of nowhere, but has been tempered and transmitted from other sources (the same way that spoken Japanese was influenced by Chinese).

No matter what his own inspirations were, Tezuka's stylistic impact is hard to deny, though most manga today do not mimic the way that Tezuka himself drew. Like all languages, JVL changes over time. Since Tezuka's initial emergence, various graphic dialects have developed under both his influence and that of many others. Truly, at this point, people around the globe can easily identify Standard JVL unconnected to any particular author's manner of drawing. The style has transcended individuals in the visual vocabulary of JVL. However, proficient readers can easily tell the difference between the more rounded *shōjo* (girls') style or the more angular *shōnen* (boys') styles. Chibi styles are easily distinguished for their short and cute figures, while various other styles also play off the abstract schema of Standard JVL in a variety of ways.

To the extent that representations from genres can be grouped into recognizable "styles," each constitutes a type of "dialect" or "accent" of JVL, since their patterns reflect varying degrees of similarity among a group of authors. It should also be no surprise that these divisions fall into separate genres. Most often, spoken languages become segmented into dialects based on geographical location. However, visual languages are predominantly a print culture, so diversity of community isn't constrained by location but established by the type of publication and its audience.

To some, the consistency of Japanese drawing styles may appear to stifle creators' innovativeness or individuality. From a VL perspective, creators each find their "visual voice" within the confines of the system they share. Focus shifts from *how* their drawings look to *what* they say with their drawings. Manga critic and theorist Fusanosuke Natsume (2001) even believes that overemphasis on images detracts from the story. As a language, using a consistent visual vocabulary allows readers the freedom to focus on the content of the expressions rather than on the expressions themselves.

Furthermore, the systematic and repetitive nature of the drawing style may be one of the many reasons manga's popularity has become so widespread across the world. This consistent visual vocabulary provides a systematic and easily accessible style for new readers to learn. If a child wanted to "draw like American comics," the follow-up question would be "Which one?" since American books feature such a diverse range of graphic dialects. In contrast, children can easily identify what it means to "draw manga" because JVL features a standard dialect across a wide range of authors. Copying this style does not just mean imitating an individual, but entering into a community of visual language speakers who share a common graphic vocabulary — and through it, a social identity as a "visual speaker" of JVL.

Indeed, Japanese children imitate Standard JVL in their figures in extremely high proportions (and increasingly outside of Japan), often leading to higher proficiency in graphic creation than children from other parts of the world (Cox et al. 2001; Wilson 2000; see example in figure 1.) Some work indicates that boys and girls influences differ as well, similar to the differences found in the genres of shonen versus shojo manga (Toku 2002a). Not only do Japanese children imitate this style, but they also appropriate methods for representing alternative viewpoints to the predominant lateral viewpoints, such as aerial and close-up views (Toku 2001, 2002b).

Contrary to the dogmatic claims that imitative drawing limits children's creativity (e.g. Arnheim 1978; Lowenfeld 1957), research suggests that most children do actually learn by emulating other sources, and indeed that it leads to increased levels of drawing ability (Wilson and Wilson 1977). Truly, copying from manga may actually prevent a drop-off in drawing ability that seems to occur during puberty for children in most cultures *except* Japan

FIGURE 11.1: Manga by a Japanese 7 year old (note the English text, used in a common language-learning script). © 2008 Neil Cohn; used by permission.

(Toku 2001). Imitative drawing, then, not only establishes a community of "visual speakers" using a common visual vocabulary but also offers an efficient way of developing proficient graphic skills, consistent with imitative learning in other domains (Tomasello 2000). However, this should be unsurprising from a visual language perspective — Japanese children are simply treating JVL in manga as a language, learning it through exposure, imitation, and practice.

GRAPHIC MEANINGS

Many graphic signs used in manga extend beyond iconic representations like those used for people, constituting what Natsume (1997) calls *Kei Yu*, which are used to represent invisible qualities such as emotions or motion. These can come in two forms, as highly conventional *graphic emblems*,[3] like sweeping lines to show motion and bubbles encapsulating text to show speech, or as nonconventional visual symbols or metaphors.

Nonconventional visual symbols and metaphors take many forms. Shōjo manga often make emotional use of nonnarrative signs in the backgrounds of their panels, using pastiches of flowers or sparkling lights to set a mood or hint at underlying symbolic meaning. Sex, especially, is often depicted through metaphoric crashing surf or blossoming flowers, or far more suggestively in erotic comics in lieu of the forbidden (in Japanese culture) depiction of genitalia (Schodt 1983, 101). Other creative uses of visual metaphor are more overt, such as a scene in Osamu Tezuka's *Buddha* where arrows pierce through the Buddha's belly to show the agonizing pain of being poisoned. A similar metaphor emerged in Rumiko Takahashi's *Maison Ikkoku* (House of Ikkoku), where an arrow shoots out of a word balloon of gossip to stab the heart of a character (Ceglia and Caldesi Valeri 2002). In most cases, symbols like these heighten the emotional impact of the representations, or creatively adapt them to better suit the graphic form.

On the other hand, conventional graphic emblems in manga vary in their transparency of meaning. In conventional depictions of rage or anger, characters grow sharp fangs and pointy claws while fire erupts behind them. This representation's meaning requires little decoding and seems to have conceptual underpinnings similar to other depictions of anger in comics (Forceville 2005), though using very different cultural conventions. Other emblems are far more opaque to those who have not learned their symbolic meaning, such as gigantic sweat drops conveying embarrassment or nervousness (Natsume and Takekuma 1995), bloody noses depicting lust (McCloud 1993), or the lengthening of the area between the nose and lips to indicate sexual thoughts (Schodt 1983). Even more unusual, some characters will suddenly become "superdeformed" — taking on a hypercartoony or deformed style — to show a spontaneous general lack of seriousness. A small sampling of these emblems and their meanings are depicted in figure 11.2. As one would expect from a visual language, many of the emblems from manga extend out to other aspects of Japanese visual culture, surfacing not only in manga but in a variety of other places like animation, street signs, and even in *kaomoji* — "emoticons" used graphically to represent nonverbal emotions and expressions online, in cell phone texting, and in other written discourse (Katsuno and Yano 2002).

Kinetic lines that show motion are another graphic emblem that has

LUST   SLEEP   ANGER OR IRRITATION

SHOCK OR EXASPERATION   ANGER   RELIEF

SUPER-DEFORMATION (CHIBI)

FIGURE 11.2. A small sample of graphic emblems from JVL. © 2008 Neil Cohn; used by permission.

historically differed between American and Japanese Visual Languages. Comic author and theorist Scott McCloud (1993) has observed that there is the potential for many different types of these motion lines, and that Japanese authors used a very different strategy than those in America in the mid- to late twentieth century. Rather than showing lines trailing the moving object, manga often show the moving object statically with lines streaming behind it. The result makes readers feel as though they are moving at the same speed as the object, and it is one of numerous techniques that McCloud claims manga uses to give a more subjective viewpoint. Indeed, the use of motion lines as a whole appears different in manga than in older American comics. Lines commonly substitute for the object itself to show a blurred motion, or surround an object in a flurry of lines (as in the example in figure 11.3). These distinctly different strategies for depicting motion were among the first characteristics appropriated by English-speaking comic authors as manga increased in readership in America throughout the 1980s and '90s (McCloud 1996).

This transmission of emblems from Japanese to American authors illustrates how language contact can initiate changes in a system graphically in the same way it can verbally. Languages only remain bound by any borders that limit their transmission. Since manga has transcended its geographic borders to a dramatic extent in recent decades, it should be unsurprising that JVL has influenced drawers in America and Europe (Horn 1996; Rommens 2000). This influence manifests in a variety of ways. The appropriation of

"OBJECTIVE" MOTION LINES   "SUBJECTIVE" MOTION LINES

FIGURE 11.3. Various strategies of motions lines. © 2008 Neil Cohn; used by permission.

graphic emblems like kinetic lines appear among the smallest instances of this influence — akin to how English has borrowed the words *tycoon* and *karaoke* from Japanese with no overarching change to English grammar. Most significant is that in recent years drawers have used the JVL dialects and emblems en masse, and in publication they are often referred to as Original English-language (OEL) manga or Manga-Influenced comics (Arrant 2006; Cha and Reid 2005). The degree to which the grammar of OEL manga truly reflects that of native Japanese manga or is merely the JVL vocabulary painted over the grammar of American Visual Language has yet to be studied. However, this influence provides a good example of the conflation of the social construct of "manga" and the visual language it is written in, and represents a prime example of how languages can transcend their culture of origins in a cognitive capacity.

JVL GRAMMAR

Although individual images can convey a great deal of information, the real power of language comes from its sequence — combining multiple units to create a cohesive meaning greater than its individual parts. The system that accomplishes this is the *grammar* of language, and visual languages draw on their sequence as much as verbal ones do. Most readers should be aware that the pages in Japanese manga are read from right to left — the opposite of Western comics. While this is an aspect of sequence, it plays a negligible role in the creation of meaning. Rather, the visual grammar is concerned with how meaning is conveyed to the reader in the content of sequential images, whether that sequence is organized right to left or left to right.

The first major approach to VL grammar was popularized by McCloud, who hypothesized that sequential meaning could be derived from the linear relationships between panels, accomplished through various types of "panel transitions." His types of transitions included:

Moment-to-moment, showing a short amount of time passing
Action-to-action, showing a whole action occurring
Subject-to-subject, showing a shift from character to character
Scene-to-scene, shifting between two different environments
Aspect-to-aspect, stepping outside of time to show aspects of the environment
Non sequitur, having no logical relationship between panels (1993, 70–72)

With these categories established, McCloud then analyzed a variety of works to find out what types of transitions they were using and uncovered some interesting results. While American comic books consistently used a high degree of Action, Subject, and Scene transitions, Japanese books introduced some Moment transitions and high numbers of Aspect transitions that were otherwise absent in American comics. His proportions are summarized in table 11.1.

TABLE 11.1
SUMMARY OF MCCLOUD'S TRANSITIONS CROSS-CULTURALLY

	American	**Japanese**
Moment-to-moment	0	~ 5%
Action-to-action	≥ 65%	~ 50%
Subject-to-subject	~ 20%	~ 25%
Scene-to-scene	~ 15%	~ 5%
Aspect-to-aspect	0	~ 15%
Non sequitur	0	0

Note: McCloud does not explicitly state percentages. The numbers cited are approximations from his illustrated graphs.
Source: McCloud 1993, 75–80.

To account for these differences, McCloud offered two explanations. In contrast to the small pamphlet-style monthly comics in the United States, he hypothesized that manga's anthology and *tankōbon* formats allowed authors to devote more panels to drawing out scenes and focusing on the setting or mood, a sentiment also echoed by Aarnoud Rommens (2000). More radically, McCloud proposed that Asian culture is less "goal-oriented" than Western culture, and that "Japanese comics . . . often emphasize *being there* over *getting there*" (McCloud 1993, 81; emphasis 2007a).

In contrast to McCloud's views, an alternative approach argues that linear relationships are not sufficient for describing how sequences of images communicate (Cohn 2003). Rather, VL grammar works in a similar way as any other language, complete with visual "parts of speech." Following modern linguistic analysis (see, for example, Chomsky 1965; Jackendoff 2002), instead of looking at the limited range of one panel's immediate linear juxtapositions, panels can combine to form larger structures in hierarchic embeddings. Several categories factor into this visual grammar, depicting various "narrative phases" within a broader "Arc" (Cohn 2007a; 2008). These phases largely reflect various states in relation to a predicate — the depiction of an event or situation. An abbreviated list of VL grammatical categories includes:

> *Establisher (E)*: setting up an interaction without acting upon it
> *Initial (I)*: depicting the nascent starting point of an event or action
> *Peak (P)*: showing the maximal point of tension of an event or action
> *Release (R)*: releasing the tension of an event or action
> *Refiner (Ref)*: acting as a modifier by honing in on information contained in
> one of the core categories

In addition to these formatives, various processes can expand the repertoire of expression by repeating the same category several times. For these purposes, the most important example is when various panels show different characters at the same narrative state, united by a process of *Environmental Conjunction (E-Conj)*. (An example of this approach applied to a manga sequence is provided in figure 11.4, in which double lines indicate main categories, modifiers indicated by single lines.)

This example from the manga *Kozure Ōkami* (Lone Wolf and Cub) opens with an Establisher setting up the situation, with the Refiner in the second panel showing more detail about the first. The third and fourth panels show close-up views of different aspects of the start of the event in the Initial Phase — the wheel and foot both stepping on *makibishi* nails — united by Environmental Conjunction (various characters denoted by subscripts). The event of jumping occurs in the Peak, again with a refiner to show the

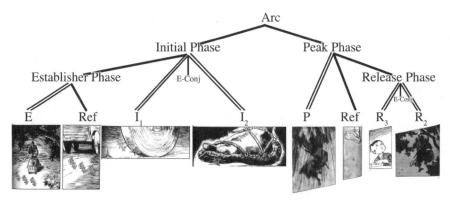

FIGURE 11.4. Visual grammar shown from a scene from *Lone Wolf and Cub*. © 1995 Kazuo Koike and Goseki Kojima, *Lone Wolf and Cub: A Taste of Poison*, vol. 20, 223–24. Milwaukie, OR: Dark Horse Comics. Courtesy of Dark Horse Comics; used by permission.

spike dropping out of the foot while in midair. It concludes with Releases, as the child looks up at his father hanging from a branch, united again by Environmental Conjunction.

From this framework, McCloud's transitional categories appear only as a "surface" structure in contrast to the deeper hierarchies of visual language grammar. How, then, can we account for the differences McCloud found between Japanese manga and American comics? Do they exist at all, or can they be explained in an alternative way? Panel transitions describe the relations between images. By thinking in terms of broader hierarchical structures, the understanding of sequences becomes far richer, though it shifts the focus away from what happens "between" the individual panels to how the content of panels fits into a larger cognitive architecture.

Since "Aspect transitions" largely refer to how panels focus on parts of a scene, these elements could potentially be captured by what is shown in actual manga panels. In addition to forming parts of a sequence, panels can serve to "window the attention" of a reader onto different parts of a narrative representation (Cohn 2007b, 64). Panels can be categorized into varying types based on how much information they contain. *Macros* are panels that show multiple characters or a whole scene, while *Monos* show only individual entities. *Micros* contain less than a whole entity, as in a close-up of a character where only part of the person is shown at a time. Finally, *Polymorphic* panels depict whole actions through the repetition of individual characters at various points in that event. These types of panels can be organized from actions to scenes to individual characters to less than a single character and are graphed in the *Lexical Representational Matrix* (LRM), shown in figure 11.5.

Using the LRM categories as a guide, a study examined the panels in various American comics and Japanese manga to see what types of panels they were using. The results revealed significant differences; percentages are summarized in table 11.2.

TABLE 11.2
PERCENTAGES OF TYPES OF PANELS IN AMERICAN COMICS VERSUS JAPANESE MANGA

	American (*N* = 12)	Japanese (*N* = 12)
Polymorphic	0.4 (SD = 0.7)	0.2 (SD = 0.3)
Macro	59.3 (SD = 14.1)	47.3 (SD = 8.5)
Mono	33 (SD = 8.3)	42.4 (SD = 5.3)
Micro	6.7 (SD = 6.5)	10.1 (SD = 5.2)

Source: Cohn 2005a

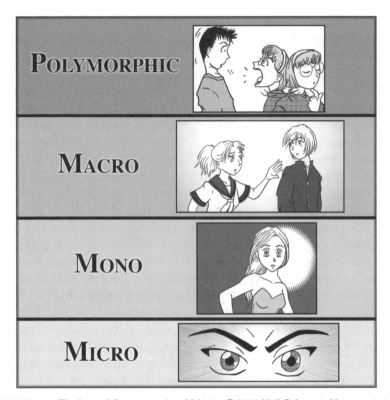

FIGURE 11.5. The Lexical Representational Matrix. © 2008 Neil Cohn; used by permission.

With higher usage of micros and monos, JVL seems to focus on individual *parts* of environments more often than on larger scenes that show the environment outright (macros), which is essentially what McCloud's approach said as well! These findings tell us that JVL tends to focus attention on individual characters almost as often as it does whole scenes.

Not only do these findings tell us about the patterns of single panels, they can also indicate possible trends in visual grammatical structures. High quantities of Monos mean that their grammar likely uses a fair amount of Environmental Conjunction. If this implication is true, then Japanese manga focus on varying parts of a scene more frequently than American comics do, carrying the necessary grammatical structures. Similarly, the larger number of Micros insinuates a greater use of Refiners as well. As can be seen quite well in the example in figure 11.4, refiners and Environmental Conjunction both show various parts of an event at a single narrative state without placing all the information into the contents of a single panel.

This expansion of information across several panels echoes McCloud's and Rommen's observations that manga draw out the representations of events instead of simply showing the actions in the setting outright. It is important to note that neither strategy is inherently "better" or "worse" than the other. More compact representations likely require less cognitive processing than those with extensive use of modifiers. On the other hand, increased panels place meaning more firmly in the graphic domain than the verbal.

Indeed, Japanese manga seems to use less text than American comics, placing more of the communicative focus on the visuals (Rommens 2000). While the appeal of a greater length in publishing format might be one explanation for this expansion of scenes, this theory rings a bit hollow without empirical verification. Just because manga authors have more pages at their disposal does not insinuate that they use it to "decompress" their scenes. They could just as easily fill that space with compact event representation and even *more* plot. An alternative viewpoint might posit that they use the visual system *as a language* — allowing the visuals to express meaning through their own capacities and thus requiring more length to do so. In fact, Paul Gravett (2004, 26) recounts that in the opening sequence of Osamu Tezuka's first hit, *Shin-Takarajima* (The New Treasure Island), his intended thirty-one-panel sequence was *shortened* to only four panels, despite launching a new, longer format of manga. However, both the published and unpublished versions rely almost solely on visual information. Placing the focus on the visuals at the expense of the verbal is consistent with other research in multimodality, which suggest that the less the verbal form dominates meaning, the more complex the nature of other modalities becomes (see, e.g., Goldin-Meadow 2006; Wilkins 1997).

As in any language, studies indicate that sequences of images also require degrees of fluency (Nakazawa 2005). In psychology experiments, subjects were asked to reconstruct four panels of a scrambled manga strip or to fill in the blank of the contents a missing panel. Results showed that performance improved with age from kindergarten through adulthood, attributed to experience with manga reading (Nakazawa 2004; Nakazawa and Nakazawa 1993). Another study compared the eye movements of manga reading between a child who reads manga frequently versus one who hardly read manga at all (Nakazawa 2002a). The expert reader's eyes moved more smoothly and focused more on the information in the images, while the nonexpert spent more time reading the words with erratic eye movements between panels on the page.

Manga reading seems to have a positive effect on education as well. Higher proficiency in manga comprehension in Japanese students correlates with achievement in language arts (Nakazawa and Nakazawa 1993) as well as heightened interest in language arts and social studies, but not "art" classes (Nakazawa 2002b). Perhaps this should be expected if we think of manga as being written in a visual language. It is just another form of writing, only in graphic form.

Just as Japanese children seem to imitate manga in their drawing styles, it also seems to have had an effect on Japanese children's creation of sequences of images. One cross-cultural study showed that two-thirds of Egyptian children, who have little exposure to comics, could not create narratives where the contents of one frame related to the next frame. In contrast, nearly all Japanese children studied were able to create coherent narratives, often using sophisticated "cinematic" techniques (Wilson and Wilson 1987).

Again, the influence manga shows on children's drawings demonstrates that JVL extends beyond just a print culture or industry. Japanese children spend time reading and drawing manga, leading to fluency that is acquired informally and spontaneously through voluntary action (Nakazawa 2005). This activity does not have to be tied to the contexts of the manga industry or *otaku* culture. Rather, in most cases, it is simply children drawing — actively participating in their society's visual language.

CONCLUSION

Finally, visual language theory can lend insight into some of the more pervasive "creation myths" surrounding manga. For many years, the origins of manga have been connected to narrative scrolls (*emaki*) from the tenth and eleventh centuries and other aspects of Japanese art history (see, e.g., Ito 2005; Schodt 1983). However, the similarities between modern manga and these ancient arts are fairly superficial in terms of their graphic features, and it was only through the influence of American comics that Japan began to engage in conventions like multiple panels (Gravett 2004; Kinsella 2000).

Indeed, structurally, the dialects of JVL in manga hardly resemble the graphic *ukiyoe* (woodblock) tradition of the 1800s — despite woodblock artist Hokusai's coining of the term *manga* (Schodt 1983) — much less to the scrolls of almost a millennia ago. As Natsume (2003, 3) succinctly observes, "there are inherent dangers in claiming manga as an outgrowth of native Japanese culture." Truly, the graphic system used by modern speakers of JVL has perhaps less connection to the graphic system depicted in emaki as modern spoken Japanese has with ancient Japanese. However, while the structural relationship of JVL to the graphic systems that preceded it may be remote, the cultural influence provided by historical graphic systems may have set the stage for how widespread manga has become (Gravett 2004, 18–23). While there may be a historical tradition of Japanese pictorial representation using sequences of images and text-image relations, it does not mean that they reflect similar cognitive patterns or the same system of expression. Indeed, with this in mind, older graphic works in Japan should be considered their own types of visual languages, bound within specific temporal and geographic constraints.

Similarly, it is also popular to argue that the "pictorial" nature of the Japanese writing system's *kanji* (Chinese characters), paired with the sound-based *kana* (syllabic signs), have attenuated the culture toward pairing words and images together throughout Japan's graphic history (Natsume 1998, 2003; Schodt 1983). While claims like this may have some feasibility,[4] it is hard to find evidence proving it. Indeed, visual language considered on its own terms need not rely on writing at all for gaining cultural influence, as it carries its own cognitive weight inherently. If the popularity of manga abroad is any indication, visual languages can develop widely and pervasively without needing a template from written language to set the stage. Truly, the global spread of Japanese popular culture in the past decades is quickly turning JVL into the most dominant form of visual language in the world, no matter which written language it is translated into. While manga may be its carrier, JVL extends beyond publishing and industry — both in Japan and across the globe. Those that engage with manga often become more than just readers and fans. They grow into "visual speakers," capable of participating in a rich graphic system, treating it like the language it truly is.

Notes

1. Peirce (1931) calls systematically understood signs "Legisigns" and those that are unique and different every time they appear "SinSigns." Thus, signs that are symbolic are technically "Symbolic Legisigns" while conventional icons are "Iconic Legisigns." I will refrain from using this jargon throughout, though his point is important to remember.
2. Several other patterned types of figures also exist in Standard JVL, depending on what type of person is being drawn. For instance, a stereotypical "big strong man" has a conventional style that is consistent yet different from the big-eyed, pointy-chin pattern.
3. The term *emblem* for this context comes from gesture research, classifying conventional signs that are consciously used and understood. Examples include the peace sign with the index and middle finger outstretched and the others folded, or the middle finger as an expletive (McNeill 1992).
4. For instance, the dual structure of the Japanese writing system may have contributed toward a unified yet split concept of writing/drawing (Cohn 2005b). The spoken verb *kaku* can mean both "writing" and "drawing," though the two senses are distinguished visually by separate kanji (書 and 描, respectively). This dual conception of graphic creation could have contributed toward rich balances of text and image usage throughout Japanese history. Though, as stated, proof of such a claim may be hard to find.

References

Arnheim, Rudolf (1978). "Expressions." *Art Education* 31(3): 37–38.
Arrant, Chris (2006). "Comic-Born, Manga-Bred." *Comic Foundry*, http://www.comicfoundry.com/modules/wfsection/article.php?articleid=210.
Ceglia, Simonetta, and Valerio Caldesi Valeri (2002). "Maison Ikkoku." *Image [&] Narrative* 1(1).

Cha, Kai-Ming, and Calvin Reid (2005, October 17). "Manga in English: Born in the USA." *Publishers Weekly*.

Chomsky, Noam (1965). *Aspects of the Theory of Syntax*. Cambridge, MA: MIT Press.

Clark, Herbert H. (1997). "Dogmas of Understanding." *Discourse Processes* 23: 567–98.

Cohn, Neil. 2003. *Early Writings on Visual Language*. Carlsbad, CA: Emaki Productions.

—— (2005a). "Cross-Cultural Space: Spatial Representation in American and Japanese Visual Language." Emaki Productions, http://www.emaki.net/essays/spatial.pdf.

—— (2005b). "¡Eye ♥ græfIk Semiosis! A Cognitive Approach to Graphic Signs and 'Writing.'" Master's thesis, University of Chicago.

—— (2005c). "Un-defining 'Comics.'" *International Journal of Comic Art* 7 (2): 236–48.

—— (2007a). "Foundations for a Natural Visual Language Grammar." Paper presented at the 2007 *Visual and Iconic Languages Conference*, University of New Mexico.

—— (2007b). "A Visual Lexicon." *Public Journal of Semiotics* 1(1): 53–84.

—— 2008. "Towards a Visual Language Grammar: The Narrative Structure of Comics, and Maybe More." Unpublished manuscript.

Cox, Maureen V., Masuo Koyasu, Hiromasa Hiranuma, and Julian Perara (2001). "Children's Human Figure Drawings in the UK and Japan: The Effects of Age, Sex, and Culture." *British Journal of Developmental Psychology* 19: 275–92.

Forceville, Charles (2005). "Visual Representations of the Idealized Cognitive Model of Anger in the Asterix Album." *La Zizanie: Journal of Pragmatics* 37: 69–88.

Goldin-Meadow, Susan (2006). "Talking and Thinking with Our Hands." *Current Directions in Psychological Science* 15(1): 34–39.

Gravett, Paul (2004). *Manga: Sixty Years of Japanese Comics*. New York: HarperCollins.

Hockett, Charles F. (1977). "Logical Considerations in the Study of Animal Communication." In *The View from Language: Selected Essays, 1948–1974*, ed. C. F. Hockett. Athens: University of Georgia Press. (Originally published 1960.)

Horn, Carl Gustav (1996, April). "American Manga." *Wizard* magazine, 53–57.

Ito, Kinko (2005). "A History of *Manga* in the Context of Japanese Culture and Society." *Journal of Popular Culture* 38(3): 456–575.

Jackendoff, Ray (2002). *Foundations of Language: Brain, Meaning, Grammar, Evolution*. Oxford: Oxford University Press.

Katsuno, Hirofumi, and Christine R. Yano (2002). "Face to Face: On-line Subjectivity in Contemporary Japan." *Asian Studies Review* 26(2): 205–31.

Kinsella, Sharon (2000). *Adult Manga: Culture and Power in Contemporary Japanese Society*. Honolulu: University of Hawaii Press.

Levi, Antonia (1996). *Samurai from Outer Space: Understanding Japanese Animation*. Chicago: Open Court.

Lowenfeld, V (1957). *Creative and Mental Growth*. 3rd ed. New York: Macmillan.

McCloud, Scott (1993). *Understanding Comics: The Invisible Art*. New York: HarperCollins.

—— (1996, April). "Understanding Manga." *Wizard* magazine, 44–48.

McNeill, David (1992). *Hand and Mind: What Gestures Reveal about Thought*. Chicago: University of Chicago Press.

Nakazawa, Jun (2002a). "Analysis of Manga (Comic) Reading Processes: Manga Literacy and Eye Movement during Manga Reading." *Manga Studies* 5: 39–49.

—— (2002b). "Effects of *Manga* Reading Comprehension Ability on Children's Learning by *Manga* Materials." *Research on Teaching Strategies and Learning Activities* 9: 13–23.

—— (2004). "Manga (Comic) Literacy Skills as Determinant Factors of Manga Story Comprehension." *Manga Studies* 5: 7–25.

—— (2005). "Development of Manga (Comic Book) Literacy in Children." In *Applied Developmental Psychology: Theory, Practice, and Research from Japan*, ed. D. W. Shwalb, J. Nakazawa and B. J. Shwalb. Greenwich, CT: Information Age.

Nakazawa, Jun, and Sayuri Nakazawa (1993). "Development of *Manga* Reading

Comprehension: How Do Children Understand *Manga*?" In *Manga and Child: How Do Children Understand Manga?*" ed. Y. Akashi. Gendai Jidobunka Kenkyukai.

Natsume, Fusanosuke (1997). *Manga wa naze omoshiroi no ka* [Why are Manga fascinating? Their visual idioms and grammar]. Tokyo: NHK Library.

—— (1998). "The Future of Manga (Japanese Comics)." Foreign Press Center, Japan, http://www.fpcj.jp/e/gyouji/br/1998/980917.html.

—— (2001). "Introduction of Manga: Short Comics from Modern Japan." In *Manga: Short Comics from Modern Japan: A Japan Foundation Touring Exhibition.* Exhibition catalog. London: Japan Foundation.

—— (2003). "Japanese Manga: Its Expression and Popularity." *ABD* 34(1): 3–5.

Natsume, Fusanosuke, and Kentaro Takekuma (1995). *Manga no Yomikata* [How to Read Manga]. Tokyo: Nagaoka Shoten.

Peirce, Charles Sanders (1931). *Collected Papers of Charles Sanders Peirce*, vol. 2, *Elements of Logic.* Cambridge, MA: Harvard University Press.

Rommens, Aarnoud (2000). "Manga Story-Telling/Showing." *Image & Narrative* 1(1).

Schodt, Frederik L. (1983). *Manga! Manga! The World of Japanese Comics.* New York: Kodansha International.

—— (1996). *Dreamland Japan: Writings on Modern Manga.* Berkeley, CA: Stonebridge Press.

Toku, Masami (2001). "What Is Manga? The Influence of Pop Culture in Adolescent Art." *Journal of National Art Education* 54(2): 11–17.

—— (2002a). "Children's Artistic and Aesthetic Development: The Influence of Pop-Culture in Children's Drawings." Paper presented at the Thirty-First International Society for Education through Art Convention, New York.

—— (2002b). "Cross-Cultural Analysis of Artistic Development: Drawing by Japanese and U.S. Children." *Visual Arts Research* 27: 46–59.

Tomasello, Michael (2000). "First Steps Toward a Usage-Based Theory of Language Acquisition." *Cognitive Linguistics* 11(1): 61–82.

Wilkins, David P. (1997). "Alternative Representations of Space: Arrernte Narratives in Sand." Paper presented at the Proceedings of the CLS Opening Academic Year 1997–98.

Wilson, Brent (2000). "Becoming Japanese: Manga, Children's Drawings, and the Construction of National Character." *Visual Arts Research* 25(2): 48–60.

Wilson, Brent, and Marjorie Wilson (1977). "An Iconoclastic View of the Imagery Sources in the Drawings of Young People." *Art Education* 30(1): 4–12.

—— (1987). "Pictorial Composition and Narrative Structure: Themes and Creation of Meaning in the Drawings of Egyptian and Japanese Children." *Visual Arts Research* 13(2): 10–21.

Manga Examples

Koike, Kazuo, and Goseki Kojima (1995). *Lone Wolf and Cub: A Taste of Poison*, vol. 20. Milwaukie, OR: Dark Horse Comics.

12

International Singularity in Sequential Art: The Graphic Novel in the United States, Europe, and Japan

N. C. Christopher Couch

Despite divergent histories of comic art publishing in the United States, Western Europe, and Japan, in recent decades there has been an apparent convergence of publication formats: the graphic novel, album, and *tankobon* (volumes of comics), respectively.[1] Although these three formats are similar in appearance, each is the product of a unique history that affects demographics of readership, patterns of distribution and sale, and cultural meanings associated with the formats.

The album collects serialized stories from weekly or monthly comic magazines. The collection of *Tintin* stories into enormously popular books created the paradigm for European works, and innovative modern creators from Moebius to Marjane Satrapi have followed the same pattern. In Japan, tankobon are collected from magazine anthologies of comics. In both Europe and Japan, comics embraced a much wider range of genres from the very beginning of the medium, and avoided the domination of the market by the superheroes characteristic of the United States. However, in both areas, comic creators were free to do either long series with continuing characters or shorter series focused on a single, novellike story. Osamu Tezuka is the paradigmatic case, creating both series like *Tetsuan Atomu* (Astroboy) and striking novels like *Adolf.* The United States was the last area to embrace complex book publication of comics. Graphic novels began to become a significant part of the market only in the 1980s, but now are close to becoming the dominant form in American comics publication.[2]

In the United States, the graphic novel is viewed as the descendant of the pamphlet-form comic book published for sale on newsstands. Comic books were invented in the 1930s by the sales department of Eastern Color Press, which printed color Sunday newspaper comic sections for newspapers. During the Great Depression, as sales of newspapers decreased, the comic book was developed as a way to increase the press's business. The size and shape of comic books was determined by the proportions of a folded and stapled newspaper page that would yield a booklet approximating the size of a newsstand magazine. Comic books were originally distributed as giveaways, promotional items for companies and their products, but soon they were sold like magazines, an innovation often credited to M. C. Gaines, who later founded EC Comics. The first comic books were anthologies of several different popular comic strips reprinted from newspapers. The stories were not complete in a single issue, but instead had the same ongoing continuity that mirrored their newspaper appearances, and thus stories were told over the course of weeks or months.

As the number of comic books increased, publishers ran out of Sunday strips and began commissioning original features. Still the comic books were collections of different stories.[3] Comic books in the United States moved away from the serialized comic strips when the superhero genre began to dominate the comic book field. They continued to be anthology publications, but the stories were in most cases complete, and in some books almost all the stories were centered on a single popular character.

The models for this kind of popular publication in the United States were American fiction magazines — mystery and detective fiction like *Black Mask* and science fiction magazines like *Amazing* and *Astounding.* Such "pulp" fiction magazines were anthologies of different, unrelated works linked only by genre.[4] *Black Mask* developed a stable of writers and characters whose names would sell the magazine, such as Dashiell Hammett, Philip Marlowe, and the Thin Man. Similarly, pulps in other genres — adventure, romance, horror, science fiction, and Westerns — developed writers like Robert Heinlein, Isaac Asimov, and Edgar Rice Burroughs; these were writers whose names and characters (like Burroughs's Tarzan) served to increase sales. There were also pulps that, like comic books, concentrated on the adventures of a single, eponymous character, such as *The Shadow* and *Doc Savage.* These magazines featured the same mix of story lengths as the other pulps, with novels, novelettes, and short stories. Unlike the other pulps, though, the stories in *The Shadow* and *Doc Savage* were credited to single authors — Walter Gibson and Kenneth Robeson, respectively — although the stories were created by multiple authors.[5]

Both these types of pulp magazines are models for the dominant form of comic in the United States, the superhero comic. Despite the growth of alternative and independent comics since the late 1960s, and the explosion of crime and horror comics from the end of World War II through the imposition of the Comics Code in 1954, superhero comic books outsold all other genres from their beginnings in the late 1930s, and continue to do so today. Superman's success led to DC Comics creating a host of imitators, including Batman and Wonder Woman, while the antecedent company of Marvel Comics, Timely, developed the Sub-Mariner, the Human Torch, and others and the Fawcett Company developed Captain Marvel. After the development of superhero comic books, the narratives in comic books departed from the format of the Sunday comic strips, with long story arcs that extended over weeks or months, and their combination of multiple genres and a variety of characters within a single publication. Like pulps, comic books featured multiple, self-contained stories in a single genre or featuring a single, usually eponymous, character. Many pulp writers also wrote for the comic books. This pattern dominated comic books in the United States through the 1970s.

Newspaper comic strips were serialized fiction, comparable in many ways to the characteristically Victorian model of publishing in installments, either periodically in magazines or as separate volumes. Pulps' serialized fiction links them to the Victorian model, and certain features of pulps link them to comic books; this separates the development of U.S. comic books from other national and regional traditions in comic art publication. The majority of the contents of pulp magazines were independent and complete stories, and the novels that were serialized were usually in relatively few parts, as few as two or three and rarely more than a half dozen. In the pulp magazines dedicated to a single character, the major feature of each magazine was usually a complete story, a short novel, appearing in only that single issue — for example, Burroughs's "Tarzan of the Apes: A Romance of the Jungle" appeared in its entirety in the October issue of *The All-Story*. Furthermore, unlike Victorian serialized fiction, or even the fiction serialized in the "slicks" such as the *Saturday Evening Post*,[6] there was no certainty that a novel serialized in a pulp fiction magazine would appear in the form of a book. Premier presses like Alfred A. Knopf picked up Dashiell Hammett and Raymond Chandler, and secondary or regional publishers like Chicago's A. C. McClurg published Edgar Rice Burroughs. But many mystery and science fiction writers' works had to await the development of specialty presses in these areas in the 1950s, or the development of major mass-market paperback lines in the 1950s and especially the 1960s before being reprinted in books. The other stories in pulp magazines were rarely collected in books, and many were never reprinted in any form.[7]

Like the shorter-format stories in pulp fiction magazines, the fiction in U.S. comic books was neither collected nor republished in any other form until the development of specialty publishers or publishing programs like DC Comics' archive series, phenomena of recent years associated with the development of a collectors' market since the 1970s. Comic book stories were available to readers only for the month that each individual issue was for sale on newsstands. The contents of the comic books were never collected, never reprinted, and disappeared within weeks of their first publication. In the United States, the development of comic books as the only form in which comics appeared on newsstands led to a separation between comic books and comic strips. Comic strips had been reprinted in books before the advent of comic books, and continued to be reprinted in book form afterward, as they are today. But these reprints are purchased in bookstores only, and even today published collections of newspaper strips are the dominant form of comic art available in bookstores.[8]

There can be little doubt that these developments affected the cultural position of comic books and comic strips in the United States. For most of the twentieth century, comic strips were considered a superior medium to comic books in tacit cultural hierarchies. Comic strips were associated with journalism, family readership, publication in books, and sale in bookstores. Comic books were associated with sensationalism, child and adolescent readership, and sale on newsstands. Although today 80 percent of comic books are sold in comic book shops, the public perception and cultural associations of such stores is perhaps even less positive than the past associations that linked newsstands to lower-class culture and publications of questionable merit.[9]

In the most influential European comic art markets — those of the United Kingdom, France, and francophone Belgium, the primary medium for the dissemination of comic art quickly became weekly comic magazines. Unlike U.S. comic books, many of the first European comic magazines were published for distribution with newspapers, and later developed into independent magazines published weekly and sold on newsstands for the entire week.

In the United States, the comic supplements of newspapers lost their early identification with humor magazines within a decade of their first appearance. The dialectical division that divided the elite humor magazines from the newspaper supplements in the United States increased over time. In Europe, the magazine format comic supplements of newspapers never lost their identification with newsstand magazines. Europe had a wider variety of humor magazines than did the United States, one aimed at a broader class and social spectrum. Some featured widely popular and long-lasting comic characters, such as Ally Sloper in England or Max und Moritz in Germany.[10] While American comic features were reprinted in Europe in these supplements within a short time of the first appearance of comic strips in the United States, original European comic features were developed as well, particularly from the 1920s on. The European magazine supplements featured American strip reprints and locally created imitations of American comic strips. Like American comic strips and the earliest comic books, European weekly comic magazines featured continuing stories starring popular characters. But throughout the 1920s, European strips were developed that soon became more popular than the U.S. strips, even before European governments began to proscribe American strips in the 1930s. For example, Hergé published the first installment of the *Tintin* strip in 1929, and this story was collected one year later in the first *Tintin* book, *Tintin in the Land of the Soviets.*

European comic magazines, like U.S. Sunday newspaper sections and the first comic books that derived from these, are anthologies that include continued stories as well as comics that are complete narratives in each strip and may or may not feature continuing characters. Unlike the American comic books, which share with their European counterparts the format of the periodical magazine, the European comics never abandoned this continuing-story format. As with Hergé's *Tintin*, other comic strips appeared in the magazines, and then each story arc was collected in a book. After *Tintin*, Alberto Uderzo's and Rene Goscinny's *Asterix* is perhaps the most popular, but the production of these collections — usually referred to in English as *albums* — numbers in the thousands of titles. Also unlike American comic books, these albums were sold from their very beginning in bookstores.

Popular titles like *Tintin* and *Asterix* have been described by critics as children's stories, and certainly the demographics of the readership of the weekly continental comic magazines included large numbers of children; the best parallel in the United States would be newspaper comic strips rather than comic books. Newspaper strips (and given their origins in newspaper supplements, the European anthology comic magazines certainly are closely allied to newspaper strips) are aimed at a readership that professional comic art publishers in the United States designate "all ages." This term, which gained importance in marketing comics in the United States after the development of the underground comics of the 1970s and independent comics in the 1980s, does not mean that the comics are not intellectually engaging and entertaining enough to attract adult as well as younger readers. Rather, it means they have no explicit sexual content or extreme violence. The continuing popularity of the *Tintin* series with adults throughout the world indicates that, although the marketing aimed at younger readers, an adult readership always existed as well.[11]

In the 1970s, fueled by political and social dislocations and developments, both in the United States and Europe, alternative comics developed. In the United States, the underground comics movement included comic strips in radical and alternative newspapers, but the most famous works of the movement appeared in comic books. The comic book may have appeared a more natural medium for radical change than the newspaper strip, a more conservative medium in the United States. In addition, comic books were a ubiquitous, inexpensive, and, in a sense, democratic media that were available on every newsstand.[12] In Europe, however, the dominant model of publishing comic art for the widest audience was the weekly or monthly comic magazine. When the currents of change flowed across Europe in the 1970s, new publishers founded alternative weekly comic magazines that imported some U.S. underground work but were the home of a new and aesthetically innovative and frequently politically radical group of artists. *Metal Hurlant* (Heavy Metal) in France and *Frigidaire* in Italy brought comics by artists like Moebius, Enki Bilal, and many others to a new public. In the United States, underground cartoonists published in thirty-two-page black and white comic books that remained in print for years and were only occasionally collected in books. In Europe, the new artists followed the publishing patterns set by Hergé and his heirs: publication in weekly or monthly comic magazines, followed by publication, usually in color, in hardcover or paperback collections. These albums, originally the province of readers of all ages, are slender, color volumes, most often in hardcover form, each containing a complete story that had been serialized.

European albums have continued to be the dominant format in the local comic market, but have had little impact in the United States. Despite the success of Heavy Metal, the American version of *Metal Hurlant*, only a few other anthology periodicals have appeared in the U.S. market — most notably, Art Spiegelman and Francoise Mouly's influential *Raw*. A few publishers have translated European albums, like *Tundra* and *Heavy Metal*, for the U.S. market. DC Comics experimented briefly with translations of albums from the prestigious French publishers Les Humanoides in 2004–5, but the series was canceled due to poor sales after less than a year. Marvel has begun a series of translations from Soleil, another French publisher specializing in science fiction comics. The most extensive and successful program of publishing albums has been that of Terry Nantier's New York-based NBM, which has successfully combined translated albums, original European-influenced U.S. work, and reprints of American comic strips.[13]

In Europe the albums drawn from the alternative comic periodicals led to a renaissance of comic art, the development of an adult readership, and an unparalleled period of artistic experimentation and growth. In the United States, similar innovation began with the underground comics movement, and received particular impetus from the return of Will Eisner to the comic art field after several decades in educational publishing.

Graphic novels have become increasingly popular in the United States over the last decade and a half. Although the term *graphic novel* had appeared in print a few times before the publication of Eisner's first book-length comic work, Eisner was not aware that the term had already been used, and independently coined the term with the publication of *A Contract with God* in 1978. Eisner has said that he grew tired of working only in the short-story format that had dominated U.S. comic books almost since the beginning. When he returned to the field, he wanted to do something new, a novel-length work published as a book. He hit upon the term *graphic novel* because it combined two words with positive meanings. *A Contract with God* was the first original, book-length work of comic art to be published with the moniker *graphic novel*. Eisner's cover design emblazoned it across the book: "A Graphic Novel by Will Eisner."[14]

Although most histories of comic art in Japan recall the traditions of visual and satirical art that developed from Japanese painting and calligraphic traditions, the primary development of comic art that concerns us is that which took place after the Second World War. The development in the Edo period of both artistic and literary works that dealt with the urban environment of the Japanese capital, and particularly the tradition of creating printed works with woodblocks that described the life of the city and its fashionable and artistic denizens — usually called *ukiyo-e*, or floating world — is often cited as the beginning of comic art in Japan. Certainly, just as long traditions of cartooning and caricature from William Hogarth, Honoré Daumier, and that of satirical magazines like *Punch*, informed and influenced the development of comic strip and later comic book art in the United States and Europe, the traditions that flourished with artists like Hiroshige Utagawa helped develop traditions and receptivity in Japan that later flourished in comic art. However, the major development of popular comic art as a mass medium took place in the periodical publications that grew in Japan in the aftermath of the devastation of World War II.

Osamu Tezuka (1928–89) was one of the most influential comic artists and animators of the twentieth century. Called in Japan "the god of manga," Tezuka's comic stories and animated films brought the tropes and storytelling techniques of American and, to a lesser extent, European comics and animation to Japan. Tezuka is reputed to have created 150,000 pages of comic art during his five-decade career as a manga artist. Tezuka's popularity and the productivity of his studio helped ensure the supremacy of comic books, as opposed to newspaper-based comic strips, in Japan in the postwar period. Although many other artists created works of importance while Tezuka was active, it was the continuing demand for his works — especially the serialized fiction and continuing characters that he created — that helped spur the development of the current Japanese system, which bears certain parallels to the European and American models of publication but which developed independently.

As in Europe, Japanese comic art is primarily published in weekly or monthly magazines that appeal to specialized audiences, with continued stories that are eventually collected in books that present entire stories appearing under the names of a single creator, or as the creations of a writer and artist. However, unlike the European model, in which contemporary creators are most often writer-artists or work is created by a single artist, in Japan the ongoing stories of the most popular artists are created in studios with many employees. In some ways, this mode of production can be compared to the shop system that provided materials for publication in comic books in the United States from the 1930s through the 1950s. The shop system of comics in the United States eventually became less anonymous, and developed into the contemporary system where writers, pencilers, inkers, and colorists create the monthly product for the most prominent titles of the major companies. In Japan, the staffs of studios usually receive credit for their work on the continued stories and collected editions that dominate the market.[15]

The reconstruction of the economy and society of Japan in the 1940s and '50s also saw the development of weekly and monthly comic magazines targeted to increasingly narrow segments of the consumer spectrum. Tezuka's work is also characteristic of related phenomena in European, U.S., and Japanese comic art: the "all-ages" comic. Like *Tintin* in Europe and the superhero comics of the United States, the work of Tezuka and similar artists who created comics ostensibly for children produced material that was engaging enough to attract adult readers. As the postwar generation matured, so too did its habit of reading comics. In Japan and Europe comics were less stigmatized by age than in the United States, but the phenomena are clearly related in all three areas.[16]

Japanese weekly comic magazines were created in the late 1950s and early 1960s and quickly became huge popular successes. By contrast, at that time comic book sales in the United States had fallen to relatively low levels after the imposition of content restrictions in the early 1950s. Sales were revived by the creation and popularity of the Marvel superheroes in the early 1960s, but still did not reach the levels attained in the heyday of the 1930s and '40s.

The Japanese weekly comic magazines of today are collections of stories by different artists featuring different characters, and are much more like European magazines than American comic books, which tend to focus on a single character. Printed cheaply on inexpensive paper, they mostly contain serialized stories that, like their European cousins, are destined to be collected in book form. The three most widely distributed are *Jump*, *Magazine*, and *Sunday*. Sales of manga have fallen since the mid-1990s, probably due to the competition for leisure time and resources from video games, the Internet and mobile devices. However, Japanese sales continue to dwarf American and European sales in terms of percentage of the population that reads comics and in monetary indexes of sales (Kinsella 2003, 30–49).

There are certain inescapable ironies in the varied histories of the publications of collections, albums, and graphic novels in the United States, Europe, and Japan. The comic books of the United States collected long, continued stories from American newspapers, but with the arrival of popular, costumed superheroes, continued stories disappeared from the comic books. American comic book readers lost the art of reading continued stories, and comic book anthologies of such stories all but disappeared. The short-story template that succeeded so well in the superhero comic books came to dominate all genres of U.S. comic books. This began to change in the early 1960s, with the reinvention of superhero comics at Marvel by writer/editor Stan Lee and artists Jack Kirby and Steve Ditko. Their new comic books, including *Fantastic Four*, *Spider-Man* and *The Incredible Hulk*, featured stories that continued through multiple issues of each title. These continued stories, called continuities in the field, were given further impetus in the late 1960s by the well-received *Green Lantern-Green Arrow* comics written by Denny O'Neil and drawn by Neil Adams. By the 1980s, the continued stories became so complex that only dedicated fans could follow all the twists and turns of the narrative, and the meaning of the term continuity gradually expanded to embrace the history of all the superheroes published by each company. In Europe, collections from magazines became the album form, which from *Tintin* to Les Humanoides remains a major and widely respected form of publication for comic books. In the United States, the rebirth of collections had to await the creation of the term *graphic novel* and the longer comic-book continuities of the modern superhero comics.

Two major developments have changed the comics market in the United States over the past fifteen years: the huge and still expanding popularity of manga and the spread of graphic novels into American bookstores. The first manga translated into English appeared as part of the underground comics movement when artist and educator Leonard Rifas founded an idealistic comic book company called Educomics in 1976 and translated and published a portion of Keiji Nakazawa's story of the bombing of Hiroshima, *Barefoot Gen*. Rifas followed the American system of publishing and released *Barefoot Gen* as a pamphlet-form comic book. Eclipse Comics, founded in 1977, also pioneered the publication of Japanese comics with the *Area 88* series and its most popular book, *Mai* (Mai the Psychic Girl). During the 1980s, as the direct-market system grew, and an increasing number of comic book stores carried independent comics, several alternative comic book companies featuring a mix of superheroes and more alternative publications developed. One of the largest of these publishers was First Comics, based in Chicago. Encouraged by Frank Miller, then famous for his work on Marvel's *Daredevil* comics, First Comics brought *Kozure Ōkami* (Lone Wolf and Cub) to America. All these publications were black and white, thirty-two-page comic books excerpted from Japanese *tankōbon* (volumes that collect story arcs of Japanese comics, reprinted from the pages in weekly or monthly manga where they originally appeared).

The real growth of manga in the United States has been led by two California-based companies (in contrast to the American mainstream comics publishers, which have always been based in New York): Viz Media and Tokyopop. Founded by Seiji Horibuchi, Viz Media began publishing translations of manga in 1987. The success of the company's publications was secured by the popularity of Rumiko Takahashi's *Ranma ½*. Japanese publishers Shogakukan and Shueisha share ownership of Viz Media, and the connection provides access to their publication lines. Tokyopop, founded in 1997, went through several changes of name and publication formats in its early history. Its first success was *Bishōjo Senshi Sērā Mūn* (Sailor Moon), marketed in a variety of formats, including magazines, pamphlet-form comic books, and graphic novels. Sales of this story, as well as the story *Gundam*, were propelled by the appearance of TV series versions on the cable channel Cartoon Network. An American company, Dark Horse comics, also contributed to the growing market for manga comic books in the United States, working with Toren Smith's Studio Proteus. Most of their products were originally released as comic books, and then collected into graphic novels; successful titles include *Mugen no Jūnin* (Blade of the Immortal), *Aa Megamisama* (Oh, My Goddess!), and *Gansumisu Kyattsu* (Gunsmith Cats). All these publishers collected their comic-book titles into graphic novels. These were distributed to and sold through comic book stores, but as the number of books published expanded and as Japanese animation on television increased awareness of the properties they were able to expand their sales through bookstores. When the *Pokemon* craze hit the United States in 1999, Viz produced a huge range of publications in a variety of formats, reaching beyond bookstores into toy stores, department stores, and retail chains like Wal-Mart. *Doragon Bōru* (Dragon Ball Z) also proved successful as an animated series, leading to extensive comic book and book sales in the same variety of outlets.

Pokemon, Sailor Moon and *Gundam* attracted viewers and readers among the teen and "tween" population of the United States. *Pokemon* and, to a lesser extent, *Dragon Ball Z*, attracted male and female fans in grade school. *Sailor Moon* and *Gundam* appealed particularly to female readers and viewers. As these new readers grew slightly older, an opportunity appeared to reach a new, broader market in the United States with Japanese graphic novels. American comic book publishers had adopted the model of creating comic books from Japanese tankōbon by "flipping," or making mirror-image copies of Japanese originals for their publications so that they would read left to right in typical Western style. This procedure seemed to meet the needs of a market that slowly adopted Japanese comics through comic book stores, in most cases adding the manga to a body of reading composed primarily of American comics, whether superhero, independent, or underground. When manga moved beyond the comic book stores in America, embraced by a new, younger and enthusiastic audience, the moment appeared ripe to bring comics to this market in a format more closely approximating the Japanese publications. This was particularly the case because a certain percentage of the fan base for these publications was interested in Japanese culture in general as well as manga and *anime* in particular. As these readers moved into high school and even college, they pursued their interests by studying Japanese language and literature. In 2002, Tokyopop began publishing unflipped manga collections, designed to be read right to left, with the sound effects untranslated. Calling this format "real" manga, the small books provided a frisson of authenticity and were embraced — particularly by teenage girls. The graphic novel sections that had begun to appear in American bookstores exploded with manga, and new readers flocked to them. Also in 2002, the Book Industry Systems Advisory Committee (BISAC), a voluntary organization composed of publishing editorial and marketing and sales professionals that maintains the standards for databases used by publishers, distributors, and bookstores, voted to give the graphic novel its own category, accelerating the development of bookstore sections and online sales.[17]

In parallel, and not coincidentally, American graphic novels were achieving previously undreamed-of favorable press coverage and increasing sales. The way into bookstores for graphic novel had been opened by what were essentially collected story arcs from comic books, and Frank Miller's *Batman: The Dark Knight Returns* (1986) and Alan Moore and Dave Gibbons's *Watchmen* (1987). In 1992, Art Spiegelman's *Maus* won a special Pulitzer Prize. This confirmed and extended the interest in graphic novels in the United States that had been building for a generation, beginning with the twin phenomena of adults buying new comics and collecting old ones as well as the underground comics revolution. In the wake of the attention paid to sales of *Maus*, publishers both within and outside the comic book industry developed graphic novel lines. DC Comics' Paradox Press used artists and writers who had long experience in the comic book industry in order to attempt to create original graphic novels of some quality. The attempt was at least creatively successful in some cases. Two from the imprint were made into critically praised films: the 1997 graphic novel *A History of Violence* by John Wagner and Vince Locke became the basis for the 2005 film by David Cronenberg, and *Road to Perdition* by Max Allen Collins and Richard Piers Rainer from 1998 (the last original graphic novel from the imprint) became the 2002 Sam Mendes film starring Tom Hanks. A variety of publishers from outside the comic book field began to experiment with graphic novel lines from the mid- to late 1990s through the early 2000s; these were unsuccessful. The comics field was not yet ready to provide the material that could fill the graphic novel shelves in bookstores and, despite the success of the exceptional *Dark Knight* and *Watchmen*, collected story arcs from superhero comics were not going to appeal to mainstream readers looking for graphic novels.

When *Maus* caught a wave of media attention, there were two impediments to following up on its success. Most comic creators were either working on mainstream superhero comics — in the specialized roles writer, penciler, or inker that American comics demanded — or were creating independent comics that the mainstream audience would never accept, such as the underground comics of R. Crumb or independent comics like the masterly works of Gilbert and Jaime Hernandez (*Love & Rockets*). In the ten to fifteen years after *Maus*, both the creators and the audience changed. Independent comics grew and developed a wider variety of titles and publishers, and readers grew more accustomed to the language of sequential art, including those readers who read manga in high school or grade school and were able to read all kinds of comics without difficulty. With more diverse creators, and more visually sophisticated readers, the graphic novel boom of the latter half of the first decade of the twenty-first century took off. In a contracting market for books, the graphic novel was one of the few media categories that was growing (Christian books was another). Well-reviewed comic book movies, like the *Spider-Man* and *Fantastic Four* series, did not lead to an increase in sales of comic books or collected story arcs, but they did help create a more favorable climate for comics in society and the media. An explosion of media coverage on graphic novels was capped by a front-page article in the *New York Times Magazine* in July 2004.[18] Growing recognition for graphic novels by American creators included the 2001 Guardian First Book Award to Chris Ware's *Jimmy Corrigan: The Smartest Kid on Earth* and Time Magazine's naming *Fun Home* by Alison Bechdel the best book of the year for 2006.[19] Both these creators had worked in the independent and alternative comics fields for years before their breakout books. Ware had created and designed a comic book series for the independent publisher Fantagraphics, the *Acme Novelty Library*, and Bechdel had syndicated the comic strip *Dykes to Watch Out For* to alternative newspapers since 1983.

The growing marketplace dominance of long-form works of comic art

— graphic novels — is frequently heralded as an indication of the aesthetic and literary development of the comic art medium in the United States. Certainly the availability in bookstores of domestically produced graphic novels by independent creators, collected story arcs from mainstream superhero publishers, translated European albums, and Japanese series in a faux tankobon format shows the wide range of tastes and interests that have grown among readers in the United States in a very short time. Just ten years ago an American bookstore with a graphic novel section was the exception, usually found in urban neighborhoods or near campuses. Now all bookstores have graphic novel sections, which continue to grow each year. The adult readership for graphic novels is confirmed in another growing bookstore practice, having a separate graphic novel section in the children's sections of bookstores featuring works for younger readers. Thanks to a combination of the importation of a increasingly wider variety of genres of manga, and more European albums, combined with the innovations of American mainstream and comics publishers, the United States is at last beginning to feature in its bookstores the same wide variety of genres of graphic novels that Europe and Japan have long enjoyed. The fact that extended stories were collected in book-length format in other national sequential art literatures made it easy to import and sell them alongside domestic productions, using the American-made rubric *graphic novel*. Although graphic novels produced by American creators have certainly become more sophisticated and varied, the cultural acceptance of long-form comics might be viewed not only as an indication of the maturation of the field here but could with equal validity be seen as a convergence of related traditions of comic art in the United States, Europe, and Japan. The convergence is not one of style or subject, at least not primarily. Rather, it is a convergence that can best be understood semiotically. As Barthes has observed:

> [T]he object is polysemous, *i.e.*, it readily offers itself to several readings of meaning; in the presence of an object, there are almost always several readings possible, and this is not only between one reader and the next, but also, sometimes, within one and the same reader. In other words, each of us has in himself, so to speak, several lexicons, several reservoirs of reading, depending on the kinds of knowledge, the cultural levels he possesses. All degrees of knowledge, of culture, and of situation are possible, facing an object and a collection of objects (Barthes 1994, 188).

The bound volume that is filled with comics is both an object – a bound book – and a collection of objects: the issues of a comic book story arc, the chapters that have appeared in weekly or monthly manga, the episodes that were serialized in a European comics magazine. Meanings associated with graphic novels, albums and tankobon differ for the readers within each sequential art tradition, but the convergence of the object in the bound volume of comics allows them to be read on many levels across cultures.

The approaching technological convergence of electronic media may be seen as parallel to the international acceptance in book format of comics from a variety of originating traditions. Like sequential art, the converging electronic media combine images and speech/text/sounds. In all of its diversity, the rapid change and development of the international graphic novel may be seen as its own form of singularity.

Notes

1. The first version of this article was presented at the International and Interdisciplinary Conference on the Graphic Novel hosted by the Institute for Cultural Studies (University of Leuven) on May 12–13, 2000, and published in *Image and Narrative: Online Magazine of the Visual Narrative* 1 (www.imageandnarrative.be/narratology/chriscouch.htm). I would like to express my gratitude to Jan Baetens, organizer of the conference and editor of *Image and Narrative*, for inviting me to present the original paper and for permission to publish this revised version.

2. The most thorough analysis of the formats of publication of comic art is Pascal Lefevre's article (2000), which emphasizes heterogeneity rather than convergence. Sabin's insightful monograph, *Comics, Comix, and Graphic Novels*, deals with formats passim, as well as highlighting them in the title. Scott McCloud's works *Understanding Comics* and *Reinventing Comics* also offer insights into publication formats, particularly in the latter volume, which extends the analysis to digital publication. Web comics have yet to supplant printed comics. Although many are widely read, particularly in the U.S., financial success for creators has continued to prove elusive and, when achieved, has followed three major avenues that rely on printed comics: selling printed collections through the comic's website, using the web comic as a springboard to better-paying work in indy or mainstream comics publishing, or selling the comic to a publisher.

3. Daniels 1971, 10–11; Steranko 1970, 13. The best statement of the legendary role of Max C. Gaines is found in Ron Mann's documentary film *Comic Book Confidential* (1988), in an interview with William Gaines, publisher of *Mad* magazine and son of Max. For the role of George Delacorte in bringing comic books to retail outlets, see See Jones 2004, 98–101. M. C. Gaines's son William Gaines became the publisher of the EC Comics line after his father's untimely death, and oversaw the creation of innovative humor, horror, crime and science fiction comics including *Mad* magazine and *Tales from the Crypt*.

4. Pulps and pulp fiction got their names from the cheap wood pulp paper on which they were printed.

5. There are many popular histories of pulp and other popular fiction magazines. The best survey is by Frank M. Robinson, best-selling author who began his career in the pulps, with Lawrence G. Davidson (1998). Other popular histories include those by Goulart (1972) and Haining (2002). Interpretive studies dealing with audience and social context include Haut (1995), McCracken (1998), and Smith (2000).

6. Slicks were the opposite of pulps and were so called because of the high-quality ("slick") paper on which they were printed.

7. On the book publication of science fiction, see Aldiss (1986), 233 and passim.

8. The connection between narrative structure in pulp magazines and comic books has not to my knowledge been discussed previously.

9. The best example of the low status of comic book stores and those who own and frequent them is the comic-book store owner in the *Simpsons* television series. I first began teaching comics as art and literature in the comparative literature program at the University of Massachusetts–Amherst in 1997. Since then, I have also taught comics and graphic novels at Haverford College in Haverford, Pennsylvania, and the School of Visual Arts in New York City. In the introductory classes, I used to ask students to rank the arts and popular arts. For the first five years, students uniformly indicated that comic strips ranked above comic books in an imagined cultural hierarchy. This is no longer true. (In classrooms I have compared comic book collecting to stamp and coin collecting to emphasize what a small hobby interest it was. Although it remains a tiny fraction of stamp and coin collecting in terms of dollar amounts in the United States, my students now tell me they know of no one their age who collects coins and/or stamps, but many who collect comics.) Comic strip artists have been media celebrities in the United States in a way comic book creators have yet to achieve. Al Capp (*Li'l Abner*), Percy Crosby (*Skippy*), and Gary Trudeau (*Doonesbury*) achieved a level of status as media magnets and social commentators that was never achieved by even the most famous comic creators such as Jack Kirby or even Will Eisner. (Stan Lee remains always the exception.) The recent extensive and laudatory coverage of a biography of Charles Schulz indicates the continuing prominence of strip creators (Michaelis 2007).

10. The best survey of comics in early European humor magazines is Kunzle (1990). On Ally Sloper and British humor magazines, see Sabin (1996), 14–19.

11. The importance of Hergé and *Tintin* in the development of the comic weekly and album is tacitly accepted by most histories of European comics, including Horn and Couperie (1971), as well as in monographs on Hergé, including those by Goddin (1988) and Peeters (1992).

12. Most general histories of comics include extensive treatment of the underground movement; Sabin (1996) includes particularly thorough coverage of Europe. Specialized histories include Estren (1987), Rosenkranz (2002), and Skinn (2004).

13. For the role of NBM in bringing European comics to American audiences, see Weiner (2003), 26–27.

14. See Andelman (2005), 291 and passim.

15. The best study in English on the production of manga is Kinsella (2000); see especially chapters 2, "The Manga Production Cycle," and 6, "Creative Editors and Unusable Artists."

16. For an appreciation of the role and importance of Tezuka, based in part on interviews with the artist, see Schodt (1983, 1996); further material on Tezuka and his publications can be found in Piovan (1996).

17. The account of the development of the market for Japanese comics and graphic novels in the United States is based on my experience in the industry. I served as editor in chief of CPM Manga, the publishing division of anime distributor Central Park Media, from 1999 to 2001, and senior editor at Kitchen Sink Press from 1994 to 1999. I also have taught comics as art and literature at a variety of colleges and universities, and was one of the guests who attended the BISAC committee meeting in 2002. Stuart Levy, founder and publisher of Tokyopop, decided to adopt the unflipped, tankōbon-size format for manga. Readers who were buying imported Japanese manga in ever greater numbers, even though they were unable to read them or were learning Japanese through reading them, were well aware of the format of Japanese comics, and were ready for an American product that would more closely resemble the originals.

18. See McGrath 2004. The article featured graphic novelists Chris Ware, Adrian

Tomine, Seth, and Chester Brown and the comics journalist Joe Sacco, as well as Art Spiegelman.

19. Grossman and Lacayo (2007), 189. Alison Bechdel's *Fun Home* (2006) was the number one book on this list of the ten best of the year. In 2007, Gene Yang's *American Born Chinese* (2006) was nominated for the National Book Award in the Young People's Literature category.

References

Aldiss, Brian (1986). *Trillion Year Spree: The History of Science Fiction*. New York: Avon.
Andelman, Bob (2005). *Will Eisner: A Spirited Life*. Milwaukie, OR: M Press.
Barthes, Roland (1994). "Semantics of the Object." In *The Semiotic Challenge*, 179–90. Berkeley: University of California Press.
Bechdel, Alison (2006). *Fun Home*. New York: Houghton Mifflin.
Coupiere, Pierre, Maurice C. Horn, Proto Destefanis, Edouard François, Claude Moliterni, and Géald Gassiot-Talabot (1971). *A History of the Comic Strip*. New York: Crown.
Daniels, Les (1971). *Comix: A History of Comic Books in America*. New York: Bonanza Books.
Eisner, Will (1978). *A Contract with God*. New York: Baronet.
Estren, Mark James (1987). *A History of Underground Comics*. Berkeley, CA: Ronin.
Goddin, Philippe (1988). *Hergé and Tintin: Reporters*. New York: Sundancer.
Goulart, Ron (1972). *Cheap Thrills: An Informal History of the Pulp Magazines*. New Rochelle, NY: Arlington House.
Grossman, Lev, and Richard Lacayo (2006). "10 Best Books." *Time* 168(26): 189.
Haining, Peter (2001). *The Classic Era of American Pulp Magazines*. Chicago: Chicago Review Press.
Haut, Woody (1995). *Pulp Culture: Hardboiled Fiction and the Cold War*. London: Serpent's Tail.
Jones, Gerard (2004). *Men of Tomorrow: Geeks, Gangsters and the Birth of the Comic Book*. New York: Basic Books.
Kunzle, David (1990). *The History of the Comic Strip*, vol. 2, *The Nineteenth Century*. Berkeley and Los Angeles: University of California Press.
Lefevre, Pascal (2000). "The Importance of Being 'Published': A Comparative Study of Different Comics Formats." In *Comics and Culture: Analytical and Theoretical Approaches to Comics*, ed. Hans Christian Christiansen and Anne Magnussen, 91–106. Copenhagen: Museum Tusculanum Press.
McCloud, Scott (1992). *Understanding Comics*. Northampton, MA: Kitchen Sink Press; New York: HarperCollins.
—— (1999). *Reinventing Comics*. New York: DC Comics.
McGrath, Charles (2004, July 11). "How Cool Is Comics Lit?" *New York Times Magazine*, 24–33, 46, 55–56.
Miller, Frank, with Klaus Janson and Lynn Varley (1986). *The Dark Knight Returns*. New York: DC Comics.
Moore, Alan, and Dave Gibbons (1987). *Watchmen*. New York: Warner Books.
Peeters, Benoit (1992). *Tintin and the World of Hergé*. Boston: Little, Brown.
Piovan, Monica (1996). *Osamu Tezuka, l'arte del Fumetto Giapponese* [Osamu Tezuka: The art of the Japanese comic]. Venice: Musa Edizioni.
Robinson, Jerry (1974). *The Comics: An Illustrated History of Comic Strip Art*. New York: Putnam.
Robinson, Frank, and Lawrence G. Davidson (1998). *Pulp Culture: The Art of Fiction Magazines*. New York: Collector's Press/St. Martin's Press.
Rosenkranz, Patrick (2002). *Rebel Visions: The Underground Comix Revolution, 1963–*

1975. Seattle: Fantagraphics Books.

Sabin, Roger (1996). *Comics, Comix and Graphic Novels: A History of Comic Art.* London: Phaidon.

Sampson, Robert (1993). *Yesterday's Faces: A Study of Series Characters in the Early Pulp Magazines.* Bowling Green, OH: Bowling Green University Popular Press.

Schodt, Frederik L. (1983). *Manga! Manga! The Word of Japanese Comics.* New York: Kodansha International.

—— (1996). *Dreamland Japan: Writings on Modern Manga.* Berkeley, CA: Stone Bridge Press.

Server, Lee (1993). *Danger Is My Business: An Illustrated History of the Fabulous Pulp Magazines, 1896–1953.* San Francisco: Chronicle Books.

Skinn, Dez (2004). *Comix: The Underground Revolution.* New York: Thunder's Mouth Press.

Smith, Erin (2000). *Hard-Boiled: Working-Class Readers and Pulp Magazines.* Philadelphia: Temple University Press.

Steranko, Jim (1970). *The Steranko History of Comics,* vol. 1. Reading, PA: Supergraphics.

Wagner, John, and Vince Locke (1997). *A History of Violence.* New York: Paradox Press.

Ware, Chris (2002). *Jimmy Corrigan, or, The Smartest Kid on Earth.* Seattle: Fantagraphics Books.

Weiner, Steve (1996). *100 Graphic Novels for Public Libraries.* Northampton, MA: Kitchen Sink Press.

—— (2003). *Faster than a Speeding Bullet: The Rise of the Graphic Novel.* New York: NBM.

Yang, Gene (2006). *American Born Chinese.* New York: First Second.

13

The Manga Polysystem: What Fans Want, Fans Get

James Rampant

INTRODUCTION

With the recent explosion in the popularity of Japanese manga there has been extensive study on the phenomenon — from the subculture groups that read it to the business strategies of companies that import and export it. However, there has been surprisingly very little academic inquiry into the translation of it, a very important process in the spread of manga to the West. Japan's lucrative comics industry is worth ¥540 billion, churning out roughly 6.08 billion publications annually (Schodt 1983). Sharron Kinsella describes manga in Japan as a ubiquitous product that reaches all demographic groups of the country's vast population, from young children to adults and even the elderly, making up "'38% of all published titles'" (quoted in Howell 2001, 59) The genres produced range from science fiction to dramas concentrating on society, as well as deviations from the mainstream such as avant-garde and erotic publications. Even stories on horse racing, mah-jongg, Japanese chess, and cooking are popular manga genres among adult readers (Schodt 1983). The majority of these genres have been exported to a Western audience, yet how did this intrinsically Japanese product make its way into the Western pop-culture mainstream? This chapter will compare published translations from the early days of the Western manga boom with *scanlations*, manga translations produced by fans and made available over the Internet, as well as manga translations published recently. By comparing the translation strategies adopted by these three distinct groups I hope to show how translational norms have developed particularly because of the impact of translation strategies adopted by *scanlation* groups and their impact on current publishers. To demonstrate this, it is important first to introduce in detail the manga translation industry in the West up to this point.

THE BEGINNINGS OF THE MANGA TRANSLATION INDUSTRY

It was not until the *anime* (Japanese animation) boom that manga began to take off in the West in the late 1980s. Frederik Schodt (1983) points out that while there were translations of Japanese comics abroad before this time, the majority were often adaptations, completely rewritten and occasionally redrawn, sold as merchandise to their anime counterparts (such as *Astro Boy* and *Kimba the White Lion*) on Western television sets at the time; this was a ham-fisted practice of naturalization to say the least. Leonard (2005) posits that the Japanese animation boom started with American fans trading their science fiction videotapes, such as those of *Star Trek* and *Battlestar Galactica*, for Japanese fans' anime videotapes. With this interest in anime fans soon turned their attention to manga and began importing it even without being able to read Japanese. To cater to this audience literate in science fiction, American manga import companies such as Dark Horse really only concentrated on importing culturally odorless, science fiction manga that they considered a safer bet. At this time, Eclipse Comics and Viz Communications, the latter an American branch of Japanese publishing conglomerate Shogakukan, began marketing titles containing an "exoticized Japan" such as Ryōichi Ikegami's *Mai the Psychic Girl* and *Crying Freeman* (Bouissou 2000) which, according to Groenstein, exerted "'a decisive influence for the successful future of manga in America'" (quoted in Bouissou 2000). With the release of the *Akira* manga series in the West in 1988, utilizing the popularity of the 1983 film, the manga boom really took off (Bouisou 2000). In 1993 a manga series, Rumiko Takahashi's *Ranma ½*, was released in America. As opposed to the culturally neutral science fiction manga that had been released previously, *Ranma ½* contained a great number of Japanese themes.

With the advancement of the Internet in the 1990s came a rise in "scanlation," which started off as a kind of New Age samizdat. Due to the lack of access to manga in the West, fans went underground and started importing the manga genres that they wanted to read even if it meant breaking the law (Deppy 2005). "Scanlators" threw off the naturalizing constraints employed by commercial translators and instead used techniques of *foreignization*, a translation concept where the author "develops a translation method along lines which are excluded by dominant cultural values in the target language" (Munday 2001, 146–8). In opposition to domesticating a text, which implies diluting its "foreignness" by adding language and cultural concepts of the target culture and thus making the text appear less of a translated product and more like a domestic product, foreignization overtly stresses the product's exoticness by retaining the cultural differences requiring knowledge from the reader, or footnotes. Such examples of foreignization in these scanlations are: leaving forms of address in their original Japanese; translating sound effects and onomatopoeia as far as romanizing them, phonetic sounds written into the English alphabet, as opposed to finding equivalents in the target language; and unflipping pages so that the reader has to read panels right to left, as is done in Japan. A comparison of both types of translation demonstrates that mainstream groups have adopted scanlation strategies.

WHAT'S INVOLVED IN MANGA TRANSLATION?

To fully understand the decisions made by scanlators and translation professionals its important to look at what's involved in the translation of manga. Separating manga translation from regular document translation is the comic-book page dynamic. One element of this — indeed, one of the most dominant elements — is page direction: Japanese books read right to left, the exact opposite of Western publications. Early published, translated manga pages were "flipped" to be read by Western audiences, left to right. However this resulted in an odd parallel universe in which samurai drew their swords with their left hands. This also led to manga artists complaining that their artwork was being altered (Randall 2005). Scanlations left the pages unflipped, though leaving no explanation as to correct reading order; it seemed assumed that their audience was part of the "in crowd" that would know the proper method for reading. Most recently published manga also leave pages unflipped, with a warning page at the back of the book (or the front, in Western terms) that the reader is reading the book backward. An intrinsic part of the comic book aesthetic that requires rethought in translation strategy is the speech "bubble." Speech bubbles in manga are taller, rather than wide, to accommodate the vertical character of the Japanese language. Leaving little room for Western horizontal text, translators have to adopt confining translation strategies, sacrificing information for brevity, to fit the speech bubble.

Sound effect translation can be costly, as it requires an artist to edit the original word out of the artwork and fit the English sound effect in. The textual representation of sound that a Japanese reader may interpret as an explosion (*DOKAN!*) or footsteps (*batabata*) are not what an English speaking audience would process as these sounds. Onomatopoeia is often used in everyday Japanese conversation to the point that onomatopoeic terms appear as verbs in dictionaries; these often become problems for translators as manga will have onomatopoeic sound effects for things that aren't generally considered to make sounds in English, such as *nikoniko* (smiling) and *shiiiin* (silence). It has become the convention with some manga translations to simply translate onomatopoeic sound effects as their verbs in English, which would ordinarily look odd in a Western comic; for example: Batman standing alone in a room with the word *silence* hanging above his head.

Other page elements that need contextualizing for English readers are culturally specific elements. Western readers are unlikely to know that when manga characters sneeze it is because they're being talked about, that spewing blood from one's nose denotes sexual excitement, that making the "okay" symbol with one's thumb and forefinger actually refers to money (i.e. the round yen coins), or that a raised pinkie finger refers to one's girlfriend. There are ubiquitous puns, especially in "gag manga," and wordplay that is often untranslatable. Foreignizing a joke by way of literal translation can impact in two ways: first, if it is explained through a footnote, the reader is interrupted from the story; second, the reader could simply not understand the cultural equivalence. As such, translators are often criticized by fans for "Americanizing" a text. There are also intrinsic elements of manga that would not necessarily be picked up by the reader. As Schodt (1983) notes, "What non-Japanese would guess, for example, that when a huge balloon of mucus billows from a character's nose it means he is sound asleep; that when a male character suddenly has blood gush from his nose he is sexually excited?" And what about important story elements? For instance, in the visually complex *shōjo manga* (girls' manga) genre, the average English-speaking reader would not know that a blank panel signifies that some time has passed between the preceding and following panels, and thus her reading of the story differs from the author's intent. In dealing with these problems the translator needs to decide upon translation strategies that satisfy not only the target audience but also stay faithful to the author's intent for the original text as well.

EARLY MANGA TRANSLATION BY PUBLISHERS

Now let's take a look at some examples of early translations produced by the publishing industry. My criteria for selection are based on translation scholar Lawrence Venuti's (1995) foreignization and domestication theory, which is built on the French translation scholar Antoine Berman's twelve deforming tendencies that he discovered as inherent in most prose translations. Berman (as cited in Venuti 2000) proposes the idea of negative analytics, an analytic of translation being the system of textual deformation that operates in every translation and prevents it from being a trial of the foreign which denotes the different translation strategies used in dealing with translating a cultural text such as "ethnocentric, annexationist translations and hyper textual translations (pastiche, imitation, adaptation and free writing), where the play of deforming forces is freely exercised" (Berman, quoted in Venuti 2000, 94). Using Berman's twelve tendencies of the negative analytic of translation (as cited in Munday 2003) we can measure how the translation deviates from a foreignizing translation to a domesticating one. The first manga we'll be looking at is Rumiko Takahashi's *Ranma ½*, which credits Gerard Jones and Matt Thorn for "English adaptation" (Takahashi 1993). Aspects of domestication are common in translated manga released at that time: honorifics are dropped from character's names, and pages are flipped to read in left-to-right order. The first example of domestication from this series is the translation of sound effects, as seen in the following table.

Japanese, Volume 1, Page 16 Text — Romanization — Explanation	English, Volume 1, Page 16 Text
1 むくっ — *muku* — onomatopoeic term expressing annoyance	rrrgg
2 すたすた — *suta suta* — sound of footsteps	tp tp
3 げいん — *gein* — gong sound effect	klong
4 どさっ — *dosah* — sound of being flung over a shoulder	hwoof
5 ざわざわ — *zawazawa* — onomatopoeic term expressing whispering	panda big one
6 ひそひそ — *hisohiso* — onomatopoeic term expressing whispering	hmm man
7 かっかっ — *kah kah* — sound of panda's growl	grrrowrr
8 ざっ — *zah* — sound of people turning away in a hurry	hwp

Here Jones and Thorn have employed *qualitative impoverishment* (Berman, cited in Munday 2003) by finding target text equivalents of these sound effects or onomatopoeia. Note that excerpts 5 and 6, which feature Japanese onomatopoeia for whispering have been translated with completely new dialogue, *expansion*, which is an example of the adaptation process that takes place in the production of the translation. There are elements of foreignization in *Ranma ½*, as Howell (2001) points out: vernacular networks are preserved in the stereotyped "foreigner talk" of the guide character who speaks in broken Japanese in the original and broken English in the translation:

English, volume 1, 42	You very strange one, no, sir?
English, volume 1, 42	This place very dangerous. Nobody use now.

Another example similar to this but an effacement of the *superimposition of languages* (Berman, cited in Munday 2003) rather than a destruction of vernacular networks of exoticization, is the adaptation of words uttered by Chinese characters in the original Japanese book into English in the translation.

Japanese, volume 3, 102	我(ウォー) (アイ)你(ニー) (Chinese word, but Japanese phoneticization given above the word) *uoo ai nii* (in Chinese *wo·ai ni* — I love you)
English, volume 3, 120	You I love!

Also a common feature in early manga, particularly in *Ranma ½*, is the use of adaptation on utterances. Here we see the English adaptation writer's influence over the translator or the original author.

Japanese, volume 2, 40	.. 早く思い出してあげなさい Hurry up and remember (for us.)
English, volume 1, 216	Don't strain your brain remembering Ranma.

SCANLATION

The first incarnation of fan translations online were in the form of translation scripts, a text-only reproductions of a manga book into English and uploaded onto the fan translator's webpage (or shared on a community site). The intended usage was that fans who had bought a copy of the Japanese book could read it in English off the computer screen with the original book in hand. With the evolution of technology — faster Internet speeds, graphics-editing software, and peer-to-peer upload/download programs — techno-savvy fans began working with Japanese-speaking fans to produce scanlations (placing the English text over the scanned image of the manga) and then distributing them online. In the early 1990s it was a lot more feasible to use Internet relay chat rooms to distribute material, to interested fans who came to their chat rooms because they saw them mentioned on a website or forum. There are still many groups who use Internet relay chat rooms in this manner today.

Scanlation groups are an organized team of translators, editors, photo-manipulators (who place the text onto the image), and scanners who digitally scan the original comics. More recently, with the drop in price of web space, scanlators have been storing onsite either as zip files available for download or displaying the page images as html pages, creating an online reading experience such as the scanlation site One Manga (http://www.onemanga.com). Scanlators show awareness of the legally ambiguous nature of their work. Some groups have been shut down by publishing companies, but most companies tolerate scanlation sites because groups that scanlate a work of manga not available in English will stop scanlating, delete their archived scanlations, and urge fans to buy the published version once a company has bought the rights to a series. However, there are scanlation groups that do continue to issue work even after its commercial release, though these groups do incur "pirate" status and are looked down on by the more reputable groups.

The first example of scanlation below is from Masashi Kishimoto's *Naruto*. This scanlation was translated by the scanlation group Toriyama's World (http://www.toriyamaworld.com) and is no longer available as the site's proprietor Ak of Troy — pseudonyms are often employed by scanlators due to the illegal nature of the trade (Deppy 2005) — removed the scanlation once the manga was published in North America. Scanlations are produced *by* manga fans *for* manga fans; as a result, these translations do not make allowances for uninitiated readers and instead tailor their translations for their "in crowd," which results in a lot of foreignization. One example is that of honorifics left untranslated, as can be seen in the following utterance.

Japanese, volume 1, 10   火影様!!!
                               Hokage sama!!!

English, volume 1, 10   Hokage-sama !!

Placed in the margin was an explanation reading, "Hokage = Fire Shadow / Sama = like 'Master'" that gave readers in English the understanding that Japanese readers would already have of the semantic meaning of characters that make up the name. Omitting such honorifics would enable the destruction of underlying networks of signification (Berman as cited in Munday 2001), as honorifics are occasionally used as plot development and to indicate to readers a character's social posistion. When characters used martial arts terminology, such as weapons or martial arts technique names, the translated text was a romanized form of the original Japanese and translation notes were written in gutters or along the border of the page. Sound effects are often replaced with English equivalents, although occasionally left untranslated, and translations often displayed the occasional spelling mistake. One important aspect to note about scanlations is that translators are not necessarily working from Japanese into English; with a greater availability of Chinese translators many scanlations are produced with the Chinese translation acting as the source text.

The Manga Translation Workshop is an alternative example of a grassroots scanlation group. My experience as a consumer/creator of scanlated material evolved through work at the Manga Library at Monash University's Japanese Studies Centre in Victoria, Australia, along with Dr. Craig Norris, who led us to create a weekly activity for 2004 whereby Australian students could cooperate with Japanese exchange students to produce scanlations of the books in the library. Though started as an enjoyable activity to help visiting Japanese students improve their English, once the Japanese students went home, Australian students studying Japanese at Monash were interested in the group and became involved, eventually leading Monash to offer a summer course jointly with the Tokyo Foundation and manga publisher TokyoPop, who provided translators to teach the course. Although the course only ran for one summer, many of the students remained involved in a weekly activity utilizing the skills learned in the workshop. What differentiates the Manga Translation Workshop from other scanlation groups was that rather than use copyrighted commercial products (translations of which are illegal to publish on the Internet) they instead approached the artists of Japanese Web comics, manga drawn by amateurs and made available for free on their websites, for their permission to translate their comics. Once translated the group made their translations available online at Lost in Scanlation (http://www.lostinscanlation.com).

The translations produced by the group differed from other scanlation groups in some ways, possibly due to their different *skopos*, their reason for translation. Where most scanlation groups aim their scanlations at their "in crowd" of manga fans, the Manga Translation Workshop, being an academic group, instead aimed to raise public awareness of manga's diversity and cultural significance by writing translations for a wider audience. One difference was in the translation of sound effects. As noted earlier, sound effects in scanlations were previously translated with an English equivalent, if translated at all. Sound effects translated by the Manga Translation Workshop were romanizations of the original Japanese sounds, but with accompanying explanations of Japanese sound effects to be found on the workshop's translation wiki (a webpage that can be viewed and edited by site users with log-in privileges). The translation wiki is itself another interesting facet of the practice; along with sound effect explanations and other translation notes, the wiki also contains a transcription of the source text alongside the translation; the website describes this feature as enabling visitors to be able to learn from and suggest new translations. This suggests that translations are overt, i.e.: translated with keeping in mind that the target text will need to be relatable to the source text by readers, and thus are translated literally, line by line.

RECENT MANGA TRANSLATIONS BY PUBLISHERS

Around 2,000 publishers have started to adopt new translation strategies. The following are examples of foreignization from a recently translated manga work by Masami Tsuda. In fact, its title alone presents interesting choices in translation. Titled in Japan as *Kareshi kanojo no jijyo* (The Circumstances of Him and Her, or The Circumstances of Boyfriends and Girlfriends) the working title of the English is *Kare Kano: His and Her Circumstances*, aimed at fans familiar with scanlations of the original who would therefore know of the Japanese title. In addition to translator Jack Niida, English adaptation was handled by Darcy Lockman and edited by Paul Morrisey. Very few sound effects are translated in *Kare Kano*, and the ones that are not are still left on the page in their original Japanese, unedited. There is no character pronunciation chart where readers might look up the readings for these sound effects themselves, or even an explanation as to what they are. Pages are, however, "flipped" in the English version. Another facet of naturalization that remains in recently translated manga is the adaptation of character dialogue.

Japanese, volume 1, 4	んー....じゃ 先生にうまく言って放課後までのばしてもらうよ Sure. . . . Okay, I'll ask the teacher to extend the deadline until after school.
English, volume 1, 8	Relax! Our teacher knows we've been super busy, so I'll just ask her to extend the deadline until after school. It'll be cool I promise.

The Japanese example contains a literal translation of the Japanese text. The English translation uses a lot of expansion and clearly domesticates the character's speech, making the character appear more like an American school student than a Japanese student.

In translating sound effects, Tokyopop left the original text on the page and put the translation in the margin. Translations of sound effects were phoneticizations of the original text rather than English equivalents, and often some sound effects were left untranslated. While Tokyopop's translation of *Kare Kano* does not preserve honorifics in the translated English; another manga released at the same time that does, however, is *Reservoir Chronicle Tsubasa*, translated and adapted by Anthony Gerard and published in Australia by Random House under the label Tanoshimi. Honorifics were kept in the English version in a similar fashion to the scanlation of *Naruto*, but a page dedicated to explaining what honorifics are was given at the beginning of the book. Cultural items were "foreignized," with translation notes given at the end of the book explaining in detail these items, such as dialects.

THE MANGA POLYSYSTEM AND TRANSLATION STRATEGIES

Munday (2001) introduces polysystem theory as a schema for studying literary works within the context of a literary system. A polysystem is "a multiple system, a system of various systems which intersect with each other and partly overlap, using concurrently different options, yet functioning as one structured whole, whose members are interdependent" (Aveling 2006, 10). Imagine a polysystem as a diagram of many circles representing literary systems and their interaction with each other. In this case Japanese literature is represented as one circle overlapping with Western literature, and occupying the space where the circles overlap are translated materials, such as manga. Munday writes, "Literature is thus part of the social, cultural, literary and historical frame-work and the key concept is that of the system, in which there is an ongoing dynamic of 'mutation' and struggle for the primary position in the literary canon" (2001, 109). Polysystems allow us to study the position of translated literature within the historical and literary context of the target culture. Aarnoud Rommens describes manga as "a subsystem within the 'ninth art's' polysystem, thereby competing with the subsystems of American and European comics" (2000) I would argue that within this polysystem, translated manga is of its own system, where manga is the main element and different publications and translation groups impact upon the translation policy norms of that system.

Itamar Even-Zohar notes that "change is considered a built in feature" of the polysystem (quoted in Aveling 2006, 6), and this is certainly the case with the manga system, as can be seen in the early translation policy adopted by publishers, one of domestication and "adaptation." While manga may be an art form and have some message to convey to the world, it is seen by Western publishers as mere entertainment and they thus feel that a "naturalization" attitude toward translation will have little consequence. Even-Zohar suggests that "the position occupied by translation in the polysystem conditions the translation strategy" (quoted in Munday 2001, 110) this can be seen in scanlation groups changing publisher's attitudes toward the domestication of cultural elements. Despite these changes, the role of adaptor is one that is still listed in the credits of most English-language manga today.

While scanlation may have shifted translation strategies in favor of the foreignization of cultural items, what about linguistic items? Michael Schreiber proposes the distinction of linguistic versus cultural foreignization and, on the linguistic side, how "translation conforms to stylistic and idiomatic norms of the target language" (quoted in Howell 2001, 59) Recent manga like Tanoshimi's *Reservoir Chronicle Tsubasa* demonstrate how honorifics were maintained in the English publication, which is an indication of linguistic foreignization. Despite this change, English adaptation of utterances from early published translation to recent translations were still commonplace. Howell describes this process of adaptation as taking place, in the case of manga publisher Viz Media, in two stages: "first a literal translation is made of the Japanese text, and then a specialist in scriptwriting adapts the dialogue to make it read more like an American comic" (2001, 60). This is, of course, impacting negatively on the foreignization of the English text, as we have seen in examples of adaptation in early manga (*Ranma ½*, 1993) and recent manga (*Kare Kano*, 2003.)

CONCLUSION

The advent of scanlation has shown how the impact of a translation group outside the publishers' market, with different goals, can change the translational norms of manga translators within that market. Comparisons of translated manga from these two translation groups show the adoption of a foreignizing translation strategy by manga publishers becase of scanlators — or, basically, because of fan and consumer pressure. This then poses the possibility that translation strategy is as much defined by the market place as it is by translators. Is this an effective, or even faithful, translation strategy? With sales of manga in the United States and Australia as high as ever, one could argue that fans are obviously enjoying and buying this product and that these translations are obviously working in that sense. Ultimately, publishers are importing and translating manga for a consumer audience, and thus that, despite Berman's criticism that naturalized translations are not adequate translations, in the world of manga publishing the successful translation is the one that the audience wants.

References

Aveling, Harry (2006). "Two Approaches to the Positioning of Translated Texts: A Comparative Study of Itamar Even-Zohar's *Polysystem Studies* and Gideon Toury's *Descriptive Translation Studies and Beyond*." *Kritika Kultura* 6: 6–25.

Bouissou, Jean-Marie (1996). "Manga Goes Global." Paper presented at the conference "The Global Meaning of Japan," University of Sheffield, March 19–22, 1996. Centre d'Études et de Recherches Internationales, http://www.ceri-sciencespo.com/archive/avril00/artjmb.pdf.

Deppey, Dirk (2005). "Scanlation Nation: Amateur Manga Translators Tell Their Stories." *Comics Journal* 269, http://www.tcj.com/index.php?option=com_content&task=view&id=343&Itemid=48.

Howell, Peter (2001) *Strategy and Style in English and French Translations of Japanese Comic Books.* Edinburgh Working Papers in Applied Linguistics. 11: 59–66.

Kishimoto, Masashi. (2001). *Naruto.* Toriyama's World, http://www.toriyamaworld.com/naruto.

Leonard, S. (2005). *Celebrating Two Decades of Unlawful Progress: Fan Distribution, Proselytization Commons, and the Explosive Growth of Japanese Animation.* Los Angeles: School of Law, University of California–Los Angeles.

Munday, J. (2001). *Introducing Translation Studies: Theories and Applications*. London : Routledge.

Randall, Bill (2005). Manga *in English, For Better or Worse*. *Comics Journal* special edition, http://www.tcj.com/sp2005/intro.html.

Rommens, Aarnoud (2000). Manga *Story-Telling/Showing*. Image [&] Narrative, http://www.imageandnarrative.be/narratology/aarnoudrommens.htm.

Schodt, Frederik L. (1983). *Manga! Manga! The World of Japanese Comics*. New York: Kodansha International.

Venuti, Lawrence (1995). *The Translator's Invisibility: A History of Translation*. London: Routledge.

Venuti, Lawrence (2000). *The Translation Studies Reader*. London: Routledge.

Suggested Manga Reading

CLAMP (S. Igarashi, N. Ohkawa, M. Nekoi, and M. Apapa) (2003). *Reservoir Chronicle Tsubasa*. New York: Del Ray.

Kishimoto, Masashi (2000). *Naruto*. Tokyo: Shueisha.

Takahashi, Rumiko (1993). *Ranma ½*, vols. 1–4. Tokyo: Shueisha.

Tsuda, Masami (1996). *Kareshi kanojyo no jijyou* [Kare kano: His and her circumstances]. Tokyo: Hakusensha.

Tsuda, Masami (2003). *Kare Kano: His and Her Circumstances*. New York: Tokyopop.

Manga in the World

14

Hybrid Manga: Implications for the Global Knowledge Economy

Jason Bainbridge and Craig Norris

INTRODUCTION

While the first manga to be translated for the American market was *Mai* (Mai, the Psychic Girl; Eclipse Comics, 1987), it would take until 2000 for manga to move from cult concern to mainstream hit in the West.[1] Indeed, as recently as ten years ago, Japanese publishers Kodansha, Shogakukan, and Shueisha still considered foreign sales "unviable" (McCarthy 2006, 15). But, as Helen McCarthy notes, "by the summer of 2003 Japanese publishers had gone beyond simply selling translation rights and formed ties with Western manga publishers" (McCarthy 2006, 15). Prominent among these was a partnership between Shueisha and Shogakukan subsidiary Viz to form Viz Media and the production of an English edition of the boys' manga *Shōnen Jump* (in 2003). In the United States, manga sales have tripled from 2000 to 2002, a market value of US$40–$50millon (McCarthy 2006, 15), with manga now accounting for one-third of the U.S. graphic novel market. Perhaps even more tellingly, this figure does not include OEL (original English-language) manga and in no way measures the impact of manga on Western popular culture more generally.

In this chapter we will look at the transnational movement of manga in terms of its *flow*. We will argue that this flow is in two stages: first, how manga is distributed and received and, second, how it is adopted/adapted for a local culture's needs in light of the cultural and economic understandings this brings to the export of Japanese cultural goods. We will be providing an overview of the Australian cultural context for manga, but since it is American popular culture that continues to dominate the global trade and exchange of popular culture (particularly in Western countries like Australia), understanding how manga became a central part of American popular culture, in terms of its distribution and adaptation, is also a crucial part of understanding how manga is similarly contextualized in Australia.

THE FLOW OF MANGA

Following on from *Mai, Kozure Ōkami* (Lone Wolf and Cub) appeared in English translation from First Comics and became a modest cult hit. But it was the *tankōbon*-like editions of *Akira* that confirmed both manga's potential and the way manga was most successfully going to be contextualized in the West; fans of the 1988 *anime* (Japanese animation) hit were keen to follow up on the characters and story line and sought out the manga as a way of supplementing their knowledge of the film; it was prelude, sequel, clarification, and adaptation all in one. Fans of *Akira* the anime sought out *Akira* the manga, and then sought out more manga with similar style and quality. A market formed to meet the demand, and so *Akira* confirmed one of the ways in which manga was increasingly going to be taken up by the West. Whereas, in Japan, it was almost invariably the manga which gave birth to the anime, in the West manga was more popularly thought of as one of the many adjuncts to anime.

In his study of the Godzilla phenomenon, William Tsutsui describes the results of a 1985 *New York Times*/CBS News poll asking fifteen hundred Americans to name a famous Japanese character; the top three results were Japanese emperor Hirohito, martial artist Bruce Lee (who is not Japanese, but from Hong Kong) and Godzilla (the fictional movie monster). Rather than using the poll as a way of exploring America's lack of knowledge about Japan, Tsutsui notes that

> the survey results also contained an important — and usually overlooked — lesson: Japanese popular culture exports have had a profound influence in America (and indeed, throughout the world) in the decades since World War II. From Godzilla in the 1950s through Astro Boy in the 1960s, Speed Racer in the 1970s, and the more recent phenomena of the Mighty Morphin Power Rangers, Hello Kitty, Nintendo, and Pokemon, creations of the Japanese imagination have been high profile and big business in the United States . . . the globalization of Japanese pop culture may well have shaped perceptions of Japan as significantly as quality control circles, just-in-time manufacturing or the once-chilling images of Honda after Honda rolling onto the docks at Long Beach. (Tsutsui 2004, 7)

Tsutsui not only makes make the point that Japanese cultural products function as a positive cultural force but actually sets up an idea of flow, of how manga is contextualized in this importing of Japanese cultural products to the West, noting that "just as the first Toyotas to hit the streets of America were followed by an ever-growing procession of Datsuns, Hondas, Subarus, Mitsubishis, Suzukis, and Mazdas, so a radioactive movie monster [Godzilla] paved the way for the global advance of Ultraman and Kikaida, manga and anime, Super Mario and Yu-Gi-Oh!, Iron Chef, Shonen Knife and Hello Kitty" (Tsutsui 2004, 178). Tsutsui's sentiment seems correct, even if the order appears wrong. The taking up of visual media (anime) by the West seems to prefigure the taking up of print (manga).

McCarthy writes, "As anime grows in popularity with American schoolchildren and college students, manga have begun to shed their cult status and break into mainstream youth publishing in the United States and Europe. Teens and preteens want more material on their favorite TV shows, and publishers want a product with a ready-made audience and its own weekly TV commercials at no extra cost" (McCarthy 2006, 15). This is precisely what happened with *Akira* in the late 1980s and early 1990s with *Pokemon* and more recently with properties like *Dragon Ball* and *Naruto*. In this way we can locate manga in a merchandising flow, commencing with anime and carrying on through ancillary products, including manga. It also means that many of the characters of *Shōnen Magazine*, like *Eightman, Kamen Rider* (Masked Rider), *Devilman*, and *Love Hina* remain better known in the West through their anime rather than their manga. The same is true for more recent iterations from *Shōnen Jump*, like *Dragon Ball* and *Naruto*.

This subordinate relationship between anime and manga was further engendered by early problems with definitions of manga in the West. This was partly a result of the Toei film studios running animation seasons in the 1970s and '80s (the "Toei Manga Festivals"), leading some to confuse manga with anime (the festival name actually referred to the manga on which the anime was based; McCarthy 2006, 8). Even more problematic was the 1990s marketing campaign of British distributor Manga Video (later, U.S. label Manga Entertainment), which McCarthy identifies as "a brilliant attempt to brand the entire medium as the product of a single distribution company. It even included a [unsuccessful] trademark application for the word 'manga'" (McCarthy 2006, 8). In both instances manga was again referred to as a subset of anime.

DISTRIBUTION IN AUSTRALIA

We can certainly see some of these themes in the distribution of manga in Australia. As in America, it was anime that prompted interest in manga (usually shown at festivals or at independent cinemas like the Valhalla in Melbourne, Victoria or the Dendy in Brisbane, Queensland) and it was texts like *Akira* and *Kozure Ōkami* that first appeared on local comic shelves. By the early 1990s, entire sections of comic stores were being labeled as selling manga (and occasionally, inaccurately, anime) which had the dual effect of abstracting manga from the other (overwhelmingly American) comics in stock while also reserving manga titles as something special and deserving of independent recognition. This was even in stores that did not distinguish between titles from rival American companies like Marvel, DC, and Dark Horse. The distinction remains in most comic stores today, though increasingly it is because customers come in seeking out manga titles; comic shop owners we spoke to characterized such readers as "not usually" being general comic readers but identified themselves as manga readers instead. Store owners also noted a gender disproportion, with many more female readers for manga than American comic titles. Such manga sections are usually located near the entrances to comic stores (to make it easier for readers to find what they are looking for) or toward the back (to encourage readers to walk past other goods in their search for manga). Most comic stores that stocked manga also carried other merchandise like plush toys, action figures, model kits and trading cards, again associating manga with a Japanese merchandising flow. Again, this was in stores that would not otherwise carry toy lines.

From 2000 on, some chain bookstores in Australia also began stocking manga, with the Dymocks book chain featuring clearly branded manga sections that were located (depending on the individual store) next to either their science fiction or children's sections (evincing either a great knowledge or complete lack of knowledge of manga readers!). Borders also features a number of manga titles but in contrast to both the comic stores and Dymocks, a number of Borders stores simply include manga in their graphic novels section; this branding actually points to manga's increasing dominance of the graphic novel market both in Australia and abroad.

Most manga in Australian comic stores is sourced from its American distributors through the ordering catalog *Previews*. This means that store owners simply take and place customer orders through Diamond Distribution along with their regular American comic orders. However, a recent distribution deal by Madman Entertainment points to the ways in which this may be changing in Australia while again seemingly confirming manga's continuing subordination to anime.

Madman Entertainment is one of the most successful DVD and merchandise distribution companies in Australia and is the leading distributor of anime in Australia and New Zealand, with close to 97 percent of the market share. It began in 1996 as an anime-only distribution company but has subsequently expanded into offering live-action and children's entertainment,

Cartoon Network and Adult Swim (animated) programs, a range of Director's Suite (primarily European art house) films, a range of Australian movies, involvement in Australian theatrical releases of (primarily) Studio Ghibli (Japanese anime) films, a youth clothing line branded as *otakuwear*[2], and most recently, a selection of manga titles. The company is owned by Funtastic Limited (one of Australia's largest distributors of toys and children's media), employs 130 people, and has an annual turnover of $AU50 million.

Madman's move into manga distribution is significant, as it means manga in Australia can now be sourced from an Australian distribution company. Furthermore, it reveals the awkward positioning of manga in the flow of Japanese cultural products into Australia. Being part of Madman seems to automatically subordinate manga to the anime that is Madman's core business, and certainly the manga releases that do relate to anime are coordinated as part of a merchandising rollout; Madman's launch of the Death Note franchise in Australia, for example, saw the first volume of the manga released along with live-action films, action figures, models, and clothing as part of the merchandising associated with Madman's release of the first volume of the anime. But, at the same time, on the manga section of their website, Madman does list manga by genre, making a clear distinction between Anime manga (described as "Everything from the world of Japanese animation! Check out the classics that started it all or start collecting a brand new series.") and comedy, drama, fantasy, romance, action, and occult — themed offerings. Such branding does suggest a genuine attempt to broaden the notion of manga, to more widely acknowledge the existence of manga as an original textual form rather than merely an anime adjunct. Furthermore, in interviews we conducted with Madman employees, the addition of manga to Madman's catalog was revealed to appeal to a larger female demographic as well, once again revealing the ways in which greater distribution and awareness of manga in Australia could lead to an increased market share among male *and* female consumers.

EXPLAINING THE EXPORT OF MANGA

In seeking to explain the success of American media texts across disparate cultures, including those with very different norms and values, Scott Robert Olson (following Bhabha 1994, among others) argues that "[a]lthough readers around the world are increasingly gaining access to the same materials to read, they do not have access to the same ways of reading" (Olson 2004, 114). Rather, Olson claims that the producers of American media texts are particularly good at making and exporting texts that easily blend into a variety of cultures. Olson calls this: "narrative transparency . . . any textual apparatus that allows audiences to project indigenous values, beliefs, rites, and rituals into imported media or the use of those devices. This transparency effect means that American cultural exports manifest narrative structures that easily blend into other cultures" (Olson 2004, 114).

We can think of Japanese manga operating in a similar way. Osamu Tezuka, the manga and anime pioneer who created *Tetsuwan Atom* (Astro Boy) and *Jungle Taitei* (Kimba the White Lion), acknowledged that manga's depictions of human bodies, objects, and basic dramatic or comic situations can be universally understood. "Comics," argues Tezuka, "regardless of what language they are printed in, are an important form of expression that crosses all national and cultural boundaries" (Tezuka 1983, 11). Clearly this works even if the manga is in Japanese, with the transparency of the visual layout still making it legible — not just in terms of literacy, but also in terms of emotional investment and enjoyment. As well-known U.S. artist and director Frank Miller has said of his delight in reading the "raw" Japanese manga *Kozure Ōkami*, "I was able to 'read' a hundred pages of a Japanese comic the other day without ever becoming confused. And it was written in Japanese! They rely totally on the visuals. They approach comics as a pure form more than American comic artists do" (quoted in Schodt 1983, 35).

Olson's idea of "narrative transparency" also has much in common with the recent work a number of scholars have been engaged in on the transnational movement of Japanese popular culture (Iwabuchi 2002a; Kenji 1997; Ueno 1999). These scholars argue that manga's popularity is a direct result of its emphasis on universally understood visuals and softened Japanese presence, making it easy to domesticate locally, ideas we will return to in more detail below. This understanding emphasizes manga's *globally* recognized qualities — and the ease of their absorption into any domestic market. Rather than claiming that manga is a particularly resilient Japanese aesthetic that can be dated back as far as the 1770s (Shimizu 1991), these scholars point to its modern history and the influence of American and European comic and animation styles on the manga form (Kinsella 2000), making manga itself a "convergent" media form, a Japanese adaptation of American and European practices.

Beyond this some argue that manga's "narrative transparency" is a deliberate strategy of the manga industry to ensure its success through overseas sales and adoption, as an American artist working at Kodansha for five years claimed: "World Comics, that's how the Japanese thought about it. They told me that their goal was to create a comics style that would be universal, the style of the 21st century" (quoted in Gravett 2004, 157). Informing the export of manga may therefore be the idea that, rather than just selling a product, Japan can also teach others how they too can creatively adapt various styles to produce a convergent cultural product such as manga (Iwabuchi 1998) — again, an idea we will return to below.

All of this means that manga, just like the American media texts that Olson describes, "seem familiar regardless of their origin [and] seem a part of one's own culture, even though they have been crafted elsewhere" (Olson 2004, 120). While our discussion here does not follow Olson's methodology of a reception study, Olson's idea of "narrative transparency" still provides a useful framework for understanding the global appeal of manga. Just as "American media do not so much encode media as become (or function as) myths themselves" (Olson 2004, 125), so too does manga reduce myths to recombinant elements, or what Olson terms "mythotypes" (Olson 2004, 126), that transcend cultural specificities. This is the way in which manga is internationally contextualized. We recognize these works of manga as "Japanese cultural products" but we can still fold them back into our own national cultures thanks to the distribution companies that deliver them to us, like Madman Entertainment.

THE SECOND STAGE OF FLOW

In many ways manga, and its more popular cousin anime, have become ideal commodities within today's global capitalism, bringing together important production techniques, marketing strategies, and cultural practices to allow manga to apparently go anywhere and tell any story, from manga versions of the works of William Shakespeare being sold in the United Kingdom to manga business manuals in the United States. As noted above, this has lead a number of scholars (including Allison 2000; Iwabuchi 1998, 2002a and 2002b; Sato 1997; Ueno 1999) to analyze the transnational movement of Japanese popular culture and, in dealing with the key cultural and economic dimensions of this flow, two key propositions have emerged. The first is that the worldwide dissemination of Japanese media marks a new form of cultural imperialism or "soft power" from Japan. The other is that these products are already somewhat hybridized and therefore familiar to a globally dispersed audience rather than representing or promoting a unitary idea of "the Japanese lifestyle" or ideals. This group argues that it is this lack of a clearly identifiable Japaneseness in terms of national, racial, or ethnic markers that undercuts the reconstruction of Japanese national/cultural identity.

Ultimately, then, the two key characteristics of manga's transnationalism seem to be its textual malleability and its financing, production, and distribution by national, multinational, and transnational organizations. This brings us to the second stage in the flow of manga: the adoption/adaptation of manga by local cultures — that is, the production of OEL manga.

Comparing the export strategies of Japanese audiovisual companies during the 1990s, Koichi Iwabuchi (1998; 2002a; 2002b) has identified three methods that Japanese cultural industries use to export cultural goods.

Sony's globalization of its Walkman product demonstrates the first method of creating standardized global products that appeal to different domestic markets. A second process is demonstrated in the way Japan's music industry "indigenizes" or assimilates foreign cultural forms into its domestic culture. Rather than exporting Japanese goods directly to the Asian market, he argues, the Japanese music industry has exported the process of successfully indigenizing foreign popular culture to create appealing local versions. This approach is not uniquely Japanese, and can be seen in many other countries where the format of a television franchise like *Big Brother* or the *Idol* series (*American Idol*, Britain's *Pop Idol*, et al.) is indigenized by using local contestants. The third process is to denationalize the product, referred to by the Japanese term *mu-kokuseki* (literally meaning "the absence of nationality"), which describes the process of removing the Japanese cultural presence from export products. We can identify each of these three processes named by Iwabuchi — globalization, indigenization, and denationalization — as enabling this second stage in the flow of manga (the adaptation/adoption of manga by local cultures) to come into being.

Globalization

Japanese cultural industries have a strong history of successfully globalizing their goods. Sony's globalization of the Walkman (originally released in 1979) demonstrated the process of creating standardized global products that appeal to different domestic markets. Asu Aksoy and Kevin Robins refer to this process as a Sony globalization strategy that "transcends vestigial national differences . . . to create standardized global markets, whilst remaining sensitive to the peculiarities of local markets and differentiated consumer segments" (1992, 18). The success of Sony's Walkman as a standardized global product that gains global relevance through marketing campaigns tailored to appeal to different domestic markets has since been applied to manga. The standardization of the manga style was established principally through a series of instructional drawing books called *How to Draw Manga*. These books, originally published in Japan, have been translated into a number of languages including English. Published since 1999 with over forty volumes in print, they cover areas such as giant robots, superdeformed characters, animals, and costumes, as well as *shōjo* (young female) and *bishōnen* (beautiful boy) characters. The series presents a simple, straightforward, and comprehensive breakdown of the manga style, effectively standardizing the manga approach to comics creation as a tool kit of drawing that anyone could use. While the manga art is far more diverse and complex than the style portrayed in the volumes of these series, the success of the *How to Draw Manga* books is in sidelining the less mainstream approaches and reinforcing what have become the standard tropes of the manga style for a global audience — the large eyes of shōjo characters, the feminine features of bishōnen, and so on.

As well as establishing a global formula for manga, the series is also significant in that it continues to be published by Japanese companies: the English-language volumes in the series were coproduced by the original Japanese publisher, Graphic-sha, and two other Japanese companies, Japanime and Japan Publications Trading. What makes the *How to Draw Manga* series so important in the flow of manga, then, is its implication that Japanese cultural industries are exporting not simply a *product* but the *process* of making a product. As Iwabuchi has argued, Japanese cultural industries have long preferred to export "the process of indigenization of the foreign" (Iwabuchi 1998, 171) and this will become more significant in the latter stages of manga's transnational flows, identified below.

Indigenization

The second important characteristic in the export strategy of Japanese cultural industries is the belief that other Asian countries can learn from Japan's knowledge of indigenizing foreign popular culture (Iwabuchi 2002a). Here, the hybridity of manga and anime — hybridity in this case referring to the processes whereby distinctive Japanese aesthetics and Western cultural forms and values coexist and are appreciated by Japanese and Western audiences — is recuperated as part of the Japanese approach to the indigenization of foreign culture.

Disney comics and animation were widely distributed and screened in Japan during and after its postwar occupation by the United States (Ono 1983), and consequently heavily influenced many elements of the manga style, such as the large eyes and cute features of characters like Astro Boy. Osamu Tezuka, one of the earliest and most famous pioneers of manga, openly acknowledged the strong influence that United States' animators — such as Walt Disney and Max Fleischer — had on his work (Schodt 1983, 63). Indeed, in his forward to Schodt's book, Tezuka writes, "The Japanese comics industry first began to show signs of heating up . . . after World War II. Western comics were imported by the bushelful, and had a tremendous impact" (Tezuka, in Schodt 1983, 11). By the mid-1960s, manga and anime had become one of the most successful forms of domestic entertainment in Japan so that popular titles, such as *Doraemon* and *Sazae san* challenged the appeal of Disney and other U.S. animation. The eclipsing of imported products by locally produced versions encouraged Japanese cultural industries to feel confident that it would be through exporting "the process of indigenization of the foreign (West) rather than the export of the product per se" (Iwabuchi 1998, 171) that they could capture the attention of international consumers.

For example, Sony Entertainment and other Japanese music industries conducted talent quests in Asia in the early 1990s. In this regard, Iwabuchi (1998, 170–73) notes that the strategy for developing a pop idol system in Asia did not involve Japanese cultural industries exporting Japanese musicians or pop music, but saw them distributing a "process whereby local contestants and audiences can appropriate and consume products of foreign origin." Iwabuchi (1998) has claimed that a dynamic process of indigenization within Asian media centers had flowed from Japan's own experience with indigenizing foreign cultures. Karaoke would be a further example of how Japanese interests developed and exported a know-how that allowed foreign songs to be reproduced with local flavor while the dissemination of local products was also enhanced.

This carries over to the adaptation of Western properties as well. *Monthly Shōnen Magazine*, for example, included the Japanese version of Spider-Man by Ryoichi Ikegami for nearly two years, from January 1970 to September 1971 (with Ikegami going on to produce Crying Freeman, Sanctuary, and *Mai.*) Spider-Man ran for thirteen story arcs and, as part of the transnational movement of manga, was later repackaged and reexported to American audiences by Marvel Comics (who had licensed their character to *Shōnen Magazine* twenty-six years earlier), though, as Steve Saffel notes, 1997's *Spider-Man: The Manga* "preceded the explosion of manga on the American scene, so it only lasted for 31 issues" (2007, 76).

Ikegami's Spider-Man (Ikegami was later joined by writer Kazumasa Hirai after the conclusion of the sixth story arc) remains a perfect example of how Japan indigenized foreign culture. It was darker, more sexual, and more violent than its American counterpart while still retaining all of the basics of the Spider-Man mythos, including the costume; notes Staffel, "Yu Komori, a high school student, was bitten by a radioactive spider and thus was granted his spider-abilities. He had an Aunt Mei, and faced Japanese versions of classic villains such as Electro and the Lizard" (2007, 76). More recently, another manga version has appeared — Akira Yamanaka's *Spider-Man J*, which has again been exported to the West as part of Marvel's 104-page anthology *Spider-Man Family* (February 2007) translated by Zeb Wells and Yuko Fakami.

Japan's ability to indigenize was again confirmed in 2001 when the Japan Foundation's Asia Centre opened a Tokyo exhibition, *Asia in Comics: Where Are We Going?* The original artwork of eleven comic artists in East Asia (including Japan) was featured, and in his exhibition catalog essay Hosogaya Atsushi (2001) praises the importance of Japan's manga industry in influencing Asian artists. More particularly, he indicates that one aim of the exhibition has been to raise awareness in Japan of the continuities and differences in comic art in the region, with Atsushi attaching importance to the ability of Japan's manga industry to provide schools to teach the process of appropriating products of foreign origin — like manga and anime — not merely exporting and consuming manga and anime per se.

However, Atsushi also acknowledges the risk that Japan might be marginalized by other Asian comic book industries, owing to its failure to realize the independence and modernity of the industry elsewhere in Asia. He mentions the Manga Summits that have been held both in Japan and internationally since 1996 as possible spaces for bringing together artists and industry personnel — spaces where the possibilities and difficulties facing exporters of Japanese cultural goods can be thrown into high relief — and warns that the general public in Japan still has very little knowledge of Asian comics. As examples, he mentions the restrictions on expression in Seoul, Korea, the challenges of educating public comic artists in Taipei, Taiwan, and the difficulties facing the integration of new media in Hong Kong, and scorns the industry's easy assumption that Japan's domestication of U.S. comic book influences might provide a useful model that can be automatically adopted in other Asian countries.

That said, within the globalization of manga, we can see that its indigenization *has* progressed smoothly. Through transnational companies such as Tokyopop, the drawing of manga has flourished and there is now talent outside of Japan that is strong enough to employ the lessons learned through the standardized manga system and to begin producing its own OEL manga. A recent example would be Tokyopop's *Jim Henson's Return to Labyrinth* (August 2006), the first in a projected series by Jake T. Forbes (writer) and Chris Lie (artist, with covers by Kouyu Shurei). It is very much a manga hybrid in that it is a sequel to a Western fantasy film, Jim Henson's *Labyrinth* (1986), rendered in a manga style. The story focuses on Toby (a character from the film who was stolen when he was just a baby by the goblin king Jareth) as he returns to the world of the labyrinth as an adolescent and thereby moves one step closer to taking his place as Jareth's heir. The text is an interesting example, then, because part of its diegesis is about appropriation and hybridity — Toby's appropriation (and reappropriation) by Jareth to become the human/goblin hybrid — the goblin king.

While the human characters and many of the goblins are rendered in a manga style (Toby, and especially Jareth, would seem to follow the bishonen form of manga) the other denizens of the labyrinth that appear toward the end of the first volume — particularly Hoggle, Ludo, and Sir Didymus — are more "literal" depictions of their filmic counterparts, fine-line representations that often seem stylistically at odds with that of the other characters. The result is an unusual hybrid in which the tools of manga are appropriated by a Western property (clearly branded as *Jim Henson's Labyrinth*) and deployed when the story requires them (Toby's routine in the real world, for example, but not the depiction of Sir Didymus at the ball). It is also a formula Tokypop clearly intends to capitalize on given their success with *Star Trek* manga and a manga *Garthim Wars* prequel to Henson's other fantasy film of the 1908s, *The Dark Crystal* (1982)

Denationalization

The third important characteristic of the export strategy of Japanese cultural industries is the denationalization of content (Iwabuchi 2002a). Once again, this assists in the reception of manga by global audiences by allowing them to engage with the text through their own particular perspectives and fantasies. Manga such as *Tetsuwan Atom* (Astro Boy) and *Hagane no Renkinjutsushi* (Fullmetal Alchemist), for example, "speak" in the different national languages of the markets into which they are translated. The visual nature of manga allows for easy translation, especially now that the right-to-left style of reading manga has been globally accepted (meaning artwork does not have to be "flopped" — printed in reverse — for translation). Moreover, the features of the manga style (big eyes and exaggerated body proportions that often mix a number of racial, cultural, and gender characteristics) make many manga characters racially, ethnically, and often sexually indeterminate.

Japanese manga artists can easily soften, erase, or replace a character's Japaneseness. The well-known manga and anime artist Mamoru Oshii, for example, suggests that artists like himself often prefer to model attractive characters on ideal Western bodies rather than "realistic" Japanese ones (Oshii et al. 1996). Consequently, many characters in Japanese manga may appear as non-Japanese, with blonde hair, as in *Bishōjo Senshi* (Sailor Moon); large eyes, as in *Pokemon*; and fantasy uniforms, as in *Dragon Ball Z*. This can also be seen in computer games developed in Japan. Mario, in the popular computer game *Super Mario Brothers*, may have an Italian name and appearance but is still rendered in a recognizable manga style at its most crude — with big eyes and a small mouth. For analysts like Iwabuchi (1998), this form of cultural shifting (i.e., the Japanese make a globally recognisable character, like Mario by appropriating Italian-ness rather than drawing upon their own cultural signifiers) is a crucial factor in explaining both the international success of manga and its position within the larger Japanese anime industry's export philosophy.

We noted earlier that manga is most often subordinated to anime in the West, that in most cases it forms part of the merchandising flow around a particular anime product. Therefore it becomes important to briefly consider how the commercial forces responsible for financing and distributing anime impact on the denationalization of manga.

This first became significant during the 1960s, when U.S. television broadcast many of the same anime as did Japan (including the *Astro Boy* series and *Gigantor*), suggesting a developing relationship between Japanese producers and U.S. distributors. Since then, Western companies and markets have become increasingly important in the globalization of anime product. During the 1980s, for example, French and Japanese animation companies coproduced a number of successful television animation series, including *Ulyssé 31/Uchu Densetsu Ulyssés XXXI* (Ulysses 31; 1981) and *Les Mystérieuses Cités d'Or/Taiyo No Ko Esteban* (The Mysterious Cities of Gold; 1982). From the 1990s on, Western (principally U.S.-based) companies increased their financing and worldwide distribution of anime, with *Ghost in the Shell* (1995) being partially financed by the U.S.-based anime distributor Manga Entertainment, and screened simultaneously in Japan, the United States, and the United Kingdom. In 1996, Buena Vista International (Disney's worldwide distribution company) undertook the worldwide distribution of Hayao Miyazaki's theatrical anime *Mononoke Hime* (Princess Mononoke) and gained the worldwide rights to distribute other anime from the Tokuma Shoten media group (parent company of Studio Ghibli, which produces Miyazaki's anime; see Pollack 1996) while in November 1999, Warner Brothers released *Pokemon the Movie: Mewtwo Strikes Back* to 3,043 theaters in the United States, making it the highest-grossing anime in U.S. history by generating a total box office taking of US$85,744,662 ("Anime," 2003). Most recently, Hollywood movie companies have acquired the rights to a number of manga and anime titles; Twentieth Century Fox produced a live-action version of *Dragon Ball*, Sony Pictures Entertainment produced a digitally animated movie of *Astro Boy* and Warner Brothers has the rights to *Akira*.

We can see the emergence of *Shōnen Weekly* in the West and the cross-licensing and cofunding relation between Japanese and international publishers such as Tokyopop as evidence that the manga industry is similarly seeking out the same distribution and coproduction opportunities of its stronger anime cousin. Just as the increasing cofinancing of anime from transnational and multinational companies — such as Buena Vista International or Manga Entertainment — reveals a tightly woven network of multinational investment in anime, so too does the sale of anime's licensing and distribution rights to foreign distributors, which increasingly includes the manga rights as part of this merchandising flow, play an increasingly significant role in Japan's anime and manga industry; *Pokemon, Naruto* and *Death Note*, for example, have all had their anime product accompanied by manga as part of a coordinated merchandising rollout.

Aside from positioning manga within this commercial flow, the more significant part of the influence of these commercial forces is in the growing denationalization of works of manga that can become standardized global icons, like *Astro Boy* or *Pokemon*. These products can be promoted by marketing campaigns and easily appropriated by audiences to become an appealing product in any market. Through this process, manga is placed within a familiar environment and becomes an everyday practice; just as you play with Naruto action figures, build Evangelion model kits and wear Death Note hoodies, so too will you read the manga that preceded the anime.

OEL MANGA IN AUSTRALIA

While the first stage of manga flow in Australia mirrors American patterns of distribution and market penetration, there have been far fewer OEL manga produced as part of this second stage of the flow in Australia than in America. Of course, part of this can be accounted for by the size of the market, but it does point to that fact that manga has yet to truly enter the Australian mainstream in the way that it has in the United Kingdom and United States. That said, a small group of Australian female artists have achieved global recognition and popularity, and in their work we can see some indication of what Australian OEL manga may look like in the future.

In describing the plot of her manga *The Dreaming*, Hong Kong-born Australian resident Queenie Chan comments, "[The story] includes some native Australian myths in it, especially in regard to the bush. The 'Australian' part is especially important to me, not least because I'm an Australian, but because it's something fresh and hasn't been done in manga before." (quoted in Kean 2005). The "something fresh" that Chan injects into her manga goes beyond simply rejuvenating the tired subgenre of the haunted house story that her narrative revolves around to symbolize the increasingly prominent role young female Australian manga artists have in defining and popularizing global manga.

Madeline Rosca provides further evidence of the broadening of manga's global relevance through the involvement of Western manga artists. Rosca was a finalist in the first International Manga Award (in 2007) with her manga *Hollow Fields*. (The heavily promoted and reported-upon International Manga Award was designed by then Japanese the then foreign minister Taro Aso to recognize the contribution of non-Japanese manga artists to the development of manga.) Rosca's placement in the award finals has helped to firmly place Australia on the map of manga creativity.

In addition to the work of these two commercial artists, female artists have also been central to the development of Australia's *dojinshi* (fan-publishing) scene that has thrived in conventions such as Manifest (http://www.manifest.org.au) and Doujicon (http://doujicon.oztaku.com). Prominent female dojinshi artists such as Komala Singh have been central to establishing the self-produced manga anthology scene, such as her *Moshi Moshi* manga anthology (2000–5), which paved the way for today's vibrant manga anthologies such as Avi Bernshaw and Kenneth Chan's ongoing *OzTAKU* (2003–).

These professional and amateur artists show the way forward for the Australian OEL manga scene — with a hybrid style drawing upon Western and Japanese sources, Chan's *The Dreaming* draws inspiration from a global horror/supernatural canon: the boardinghouse in the bush evokes Australian director Peter Weir's *Picnic at Hanging Rock* (1975); supernatural forces connected to a past violence suggest Japan's *Ringu* and *Ju-on* series; the possession of innocent youth that reminds one of the U.S films *The Exorcist* (dir. William Friedkin, 1973) and *The Shining* (dir. Stanley Kubrick, 1980); and a truly global outlook reaching out to overseas publishers and audience (Chan and Rosca are both published through U.S.-based publishers — TokyoPop and Seven Seas, respectively).

The success of these two Australian female manga artists (Chan's *The Dreaming* has gone on to become one of TokyoPop's best-selling titles) has placed them at the forefront of innovative OEL manga. Their work brings into focus the new role of globally dispersed artists rejuvenating the manga form and the role Australia plays in this phenomenon, the changes to the nature of manga as it accommodates non-Japanese artists with new stories to tell, and the role of young female artists in the adaptation and adoption of manga.

CONCLUSIONS

The first and second stages in the flow of manga do seem to meet the three conditions outlined by Iwabuchi in relation to the export of Japanese cultural products. Most observers would acknowledge that the *How To Draw Manga* volumes have become one of the most popular products of manga's global market and have effectively standardized manga aesthetics for a global amateur manga-drawing community, with the export of this model of manga style providing a framework within which a number of stories and topics can be "indiginized" for a global audience through OEL manga, including that of *Star Trek* and *Hamlet*. The increasing number of these indigenized titles further suggests that manga is becoming part of a "perfect" global commodity — being both transnational and, as a result, increasingly denationalized.

The argument regarding manga's Japaneseness (or lack of it) opens up a space to consider what local industries are actually doing with the comic form. One reading of the removal of Japaneseness seems to declare that because manga characters don't look Japanese, any cultural or lifestyle association is suspect because it is conveyed through a body that has a softened Japanese cultural presence (looking more Caucasian than Japanese). However, we would question whether it is helpful to reduce the issue of cultural influence to such a superficial level as this. Such critiques tend to minimize the significance of the fan experience of manga and overlook the examples of foreigners, such as Fredrik Schodt (1996), who have developed a sophisticated understanding of manga's place within Japan while avoiding the heavily stereotyped image of Japan that can dominate some Western discourses around manga. For instance, Schodt (1996, 59–62) places the contested Caucasian or Japanese interpretation of manga bodies within specific historical and cultural contexts. Schott is definitely aware of the problems associated with the positioning of the Japaneseness of manga, but also acknowledges manga's lack of Japaneseness in its domesticated form:

> There is an element of risk in promoting manga, as there is no guarantee foreigners will get a better impression of Japan from reading them. The material foreigners prefer, moreover, may not be what is preferred in Japan, and it may be interpreted differently. . . . however, manga will give a far truer picture of Japan, warts and all, than "highbrow" tea ceremony or Zen ever could. As a form of popular culture, comics of all nations tend to be tightly woven with local culture and thought. In translation, manga — especially — can be both a medium of entertainment and a Rosetta stone for mutual understanding. (1996, 340)

This idea of manga in translation is one that encourages recognition of the competing and mutual engagements that exist within manga flows today, both in America and Australia.

Perhaps most importantly, what is at the heart of these transnational manga flows is the increasingly important role Asia will play in the new cultural world order, something that is perhaps felt even more keenly in Australia. The hybridity of manga — where distinctive Japanese aesthetics and Western cultural forms and values coexist and are appreciated by both Japanese and Western audiences — may be recuperated as part of a global approach to the indigenization of foreign culture. As a commercial product, manga increasingly becomes denationalized as non-Japanese production, distribution, and adoption/adaptation increases — through, for instance, publisher Tokyopop and the OEL manga of Queenie Chan. However, debate will certainly continue within fan cultures regarding the status and value of authentic Japanese manga compared to its OEL iterations and around its subordinate role to anime.

In the meantime, any concerns Japan may have with the future of the cultural ownership of manga will need to be addressed by developing new ways to accommodate such hybridity. Such moves can already be seen as recently as July 2007, when the Japanese government established the International Manga Award to recognize the contribution foreign manga artists are making to manga's development. That a Tasmanian-based manga artist Madeline

Rosca was named as a finalist in these awards confirms that Australia's place in these transnational manga flows will be something to watch in the future.

Notes

Thanks to Tim Anderson and Madman Entertainment for their assistance with this chapter. Thanks also to the staff of Area 52 and the Dymocks bookshop in Hobart, Tasmania; and the staffs of the Comics Etc., Ace Comics and Games, Borders, and Dymocks bookshops in Brisbane, Australia.

1. This is not true of all of the West. Italy, Spain and France, for example, have been translating and publishing their own manga for the past four decades.
2. In Japan, the term "otaku" commonly refers to someone with an obsessive interest in any area, for example, cars, video games and so on. Within the West "otaku" has been associated with fans of manga and anime where the term means more than simply being up-to-date or knowledgeable, but also valuing the Japanese-ness of these texts.
3. Tankōbon are collected volumes of comics.

References

Aksoy, Asu, and Kevin Robins (1992). "Hollywood for the 21st Century: Global Competition for Critical Mass in Image Markets." *Cambridge Journal of Economics* 16: 1–22.

Allison, Anne (2000). "A Challenge to Hollywood? Japanese Character Goods Hit the US." *Japanese studies* 20(1): 67–88.

"Anime" (2003, May). Box Office Mojo, http://www.boxofficemojo.com/genres/anime.htm.

Atsushi, Hosogaya (2001). "Comic Exchanges between Asia and Japan: Past and Future." In *Asia in Comics: Where Are We Going?* (exhibition catalog), 50–51. Tokyo: Japan Foundation Asia Center.

Bhabha, Homi K. (1994). *The Location of Culture*. London: Routledge.

Gravett, Paul. (2004). *Manga: Sixty Years of Japanese Comics*. London: Laurence King Publishing.

Iwabuchi, Koichi (1998). "Marketing 'Japan': Japanese Cultural Presence under a Global Gaze." *Japanese Studies* 18(2): 165–80.

—— (2002a). *Recentering Globalization: Popular Culture and Japanese Transnationalism*. Durham, NC: Duke University Press.

—— (2002b). "'Soft" Nationalism and Narcissism: Japanese Popular Culture Goes Global." *Asian Studies Review* 26(4): 447–68.

Kean, Benjamin Ong Pang (2005). "Queenie Chan on *The Dreaming*". Tokyo Pop, http://www.tokyopop.com/Robofish/tp_article/286686.html.

Kinsella, Sharon (2000). *Adult Manga: Culture and Power in Contemporary Japanese Society*. Honolulu: University of Hawaii Press.

McCarthy, Helen (2006). *500 Manga Heroes and Villains*. London: Chrysalis Books.

Olson, Scott Robert (2004). "Hollywood Planet: Global Media and the Competitive Advantage of Narrative Transparency." In *The Television Studies Reader*, eds Annette Hill and Robert C. Allen, 111–29. London: Routledge.

Ono, Kosei (1983). Disney and the Japanese. *Look Japan*, 6–12.

Oshii, Mamoru, Kazunori Ito, Toshiya Ueno (1996, Vol. 28, Iss. 9). "Eiga to wa jitsu wa animeshon data" [Film was actually a form of animation]. *Yuriika*, 50–81.

Pollack, Andrew (1996, July 24). "Disney in Pact for Films of Top Animator in Japan." *New York Times.*

Saffel, Steve (2007). *Spider-Man: The Icon.* London: Titan Books.

Sato, Kenji (1997). "More Animated than Life: A Critical Overview of Japanese Animated Films." *Japan Echo* 24(5): 50–53.

Schodt, Frederik L. (1983). *Manga! Manga! The World of Japanese Comics.* New York: Kodansha International.

—— (1996). *Dreamland Japan: Writings on Modern Manga.* Berkeley, CA: Stone Bridge Press.

Shimizu, Isao (1991). *Manga no Rekishi (The History of Manga),* Iwanami Shoten, Tokyo.

Tezuka, Osamu (1983). "Foreword." In Fredrik L. Schodt, *Manga! Manga! The World of Japanese Comics,* 10–11. New York: Kodansha International.

Tsutsui, William (2004). *Godzilla On My Mind: Fifty Years of the King of Monsters.* New York: Palgrave Macmillan.

Ueno, Toshiya (1999). "Techno-Orientalism and Media-Tribalism: On Japanese Animation and Rave Culture." *Third text* 47: 95–106.

Suggested Manga Reading

Chan, Queenie (2005). *The Dreaming.* Los Angeles: Tokyopop.

Rosca, Madeline (2007). *Hollow Fields.* Los Angeles: Seven Seas Entertainment.

15

Manga in Europe: A Short Study of Market and Fandom

Jean-Marie Bouissou, Marco Pellitteri, and Bernd Dolle-Weinkauff with Ariane Beldi

This chapter is a collective work by the Manga Network, an international study group comprising academics and PhD students.[1] This group was launched in 2006 by Jean-Marie Bouissou, a French Japanologist; Bernd Dolle-Weinkauff, a German comics specialist; and Marco Pellitteri, an Italian sociologist and manga specialist, with the help of the Japan Foundation. The Manga Network has held international conferences on manga and Japanese popular culture in Paris in 2007 and 2008.

For this chapter, Bouissou, Dolle-Weinkauff, and Pellitteri have been joined by Ariane Beldi, a Swiss PhD student at the University of Geneva. Beldi wrote the "Survey Method" section, while Pellitteri wrote "The Manga Market in Europe Today." The four authors then joined hands for "An Analysis of Core Manga Fandom in France, Italy, Germany, and Switzerland."

THE MANGA MARKET IN EUROPE TODAY

The manga market abroad is thriving: in 2005, Asia (excepting Japan) comprised 42 percent of it, the United States 36 percent, and the rest of the world 22 percent (Japan External Trade Organization, 2005).[2] What is not clear, in these percentages, is the impact of manga according to such variables as the population's size and the volume of the actual manga readership basis in single countries, or levels of income. With more circumstantial data it would be possible to realize better the impact of manga in each nation,[3] especially in Europe, where the market comprises many countries, each one with its own manga culture and history.

Italy used to be the largest manga market in Europe, but official sales figures are not made public. One of the few verifiable facts is that in 2005, 58 percent of the about 2,800 comics titles published were manga and Korean *manhwa* (1,624; see Zaccagnino and Contrari 2007, 2).[4] The all-time bestselling manga is the *Dragon Ball* deluxe edition, with each issue having sold about 150,000 copies by the end of the 1990s; later best-sellers — *Inu Yasha* and *One Piece* — sold no more than 75,000 copies per volume, partly because there is a larger range of general manga titles available with a wider appeal. Ten houses publish manga in Italy: Dinyt, D/Visual, and Shin Vision (only manga); Star Comics, Flashbook, Hazard (mainly manga); and Coconino Press, Panini, Kappa, and Play Press (manga among other kinds of comics). Occasionally also publishers like Einaudi, Mondadori, or Rizzoli, which normally do not deal with manga, publish some titles.

France used to lag behind Italy: until 2000, the total number of new manga titles published each year in Italy was five times higher than in France. But between 2000 and 2008, the supply of new manga titles in France increased by 567 percent, from 227 to 1288 (plus 98 new manhwa titles). In 2008, manga accounted for 35.8% of the new comics titles published in France, and manga grabbed 37% of the French comics market, by selling 12.3 million books sold for a value of more than 160 million euros (about 210 millions US $) Kishimoto Masashi's *Naruto* was the biggest manga best-seller, with 220,000 copies sold for each of its six new volumes. This now maybe makes France the largest European manga market (Rattier 2000, 2008).

The structure of the French manga publishing business is unique. From 1988 to 2004, no less than thirty-seven publishing houses entered the field;[6] 20 percent of these either closed down or left the manga business. Most of them were started by manga fans — among them people who had accumulated business school diplomas and some experience in bookstores and/or fanzines — whereas traditional publishing houses shunned manga. The most famous "first generation" manga publishing houses are Glénat, Tonkam, Delcourt, and Soleil.[7] Not surprisingly, perhaps, as soon as manga proved to be profitable, well-known companies such as Hachette, Dargaud, Casterman, Flammarion, Le Seuil, and Philippe Picquier entered the market. At the same time, new, smaller publishers specializing in manga, such as Imho and Cornelius, continued to emerge and claimed their share of the pie.

Today Germany is the third and arguably most interesting European market for manga (Dolle-Weinkauff 2006). Due to the lack of strong local production there, imported Japanese comics account for about 70 percent of all comics sold. A peculiar feature is that Germany's manga audience is mostly female, whereas in other countries readership is more evenly divided between the sexes. Also, the lack of polemics on manga's futility or (im) morality has allowed an almost undisturbed increase of sales. In ten years (1997–2006), the total revenue in manga sales rose exponentially from three to seventy million euros. The best-sellers are *Dragon Ball, Bishôjo senshi* (Sailor Moon), *Inu Yasha,* and *Case Closed: Meitantei Conan (Detective Conan).* The latter two sold one million copies each in 2005; however, *Dragon Ball* beat both with six million copies between 1997 and 2006, and still does well. Today the main publishers active on the German market are Carlsen (Germany), Egmont (Denmark), Panini (Italy) and Tokyopop (head-quartered in Hamburg).

In Spain, since the 1990s, the most important manga publishers are Norma Editorial, Glénat España, Planeta DeAgostini, Mangaline, Ivrea, and Selecta. At first, they made a strategic marketing mistake — this also happened in Germany and the United States — by reprinting manga in traditional comics book format and selling it at high prices (Rodriguez de León 2005). The market stagnated at a very low level, forcing the publishers to stop publication. Only since works of manga have been published in lower-priced *tankōbon* (soft covered books in small format) have it gained commercial success.

Belgium is a multilingual country with a strong local tradition of *bande dessinée* as the home of Hergé's famed *Tintin* series.[8] Although figures are unavailable, circumstantial evidence — even a simple look at the book-stores — clearly shows that the manga market has been steadily growing since the late 1990s. All major manga publishers are distributed in Belgium, with Glénat, Dargaud, and Casterman enjoying the advantage of having local roots in Wallonia. The range of titles on offer is much wider for French-speaking fans than for Flemish ones, if only because more manga are now translated into French than any other European language. In a country with a rich comics culture, most titles aim at general, sophisticated audiences — like Tezuka Osamu's *Buddha,* Urasawa Naoki's *Monster,* and the work of Taniguchi Jirô.

Manga was unintentionally introduced in Russia in the 1980s by some foreign diplomats who visited Japan and took home copies of some manga works (Alaniz 2005). The first fans were the children of employees at the diplomatic local offices. However, the "market" has been limited to hand-to-hand circulation of manga among a small circle of fans for twenty years, until it exploded at the turn of the twenty-first century, above all thanks to *anime* (Japnese animation) on TV and DVD, as elsewhere.[9] Similarly to what hap-pened in the United States (Leonard 2005), manga has grown from the grass roots, from the fans — at first, thanks to underground imports and home-made copies, and then with professional publishers. The very first manga officially published was *Ranma ½,* by local venture Sakura Press in 2005.

In Poland the comics have been struggling for years, between bad reputation and censorship. Nowadays, such internationally known Polish artists as Grzegrorz Rosinski, author of the *Thorgal* saga, sell very well.[10] At present, European comics account for 20 percent of the Polish market, but manga, which entered it in 2005, has a 70 percent share (Pasamonik 2005). This success owes much to Japanese entrepreneurs Yasuda Shin and Watanuki Ken'ichirō, who started two Japanese-Polish publishing ventures — respectively Japonica Polonica Fantastica, and Waneko. They have been joined by the Danish Egmont, which offers about one-half of Poland's manga catalog.

The trend of Japanese publishers entering the market — a process begun in the United States in the 1980s — has also been at work elsewhere in Europe. For example, Gō Nagai's Dynamic Planning created Dynamic Italia and Dynamic Vision in France as direct subsidiaries. However, because of the vigor of the locally generated manga business, the Japanese publishers had little success except in Germany, thanks to Tokyopop's Hamburg headquarters and entrepreneurial strength.

Several new trends have emerged in the European market since the turn of the twenty-first century, and manga has gained acceptance, and even praise. Since 2003, manga has regularly won prizes at France's Festival d'Angoulême;[11] for example, Mizuki Shigeru's *NonNonBā* (*NonNonBā to ore*) won the Best Series Award in 2007. And manga genres have evolved. In France, Italy, and Germany some locally produced material has been dubbed *Euromanga* (Pellitteri, 2006, 2008). In 2006, Dargaud launched *Cosmo*, a line of comics in which authors blend styles from bande dessinée, American comics, and manga (Pasamonik 2006). Also, as the first generation of fans is now in their thirties,[12] manga culture is becoming deeper and more refined. Manga for teenagers still provides the bulk of the best-selling series, but increasingly it is yielding ground to an ever-expanding range of serious and sophisticated series for adult, demanding readers who appreciate the deluxe edition of Tezuka's *Buddha*, the austere *Au temps de Bōchan* (*Bōchan no jidai*) by Taniguchi (Le Seuil),[13] and Hiroshi Hirata's *Satsuma* (*Satsuma gishi den*), which Mishima Yukio himself praised to the skies (Delcourt). Although the teenage base remains all-important, the European manga fandom now extends to sophisticated adult readers who make it much stronger, as shown by the European survey conducted in 2006–7 by the Manga Network.

AN ANALYSIS OF CORE MANGA FANDOM IN FRANCE, ITALY, GERMANY, AND SWITZERLAND

The 2006–7 Survey by the Manga Network

In 2006–7, the four authors of this chapter circulated a fifteen-page questionnaire in France, Germany, Italy, and Switzerland that covered social, cultural, psychological and economical aspects of manga fans' practices.[14]

Although the questionnaire used in each country was the same, the methods of collection and analysis varied. In France, the questionnaire was published in two ways: first, in 2006, as a Microsoft Word document to members of online manga forums; and second, in July 2007, to people attending the Japon Expo convention.[15] About 370 responses were submitted. In Italy (about 420 surveys) and Germany (about 340), the questionnaire was circulated online. In Switzerland, the questionnaire was published online using SurveyMonkey. com (http://www.surveymonkey.com); 76 people from the three linguistic regions (German, French, Italian) completed it.

The main biases of these modes of distributions are obvious. The statistic samples are neither random nor generally representative, but "auto-selected." The respondents stem from the most sophisticated and hard-core fans, those who spend time on online manga forums and/or go to conventions, and who are passionate enough to spend up to thirty minutes to complete a very detailed questionnaire. Younger readers may be underrepresented because the questionnaire was not designed for them.[16] Despite these biases, the results of the survey can be used for explorative/descriptive purpose. The following analysis, though, cannot be generalized to the vast universe of European manga fans. Nonetheless, it provides preliminary data that can form the basis of further research and will be followed by further enquiries.

The Sociology of Manga Fans

In France and Italy, the majority of the respondents were male (57 percent and 56.5 percent, respectively). The opposite is true in Germany, where 80 percent of the respondents were female, while in Switzerland this was 50 percent.[17] One possible explanation is that in the past Germany offered few comics for girls, so they have welcomed the rich offerings of *shōjo manga* (girls' manga). However, it should be stressed that in Italy and France, female respondents outnumbered male ones in the younger (or youngest) age groups. Furthermore, regardless of country, all female fans were more active participants in manga fandom. They regularly scored higher in almost every category: frequency of reading manga, manga-related activity on Internet, attending conventions, and cosplay[18]. Therefore, female readership is presently the most dynamic part of the European manga market.

The median age of the respondents was 20 in Switzerland, 20.5 in both Germany and France, and 22 in Italy. Respondents were divided into three socioeconomic categories: those still attending primary school (hereafter referred to as "schoolgoers"); those attending university or specialized/voca-tional schools (hereafter referred to as "students"); and those who were either working or looking for a full-time job (hereafter referred to as "young profes-sionals"). France and Italy shared similar statistics: respectively, 27.5 percent and 20.5 percent belonged to the schoolgoers' cohort; and 42 percent were students and 31 percent were young professionals in both countries.[19] On the other hand, in Germany, the younger, schoolgoers' cohort (39 percent) outnumbered those of students (20.5 percent) and young professionals (25.5 percent)[20] — like in Switzerland (40.5 percent, 33 percent, 26.5 percent). The explanation for this probably lies in the fact that Japanese TV series were aired in Germany later — not until the early 1990s, versus the 1970s in France and Italy: since almost all the fans in every country came to read manga after discovering *Goldorak, Candy*, and *Dragon Balls* on TV, it follows that the fandom would "automatically" be younger in the country where the big robot, the young damsel, and Sangokū arrived later. Another reason might be the fact that because of the relative weakness of the German comics culture in comparison to that of France and Italy, reading comics was mostly regarded by Germans as "for children only," whereas in France it was "Pour les jeunes de 7 à 77 ans."[21] However, whatever they are, those numbers probably underestimate the younger cohort, because of the biases in the poll.[22]

In regard to social position, as far as the survey permits a grasp of it,[23] a majority of the respondents were from the middle class. They were raised in a stable family and a rather affluent environment that allows for a postmaterialist consumption style and thus varied cultural consumptions. They were educated to the various uses of media, and had a medium-high education level conducive to interest for such "far away topics" as Asia or Japan. Those fans who were employed most often had white-collar jobs, often creative ones, and they were sometimes very well paid.

Here again, the manner of conducting the survey (via the Internet) and the length and complexity of the questionnaire have biases against the less affluent and less educated. This category appears more clearly in the Japon Expo part of the French Survey, where a profile made of low-income, broken-family, low-education-level and jobless respondents accounted for about 15 percent of the whole. Furthermore, many respondents did not answer questions about their parents' jobs or gave unclear answers[24] — a reluctance that most likely concealed a lower social status (although we can't, of course, be certain of this). However, what the survey reveals about the specific group of manga fans who answered it is far away from the long-held but now vanishing prejudice that has stigmatized Japanese comics and TV series as cheap entertainment for low-class, undereducated youngsters looking for escape from a depressing daily life.

How Did They Come to Read Manga?

In every country, Japanese TV series have by and large been the catalyst for the uptake of manga.[25] But manga didn't appear in a vacuum. Only 29.5 percent of the respondents said they had not been reading comics prior to the arrival of manga in their country. The others had all been reading either a "lot" or a "few" European or U.S. comics. These percentages reflect the existence of strong local traditions of comics creation and readership that contributed to the success of manga. However, in attracting these 29.5 percent new customers, the manga boom enlarged the comics market as a whole. At the same time, there is no doubt that manga encroached on traditional European and American comics' share, since the percentage of respondents who didn't read these comics anymore (51 percent) was larger by 21.5 points than the percentage of those who did not read them before discovering manga.

In every country, the manga-reading habit came at an early age: 12.5 percent of the respondents began before the age of ten, 44.5 percent between ages ten and fourteen, and 29 percent during their high school years. As the age of respondents increased, so did the age of the beginning of reading manga, but only slightly, since even the oldest respondents within the cohort under 25, who account for about 70 percent of the whole sample, were still in middle school when *Akira* — the first best-seller that opened Europe to paper manga after the wave of TV anime series — was translated in French, Italian, and German between 1989 and 1991.

Reading Habits and Practices

The respondents were avid readers, as far as their favorite material was concerned. On average, 26.5 percent of them indulged in their passion every day; 29 percent read manga three or four times a week, and 21.5 percent at least once a week; 75.5 percent said they would spend much more time reading manga if possible. Furthermore, they were educated enough to read manga in one or more foreign languages. Those who read manga in both their native tongue and English accounted for 51 percent of the respondents; in both France and Germany, up to 22 percent also "sometimes" read their favorite titles in Japanese. These numbers judge the too-common prejudice against manga fans as semi-illiterate for what it is.

Manga fans are also manga buyers: about three-quarters of the respondents in every country own more than 50 volumes apiece. This is not enough to characterize them as "collectors," but in both France and Switzerland, a significant percentage (16 percent and 19 percent) had amassed more than 500 volumes apiece. The biggest spender was a German fan who reported a collection of around 2,500 titles — more titles than had ever appeared in the German language to the time of our survey.

It should be noted that despite the defiance long aroused by manga among educators and parents, public libraries now play an important role in the dissemination of manga; in France 28 percent and in Germany and German-speaking Switzerland 37 percent borrow manga works from these institutions. These numbers, as well as the multiple experiences of several authors of this chapter with librarians wishing to acquire some competence in the field of manga, bear witness to the growing acceptance of this genre by the authorities, and even to a liking for it among the librarians. This is especially the case in Germany, where there have been few outcries against the "danger" or "vulgarity" of Japanese comics.

The Social Dimensions of Fandom

Manga is not just a reading format. According to our survey results, it also allows fans to interact with like-minded people. The social dimension of the fandom as a community seemed of great importance for a significant majority of the fans. This was perceptible in the high percentage of those who were introduced to manga through friends (39 percent) and those who actively introduce manga to their friends (66 percent). "Discussion with other fans" ranked high among the reasons why they liked manga, at least in Italy and France (32 percent). A large percentage of the respondents also discussed manga within their family circle "often" or "sometimes" (70.5 percent). Book sharing was also a prevalent form of social interaction — be it "always/often" or "sometimes" (78 percent); more than that, book sharing was also a matter of principle, since "manga is a pleasure that must be shared" (56 percent).

The Internet was of utmost importance. Of course, the way the survey was conducted induced an enormous bias, but even in the small part of the population sample that was handed the questionnaire in person,[26] 95 percent visited manga sites on the Web and 62.5 percent chatted in Web forums — that is, only 7 points less than those surveyed through the Internet. The Web was the place for getting information; chatting (72 percent of the respondents visited forums for that purpose, 48 percent of them as registered members); copying Japanimation or scanned manga series (73 percent); buying manga titles (50 percent); and accessing manga in foreign language through "scanlations" (65.5 percent).

Manga events were another place to share and, for some fans, to express themselves to others. An average of 64 percent of the respondents took part in manga conventions "often" or "sometimes," and 13.5 percent of them took part in cosplay events.

The respondents were definitely not lonely figures: 81 percent of the respondents shared their passion with other family members and 72 percent with their spouse or companion when part of a couple. A large majority (67 percent) of the respondents knew other fans at school or the workplace,[28] and almost all of those (86 percent) actively interacted with others who shared their passion. These results clearly show that manga — often criticized as a solitary, if not masturbatory, activity for *otaku*[29] confined to their rooms in escapist fantasy — is in fact a means for socialization and active interaction with others.

Furthermore, according to the respondents, manga reading reverberated to a significant degree upon their conduct and their state of mind — hence, their relationship to others. A whopping 89 percent of the respondents asserted that manga reading had a degree of influence upon their life (among them, 49 percent said "extremely" or "a lot"), and even more said it influenced their state of mind. According to the respondents, the influence of their favorite reading material is highly positive: owing to manga they encountered new friends (54 percent), felt less stressed (53.5 percent), felt more dynamic (52 percent), and had learned new values (32.5 percent). Whatever the degree of self-deception may have been in passing such judgments, even this fantasy could be considered as a positive effect of manga reading because, in the end, it made the manga fans more comfortable with themselves.

Motivations for Reading Manga: Escapism Is Not the End of the Story

As for motivations for reading manga, a commanding majority of the respondents claimed they were doing so because it gave them an escape from everyday life (67 percent), and because "it's fun and relieves stress" (42 percent) — whereas only a small minority (15 percent) appreciated manga because they felt it reflected their own problems and experiences.

These results broadly converge with the common image of manga as a literature of escapism and manga readers as people looking primarily for (supposedly cheap) entertainment. However, other findings showed that this was only half of the story, because a significant percentage of respondents (44.5 percent) felt that manga protagonists were "easy to identify oneself with," 36.5 percent thought that manga stories were able to encourage reflection about life and society, and 34 percent also stated that manga characters showed qualities that they as readers would like to have. However, this is not as paradoxical as it might seem. For one thing, fantastic manga stories often require a high degree of attention and seriousness from the reader, because of a complex narrative together with syncretistic associations of themes, figures, and objects coming from many different cultures. On the other hand, behind the fantastic facades, very realistic conflicts often appear. Manga fantasy frequently supplies the thrill within absolutely familiar and everyday conflict plots — a strategy which indeed increases the reader's interest.

The issue of motivations looks even more complex in the light of another set of questions that invited the respondents to compare manga and European comics. For that set, 41.5 percent of the respondents rated manga characters as "more emotionally attractive" than those of European comics rather than "more extraordinary" (33 percent).

As for gender, significantly more females than males feel this proximity with manga protagnists and familiarity with the plots. Obviously, this relates to the large number of shōnen (boys') and shōjo (girls') manga whose plot takes place in the familiar setting of school, and with the fact that shōjo manga are the only kind of comics (mostly) made by women for women. This shows clearly that the success of manga in Europe derives partly from the inability of European and American comics — mostly created by men and imbued with a "sophisticated and artistic" mentality appealing to an intellectual readership rather than a popular one, especially in France from the 1970s to the '90s (Bouissou 2008) — to address the concerns and please the peculiar sensitivity of the young female audience.

Comparison between manga and traditional comics revealed other significant aspects of the attraction to manga. The three cohorts of respondents unanimously praised manga drawing as "more dynamic" than that of traditional comics — with the older ones being less sanguine about its "beauty." More generally, manga was perceived as "dynamic" and "modern," whereas traditional comics were belittled as "more conservative" and — perhaps as a result — Japan itself looked "more modern" to the respondents than their own country. Thus, reading manga might be equated to "being modern and dynamic" while reading comics looked somewhat "uncool."

Other significant factors for the success of manga were linked to marketing strategy, beginning with the pace of publication. In France, whereas most comic series progress at the very frustrating pace of only one 56-page album per year (if not every two years), successful manga series are published at a steady pace of 250-page volumes every two or three months. The ability of manga to generate addiction to a bargain, especially since the advent in 1959 of the 250-page-plus weeklies, has been well-documented in Japan (Yokota 2006). In Europe, addiction was perceptible in the percentage of respondents who confess that the manga habit "is costly for me" (20 percent) and those who would like the publishers to accelerate the pace of publication (33 percent). It's clear that the success of manga is also linked to this basic competitive advantage in terms of marketing.

Price was another factor in the success of manga, especially in France. In Japan, the fact that many manga magazines cost no more than a cup of coffee has been decisive for turning manga into a mass-consumed product. The price factor was also important in the eyes of 29 percent of the respondents in France, where most standard bande dessinée albums offer no more than 56 pages for as much as 12 euros (US$18), whereas manga offers at least 250 pages at only 60 percent of this cost. However, the price factor seemed negligible in the other three countries, where there is not such a differential in price between local comics and manga.[30]

Last but not least are the questions of violence and pornography in manga, which have been so often condemned by the authorities and the alarmed parents of European fans. Sex scenes ranked at the very bottom of the respondents' reasons for reading manga (15.5 percent).[31] Twenty-seven percent (and 39 percent in France) confessed a liking for "fight scenes," but there is nothing new in this penchant for violence among those interested in things Japanese: before the advent of manga, the image of Japan as the country of martial arts used to be the highest-ranking motivation for French university students engaging in Japanese studies. Manga simply capitalizes upon a very deep-rooted imaginary touching the country of samurais — an imaginary that evokes violence but associates it with aestheticism, self-control, and sophistication.

Thus, the motivations for reading manga in Europe are much more complicated than the simplistic set of escapism, sex, and violence to which they have been too often reduced. They have much more to do with social interaction, with the very basics of marketing (available and affordable products tailored to answer to demands that the local producers did not care for), and with the unparalleled sophistication of series able to mix fantasy and reality, fun and drama, and violence with *kawaii* (exceptionally cute or adorable) (Bouissou 2006).

Notes

1. The Manga Network's website can be accessed at http://www.ceri-sciences-po.org/themes/manga/index.php.
2. In this paragraph we neglect some areas where manga is actually successfully marketed, because of lack of space and/or data, or because — as for Great Britain — of a discourse that would be more fitting in comparison to the United States. A more detailed panorama of European manga market can be found in Pellitteri (2008).
3. In the United States (with a population of about 300 milion), the best-selling manga in 2006 was *Naruto* #9, which sold about 100,000 copies (Hibbs 2007), whereas in France (population: ±64 million) each new volume of the young ninja's adventures sold around 130,000 during its first year on the market; in Italy (population: ±58 million), single issues of such series as *Dragon Ball* have regularly sold more than 150,000 copies.
4. For every country, these statistics include new volumes of already running series.
5. Information compiled from Pasamonik (2005; 2006a) and Zaccagnino and Contrari (2007, 2).
6. For a complete list see Dunis and Krecina (2004).
7. Delcourt and Tonkam merged in 2006, and Soleil now heads a consortium of six publishers.
8. *Bande dessinée* is the Franco-Belgian school of comics.
9. See the section "How Did They Come to Read Manga?" later in this chapter.
10. The saga, which began in 1980, comprised thirty volumes as of 2007. The last volume sold 30,000 copies in Poland and 119,000 in France.
11. The Festival d'Angoulême is the biggest festival in Europe for bande dessinée, with an attendance in 2008 of 220,000.
12. Those born between 1965 and 1970 had their first (indirect) contact with Japanese manga when such TV series as *Alps no shōjo Heidi*, *UFO Robo Grendizer*, or

Candy Candy were aired in Europe, first in Spain (1975), and then Italy (1977) and France (1978).

13.   A historical French version comes from the Japanese *Bōchan no jidai*, a historical work about Japanese intelligentsia at the turn of the twentieth century.

14.   This survey has been supported by the Japan Foundation and the French Fondation Nationale des Sciences Politiques (aka Sciences Po; see its website at http://www.sciences-po.fr) as a means of studying the phenomenon of cultural globalization and the "soft power" derived from exports of popular culture goods. The French version of the questionnaire can be found at the Manga Network website, http://www.ceri-sciencespo.com/themes/manga/documents/sondage.pdf. German and Italian versions are also available upon request from bouissou. manganet@yahoo.fr.

15.   134,000 people attending in four days in 2008, Japon Expo — which started in 2000 with a first-time attendance of 3,200 — is the largest manga convention in France.

16.   However, when standing in line for a long time with nothing else to do, as the French fans were at the entrance to Japon Expo, the younger cohort did answer in large numbers.

17.   Significantly, in the Italian- and French-speaking regions of Switzerland, the gender pattern is similar to those in Italy and France, whereas it is similar to that of Germany in the German-speaking region.

18.   Short for "costume play": outfit oneself, with elaborate costume and accessories, as a specific manga character, for either fun or competition.

19.   The younger cohort is better represented in the French sample because of the way the survey has been distributed at the Japon Expo. For unknown reasons, in Italy the level of "not applicable" answers to that question reached 7.5 percent.

20.   Whether those who did not answer (6.7 percent in Italy and 14 percent in Germany) were searching for a job or were in transition phase between the end of schooling and a professional or university career cannot be determined.

21.   "For the young (at heart)" from 7 to 77": this was the advertising slogan on the leading comics weekly *Tintin* (1946–93).

22.   The ratio of 36 percent in the survey conducted at the Japan Expo in France — where the questionnaire was welcomed as a kind of game by the young people waiting in the entrance line — is probably more accurate, but might still underestimate the youngest cohort due to several reasons (the cost of entry, the need for a means of transportation for those living outside of Paris and its suburbs, etc.).

23.   There was no question about the level of income of either the young professional respondents or their parents, because this would certainly have resulted in many would-be respondents dropping the questionnaire altogether. We had to somewhat "guess" the social status of the respondents by using "indirect" questions about the nature of profession, incidence of joblessness in the family, level of education, and place of residence and combining them with some economic factors (the amount of money spent on manga, DVDs, and other "goodies" every month).

24.   This was as high as 37 percent in Italy.

25.   Detailed data for the four countries will be available on Manga Network's Website at http://www.ceri-sciences-po.org/themes/manga/index.php in the future. Since there is no space here to discuss in detail the differences among the four countries, we present only aggregated statistics for this chapter.

26.   This was 66 percent of the French sample that was surveyed during Japon Expo.

27.   The bias introduced in the French survey by the fact that two-thirds of those surveyed had been contacted at the entrance of Japon Expo is limited, because those who were attending a convention for the first time were instructed to answer "never."

28. This was 76 percent of the students and 55 percent of the young professionals.
29. "Your home" in Japanese. This term is now commonly used to refer to people with obsessive interests, particularly in anime, manga, or video games.
30. Only 8 percent of the Germans and 6.5 percent of the Italians defined manga as "less expensive" than other comics. This difference probably results from the fact that German and Italian respondents compared the price of manga paperbacks to that of comics magazines — of which there are plenty in both countries — whereas the French compared them to the price of hardcover albums, due to the scarcity of comics magazines in that country.
31. Of course, a certain degree of self-censorship may be suspected.

References

Alaniz, José (2005). "Compagni *mangafan* di Russia" [Fellow *Manga-fans* of Russia]. *Kappa* 168: 4.

Bouissou, Jean-Marie (2008). "*Global Manga.* Perché il fumetto giapponese è divenuto un prodotto culturale mondiale" (Global manga: Why Japanese comics have become a worldwide cultural product). In *Il Drago e la Saetta. Modelli, strategie e identità dell'immaginario giapponese* (The dragon and the dazzle: Models, strategies and identities of Japanese imagination), edited by Marco Pelliteri, 493–507. Latina, Italy: Tunué.

—— (2006). "Japan's Growing Cultural Power: The Example of Manga in France." In *Reading Manga from Multiple Perspectives: Local and Global Perceptions of Japanese Comics*, edited by Jaqueline Berndt and Steffi Richter, 149–65. Leipzig, Germany: Universitätverlag Leipzig.

Dolle-Weinkauff, Bernd (2006). "Comics und kulturelle Globalisierung" (Comics and cultural globalization), Paper presented at the *Forschungsberichte zu Struktur und Geschichte der Comics in Deutschland* conference, November 17–18, Koblenz-Landau university. Available at http://www.comicforschung.de/tagungen/06nov/06nov_dolle.html.

Dunis, Fabrice, and Florence Krecina (2004). *Guide du manga. France : des origines à 2004* (A guide to manga in France: From its origins to 2004). Strasbourg, France: Editions du Camphrier.

Hibbs, Brian (2007). "Tilting @ Windmills #37: Bookscan 2006." Newsarama, http://www.newsarama.com/tilting2_0/tilting37.html.

Japan External Trade Organization (2005, July). *Japan Economic Monthly* (industry report). Tokyo: Japan External Trade Organization.

Leonard, Sean (2005). "Progress against the Law: Anime and Fandom, with the Key to the Globalization of Culture." *International Journal of Cultural Studies* 8(9), http://ics.sagepub.com/cgi/reprint/8/3/281.

Pasamonik, Didier (2006, June 26). "'Shōgun,'" un magazine de mangas . . . européens!" ("Shōgun," a magazine with manga . . . from Europe!). ActuaBD, http://www.actuabd.com/spip.php?article3875.

Pellitteri, Marco (2006). "Manga in Italy: History of a Powerful Cultural Hybridization." *International Journal of Comic Art* 8(2): 56–76.

——, ed. (2008). *Il Drago e la Saetta. Modelli, strategie e identità dell'immaginario giapponese* (The dragon and the dazzle: Models, strategies and identities of Japanese imagination). Latina, Italy: Tunué.

Rattier, Gilles (2000), "2000: L'année des confirmations" (2000, the year of confirmations), http://www.acbd.fr/bilan-2000.html

—— (2008), "2008: Recherche nouveaux marchés . . . désespérément" (2008: Looking for new markets . . . desperately) http://www.actuabd.com/IMG/pdf/ACBD-Rapport_2008.pdf

Rodriguez de León, Rolando José (2005). *"Anime e flamenco"* [Anime and flamenco]. *Kappa* 156: 2.

Yokota, Masao (2006). *Animation no rinō shinri gaku* (The clinical psychology of animation). Tokyo: Seishin shobô.

Zaccagnino, Marcella, and Sebastiano Contrari (2007, October 31). "Manga: il Giappone alla conquista del mondo" (Manga: Japan conquering the world). *Limes, rivista italiana di geopolitica*, http://www.limesonline.com.

16

Manga Shakespeare

Emma Hayley

CONCEPTUALIZATION AND COMMERCIAL OPPORTUNITY

In 2005, *Manga Shakespeare* was a new and innovative concept in the United Kingdom spearheaded by the yet-to-be launched publishing house SelfMadeHero. Fusing manga visuals with original Shakespearean texts was a logical development in book publishing from both the creative and commercial perspectives. SelfMadeHero, a manga and graphic novel imprint whose principal aim is to breathe new life into the classics, was conceived in 2004 and launched in 2007. Developments in the graphic novel market during this period were significant.

In the UK, there was a 98 percent increase in the volume of sales of graphic novels from 2004 to 2005 — an increase from approximately 290,000 to 577,000 copies.[1] This statistic subsumes manga under the broader category of graphic novels. In the same period the sales volume for Titan books — a (non-manga-focused) comic book publisher in the UK — went down from 71 percent to 45 percent, and volume of sales for Tokyopop (a publisher exclusively of manga) went up from 2 percent to 20 percent, with others, such as manga publisher Gollanz, rising from 0.6 percent to 6 percent. This was an indication that manga was undergoing a rapid growth in sales in the UK. Previous years had seen a year-by-year growth from 2001 in sales of graphic novels.[2] The value of graphic novels sales rose from approximately £1 million in 2001 to £5 million in 2005.[3]

The ever-increasing rise of manga outside Japan was not ignored by the book industry. One industry publication noted, "As the UK graphic novels market grows, more publishers are entering the market, including Book House, HarperCollins, Tanoshimi (Random House) and Weidenfeld & Nicolson" (*The Bookseller*, October 27, 2006). "Manga is the most popular form of graphic novels among the young, with a generation of British youth weaned on watching animation from Japan and reading manga." (*The*

Bookseller, November 2008). The manga that was being distributed in the UK was almost exclusively imported from Japan and translated into English. In 2006, Tokyopop launched a competition called Rising Stars of Manga; for the first time it seemed that manga artists in the UK and Ireland would get recognition for their talents. As well, it might provide a stepping stone through which UK manga artists could get their own manga commissioned.

The manga boom is a result of a variety of factors — one, I would suggest, is the influence of the *anime*, or Japanese animation, market. While manga and anime have a relatively long history in Japanese culture, both art forms have only recently spread to the West. It was in 1988 that the UK distribution company Manga Entertainment released *Akira*, an apocalyptic science fiction film directed by Katsuhiro Otomo. A number of popular anime titles followed *Akira*, and together with Hayao Miyasaki's award-winning *Sen to Chihiro no Kamikakushi (Spirited Away)* this art form was quite clearly becoming embraced by the West. While the market for manga and anime are not synonymous, the success of one will inevitably influence sales in the same way that a successful screen adaptation of a book may see the book hurtling toward the bestseller list. The popularity of manga will, therefore, in part, have been helped by the various translations of anime titles for a Western audience. As well as animes, Japanese mangas were also being translated into different languages by Scanlators and distributed through the Internet. This also contributed to the growth in popularity of manga outside Japan.

In a broader sense, it is the intensification of our visual culture that must also be a factor in influencing manga's popularity in the West. While a Japanese audience has a head start in visual literacy because of the graphic nature of its language, in which ideographic characters and phonetic symbols coexist, the Western approach to reading is linear. We are, however, becoming influenced by the visual arts more than ever before. Children are growing up in a digital age and as such are far more visually literate than those of previous generations.

In the context of this rapidly rising sector of the book industry in 2005, I saw an opportunity and conceived the idea of launching SelfMadeHero with the *Manga Shakespeare* series. During this period I went to numerous international book fairs and met editors from around the world. I realized that a new role had developed in publishing houses — the role of the "manga editor." Editors in France, for example, who used to deal only with *bande desinée*,[4] now had to become experts in manga. Manga was the hot format in the publishing industry. I felt that the time was right for a UK publisher to start commissioning full-length mangas with a UK team.

My primary aim with the *Manga Shakespeare* series was to introduce teenagers or first-time readers to the work of William Shakespeare via a medium they understood. Manga, with its pace and vigor, was particularly appropriate for Shakespeare, who intended his plays to be seen rather than read. *Manga Shakespeare* provided a bridge between the world of performance and linear text, a way of bringing Shakespeare to life in a visual way for a new audience. I wanted these mangas to be seen as entertainment rather than as primarily educational.

THE CREATIVE PROCESS

With the manga market becoming the fastest growing sector of the book industry, *Manga Shakespeare* seemed inevitable. However, SelfMadeHero was not the first publisher with the idea of reinventing the classics visually — many will remember the Graphics Illustrated series begun in the 1950s, and there have been a number of publishers since. We were, however, the first UK publisher to commission full-length English language versions of Shakespeare's plays as works of manga.[5] There were a number of key ingredients needed to make the *Manga Shakespeare* series a credible venture. I needed a creative team made up of a script adaptor/editor, artist, textual consultant, and layout designer. I contacted Richard Appignanesi, who was key in pioneering Icon Books' successful *Introducing* series. Appignanesi was used to editing books that married words with images. The script adaptor needed to be able to see each page visually and Appignanesi was perfect for the job — an avid comic reader since youth, he also had a proven track record as an editor of a series of visual books.[6]

We discussed the series at length, looking at the many ways in which we could produce the books: Would we print it in the Japanese manner, from right to left? Would we modernize the text? Would we abridge the text? Which artists would we use, and would they be Japanese mangaka?

We decided that keeping the original Shakespearean text was crucial, but in an abridged form. The reason Shakespeare is still the most widely read playwright today is because of many factors, but one is the beauty of the language he uses. To modernize the text would mean losing that element unnecessarily. I brought a man called Nick de Somogyi on board as our textual consultant. Among many other accolades he was the founding editor for the Globe Quartos series, author of *Shakespeare's Theatre of War* and editor (since 2001) of Nick Hern Books' *Shakespeare Folios* series. He would make sure that the abridged text maintained a consistency in style and fluidity.

The abridgement of the text was necessary because it needed to work with the medium. The point of this beautiful medium is not to have pages of talking heads, but to "show" and not "tell," combining visual poetry with textual poetry. To use the full text would have meant ignoring the nature of manga. Imagine pages and pages of the talking head of Hamlet as he delivers his monologues! We wanted to create books that engaged readers, keeping their attention in spite of the sometimes difficult language. As a prime example, we looked to Baz Luhrmann's film *Romeo and Juliet* (1996) in which he kept true to the original Shakespearean language and used visual imagery to refashion the story for a contemporary audience.

While the imported manga we saw in the UK stayed in its original format and read from right to left, we decided that our manga would be "flipped" to read from left to right. Our aim was to appeal to an audience used to reading from left to right, and the aim was also for the series to cross over into the mainstream. We did not see the advantage of creating a new manga in the Japanese way other than for novelty. Also, as a manga audience expects their mangas to be in black and white as tradition dictates, we saw no advantage in changing this. Our books include the expected splash of color with the inclusion of eight to nine color pages at the beginning that serves to establish the setting of the manga and introduces the characters — much like a dramatis personae.

With the format decided upon, we set about finding the artists. There are many talented manga-kas in Japan and a collaboration between a Japanese artist and a UK editorial team could have been interesting; however, we decided on a different approach. With the ever-increasing popularity of manga outside Japan, there was a growing number of young artists in the UK who considered themselves to be mangaka. Some ten years ago this pool of talent would not have existed in the UK, or at least it would have been at an embryonic stage. In 2005, creating a UK homegrown manga was possible and resulted in a UK publisher supporting its own new emerging talent.

I contacted a collective of UK manga artists, Sweatdrop Studios, who had been self-publishing a number of titles. Various members of the collective did some samples of plays of their choice, creating covers and pages and suggesting alternative settings. Based on these trials, we picked two artists — Sonia Leong for *Romeo and Juliet* and Emma Vieceli for *Hamlet*. We signed up both the artists based on an advance-and-royalties agreement. We were on the same wavelength as far as the creative vision for each of the books was concerned, and the team collaborated on appropriate settings for the plays. The artists would sketch out their character designs based on these discussions.

Our version of *Romeo and Juliet* would be set in modern-day Japan. The setting was appropriate — Romeo and Juliet's respective families could be part of warring *yakuza* (members of an organised crime syndicate); and the story line was feasible in present-day Japan, where very traditional values sometimes clash with a younger generation's ideals.

Character and costume design developed and changed in the early stages of commissioning. Leong, for example, first of all depicted Juliet as a traditional girl wearing a typical Japanese kimono. But Juliet then developed into a sassy, young Shibuya-district trendsetter dressed in the latest Japanese fashions, contrasting with her more traditionally dressed parents. We can see why Juliet would fall for Romeo, a cool Japanese pop-rock star, over her parents' preferred suitor Paris, a rich banker.

We decided to set *Hamlet* in a cyberpunk future with advanced communication devices and holograms. Vieceli's depiction of Ophelia started out as a spanner-wielding technician in an attempt to make her a dominant character, but this approach changed and she developed into a more feminine figure, which showed that Ophelia's strength as a character was her femininity. "In *Hamlet*, I focused less on what's happening but more on who it's happening to," explains Vieceli, "for instance, I used lots of close-ups to express the emotions of the characters. It was important for getting a story as cerebral as *Hamlet* across effectively" (Vieceli, interview with the author, 2008). These approaches to the characterization were very important to get right in the early stages of the creative process. They also indicated what sort of manga — *shōjo manga* (girls' manga), *shōnen manga* (boys' manga), or another sort — we were creating.

FIGURE 16.1: Feuding Families.

FIGURE 16.2: "Contemporary" Romeo and Juliet.

THE INFLUENCE OF JAPAN

Brandishing covers and spreads of these first two *Manga Shakespeare* issues, I joined a delegation of small to medium-sized independent UK publishers on a UK Department of Trade and Industry (UKDTI)–sponsored mission to Japan. With my plans to launch my book imprint SelfMadeHero in 2007, and to launch it with the *Manga Shakespeare* series, this became a valuable fact-finding mission. This was the first time I had ever been to Japan and I quickly realized that manga was everywhere. It bore no comparison with the few comic book shops that we had scattered around the UK — manga was very much a part of Japanese culture, not a niche market. Everything from cookbooks to car manuals were manga works, and there was manga for every social group and age. It was quite obviously a medium rather than a genre, with each work created specifically for a very narrow, well-defined demographic.[7]

This fact-finding mission to Japan was tremendously helpful in under-standing manga within the context of Japan and raised certain questions that

FIGURE 16.3 (Above left): Horatio.

FIGURE 16.4 (Above right): The characters of *Hamlet*.

further influenced my approach to the *Manga Shakespeare* series. My partici-pation in the mission also drew the importance of manga in a trading sense to the attention of the UKDTI who wrote a case study on SelfMadeHero: "With their dramatic speech bubbles, enormous eyes and big hair, 'manga' comics and characters are becoming increasingly popular around the world" (UKDTI, 2008).

Various questions were raised in my mind: Would our *Manga Shakespeare* series have a clearly defined audience? Should the adaptations conform to what a shōjo or a shōnen audience might want? Could what we were about to do qualify as being manga at all, since it was not to be drawn by Japanese artists? Would manga enthusiasts be put off because it was Shakespeare, and would Shakespeare lovers be put off because it was manga?

Many of Shakespeare's plays do not easily fit into the conventional manga categories both because of the nature of the plays themselves and also because Shakespeare has a wide-reaching readership both in terms of age and gender. Take *Hamlet* for example: does it appeal more to male or to female read-ers? If you give a boy a choice of either reading *Romeo and Juliet* or *Hamlet*, nine times out of ten I have found that the boy will choose *Hamlet*, perhaps wanting to steer clear of "girly" romance and instead identifying more with a male protagonist. However, our version of the protagonist was created as a *bishōnen* (beautiful boy) character, with the aim of appealing to girls as well as boys. Indeed, the artist Vieceli received many comments from female fans who considered her Hamlet to be their ideal pinup. While our manga version of *Hamlet* possesses characteristics of shōjo manga, it is not typically shōjo because of the nature of the narrative. There is an unwritten code in shōjo manga that males cannot be protagonists, or at least, they are rare (there are, of course, exceptions to this rule).

Japanese artists have been experimenting with Shakespeare as manga for decades. Certain original works of Shakespeare were adapted to focus on the female character such as Riyoko Ikeda's adaptation of *Othello* (1969), which shifts the central focus from Othello to Desdemona so that the reader is given the chance to identify with both protagonists. Double heroines, which became a feature of some manga (such as Ikeda's *Oscar and Marie Antoinette*) meant that certain plays such as *The Merchant of Venice* and *Twelfth Night* were ideal candidates for shōjo manga. Osamu Tezuka himself did an adaptation of *The Merchant of Venice* in 1959, as did Machiko Satonaka in 2001; and Kumi Morikawa did a version of *Twelfth Night* in 1978.

Romeo and Juliet is clearly a shōjo title. Since the popularity in Japan of director Franco Zeffirelli's *Romeo and Juliet* (1968), Japanese adaptations of the play include stage versions and lesbian manga. In various dramatic

FIGURE 16.5: Hamlet.

versions, boys have played Juliet, and this gender-bending is something that manga shares. Some of the story lines of plays such as *Twelfth Night* and *The Merchant of Venice*, where sexual identities become blurred, have a lot in common with shōjo manga, and this explains why these plays are so popular in Japan — particularly in Kabuki theaters and in the Takarazuka all-female theater, where all parts are played by women.

Osamu Tezuka was a great fan of the Takarazuka revue and obviously very conscious of gender,[8] and the works of both Tezuka and Shakespeare share the changing of identities. Tezuka knew a lot about performance and must have learned a lot from Shakespeare's works.[9] So while Shakespeare had an influence on manga in Japan, now manga was to have an influence on the interpretation of Shakespeare in the UK.

The manga genres that have been identified in Japan influenced our *Manga Shakespeare* adaptations to a certain degree. Stylistically, both *Hamlet* and *Romeo and Juliet* follow the shōjo variety of manga, and this is particularly obvious in the panel layouts, pacing, and emphasis on characters' emotions. When choosing artists for later titles in our series, it became obvious that specific styles suited specific stories. Our version of *Richard III*, set in medieval England, would have much in common with a shonen style, where fast-paced action-packed story lines are common. Our adaptation concentrated on the action, focusing on the bloodthirsty exploits of its evil male protagonist, who was responsible for the bloodiest chapter of the English monarchy. *A Midsummer Night's Dream*, which we set in an alternate modern-day Athens with much of the action taking place in the forest outside the city, would have a shōjo quality with its theme of romances, its double heroines, and so on. *The Tempest*, set in the future after a global energy crisis has plunged mankind into a second dark age, nestles somewhere in between the two genres both stylistically and in terms of story line.

Do all of Shakespeare's plays lend themselves to manga? When Appignanesi adapts the plays, he always looks to uncover the kernel of action often hidden by a long speech. It is, in part, down to the skill of the adaptor to make a good manga from the original. As Appignanesi explains:

> There is no *uni-fit* formula for all of Shakespeare's plays, but in principle any one can be adapted to the manga form because of the dramatic potential. The problem is transformation from theater of poetry to the genre of the manga-style graphic novel. Does adaptation of Shakespeare's original script betray the poetry on which his theater relies? My answer is that the integrity of the manga genre must be preserved if the adaptation is going to work at all. In that sense, what I do is very like Verdi's adaptation of Shakespeare for the genre of opera, where similarly much of Shakespeare's script has been sacrificed to the needs of musical theater, but the end product succeeds to maintain the spirit of the original. (Interview with the author, 2008)

Appignanesi found *Macbeth* to be one of the easier plays to adapt effectively. "Plays with more action, such as *Macbeth*, lend themselves with more ease to illustration," he comments. "The reason for that is self-evident: graphic novels must avoid being 'word heavy' as this interferes with framing and tempos of reading which is specific to the graphic novel genre."

In our *shonen* manga version of *Macbeth*, Samurai warriors have reclaimed a future postnuclear world of mutants, making for a visual feast of action-packed fight scenes. Our *Julius Caesar* is set in an imaginary world somewhere between Rome and Baghdad — we allude to recent history and to the fall of a mighty dictator. Our manga version of *As You Like It* (2009) is set in modern-day China, where the reader can see the clash between the rural and urban — a modern-day reality. We change Shakespeare's settings where it is appropriate to do so, in the same way that directors reinvent Shakespeare for the screen or stage. While not all our mangas have been recast in modern-day settings, the main aim is for the setting to aid in the readers' identification with the narrative and thereby encourage readers to see the relevancy of the story in today's society.

THE REACTION TO *MANGA SHAKESPEARE*

At the London Book Fair in March 2006, SelfMadeHero sold the North American rights to the *Manga Shakespeare* series to U.S. publisher Harry N. Abrams, which publishes the series under their Amulet Books imprint. We convinced buyers at most of the major UK bookstore chains to commit to taking copies before their release and, following extensive press coverage, the books sold out rapidly and reprints were requested within five months of publication. During this period, SelfMadeHero appointed sales agents and distribution companies globally for export markets — including Australia, New Zealand, Asia, and Europe. Translation rights were granted to Italian and Korean publishers in the first year and other translations followed.

Our goal is to make manga more accessible to the mainstream while making Shakespeare more accessible through manga, and we appeal to two different markets — the trade and the educational. While the main focus of the *Manga Shakespeare* series has been for entertainment (just as Shakespeare intended his plays to be), we have not ignored the value of the books on an educational level. In 2007, we developed educational resources that teachers and students will be able to use alongside our books in the classroom. Our marketing approach in the educational market has been novel. While we have been intermittently direct mailing UK secondary schools with our promotional leaflets, we have also developed a series of workshops using interactive white board (IWB) technology.

Manga Shakespeare attracted worldwide attention when the first books were published in March 2007. Rather than only attaining reviews in the comic press, our manga received critical acclaim in influential mainstream newspapers such as the *Financial Times*, which wrote, "The manga versions are . . . visually appealing, intelligently adapted, and demonstrate that Shakespeare is a writer for every age. A cartoon version of Shakespeare is in some ways truer to the original than reading the text alone; the visual element was always supposed to be part of the experience" (*Financial Times*, March 2007).

In addition, The *Independent on Sunday* and the *Times* offered these reviews:

> This new series does in book form what film director Baz Luhrmann did on screen — make Shakespeare cool and accessible to a younger generation. . . . Just as Leonardo DiCaprio made Shakespeare sound like urban American dialect, so it seems entirely plausible that Japanese mobsters should shout "Have at thee coward!" before launching into a street fight . . . (the) artists use the dynamic flow of manga to give Shakespeare's plots an addictive page turning energy. (*Independent on Sunday*, March 2007)
>
> These artists demonstrate how vividly manga techniques and pacing can convey motion and emotion . . . the appetite for manga culture in this country shows no sign of abating . . . a Japanese export has become the future of comics. (*Times*, October 2007)

We have had further features in UK magazines and webzines, and on television and radio. The Japanese press has also shown huge interest in the idea — TV Tokyo visited our offices in central London and the story went out on a Japanese breakfast TV show.

Amid all this publicity, academics have also shown interest. Ryuta Minami of Aichi University of Education in Japan began using our texts to introduce his literature students to Shakespeare. Minami and Yukari Yoshihara from the University of Tsukuba invited Leong, Vieceli, and me to Japan in July 2007 to do a series of presentations about *Manga Shakespeare* at Tsukuba University, Nagoya University, and the Kyoto International Museum of Manga. Only five months after the launch of *Romeo and Juliet* we realized we were making manga history; our books were being used in universities as textbooks, our artists' work was stored in the Museum of Manga in Kyoto, and we had given talks at seminars in several universities on the fusion of Shakespeare, manga, and Japan. We all felt truly honored.

THE FUTURE OF GLOBAL MANGA

The same year we were doing the seminar circuit in Japan, the Ministry of Foreign Affairs of Japan, with a view to raising awareness of the attractions of Japanese contemporary culture, established the International Manga Award, which was designed to honor manga artists who contributed to the promotion of manga overseas. There were 146 entries from twenty-six countries all over the world, including fifteen entries from the UK. The scheme was the result of an idea raised in a policy speech on cultural diplomacy, "A New Look at Cultural Diplomacy: A Call to Japan's Cultural Practitioners," delivered on April 28, 2006 by the then foreign minister Taro Aso.[10] This award was significant, as it was an official recognition that manga artists could be non-Japanese.

Furthermore, in celebration of the rapid growth in popularity of Japanese-inspired manga in the UK, a manga-writing contest, the Manga Jiman Competition,[11] was held by the Embassy of Japan in London 2007.

On launching the competition, Japan Information and Culture Center (JICC) director Mami Mizutori commented, "At present, most manga on sale in the UK are translations of Japanese works or are imported from the U.S. However, recently some original manga works have begun appearing in the UK, such as the *Manga Shakespeare*, brought out by a British publisher. We at the Embassy very much hope that UK-produced manga will come to play its part in raising interest in Japan among British people.[12]

The manga we see today in Japan is a hybrid of Japanese and American aesthetic. It is influenced by Western television, film, and comics. In the West, manga has evolved rapidly; it has become a hybrid within a hybrid. New European styles will influence a new breed of "global" manga that is created outside Japan. With each new work of manga comes the potential for a new fan base for non-Japanese mangaka, and this fanbase will have its own expectations of its artists. This, I propose, is just the beginning for global manga.

With the terrific response to the *Manga Shakespeare* series in the UK and internationally, SelfMadeHero has brought more of Shakespeare's great works to life through manga, including *King Lear, Much Ado about Nothing, Twelfth Night, Othello*, and *The Merchant of Venice*. We continue to see our series as having a global appeal, and in early 2008, I completed a tour of Malaysia, Singapore, and India (as a guest of the British Council), putting on *Manga Shakespeare* workshops and talks for teachers and students.

As Sunitha Janamohanan, the arts manager for the British Council in Malaysia comments, "SelfMadeHero has been breaking ground in literature education, making Shakespeare more accessible in the classroom and showing teachers how to use visual literacy to aid in their pupils' understanding" (2008). Following a *Manga Shakespeare* workshop at the Ministry of Education Malaysia, one official said, "(Manga) would serve as a great tool in teaching literature in schools to students who find it hard to learn Shakespearean text." The Malaysia Curriculum Board is now considering the inclusion of graphic novels in its school syllabi.

While we made important inroads with our program of seminars and work-shops, our tours also revealed that many of the myths of manga — such as the common one asserting that manga is violent — and conservative approaches to graphic novels/comic books are still prevalent. While attitudes are changing, this conservatism also exists in the UK. It seems so strange to me that some people are unable to see the medium of manga as a form of literature with intrinsic value and instead blindly perceive it as a conduit for "dumbing down" great works; the divide between the visually literate and illiterate is obvious in this respect. I hope that SelfMadeHero has managed to change some people's attitudes when we stress to our audiences that this is an important, influential and "grown-up" medium that is here to stay.

Notes

1. These numbers reflect sales through Nielsen BookScan's Total Consumer Market index (25 July, 2007).
2. There was an increase in sales volume of graphic novels in the UK in 2001–2 by 40.7 percent; in 2002–3 by 37.5 percent, and in 2003–4 by 31.7 percent (Nielsen BookScan, 25 July, 2007).
3. Exact figures for the value of the graphic novel market in the UK were £1,279,764 in 2001; £1,738,022 in 2002; £2,456,288 in 2003; £3,252,918 in 2004; and £5,326,508 in 2005 (Nielsen BookScan, 25 July, 2007).
4. The term *bande desinée* refers to French graphic novels.
5. Here I must make the distinction between manga and Western graphic novels.
6. Appignanesi's own best-selling titles written for Icon Books include *Freud*, *Postmodernism*, and *Existentialism*. His interest in Japanese culture was evident before his involvement with the *Manga Shakespeare* series as author of the novel *Yukio Mishima's Report to the Emperor*.
7. While a lot of manga conforms quite closely to genre, there is plenty of work that does not naturally fit into any genre, either demographically or stylistically.
8. Tomoko Yamada, curator of the Kawasaki City Museum, talk delivered July 8, 2007, at Tsukuba University in Tokyo.
9. Yukari Fujimoto, editor and manga specialist, talk delivered on July 8, 2007, at Tsukuba University in Tokyo.
10. In 2008 Aso became the president of Japan — he is well known as a manga enthusiast.
11. *Manga Jiman* can be roughly translated as "having pride in manga."
12. This was published on the Embassy of Japan in the UK website (http://www.uk.emb-japan.go.jp/en/japanUK/exchange/070712manga.html), on February 5, 2008.

Suggested Manga Reading

Shakespeare, William (2007a). *Hamlet*. London: SelfMadeHero.
—— (2007b). *Romeo and Juliet*. London: SelfMadeHero.
—— (2007c). *Richard III*. London: SelfMadeHero
—— (2007d). *The Tempest*. London: SelfMadeHero
—— (2008a). *As You Like It*. London: SelfMadeHero.
—— (2008b). *Julius Caesar*. London: SelfMadeHero.

—— (2008c). *Macbeth*. London: SelfMadeHero.

—— (2008e). *A Midsummer Night's Dream*. London: SelfMadeHero.

—— (2008f). *Othello*. London: SelfMadeHero.

—— (2009a). *Henry VIII*. London: SelfMadeHero.

—— (2009b). *Much Ado About Nothing*. London: SelfMadeHero.

—— (2009c). *King Lear*. London: SelfMadeHero.

—— (2009d). *Twelfth Night*. London: SelfMadeHero.

—— (2009e). *The Merchant of Venice*. London: SelfMadeHero.

17

The Manga Phenomenon in America

Wendy Goldberg

Manga sales have skyrocketed in America and show little sign of slowing down, rising even as sales of *anime* (Japanese animation) falter.[1] One cannot go into a big bookstore without seeing several aisles dedicated to manga and comics books, with several kids sitting on the floor, speed-reading the latest volume of their favorite series. In this essay, I will explore several reasons why, at first, manga took so long to reach an audience in America and then why it became so popular. I will then examine different publishing models by successful companies and the growing specialization in the market.[2]

THE EARLY HISTORY OF MANGA IN AMERICA

There are several things that contributed to the initial failure of manga in the 1980s and early 1990s in America. Publishers and bookstores had not defined an audience that would appreciate manga. It took several critical successes in American comics to show that the format did not have to be for a narrow market, that of teenage boys. Comics were seen as mostly "superhero" fare and a "safe bet" for comic book stores; the big companies, DC and Marvel, created insular universes in which their characters could cross over to different titles, forcing readers to buy these different titles to keep up with their story lines. Publishing and marketing expectations that comics be equated with superheroes initially eclipsed any chance for the diversity of manga genres to flourish. Second, the distribution of comic books in America from the newsstand to specialty comic book shops also stifled manga. Most comic book stores needed assurances that titles would sell, and DC and Marvel made exclusive deals to distributors, such as

Diamond, that would sell their books to stores.

Since manga did not fit into these superhero universes, publishers had difficulties in figuring out an audience that would buy and read these Japanese books. Initially, the manga titles that made it to America were not considered comic books in the sense that their story and art transcended childish stories. One example was Nakazawa Keiji's *Hadeshi no Gen* (Barefoot Gen: A Cartoon History of Hiroshima).[3] This serious story about life in Hiroshima after the atomic bomb was marketed as serious literature, not as a comic. To break out of this comic book "ghetto" and show that comics could be serious — a resounding theme from independent publishers from the late 1980s and early 1990s — some American comic book creators lent their popularity and critical success to fledgling manga. For example, the first four volumes of *Gen* were published by New Society Publishers, and included in later editions was an introduction written by American graphic artist Art Spiegelman, who was gaining critical attention for his Holocaust comic book memoir, *Maus*, which would receive a special Pulitzer Prize in 1992, giving more credibility for comics as literature. Spiegelman argues that comics were a "highly-charged medium" for important stories, "delivering densely concentrated information in relatively few words and simplified code-images" (Spiegelman 1990, v and vi).

While promoting comics as serious art, publishers also had to acknowledge and prepare American audiences for the different conventions in manga storytelling. Spiegelman acknowledges in his introduction to *Gen* that manga is different than American comics: "Japanese comics have stylistic quirks and idioms that are quite different from ours, and these must be learned and accepted as part of the process of reading *Gen*" (1990, vi) Because manga, in some ways, "looked" like American comics but had qualities that were foreign to American readers, Spiegelman more or less apologizes for the strangeness of manga — a quality that would become its main selling point to readers after the year 2000.

Though *Gen* failed to find an audience, publishers still looked to market manga. Before that was to happen, they had to know that American readers could embrace nontraditional comics. Alternative American books showed that U.S. readers could embrace nontraditional comics. The "black and white" boom started by the popular 1984 comic book *Teenage Mutant Ninja Turtles* by Kevin Eastman and Peter Laird (which then found an even larger audience through its animated television series and movies), showed that noncolor comics could find an active readership.[4] Manga also had its advocates in the comics community — especially writer and artist Frank Miller who, after becoming famous for his popular graphic novel *Batman: The Dark Knight Returns*, drew the cover art for Dark Horse's *Kozure Ôkami* (Lone Wolf and Cub) by Koike Kazuo.[5]

In searching for a best-seller, publishers selected some titles based on the fame of the manga's creator, and one obvious example was the science-fiction epic *Kaze no Tani no Naushika* (Nausicaä of the Valley of the Wind), drawn by the famous anime director and cofounder of Studio Ghibli, Miyazaki Hayao, who had started the series in 1982 and finally finished it 1995 ("Nausicaä around the World" 2008). In America, the series was first published in monthly installments from 1988 to 1996 by VIZ Communications (later, VIZ Media).[6] Like other titles of that time, *Nausicaä* relied on the comic book store for distribution.

Comics could only reach the stores through direct sale distributors who limited what could be ordered. Comics scholar Mark Rogers notes that "at the end of the 1980s, direct sales would represent more than eighty percent of all comics sold." The centralization of the marketing of comic books, argues Rogers, catered to a niche market of specialized readers (Rogers 197, 8). In this model, those who wanted to buy comics could place their orders through the store, which would then order the comics through the distributor. It seemed successful for both ends of the market — readers could get exactly what they wanted and the big comics companies, like DC and Marvel, could print enough to fulfill that demand. But instead of reaching new readers with different material, publishers chose to fill dominated store shelves with collectible superhero comics.[7]

When manga finally broke through this deadlock, it did not occur in the comic book store, and it was not because of the traditional male market for superhero fare. Takeuchi Naoko's *Bishôjo Senshi Sailor Moon* (Sailor Moon), in the pages of *MixxZine*, introduced female readers to the *shōjo manga* (girls' manga) genre.[8] Online trade website ICv2.com claims that "It was *Sailor Moon's* presence on American television screens that gave shōjo manga a beachhead in the U.S. pop culture landscape" ("Shōjo Manga and Anime — Big Business in Japan" 2001).[9] Even though the series was cancelled, toy sales and an active online community helped this phenomenon to grow.[10] *Sailor Moon* was soon followed by popular titles from Watase Yū and the manga artist collective CLAMP.[11] Currently, Takuya Natsuki's shōjo manga *Fruits Basket* (2004–) dominates, with its publisher Tokyopop claiming to have sold two million copies of this title as of December 2006 ("Fruits Basket Reaches Two Million Units" 2006). However, such sales figures do not account for readers who flip through manga while sitting in a bookstore or library, or those who trade titles with each other.[12] Following *Sailor Moon's* successful introduction through the anime, shōnen (boys') titles such as Toriyama Akira's *Dragon Ball* and *Dragon Ball Z* also saw their sales rise from airing on U.S. televisions's Cartoon Network, and anime aimed at younger children, such as *Pokémon*, raised toy and game sales.[13]

Manga has grown from a few titles sold exclusively in comic book stores to many shelves in bookstore chains. In March 2001, the highest-ranked manga on comic book distributor Diamond's list was Stan Sakai's *Usagi Yojimbo* (Dark Horse) at position 159. Other titles included Yatate Hajime and Tomino Yoshiyuki's *Shin Kidô Senki Gundam Wing* at 167 and Rumiko Takahashi's *Ranma ½* at 173; these were among a total of twelve manga titles, most of them at the lower end of the best-selling spectrum ("Top 200 Comics" 2001). As of November 2007, manga dominated the graphic novel market: Tokyopop's *Fruits Basket* was at number 9; VIZ Media's *Naruto* volumes 22, 23, and 24 were respectively at 10, 15 and 17; Dark Horse's *Berserk* was at number 20 ("Top 100 Graphic Novels Actual" 2007). These numbers, however, do not include sales at bookstores, which have consistently been higher for manga than for other comic books. *Fruits Basket* and *Naruto* have even made inroads into mainstream book sales by entering *USA Today's* Booklist in 2006 ("Naruto 11 Sets Booklist Record" 2006; "Fruits Basket Sets Booklist Record" 2006).[14]

Despite many false starts, manga has finally become a solid market in America. In the following sections I will examine different models used by the major manga publishers in America in order to probe more deeply how manga found its readers.

THE COMIC BOOK MODEL (DARK HORSE)

In the late 1980s comics publisher Dark Horse, was one of the few independents that competed with the giants DC and Marvel for comic book store shelf space. Unlike its large competitors, Dark Horse took more risks in selecting, licensing, and marketing titles, and they were one of the first publishers to include manga in their catalog with varying degrees of success.

Dark Horse initially imitated American comic book publishers by releasing titles monthly in a "pamphlet form" of thirty-two pages. The pages were colored and "flipped" to read left to right in traditional Western fashion. Dark Horse then collected monthly issues together into a graphic novel. The manga that Dark Horse chose to publish were selected for subjects that might appeal to a superhero comic book reader.

One of their first titles, Manabe Johji's *Outlanders*, published from 1988 to 1992, was a science fiction story featuring a female protagonist who dressed and posed provocatively on the covers. The intended audience for the manga and others like it in Dark Horse's catalog at the time would have been teenage boys.[15] Next, Dark Horse published *Dirty Pair* in 1993 and *Bubblegum Crisis* from 1994 to 1995, which also featured sexy female characters wielding guns and riding motorcycles. In these titles Dark Horse licensed the manga characters and created original stories that might appeal to American readers.[16] In the mid-1990s, Dark Horse's catalog grew with the addition of

Studio Proteus, a company Dark Horse had worked with since 1988 ("Dark Horse Acquires Studio Proteus" 2004). They added Shirow Masamune's *Appleseed*, and then his *Kôkaku Kidôtai* (Ghost in the Shell) in 1995.[17] They also published the popular *Aa! Megami-sama!* (Oh My Goddess) by Fujishima Kosuke (1994–).

Critic Frederik Schodt argues that one reason for Dark Horse's success with manga in the 1990s was because the company looked for "Japanese artists who draw in a rather non-Japanese style" (Schodt 1996, 13). Though Dark Horse tended to develop projects that featured female sex appeal in order to sell books, they showed a diversity of manga art forms, from the detailed, somewhat more realistic figures of Shirow to the traditional, idealized "big-eyed" characters of Fujishima.[18]

Although still maintaining a presence in comic book stores, Dark Horse has begun to abandon the traditional comic book model for manga and to look to other ways of generating sales. Their perennial best-seller, Samura Hiroaki's *Mugen no Jûnin* (Blade of the Immortal), was the last manga to be published in the monthly format ("Philip Simon on 'Blade of the Immortal'" 2007). Recognizing that their buyers had changed from comic book readers who wanted high-quality, collectible issues, to readers more interested in content, Dark Horse also decided to reprint their back catalog in inexpensive omnibus editions. Ironically, they are following the pattern of American comics publishers who have taken advantage of the extra shelf space in bookstores to release thick, inexpensive, black-and-white reprints of their superhero titles. Dark Horse CEO Mike Richardson states that this move is partly because of American comic publishers' success with the reprint, and because readers "see great value in it" ("Interview with Dark Horse CEO Mike Richardson" 2008).

In the future, Dark Horse will publish a title by the popular women's collective CLAMP at the same time it is released in Japan. The title and subject were not known at the time of this writing, but Dark Horse has faith in the group's popularity in America, and the novelty of receiving a desired title so quickly will most likely appeal to readers. In the past, it has taken years for Japanese titles to be published in the States, but editor Carl Horn states that "no longer should fans wait a year or two."[19]

Dark Horse remains a prominent manga publisher because it has shown flexibility in the altering of its comic book model. Nonetheless, the next two publishers I will discuss consistently outsell Dark Horse.

THE JAPANESE MODEL (VIZ MEDIA)

Founded in 1987 by Horibuchi Seiji and owned by Japanese publisher Shogakukan, VIZ Media has become one of the powerhouses of manga publishing in America. Initially, feeling the pressure to adapt manga to American standards, such as including word balloons and colored pages, VIZ eventually went independent to try to reproduce the Japanese comics model in America (Schodt 1996). One of their first successes was the manga version of the very popular *Pokémon* anime and video game; it became "the first time any comic of Japanese origin or even any black and white comic has been number one" (Pokemon is America's Best-Selling Comic" 1999). VIZ discovered that their titles were not only potential blockbusters in the States but also that readers could learn to embrace the Japanese model and culture of manga.

With *Shōnen Jump*, VIZ successfully sold the manga magazine format to American readers. In Japan, manga publishers print all of their comics weekly, biweekly, or monthly, then collect them into a graphic novel called a *tankōbon* (Thompson 2007). Comics and manga anthologies have generally not fared well in the American market,[20] but this all changed in 2002 when another Japanese manga publisher, Shueisha, bought an interest in VIZ ("Shueisha Buys Equity Interest in VIZ" 2002). In January 2003, VIZ published an American version of Shueisha's popular weekly manga magazine, *Shōnen Jump*. The magazine benefited by having some high-profile "anchor" titles that were being aired on the Cartoon Network as anime, including *Dragon Ball Z* and *Yu-gi-oh*. Readers did not seem to mind the lower-quality paper in the magazine, different from the glossy pages of American comic books; nor were they bothered that the stories were published in black and white. These readers were not the collectors from comic book stores — although they did collect anime-based trading card games. The magazine featured articles on tips and tricks for beating opponents in card games and sometimes included special cards available only in *Shōnen Jump*. By the end of 2003, thanks to heavy marketing tie-ins with video and card games, *Shōnen Jump* sold "more than 60% since midyear, increasing from 190,000 to 305,000" ("Shonen Jump Sales Skyrocket to 305,000! 2003).[21]

As *Shōnen Jump* appealed to boys, VIZ attempted to capture the girls' market by publishing *Shōjo Beat* in 2005. While *Shōnen Jump* had offered, in addition to its series, information on card and video games, *Shōjo Beat* looked more like a girls' fashion magazine with sections titled "Culture and Trends" and "Fashion and Beauty." Its ads included clothing companies alongside ones promoting VIZ shojo titles. While not "colored" in a traditional comic book sense, *Shōjo Beat* follows the Japanese model by washing each serialized story in a different color.[22]

The covers of both *Shōnen Jump* and *Shōjo Beat* usually feature an anchor title, like Kishimoto Masashi's *Naruto*, which has already shown to be a popular draw for readers. For the other series included in the magazine, VIZ could afford to experiment with titles, replacing unpopular stories with others.[23] This information would help them decide which titles should be collected into graphic novels for sale at bookstores, and which titles they should heavily promote. By the end of 2007, VIZ put out three *Naruto* books a month amid massive marketing, with all three volumes making it into Diamond's Top 100 Graphic Novels list ("Top 100 Graphic Novels Actual" 2007).[24]

With their manga anthologies, marketing tie-ins to card and video games, and exclusive access to popular Japanese titles, VIZ Media continues to grow.

THE BOOKSTORE AND LIBRARY MODEL (TOKYOPOP)

In 1996, Stuart Levy founded Mixx Entertainment, which would become the major manga seller Tokyopop in 1998 ("Interview with Tokyopop VP Mike Kiley" 2002). Most famously, Mixx Entertainment put out the magazine *MixxZine*, which first published *Sailor Moon*. Though Tokyopop benefited from the growing shōjo fandom, they believed their material would appeal to nontraditional readers of comic books and manga. To reach this readership, bookstores were going to be an important part of their business. In 2002, Tokyopop vice president Mike Kiley noted that "there are people in strip malls in Topeka, Kansas and Madison, Wisconsin that are buying these books now that are not part of this core *otaku* crowd."[25]

Ironically, in targeting non-otaku fans, Tokyopop used a marketing strategy that would appeal to otaku. In January 2002, Tokyopop issued a press release, stating that they would not "flip" the pages of their manga. This was seen in the industry as a master stroke, since "avoiding all the adaptation chores involved in reversing the images" would "allow Tokyopop to publish its growing number of key manga titles with three-to-six times greater frequency than the current industry standard" ("Tokyopop to Publish Manga in Japanese Format" 2002). The only other title to be "unflipped" at this time was VIZ's *Dragon Ball* series because creator Toriyama Akira preferred this format ("Tokyopop to Publish Manga in Japanese Format" 2002). Tokyopop pushed the "authentic" experience of their manga by creating bookstore floor displays to hold their titles (which also appealed to stores by creating more shelf space). In big red letters at the top of the display was the word *AUTHENTIC* ("Tokyopop Plans 'Authentic' Book Dumps in April" 2002).

Though they were not targeting an otaku audience, Tokyopop was teaching the audience how to be otaku. First, they had to explain this way of reading the sequence of text and image. At the back of each novel they posted a warning that the reader was beginning in the wrong direction and provided a small how-to guide to familiarize readers with this format, sometimes even providing arrows in text at the end of pages and panels. Like VIZ Media and other manga publishers, Tokyopop included extras in their graphic novels such as *omake*,[26] plot summaries, character descriptions, and glossaries of Japanese terms and culture.

Though other publishers did not initially employ Tokyopop's format, they eventually followed its lead. Dark Horse has started to reprint "unflipped" versions of their back catalog.[27] Tokyopop's entry into the bookstore and its alteration of the book's format changed manga publishing completely, since other companies were forced to compete with their success. Though not in the business as long as Dark Horse or VIZ Media, Tokyopop currently publishes more volumes of manga than the other publishers. In 2007 they put out 510 volumes, compared to Dark Horse's 75 and VIZ's 384. Their bestseller is Takuya's *Fruits Basket*, but they have many strong sellers.[28]

THE LITERARY MODEL (VERTICAL)

New York-based Vertical is a latecomer to manga publishing but the expansion of their catalog to include manga in 2004 seemed a natural fit. Started in 2001, the company initially published contemporary Japanese genre and popular fiction and nonfiction. According to editorial director Ioannis Mentzas, they saw that classic manga titles were not being published and decided to fill this gap.[29] Vertical marketed their books as literature for an audience interested in "serious" graphic novels.[30]

Their first project was an ambitious one — Tezuka Osamu's eight-volume *Buddha* series. In bringing the "godfather" of manga's more adult work to America, Tezuka Productions put their faith in this new company. Vertical put out high-quality, hardcover editions of Tezuka's work, at $24.95 each, with paperback editions following in 2006. Beautifully designed by Chip Kidd, *Buddha* was a commercial and critical success; their first print run of 10,000 copies sold out, and the series won a Will Eisner Comic Industry Award in 2004 (Reid 2004). Their editions must have pleased Tezuka Productions, because Vertical then released Tezuka's *Kirihito Sanka* (Ode to Kirihito; October 2006); *Apollo no Uta* (Apollo's Song; June 2007); and *MW* (October 2007). They will also release Tezuka's *Black Jack*, beginning in late 2008.[31] In the book description of *MW*, Vertical exclaims that "with his sweeping vision, deftly intertwined plots, and indefatigable commitment to human dignity, Tezuka elevated manga to an art form."[32]

In appealing to a literary-minded audience, including those who might buy other Japanese books in their catalog, they made the editorial decision — quite against the norm from other manga publishers at this time — to "flip" their pages. Mentzas believes that the target audience for these books would not know how to read in the opposite direction. However, they understand that younger readers have certain expectations about how manga should look; they will leave "unflipped" those titles that they feel will appeal to this audience, including Tezuka's *Dororo* (April 2008–).

Vertical has also published early important shōjo work by Takemiya Keiko, *Terra e* (To Terra; 2007) and *Andromeda Stories* (2007–8).[33] Their latest project includes simultaneously publishing the original prose version and the manga version of the fantasy series *The Guin Saga* by Kurimoto Kaoru (manga illustrated by Yanagisawa Kazuaki; 2007–). Vertical hopes to publish more early shojo and classic manga, and their plan is that 50 percent of their current catalog will be manga titles.[34] Their entry into manga publishing reveals that companies other than VIZ and Tokyopop can find success with a niche readership.

INCREASED SPECIALIZATION AND NICHE MARKETING (OTHER PUBLISHERS)

With the success of manga in bookstores, several independent publishers as well as imprints of American publishing houses began to appear in 2004. Del Rey Manga, an imprint of the American publisher Del Rey, owned by Random House, made an impressive debut with two CLAMP titles, Tsubasa: RESERvoir CHRoNiCLE (2004–) and *xxxHolic* (2004–). Del Rey Manga managed to get these titles by forming a partnership with Japanese publisher Kodansha, and has tapped into that company's diverse catalog.[35] They currently publish more manga volumes than some other publishers, including Dark Horse (see the appendix to this chapter).[36]

Rather than competing with the big publishing houses, other publishers search for smaller, specialized audiences. One such area for potential growth are *yaoi*[37] and *josei* (women's) titles. Aurora, founded in 1996 and owned by the Ohzora publishing company, plans to expand its market to include more titles to attract older, female readers. Current releases include Tamaki Chihiro's josei title *Walkin' Butterfly* (2007–) as well as yaoi titles through their imprints Deux Press and Luv Luv Press. Even Broccoli Books, which split from Digital Manga Publishing in 2002 to focus on "supercute" manga such as Koge-Donbo's *Di Gi Charat: Dejiko's Adventure* (2004–7) and other *Di Gi Charat* titles (Cha 2006), has launched a boys' love imprint, Boysenberry, in 2007 ("Broccoli Launches 'Boys' Love' Imprint 'Boysenberry Books'" 2007).[38]

Now that manga has been shown to be a successful seller thanks to the inroads made by Dark Horse, VIZ Media, and Tokyopop, smaller companies can afford to take more risks, bringing diverse titles to American readers. One of the newest manga publishers, Yen Press, launched in 2007 and a subsidiary of Hachette Books,[39] has put out an unusual title, Tobe Keiko's *Hikari to Tomoni . . . Jiheishouji Wo Kakaete* (With the Light . . . Raising an Autistic

Child; 2007–), about a mother's relationship with her autistic child.[40]

As the manga market grows, smaller manga companies are experimenting with different stories, art, and genres to appeal to a hungry readership. Unlike the comic book stores that featured one type of book geared repeatedly to the same readership, these publishers are bringing new titles searching for new readers.

APPENDIX: FROM *THE ICv2 GUIDE TO MANGA* 50 (MARCH/APRIL 2008)
RELEASES BY YEAR (IN TOTAL NUMBER OF VOLUMES)

Publisher	2005	2006	2007	2008
Aurora	0	0	6	36
Bandai	0	0	15	18
Broccoli Books	7	9	24	27
CMX	60	85	100	114
CPM	17	8	11	17
Dark Horse	30	62	75	88
Del Rey	37	72	104	143
Digital Manga	0	0	78	102
Dr. Master	0	0	34	36
Go Comi!	4	23	33	60
Media Blasters	0	0	12	24
Seven Seas	0	0	25	40
Tokyopop	380	400	510	504
Udon	6	13	25	40
VIZ	400	415	384	400
Vertical	0	0	12	12
Yaoi Press	0	0	14	10
Yen Press	0	0	6	60
Total	941	1087	1468	1731

Source: ICv2.com (http://www.icv2.com)

Notes

1. When I first wrote this essay, the manga market was growing; however, as of Fall 2008, the American economy had faltered, affecting nearly every industry,

including publishing. According to ICv2.com, "The number of volumes of manga that publishers are planning to release in 2009 is down nearly 10% from the number actually released in 2008" ("Projected Manga Releases Down in 2009" 2008). It remains to be seen what the full effect of a recession will do to this market.

2. According to ICv2's *Guide to Anime* 50 (2008), "the number of anime releases are decreasing compared to 2006, while the number of new manga new volumes continue to rise." See this chapter's appendix for the growing number of manga volumes released from 2005 to 2008.

3. *Barefoot Gen* was initially translated by Project Gen, "a non-profit, all-volunteer group of young Japanese and Americans living in Tokyo" (Asazuma 2004, 237). From 1980 to 1982 Leonard Rifas, founder of Educomics, published the first two volumes of *Gen* and *Ore wa Mita* (I Saw It), the author's autobiographical account of Hiroshima. *Gen's* "repeated failures," according to Rifas, came because "the mainstream American comic book industry was heavily dominated by two comic book companies, both of them specializing in superhero stories, and neither of them demonstrating much interest in the risks of publishing other kinds of material" (Rifas, 2004, 144).

4. Carl Horn, interview with the editor, December 10, 2007. For more on the black-and-white comic boom/bust in the 1980s, see Groth 2006.

5. This was originally published by First Comics in the 1980s; Dark Horse picked up the license and published the twenty-eight-volume set from 2000 to 2002. The series consistently broke into the top twenty-five selling graphic novels according to ICv2.com ("Dark Horse Releases Retro Manga Sales: Lone Wolf, Akira Blowing the Doors Off" 2001). The first volume "sold over 27,000 copies, a big number for a graphic novel" ("Dark Horse Retro Manga Boffo: Old School Material, Format Finds Fans" 2001). Dark Horse has also published other Koike titles, including *Shurayukihime* (Lady Snowblood; 4 vols., 2005–6); *Kubikiri Asa* (Samurai Executioner; 10 vols., 2004–6), and is currently publishing Koike's *Hanzo no Mon* (Path of the Assassin; 2006–) and *Crying Freeman* (2006–; originally published by VIZ Media,1995–96).

6. VIZ also issued the series in graphic novel form as a *Perfect Collection* (1995–97). An "Editor's Choice Edition" came out in 2004.

7. "Instead of producing a variety of comics for a variety of people, the industry increasingly produced a single kind of comics for an insular, though devoted, audience," notes Rogers, focusing particularly on "reader-collectors" (1997, 2). In the early 1990s, comics not only became equated with superheroes but also became investments or relics to be preserved. In order to create demand, Marvel published new series for their flagship titles such as Chris Claremont and Jim Lee's *X-Men* and Todd McFarlane's *Spider-Man*. These issues started with the "coveted" first issue and had varying cover designs. Collectors bought multiples in the hope that the price would eventually reach the levels of the golden age of comics. In turn, comic book stores, fueled by high sales, bought more and more to fill this artificial need. The shelves were crowded with superhero comics.

8. *Sailor Moon* was then published in graphic novel format in April 1998 by Tokyopop.

9. See also "Sailor Moon Graphic Novels Top Bookstore Sales" (2008), in which the writer notes that *Sailor Moon* outsold mainstream superhero comics: "Book Scan, the professional service that tracks sell-through in the book market lists *Sailor Moon* books with juvenile titles where it has to compete with *Harry Potter*, *Goosebumps,* and *Anamorphs . . .* if *Sailor Moon* were listed with graphic novels, it would easily have topped Marvel's *Ultimate X-Men* collection, which did head Book Scan's most recent list of graphic novel bestsellers."

10. Though online fandom (most notably the "Save Our Sailors" campaign, started

in 1996; see http://www.saveoursailors.org) expressed great disappointment with DC Entertainment's editing of the *Sailor Moon* anime, most notably changing the gender of certain characters to avoid *shōnen-ai* (Boys' Love) and *shōjo-ai* (Girls' Love) overtones, the outcry not only showed that there was an audience for a title like *Sailor Moon* but revealed that these readers desired *unedited* shōjo anime and manga. To show how much time has changed, as of this writing, Amazon.com prominently displays a yaoi category in their graphic novel section.

11.   Some CLAMP titles include: *Cardcaptor Sakura* (Tokyopop 1999–2003) and *Mahô Kishi Rayearth* (Magic Knight Rayearth; Tokyopop 1999–2001). Watase Yū's books include *Fushigi Yûgi* (Fushigi Yugi: The Mysterious Play; VIZ Media, 1998–2006) and *Ayashi no Ceres* (Ceres: Celestial Legend; VIZ Media 2001–6).

12.   See "The Hidden Manga Consumer: In Stores and Libraries" (2005). Dark Horse editor Carl Horn relates that while on a long plane ride he noticed two young girls reading manga, and upon finishing, exchanged their titles (interview with the editor, December 10, 2007). Because of the rising numbers of teen readers demanding more manga in their libraries, librarians have scrambled to educate themselves about graphic novels. There are numerous resources available to them online and in print. Some examples include Steve Miller, "Graphic Novels on the Web" (www.angelfire.com/comics/gnlib/); Michael R. Lavin, "Comic Books for Young Adults" (ublib.buffalo.edu/libraries/units/lml/comics/pages/); and Gilles Poitras's "The Librarian's Guide to Anime and Manga" (www.koyagi.com/Libguide. html). Recent printed guides for librarians include two new books: Brenner's *Understanding Manga and Anime* (2007) and Pawuk's *A Genre Guide to Comic Books, Manga, and More* (2007).

13.   *Pokémon* manga are fewer in number and are mostly spinoffs from the anime and games.

14.   According to *USA Today* their booklist "is based on a computer analysis of retail sales nationwide last week. Included are more than 1.5 million volumes from about 4,700 independent, chain, discount and online booksellers" ("About the Best-Selling Booklist" 2006). Anime News Network reports, "Of the 27 volumes of the manga that VIZ Media has published in English so far, 24 have made it onto *USA Today's* list" ("*USA Today* Booklist December 31–January 6" 2008).

15.   The hypercollecting boom in the early 1990s also affected Dark Horse, which released *Outlanders* issue no. 0 on March 1, 1992. This was a common ploy at this time. If issue number 1 titles were collectible, then issue no. 0 could be even more so.

16.   Both titles were written and drawn by Adam Warren.

17.   Because the *Ghost in the Shell* movie was released the same year that the manga came out, Dark Horse was able to take advantage of what would become very important to companies like VIZ Media — the marketing of a product across different platforms. Dark Horse later published the second *Ghost in the Shell* series in 2003 and *Ghost in the Shell* 1.5 in 2006–7.

18.   Dark Horse broadened their catalog with *Legend of Mother Sarah* (1995–97) by Ōtomo Katsuhiro, most famously known for *Akira*. The publisher later picked up *Akira*, reprinting it in six volumes in 2000. *Akira* was originally published by Epic Comics, an imprint of Marvel, in 1989 through the mid-1990s, where it was colored and edited. Marvel even asked Ōtomo to provide an alternate ending.

19.   Carl Horn, interview with the editor, December 10, 2007.

20.   For more on manga anthologies see Farago (2007). Examples of manga anthologies include *Animerica* (VIZ Media, 1993–2005), published for free and distributed through bookstores and Best Buy; *Manga VIZion* (VIZ Media) 1995–98; *MixxZine* (Mixx Entertainment, 1997); *Smile* (Mixx Entertainment/ Tokyopop, 1998–2000; see Arnold 2000); *Pulp* (VIZ Media, 1997–2002, featuring mature, *seinen manga* titles; *Manga* (Tokyopop, 1999–2000, a culture magazine

with manga); *Chibi Pop Manga* (Chibi Pop Manga, 1999–2000); *Raijin Comics* (Gutsoon! Entertainment, 2002–4); *Super Manga Blast* (Dark Horse, 2000–6, serializing *Ah! My Goddess* and *What's Michael*); *Animerica Extra* (VIZ Media, 1998–2004, which became a shojo publication only in 2003, later to be replaced by VIZ's *Shojo Beat*); and *Newtype USA* (ADV, 2002–8; though it published excerpts, it was not truly a manga anthology, but was an important magazine about manga and anime releases and was replaced by *PiQ* magazine; see "Newtype USA Ending 'PiQ' Launching" 2008).

21.   Current popular titles in the magazine include Kishimoto Masashi's *Naruto* (2003–), Oda Eīchirō's *One Piece* (2003–), Tite Kubo's *Bleach* (2007–); Takahashi Kazuki's *Yu-gi-oh GX* (2007–), and Ohba Tsugumi's *Death Note* (2007–8).

22.   Currently featured titles include Watase Yū's *Zettai Kareshi* (Absolute Boyfriend; 2006–) and Umino Chica's *Honey and Clover* (2008).

23.   For example, VIZ dropped *Shaman King* from *Shōnen Jump* and replaced it with *Bleach* in 2007. Unlike *Shaman King*, *Bleach* greatly benefited from the anime series airing on the Cartoon Network.

24.   Other popular VIZ titles include Arakawa Hiromu's *Fullmetal Alchemist* (2005–); Ohba Tsugumi and Obata Takeshi's Death Note (2005–7); Watsuki Nobuhiro's *Rurōuni Kenshin* (2003–6); and Takahashi Rumiko's *Ranma ½* (2003–).

25.   Kiley also commented, "The comic book business was the foundation for Tokyopop and it continues to be very important to us but the leaps-and-bounds gains are totally in the bookstores — big chains." ("Interview with Tokyopop VP Mike Kiley" 2002). Tokyopop President Levy also stated that the company could not rely on comic book stores to push their titles, that "specialty shops [were] too much of a niche to be the company's sole outlet" ("Stu Levy: Founder of Tokyopop" 2007).

26.   *Omake* are extra, often humorous, stories that may feature the characters in silly situations or may even be a story about the manga's author.

27.   In the 2007 book description of Dark Horse's reprinted *Appleseed*, they write, "produced in the authentic right-to-left reading format, as originally published in Japan."

28.   Other titles include CLAMP's *Chobits* (2002–3) and *Cardcaptor Sakura* (1999–2003); Akamatsu Ken's *Love Hina* (2002–3); Kamijyo Akimine's shōnen manga *Samurai Deeper Kyo* (2003–); and Kōga Yun's *Loveless* (2006–).

29.   Ioannis Mentzas, interview with the editor, December 21, 2007.

30.   The rise of the American graphic novel has definitely contributed to Vertical's success. Once bookstores could promote comic book titles to adult readers, Vertical could target this same audience. As mentioned earlier in this essay, Art Spiegelman's *Maus* was the most prominent graphic novel to show that the medium could tell serious stories. Other award-winning graphic fiction included Marjane Satrapi's *Persepolis*, Alison Bechdal's *Fun Home*, Harvey Pekar's *American Splendor*, amd Chris Ware's *Acme Novelty Library*, to name a few.

31.   Previously, two volumes of this series had been published by VIZ, in 1997 and 1999; see Thompson 2007, 31.

32.   See http://www.vertical-inc.com/books/MW/MW_preview01.html.

33.   Kai-Ming Cha writes, "Takemiya is considered one of the pillars of shōjo manga, having been part of the Fabulous 49ers, the group of women artists and writers who established and solidified the girls' comics industry in Japan in the mid and late 1970s." Cha notes that Takeyima was especially important in the growth of "boys' love and yaoi titles although *To Terra* is not of this genre" (Cha 2007).

34.   Mentzas interview.

35.   Their catalog includes Hayakawa Tomoko's shōjo title *Yamatonadeshiko Shichihenge* (The Wallflower; 2004–), Shimoku Kio's otaku-training *Genshiken* (2005–7), Urushibara Yuki's lyrical *Mushishi* (2007–) and Iwaaki Hitoshi's horror

comic *Kiseiju* (Parasyte; 2007–; originally released by Tokyopop, 1997–2002; see Thompson 2007, 264).

36. Another manga publisher is CMX Manga, an imprint of DC comics, launched in 2004. Marvel Comics, on the other hand, has made its comics looks more like manga. In January 2002 it launched the Marvel Mangaverse line, in which traditional titles such as *Spider-Man* and the *X-Men* are drawn in manga style. In late 2007, Marvel announced a further experimentation with a short shonen series featuring Wolverine. ("Marvel and Del Rey Announce Manga Pact" pwbeat. publishersweekly.com/blog/2007/12/10/marvel-and-del-rey-announce-manga-pact 12/10/07).

37. Unfortunately, due to economic realities, Broccoli Books closed its doors in November 2008.

38. Yaoi describes manga subgenre written for women, featuring male-male love stories. They are usually erotically charged with very little narrative. Yaoi is an acronym for yamanashi, ochinashi, iminashi, which translates as "no climax, no conclusion, no meaning" (see Thompson 2007, 415).

39. See the Yen Press website, http://www.hachettebookgroupusa.com/features/yenpress/index.html.

40. They also publish more mainstream titles, like Peach-Pit's *Zombie-Loan* (2007–).

References

"About the Best-Selling Booklist" (2006). *USA Today*, http://www.usatoday.com/life/books/booksdatabase/2006-06-14-bookslist-about_x.htm.

Arnold, Adam "Omega" (2000). "*Full Circle: The Unofficial History of MixxZine*." *ANIMEfringe: An Online Anime/Manga E-Zine*, http://www.animefringe.com/magazine/00.06/feature/1/index.php.

Asazuma, Namie (2004). "About Project Gen." *Barefoote Gen Volume 2*. San Francisco: Last Gasp. 278–8.

Brenner, Robin E. (2007). *Understanding Manga and Anime*. Westport, CT: Libraries Unlimited.

"Broccoli Launches 'Boys' Love' Imprint 'Boysenberry Books'" (2007). ICv2.com, http://www.icv2.com/articles/news/10126.html.

Cha, Kai-Ming (2006). "Super-Cute Broccoli Grows in the U.S." *Publisher's Weekly*, http://www.publishersweekly.com/article/CA6375151.html.

—— (2007). "Takemiya's Classic Manga, *To Terra*." *Publisher's Weekly*, http://www.publishersweekly.com/article/CA6416132.html?q=shojo+%22Takemiya%22.

"Dark Horse Acquires Studio Proteus: Including Manga Titles by Eclipse and Innovation" (2004). ICv2.com, http://www.icv2.com/articles/news/4230.html.

"Dark Horse Releases Retro Manga Sales: Lone Wolf, Akira Blowing the Doors Off" (2001). ICv2.com, http://www.icv2.com/articles/news/785.html.

"Dark Horse Retro Manga Boffo: Old School Material, Format Finds Fans" (2001). ICv2, http://www.icv2.com/articles/news/69.html.

Farago, Andrew (2007). "Jason Thompson." *Comics Journal*, http://www.tcj.com/index.php?option=com_content&task=view&id=697&Itemid=70.

"Fruits Basket Reaches Two Million Units" (2006). Anime News Network, http://www.animenewsnetwork.com/press-release/2006-12-06/fruits-basket-reaches-two-million-units.

"Fruits Basket Sets Booklist Record" (2006). Anime News Network, http://www.animenewsnetwork.com/news/2006-08-17/fruits-basket-sets-booklist-record.

Gravett, Paul (2004). *Manga: Sixty Years of Japanese Comics*. New York: HarperCollins.

Groth, Gary (2006). "Black and White and Dead All Over." *Comics Journal*, http://www.tcj.com/index.php?option=com_content&task=view&id=366&Itemid=48.

"The Hidden Manga Consumer: In Stores and Libraries" (2005). ICv2.com, http://www.icv2.com/articles/news/7049.html.

"Interview with Dark Horse CEO Mike Richardson" (2008). ICv2.com, http://www.icv2.com/articles/news/11807.html.

"Interview with Tokyopop VP Mike Kiley: The Growth Is In Bookstores" (2002). ICv2.com, http://www.icv2.com/articles/news/1614.html.

"Marvel and Del Rey Announce Manga Pact" (2007). *Publisher's Weekly*, pwbeat. publishersweekly.com/blog/2007/12/10/marvel-and-del-rey-announce-manga-pact.

"Nausicaa around the World" (2008). *Nausicaa Net*, http://www.nausicaa.net/miyazaki/manga/nausicaaworld.html#japan.

"'Newtype USA' Ending; 'PiQ' Launching" (2008). ICv2.com, http://www.icv2.com/articles/news/11893.html.

Pawuk, Michael (2006). *Graphic Novels: A Genre Guide to Comic Books, Manga, and More*. Westport, CT: Libraries Unlimited.

"Philip Simon on 'Blade of the Immortal': Dark Horse Editor Explains the Transition to 'Trades Only'" (2007). ICv2.com, http://www.icv2.com/articles/news/11490.html.

"Pokemon is America's Best-Selling Comic Book" (1999). AnimeNewsNetwork, http://www.animenewsnetwork.com/news/1999-06-24/pokemon-is-america's-best-selling-comic-book.

"Projected Manag Releases Down in 2009" (2008). ICv2.com, http://www.icv2.com/articles/news/13982.html.

Reid, Calvin (2004). "Vertical Concedes It Went Too Far, Spent Too Much." *Publishers' Weekly*, http://www.publishersweekly.com/article/CA444796.html.

Rifas, Leonard. (2004) "Globalizing Comic Books from Below: How Manga Came to America." *International Journal of Comic Art* 6(2): 138–71.

Rogers, Mark Christiancy. (1997). *Beyond Bang! Pow! Zap!: Genre and the Evolution of the American Comic Book Industry*. University of Michigan, Program in American Culture. Dissertation Abstracts International, Section A: The Humanities and Social Sciences, 1997 Nov; 58(5): 1783–84.

"Sailor Moon Graphic Novels Top Bookstore Sales" (2001). ICv2.com, http://www.icv2.com/articles/news/625.html.

Schodt, Frederik L. (1996). *Dreamland Japan: Writings on Modern Manga*. Berkeley, CA: Stone Bridge Press.

"Shojo Manga and Anime — Big Business in Japan: Rapidly Growing in North America" (2001). ICv2.com, http://www.icv2.com/articles/news/605.html.

"Shonen Jump Sales Skyrocket to 305,000! Single Issue Hits 540,000 Copies Sold" (2003). ICv2.com, http://www.icv2.com/articles/news/3867.html.

"Shueisha Buys Equity Interest in VIZ: Links to Two of Japan's Top Three Publishers" (2002). ICv2.com, http://www.icv2.com/articles/news/1679.html.

Spiegelman, Art (1990). "Barefoot Gen: Comics After the Bomb." *Barefoot Gen: Out of the Ashes*. Philadelphia, PA: New Society Publishers. v–vii.

"Stu Levy: Founder of Tokyopop" (2007). Variety Asia Online, http://www.varietyasiaonline.com/content/view/4793.

Thompson, Jason (2007). *The Complete Guide to Manga*. New York: Ballantine Books.

"Tokyopop Plans 'Authentic' Book Dumps in April: With Special Pricing to Support Manga Launch" (2002). ICv2.com, http://www.icv2.com/articles/news/1073.html.

"Tokyopop to Publish Manga in Japanese Format: Change Will Affect Publisher's Entire Line-Up" (2002). ICv2.com, http://www.icv2.com/articles/news/1067.html.

"Top 200 Comics — March, 2001: Quantity Estimates Based on Diamond Indexes and External Title Data" (2001). ICv2.com, http://www.icv2.com/articles/home/192.html.

"Top 100 Graphic Novels Actual — November 2007: Sales Estimates for November Based on Diamond Indexes and Publisher Title Data: Sales Estimates for November

Based on Diamond Indexes and Publisher Title Data" (2007). ICv2.com, http://www.icv2.com/articles/home/11778.html.

"*USA Today* Booklist December 31–January 6" (2008). Anime News Network, http://www.animenewsnetwork.com/news/2008-01-11/usa-today-booklist-december-31-january-6.

18
Manga in East Asia

John A. Lent

During the past twenty to thirty years, manga culture has inundated parts of East and Southeast Asia and to varying degrees has changed leisure time activities, decimated local comics industries in some instances and hybridized them in others, and occasionally nourished new interest in an entertainment form that had wilted under the strains of competition from other media, overused writing/drawing formulas, and societal neglect.

The survival of manga in Asia outside Japan was not always a certainty; at times, it faced a Sisyphean task, dodging denouncements from high government officials, cartoonists, parents, and teachers and facing censorship and bannings. Manga usually endured because of the illegal piracy rampant in the region and the persistence of Japanese economic and cultural strategists.

One big boost for the export of manga came in the mid-1990s, when Japan's economic bubble burst and the country looked feverishly for foreign markets, among them the markets for its popular culture products (Lent 2004, 40). The *Japan Times* gave as another reason for the huge exportation of manga the government's eagerness to use comics subculture to promote the Japanese image, still tarnished in parts of Asia by World War II atrocities. Calling manga and anime Japan's new ambassadors, the *Japan Times* noted that "as Japanese manga and anime become loved beyond expectations, they have also come to represent the culture as cameras or Mount Fuji did in previous generations" ("Ambassadors Manga and Anime" 2007).

Japanese popular culture made inroads into East Asia long before the arrival of manga. Both Korea and Taiwan were under decades of Japanese colonialization, and like the rest of East Asia and almost all of Southeast Asia, were occupied by Japan during World War II. However, though Japanese popular culture existed in these territories, it was not readily embraced by populations that remembered wartime atrocities and deprivation. For example, relative to manga, both South Korea and Taiwan had government

policies and bodies to curb their importation, none of which was very effective because of the widespread piracy. In fact, for decades, Taiwan has served
as an intermediary station on the routing of manga from Japan to other parts
of Asia.

In an effort to explain the current popularity of Japanese popular culture
in Asia given this history, Koichi Iwabuchi notes two factors: (1) it appeals
to the new rich youth of Asia, and (2) Japanese cultural industries in Asian
markets are informed by Japan's reflections on its own experience of indigenization of United States popular cultural influences since World War II
— the Japanese appropriated U.S. popular culture and were not colonized
by it (2001, 25). He adds, "If Japanese popular culture is well-received by
Hong Kong, Taiwanese and South Korean media industries and consumers,
it might be because it lucidly represents intertwined composition of global
homogenization and heteregenization in East Asian context" (2001, 27).

HISTORY AND DEVELOPMENT

The newest East Asian country in the manga phenomenon is China, which,
until the 1980s, operated under a closed economy, with a Chinese type of
comic book, *lianhuanhua*, prevailing. Manga became popular in the late
1990s, partly because of the amount of *anime* (Japanese animation) shown
on Chinese television and because of more Japanese-Chinese interaction
through business and tourism. Now manga can be found in abundance on
newsstands and in bookstores in China. One modern comics café I visited in
Shanghai carried mostly manga and manga paraphernalia as well as Japanese
videos, with small sections devoted to comics from Hong Kong, Taiwan, and
Korea but absolutely nothing produced in China.

China's tie-ins with manga precede liberation in 1949, going back to 1921,
when master cartoonist Feng Zikai studied in Tokyo for ten months. There
he was exposed to the "poetic resonance" of Yumeji Takehisa's sketches
and the "casual essays executed as paintings" of nineteenth century painter
Hokusai. Although manga as comic book did not exist, manga denoting cartoons or caricatures was in wide use (Barmé 2002, 93). Feng was enthralled
by manga, fitting it to his own artistic and philosophical perspectives.
Biographer Christophe Harbsmeier notes, "It [manga] was basically a popular, an 'unbuttoned' art form which stood in defiant opposition to official
and 'respectable' art. The *manga* represented an alternative tradition, an
iconoclastic subculture that valued spontaneity not perfectionist virtuos-
ity. Often the *manga* were provocatively vulgar in subject matter. They were
concerned with everyday things or with grotesque fantasies" (1984, 19).

Upon his return to China, Feng imitated this style, publishing his drawings in *Women* (We) and *Wenxuezhoubao* (Literary Review). Harbsmeier

has noted that, because of Feng's stylistic links to manga, *Wenxuezhoubao* editors termed his sketches *manhua* (1984, 20). However, contrary to popular belief, *manhua* is probably not a term derived from the term *manga*; evidence reveals the word was used in China since at least the twelfth century, and as a reference to casual, impromptu paintings in the early eighteenth century.

Japanese manga was thriving in Hong Kong before the territory reverted to China in 1997. Initially influenced by Chinese models, Hong Kong's comics began to change in the late 1960s as pirated copies of manga translated and reprinted in Taiwan came in and Japanese animation for children was broadcast on local television. The pirated versions were either directly reproduced from the originals without mention of the creators' names or were completely redrawn by local artists (Wong 2006, 30). Local comics' stories, plots, character design, and drawing styles began to take on Japanese characteristics by the late 1960s. Ng Wai-ming coments that Hong Kong comics at that time adopted manga's penchant for longer stories, cinematic angles, and particular human features such as girls with big eyes and long legs (2003, 184).

Giants of early Hong Kong comics, such as Tony Wong (Wong Yuk-long), Ma Wing-shing, and the brothers Kwong Tung-yuen and Kwong Nam-lun, were mainly inspired by manga. Wong's company Jademan (Yuk-long) even adopted assembly line production techniques common to Japanese publishing in which each person has a specific function. Wong refined the system, putting as many as twenty artists on each book (five times the number used by the Japanese) and tiering employees according to skills and functions, notes Liu Sui Yin, Jademan production controller (Liu interview 1992). Wong was also credited with putting his comics in a Hong Kong context. His career was deterred in the early 1990s when he was imprisoned for fraudulent business dealings.

Ronnie Ma Shuk Chu, sister of Ma Wing-shing and general manager of his comic book company, Tin Ha (Jonesky), has said that Ma learned much from the Japanese but felt he and some others had developed their "own style, own feeling." She did not see the importation of manga as unhealthy or competitive but as an opportunity for artists to see new trends and to "put something new in their work as a result" (Ma interview 1992). Ma Wing-shing himself admitted to being a big fan of manga and learning much from it and from manga creators Ryōichi Ikegami, Tadashi Matsumori, and Kazuo Koike (Ng 2003, 187).

Old guard comics publishers the Kwong brothers published four weeklies, translated and printed forty pirated Japanese manga, and owned a comic book store by the 1990s. Kwong Nam-lun, considered one of Hong Kong's most active comics pirates, explains that bringing out illegal Japanese comics was relatively easy: "I'd just buy a copy of a Japanese comic in a department store, pay someone to translate it, and print it. There would be at least five hundred buyers for each pirated title" (Kwong interview 1992). He explains that the piracy business had suffered by the 1990s because local comics had become more popular than those from Japan and because local publishers had started paying for the rights to certain manga titles, and that once that was done he could no longer pirate those titles.

Among the first to purchase Japanese sublicenses were the Freeman Collective and Tony Wong, after his release from prison in April 1993. That same month, Freeman purchased several sets of Cantonese-language rights to Japanese manga; Wong later bought the Cantonese-language rights to *Dragon Ball*, *Ranma ½*, *Patlabor*, and *Doraemon*, all of which were also televised (Clements 1996).

In the past the Hong Kong authorities had turned a blind eye toward piracy. One critic of the comics, Yuen Kin-to, editor of *Monthly Comic Magazine*, comments, "You can do all the illegal pirating you want as the law allows you to escape. No company has been penalized; they just stop doing business and then start up again later on" (Yuen interview 1992). As *Monthly Comic Magazine* Publisher C. Ming Pang explains, "It is easy to start a company here; costs [HK]$1150, so if a pirate is sued, he closes down and starts a new company" (Pang interview 1992) .

Similar ruses were prevalent in the mid-1990s. One, as previously mentioned, was to import Chinese translations of manga reproduced in Taiwan. Technically these were Taiwanese publications so there was no need to buy the Hong Kong rights. One result was that the Taiwanese edition of the manga *Crayon Shin-Chan* (Crayon Shin-Chan), was released in Hong Kong one full month before the Hong Kong edition appeared (Clements 1996, 19).

Since the 1990s, some Hong Kong comics publishers, particularly Jademan, have collaborated with the Japanese, mainly providing artists to draw their manga in Chinese style (Liu interview 1992). In exchange, Scholar, the Japanese subsidiary of Kodansha, sold Jademan titles in Japan (Wan interview 1992). David Ki, former general manager of Jademan, comments, "We started to cooperate with the Japanese not to have Hong Kong comics land in Japan. I think Japan is using Hong Kong as a stepping stone to enter China's market. . . . The Japanese try to control all quality. They prepare all scripts, and the Hong Kong artists do the drawing and inking only. The enterprise of the Japanese is to use Hong Kong labor and become a distributor to other countries" (Ki interview 1992).

The manga market in Hong Kong has been greatly expanded since the early 1990s, especially with Wong's new company Jade Dynasty and Ma's Jonesky both publishing licensed Chinese-version manga to diversify their revenue sources. A third company, Culture Comics, had published more than three hundred licensed manga titles from its founding in 1992 until 2005 (Wong 2006, 32–33). During that period, the format, size, and frequency of Hong Kong comic books changed to the Japanese style, and many aspects of manga culture — rental shops, comics Internet cafés, *dōjinshi* (fanzine), cosplay (dress as favorite characters) — became very popular in Hong Kong. Additionally, Hong Kong publishers and artists experimented with *shōjo* (girls'), erotic, and scatological comics, and Japanese methods of drawing and presentation became "clichés" in Hong Kong comics. Among the latter were different-shaped speech balloons to denote loudness and the emotions of speakers; the "cute version" or "Q version," where the size of the protagonist suddenly becomes small and distorted, used for humorous effect; sound used to depict activities and emotions; and the Japanese methods of portraying facial expressions (Ng 2003, 190). Many Hong Kong comics about car racing, soccer, and yoyo playing are modified from the bestselling manga titles *Initial D*, *Captain Tsubasa*, and *Beyblade*; adaptations of Japanese video games are also very popular. *Street Fighter* and *King of Fighters* have evolved into more than ten comic books in Hong Kong (Ng 2003, 189). Much of the artistry of the late 1990s and early 2000s was done by cartoonists who grew up with manga and anime — for example, Situ Jianqiao, who mixes Japanese science fiction with Hong Kong kung fu comics and even sends his work to Japanese masters for critiquing, and Li Zhida, whose work combines "Otomo Katsuhiro's drawings and post-modern feel, Mochizuki Minetaro's and Murakami Haruki's imaginative, unconventional and discursive plots, and Maruo Suehiro's sense of craziness" (Ng 2003, 189).

Alan Wan, deputy chairman of the Jade Dynasty Group, comments that after the copyright concept was well established in Hong Kong in the 1990s, Japanese comics became more important and anime and Japanese merchandise (especially interactive games) even more pervasive than manga. He said he quit drawing in 1990 to concentrate on marketing and developing licensed works from Japan, which, in turn, expanded the market, bringing in more readers while at the same time not taking away from local comics. Wan pinpointed 1994–96 as the top period of Hong Kong comics; saying that both those who imported manga and those who produced local comics made money easily. In 2007, Jade Dynasty, which controlled more than half the comics market, published nine local titles weekly and thirty issues of manga (Cha 2007).

Koreans have been schizophrenic in their relationship with manga, torn between being attracted to it and feeling obliged to boycott it. Some Japanese influence on Korean cartooning came about in the earliest part of the twentieth century when Japan occupied the Korean Peninsula; by the 1920s, *manhwa*, a word derived from the Japanese, was applied to cartoons (for a history of Korean cartooning, see Lent 1995).

Serious importation of manga began in the late 1970s, with the opening up of a market for adult comics, also fueled by a number of domestic publications. The earliest manga titles brought to Korea were adapted to the local culture, providing a patchwork made up of different endings to suit Korea, a change of settings, and even switching a character from male to female or vice versa (Yamanaka 2006, 196). In 1980, the Korean Social Purification Committee cracked down on adult manga and manhwa, resulting in the indictment or arrest of scores of publishers and cartoonists, the withdrawal of authorization permits from nineteen publishing companies, and confiscation of 28,000 offensive (violent or obscene) comic books ("Dirty Strips" 1980, 17; "It's Not So Funny" 1986, 6).

The situation was only aggravated in 1987 when, in the throes of democratization, a government measure allowed local publishers to print anything they wished without prior censorship, as long as they first registered with the authorities. Adaptations of manga disappeared, replaced by copies — that is, manga that was mechanically copied, their pages "flipped" to read left to right, and lines translated word for word (Yamanaka 2006, 196). The influx of manga copies gave rise to an increase in quickly drawn series of the most successful Japanese comics weeklies, a result of which was that domestic artists had to discard the traditional comics rental system in favor of weekly serialization (Yamanaka 2006, 197).

The outcome of this loosening up was that, "From then on, money-grubbing publishers eager to get on the commercial bandwagon began to indiscriminately copy vulgar comics which appeared in Japanese weeklies, or substandard adult comic books published in single editions in Japan" ("Japanese Cartoons Flood Korea" 1991, 28). The following year, at least 134 comic book duplicates appeared.

Domestic publishers changed their routine in the early 1990s, either serializing Japanese comics in local cartoon weeklies or publishing them in single editions. The Korea Ethics Committee on Books, Magazines, and Weekly Newspapers, which in 1991 began serious scrutiny of the publication of Japanese comics in Korea, reported that during the 1987 to October 1990 period, 200 kinds of Japanese comics were imported and published by thirty-four local publishers. Only 21 were written for children; the remaining 179 were designed for adults, with violent or sports stories. All but 4 of the books were reproduced without the permission of the original authors or publishers ("Japanese Cartoons Flood Korea" 1991, 28).

Despite efforts to monitor the comics industry more closely, cutthroat competition among publishers continued, often resulting in "publication pollution," with popular Japanese comic book stories brought out under title variations. For example, *Dragon Ball*, a Japanese comic story by Toriyama Akira first published in Korea by Seoul Publishing, had fifteen additional versions by other publishers, including *Dragon Ball Z, Dragon Ball Q, Dragon Ball Cabal of Taoist Magic*, and so on.

In the early 1990s, the Ethics Committee was stymied in its efforts to clean up the industry because of the size of the task and their limited monitoring capability (one full-time and five part-time members meeting twice monthly), the changing nature of vaguely written regulations, and the gradual liberalization of the importation of Japanese cultural products such as manga (Cha interview 1994). For a time, the committee precensored manga, which was contradictory to the government's total ban on Japanese cultural imports. The only permanent member of the committee, Cha Ae-ock, estimated that three hundred illegal manga titles got into Japan between 1990 and 1994, many translated and reprinted by Korean comics firms. The committee was looking for, she explains, "cases of obscenity and violent content. Some kisses are all right, but deep kisses are not. Generally, however, kissing is okay. But, there can be no nudity, profanity, stabbing, blood, shootings, amputations, et cetera. In children's comics, showing a weapon is allowed, but not its use" (Cha interview 1994).

Because of manga's immense profits, publishers continued to mold their business practices and their books' contents after the Japanese pattern. Hwang Kyung Tae, head of the huge Dai Won Publishing Company, comments, "Since Japanese comic books started much earlier, we must study them to be successful; we try to approach the comics industry like the Japanese" (Hwang interview 1994). In cases where Korean comics publishers translated and reprinted manga or used Japanese stories in their comics magazines, cost definitely was the major factor. Critic Choi Suk Tae said that the many manga in bookstores often were translated, pirated versions, and as such, allowed the stores to skim 75 percent of the book prices as profit. As a result, he added, the stores were not keen to carry Korean artists' works (Choi interview 1994). For the same profitability reason, Korean comics magazines usually consisted of 20 percent Japanese stories (Jung interview 1994).

A number of efforts were made in the 1980s and '90s to profoundly change the local comics industry. Among them were the birth of comics magazines in the mid-1980s and, slightly later, the use of retail bookstores (in addition to rental shops) as comics outlets. The expected result of higher quality comics and a lessened use of manga did not materialize. Concerning the latter, where Korean comics did not fill voids in genres, those from Japan were substituted and, as already mentioned, the new magazines had considerable Japanese content.

As at other times, the Korean public and parts of the cartooning profession in the late 1980s and early '90s railed against the onslaught of manga. Particularly involved were the Korean Cartoonists Association and Uri

Manhwa Myophoe (Our Cartoon Association), a group of cartoonists and friends formed in 1992. Members of the latter body led a public demonstration in July 1992, at which manga was denounced and Korean cartoonists considered unduly influenced by it were identified and ridiculed. Uri Manhwa Myophoe staged other anti-Japanese comics events, including an awareness-building exhibition/screening in July 1994, and lobbied for government action. The two-week *Active Cartoon* exhibition, which I attended, featured Korean cartoonists who did not want to compromise their work because of manga, displayed early manhwa with Japanese influences, and castigated manga in displays. Major organizer, political cartoonist Pak Jae-Dong, said a key motivation of the group was to stir the government into action concerning Korean comics. To avoid being inundated by manga, he notes, there must be a quality-assured selection process of importation and a conscious effort on the part of local artists to create better Korean comics (Pak interview 1994).

Subsequently, when the Korean government realized animation was one of the country's major exports, it began a number of initiatives, first in 1994–95 and then again in 1997, to promote indigenous production — including that of comics. These included festivals, competitions, educational facilities, libraries, museums, government subsidies and grants, ministerial agencies devoted to comics contents and character design, and a drive to sell Korean animation and comics abroad.

These endeavors paid off as the manhwa industry mushroomed (even abroad) by the early 2000s. Between 1990 and 2001, the number of comics titles in Korea more than doubled, from 4,130 to 9,177, accounting for 21.5 percent of all periodicals published in Korea, up from 9 percent. The number of total copies published increased during this decade from 6.83 million to 42.1 million, from 2.7 percent of total sales of all periodicals published in Korea to 36 percent (Kim interview 2003).

What these drives did not do was stem the tide of manga importation or imitation. In 2001, 44 percent of all comics titles and 62 percent of all copies circulated were non-Korean (namely, Japanese). By May 2002, the number of manga titles circulating was 4,562, compared to 2,579 Korean. Kim Nak-Ho (interview 2003) explains that the figure was stable after that because so many manga titles had been imported — that is, there were not many more that could be brought in.

Japanese manga was already available in Taiwan when the Nationalists arrived in 1949, and it became a formidable competitor for the first domestic comics, which appeared in the late 1940s and early '50s. In fact, manga was to become the bane of Taiwanese cartooning henceforth. In the 1950s and early '60s Taiwan experienced its golden age of domestic comics, but the euphoria was brief, cut short in 1962 when the Ministry of Education, reacting to parents' complaints, effected a precensorship system.

Although the explicit portrayals of sex and violence in imported Japanese comics must have been the major concern of parents and teachers, manga were not scrutinized as closely by the Censorship Board as local comics were. One can only surmise that the Censorship Board was looking for something more than depictions of sex and violence, perhaps materials that opposed the rule of Chiang Kai-shek, supported communism, or otherwise threatened Taiwan's national security. Nevertheless, cartoonists were quick to denounce the biased and inconsistent nature of the censorship board's work. Of course, the double standard was profitable to investors in Japanese comic books, for Taiwanese publishers resorted to tracing over or copying them outright; the only change required was substitution of Chinese dialogue. In the process, local cartoonists were edged out, and the quality of the comics was shortchanged. Rather than contend with these conditions, many cartoonists quit the profession, some for as long as twenty years. The last straw for cartoonist Chiu Hsi-hsun occurred when a board member assessed his work by asking, "Since when can dogs talk? Any child who reads this would end up in a straightjacket" (quoted in Lent 1993, 4) On the other hand, according to famed cartoonist Niu Ko, "nobody minded if Japanese dogs talked. They could be singing songs for that matter, and they'd still get through" (quoted in Lent 1993, 4; see also Lu 1990, 33–41).

Another factor that contributed to this dismal period in the history of cartooning was the stronger control wielded by the National Institute for Compilation and Translation (NICT), put in charge of comics censorship from 1967 to 1987. The NICT came under much angry criticism as it was accused of collaborating with publishers in flooding the market with Japanese comics. Hua Jen Publisher of Taichung was the first to submit Japanese comics to the committee for approval, and when their comics were approved, other local publishers saw the door was open to dealing with Japanese comics distributors (Chen 1981).

Although it was illegal to import Japanese comics, publishers found ways of smuggling them in. Apparently, the NICT did not interfere once they were translated and reprinted. In fact, one member of the government body even talked about the advantages of importing illegal Japanese comics, saying they promoted cultural exchange, absorbed the advantages of an "exotic culture," and stimulated higher-quality domestic cartoons (Chiang Tzu-hua, cited in Chen 1981).

The NICT remained a hotbed of controversy into the early 1980s, and its perceived double standard turned more local cartoonists away, with some even joining movements to prohibit Japanese comics in Taiwan. One such campaign was "Following Wind" in 1983, when 45,500 Japanese manga considered pornographic were confiscated. "Following Wind" came on the heels of a public outcry about the NICT's approval of a manga that had sexually explicit scenes, including the rape of a policewoman (Chi 1980).

With increased public reaction against manga, NICT policies, and irresponsible Taiwanese comics publishers, changes appeared, first in 1984, with the China Times Publishing Company establishing a cartoon department, publishing local comic books, and encouraging Taiwanese cartoonists through competitions; and then in 1992, through passage of stiff copyright regulations meant to close down pirated manga operations. Both legitimate and pirating publishers went to Japan to discuss copyrights, resulting in a bilateral agreement (Kid Jerry interview 1992). Under new terms, Japanese publishers could license their copyrights to Taiwanese publishers through bidding; those that could guarantee the largest sales were awarded contracts. Taiwanese companies would pay an 8 percent of sales royalty to their Japanese counterparts.

One of the companies that wrapped up its lucrative pirate business in 1992 was Tong Li, the largest manga publisher in Taiwan. The president of Tong Li, Fang Wan-nan, who called himself the "king of the pirates," was initially worried about his chances for survival in the legitimate comics market. For fifteen years, he had had a steady cash flow, bringing out fifty Japanese comic books monthly and more than a thousand different titles over the years, some of which sold more than 100,000 copies each (Fang interview 1992).

For four and a half years in the late 1980s and early '90s, the ten or more comics pirates had an agreement with Japanese distributors that was particularly beneficial to Tong Li but supported other pirates not among the ten. The Japanese released their latest comic book list to all Taiwanese pirate publishers, who drew by lot to see which titles they received. Through the agreement, Tong Li received 44 percent of all new titles and thus had the best chance of garnering the prime comics. The Japanese distributor was paid US$12.50 per title.

Once a comic book was obtained by Tong Li, Fang tore out the pages and distributed them to his editors to make them appropriate and readable for a Taiwanese audience. They did this by whitening out the Japanese language and replacing it with Chinese, and by modifying pictures of explicit sex and violence (during my tour of the Tong Li offices, I watched as a young employee pasted a bra over bare breasts in a Japanese book). After the revised books were printed, they were sent throughout the island via Tong Li's distribution system of sixty vans and one hundred salespeople. Tong Li also exported twenty to thirty titles (two or three hundred copies of each) monthly to Singapore, which in turn sent some to Malaysia.

At least eight pirated comics weeklies existed in Taiwan when the bilateral agreement was struck. The most popular, *Teenager Weekly*, pirated the work of Japan's top ten cartoonists and sold at US$1.35 per copy, underselling local comic books by nearly six times. Another, *Comics Express*, which combined seven of Japan's most popular strips, illegally sold 180,000 copies weekly, netting its publisher US$4.3 million yearly (Chang 1992, 14). The availability of facsimile allowed an illegal printing of the strips to occur the same day they appeared in Japanese newspapers. Lu, pointing out the unfair situation pirated comics created, comments, "Publishers of pirated comics evade taxes, they use cheap paper and printing, and they skim off the cream of the crop to purvey to readers only too willing to plop down for whatever's bigger and cheaper. How can local cartoon magazines compete with opponents who don't play by the rules?" (1990).

In the dog-eat-dog world of Chinese version manga, even comics publisher pirates had their illegal books "hijacked," as many rental shops and wholesalers copied these works and put their own versions of them in circulation instead.

Though today manga sales represent about 80 percent of the comics market in Taiwan, the numbers of copies sold have dropped sharply by 40 percent since 1996. This is in line with overall trends, as sales of all comics in Taiwan dropped by a total of 60 percent in the three years after 1997. Between 1996 and 1998, one-half of all comics specialty stores closed and three of the seven comics publishers folded. According to the Taipei Comic Art Labor Union, the number of new manga titles licensed yearly in Taiwan is 220, each at 6,000–10,000 copies, down considerably from pre-1992 figures. Yet they still are more attractive to consumers and publishers than Taiwanese titles, grossing annual revenues of NT$2.1 billion (US$70 million). Manga can sell 10,000 copies, but fewer and fewer local comics reach the break-even point of 2,000.

The tenuous nature of Taiwanese comic books and the financial viability of the manga industry have led to a number of local cartoonists drawing for Japanese publishers. Most prominent of this group is Cheng Wen, who works for a Japanese publisher, every month doing seventy pages in two stories on his popular *Legendary Heroes of Chou Dynasty*, a comic book with a circulation of 300,000 in 1992 at the time of my interview with him. Cheng explains that he uses varying styles for different markets; for the Taiwanese market, he "puts clothes on the women characters in *Legendary Heroes*," but for the manga version, he draws sexually, for which, he comments, "I feel guilty because of the Taiwan tradition on sex." His style is to modernize ancient Chinese stories, using cinematic techniques, emphasizing the main traits of characters, and putting human frailties into characters who for centuries were held to be perfect (Cheng interview 1992). He favors drawing for the Japanese because of audience appreciation and acceptance of new ideas and the hands-off policy of Japan's government. One writer described Cheng's style as combining Japanese and Western comics with Chinese painting and calligraphic skills (Wong 2006, 33). Zhong Meng Shun is another Taiwanese artist working for the Japanese. He notes that the Japanese write the stories, find a translator, and hire him to draw the panels based on their ideas, which is different from the Taiwan situation, in which both the publisher and artist share ideas (Zhong interview 2005).

As in other Asian countries, the government has gotten involved in trying to stimulate comics production with a national character. The Government Information Office offers annual graphic novel awards, and the NICT has programs to encourage new talent and hire cartoonists to draw comic books that it prints and distributes to schools, and sponsors "excellent comic book" competitions and youngster cartoon weekend camps. Often, the winning graphic novels and comic books of these competitions look very much like manga.

If one is not convinced of the dominant presence of manga in Taiwan, a stroll through any major bookstore will dissolve the uncertainty. For example, the largest Taipei bookstore, Kinnokuniya, has one very long wall and many racks of thousands of manga titles, compared to about one hundred or fewer U.S. superhero and Taiwanese titles.

CONCLUDING REMARKS

The Appeal of Manga

East Asian comics professionals venture a number of reasons why their audiences are enamored of manga. At the height of the piracy plague in its country, the Korea Ethics Committee for Books, Magazines, and Weekly Newspapers said Japanese comics were popular among Koreans because of their "high readability and superiority of layout and techniques," as well as their intelligibility in a society that has many language, culture, and lifestyle similarities with Japan. The committee also stated that Korean cartoonists, because of insufficient support, cannot provide readers with a domestic product that is competitive (see Lent 1995, 17).

Korean historian and comics creator Lee Won Bok believes that an appeal was the sexual and violent content of many manga and warns that Korea "must open its moral door or Japanese comics will beat out Korean" (Lee interview 1992). The head of Bucheon Cartoon Information Center, Cho Kwan Je voices a similar viewpoint, noting that since manga were allowed to be imported in the late 1980s, Korean audiences found manhwa titles to be less funny, as they became more infatuated with the enormous amount of funny and sexy manga available (Cho interview 2003). One comics editor explained that manga is favored by Koreans over U.S. or European comics, because the latter are enhanced as an art form while manga is strictly for public entertainment. He elaborated, "Comic book artists in [the] U.S. and Europe are treated as artists and don't get close to the masses. It is like the difference between French and Hollywood films — artistic versus public" (Hwang interview 1994).

A Hong Kong comics publisher credits Japanese manga style as being "more elegant, more pleasant" to local people. He also feels that Japanese artists are free and willing to draw a variety of topics, saying that in Hong Kong, one "cannot find artists who can spend time specializing in science fiction" (Pang interview 1992).

The Impacts of Manga

One worry, particularly in South Korea and Taiwan, has been the potential impacts of manga on national identity and cultural values.

When the Korea Ethics Committee tried to clamp down on manga after 1991, it declared the comics had deleterious effects upon the Korean value system, on traditional morals, manners, culture, and discipline. The committee pointed out that children's books "unnecessarily overemphasized such horny and cruel [subjects] as a naked girl having a bath and a guy skewering a dragon to make a barbecue of it" and carried lines such as, "It feels really good to kill someone." Adult titles, according to the committee, featured characters who were "usually merciless hitmen, detectives with the authority to kill offenders and men keen on decadent womanizing." One source describes adult comics dealing with Japanese history as "shot through with hanky-panky, flagrant violence, and eerie killing scenes by 'samurai', or 'ninja'. Blood-and-thunder comics have graphic lines and drawings which detract from the sanctity of human life. Love cartoons can't do without homosexuality, sexual perversion and bawdy love scenes" ("Japanese Cartoons Flood Korea" 1991, 28).

As already indicated, such concerns have been prominent in Taiwan for decades, resulting in many press editorials and opinion articles denouncing manga and occasional campaigns where manga was rounded up and destroyed. Throughout the 1980s and '90s, parents and teachers worried about the moral influences of Japanese sex- and violence-oriented comics; in 1991–92, the Modern Women's Foundation spearheaded a campaign to seek government action after a survey it conducted in five Taipei junior high schools found that 72.5 percent of the students had read pornographic and violent comics (see Lent 1999a, 192–93).

Many manga and their characters are so embraced by East Asian cultures that they feature in commercial and government promotional campaigns. For example, *Doraemon*, popular in East and Southeast Asia since the 1970s, has been used to promote everything from a fast food chain to local government bodies (Nakamura 2005, 2–3). A more recent example is *Kami no Shizuku*

(The Drops of God), a manga series on wines that took Japan, Korea, China, and parts of Europe by storm in 2007. The main character learns about wine after his father, a famous wine critic, dies and leaves a will describing the top twelve wines of the world. Sales of specific wines mentioned increased by as much as 30 percent after the manga appeared.

Japanese comics have been resisted in East Asia at times because of effects upon the indigenous comics markets. As has been mentioned already, manga does make up large portions of the East Asian comics industries. However, there is an upside as well in that manga has played a role in rejuvenating comics readership in places where it had waned and kept artists and businessmen employed when local comics could no longer do that.

Finally, manga's impact on artistic and cartoon and comic book styles regularly comes up for discussion. Some critics claim manga and other East Asian comics are indistinguishable; most, however, contend the opposite, or at least, believe that hybridization is at work.

In some instances, the differences are in areas other than style, such as psychological or sociological backgrounds, marketing practices, or importation patterns. Talking about manhwa and manga, Korean researcher Nak-ho Kim comments,

> Publishers say Korean comics do not have a manga style but that is trash. You can't tell Japanese and Korean comics apart. Both have an Asian traditional way of drawing — using black and white lines and emptiness between panels and lines. All share the basic principles. . . . The difference between Korean and Japanese is what lies beneath the comics style. Mainstream Korean comics use more drama and narrative. Mainstream Japanese are more concerned with building up individual characters and personalities. It is a cultural difference. Korea, through its cultural background, emphasizes more the forces of society and history beyond the individual. In Japan, the focus is more on the individual. (Kim interview 2003)

Differences between manga and Taiwanese comics also relate to cultural traits. Taiwanese comics are considered healthier, more positive, and humane, with some comics personnel claiming they concentrate on virtues such as loyalty and perseverance, while manga conveys a sense of obsession with perfection that is almost pathological. Taiwanese characters of all types are portrayed as not extremely smart or skilled at a top-tier level, but they tend to be nobodies with a good sense of humor and the ability to survive hard times (Lent and Shiau 2008, 729).

In Hong Kong and South Korea, publishers have worked at domestication of manga. The result, according to Ng (in reference to Hong Kong comics), is that they are not "blindly copying," but instead, they "skillfully and selectively incorporate some Japanese elements into their works, such elements enriching, but not replacing, local aspects" (2003, 192). Based on their textual analysis, Wood-hung Lee and and Yomei Shaw concluded that Hong Kong consumption of manga is "by no means passive and dependent," that publishers and readers alter manga to suit their own language and culture (2006, 53). This, they report, is accomplished through translating onomatopoeia (through literal translation, coinage of new expressions, omission of onomatopoeia in translation, and treating onomatopoeia as part of the illustration, left unedited and not translated), dealing with puns (by substituting similar Chinese puns, using footnotes and explanations, and ignoring the original text and its pun), and editing to suit Hong Kong societal taboos concerning portrayal of excrement, sexual activity, or indecent behavior. Despite these efforts, Lee and Shaw note that Hong Kong culture is being shaped by Japanese popular culture.

Seoul Cultural Publishers director Kim Mun Hwan points out that differences between manhwa and manga are becoming apparent; namely, "The shapes of Korean eyes and faces are drawn more softly than Japanese; Korean comics have round lines while manga have sharper, straighter ones. Korean books are read front to back; Japanese from back to front, and Korean comics do not have the blatant violence and sex, bleeding scenes, amputations, and so on" (Kim interview 1994).

In her interviews with Korea's top ten *soonjung manhwa* (girls' comics) artists, Sueen Noh found that all were influenced by manga in character design, depiction of human bodies, mood expression, page layout, scene transition, and theme selection. However, the artists asserted that "once the author obtains his/her own originality, s/he would eventually come to gain a uniqueness relieved from manga influence" (2004, 284). They also pointed to differences between Japanese and Korean comics, among which were that manga are "highly planned and specialized in various genres," are indistinguishable for they imitate one another, are more commercialized, and have more freedom relative to sexual and violent themes. They also felt Korean artists were more autonomous in that they were not required to show scripts to editors (291–93). David Walsh agrees with the latter point, noting that "thanks in part to a comics industry that tends to cede more control to artists, manhwa allows for a level of individual expression, in storytelling and style, that is not always found in manga" (2007).

Seon Jeong-U, the cocurator of an important Korean comics retrospective in Angoulême, France, maintains that the real difference lies in how Japan and Korea interacted with outside forces. "Japanese comics went their own way after initial influences from outside, but manhwa just kept being influenced from outside," Seon explains. "Korean comics are open to influences from many sectors, especially Japan. More European comics are imported into Korea than Japan, because the Japanese do not import much as they have so many of their own comics. Someone called manga the comics of Galapalos Islands, in that they isolate themselves. Japan opens a little, sucks up some things from outside and closes" (Seon interview 2003).

Others are not convinced about distinctions between Korean and Japanese comics, notes Chie Yamanaka declaring, "the pursuit of an essential 'Koreanness' resulted in the discovery that such a thing does not exist. Nevertheless, the producers of manhwa still cling to it . . . " (2006, 193). Korean newspaper critic Lim Bum feels that Korean characters and cartoon styles are still very Japanese, and in cases where Koreanization has occurred, the cartoonists responsible for the work are not popular and the effort is lost. He explains that cartoonists "don't have to put characters in traditional garb and settings, but they have to draw with a sense of familiarity and originality and touch Korean feelings" (Lim interview 1994). He had suggested that the government and *chaebols* (Korean conglomerates) promote and use Korean cartoon characters and, since 1995, this has happened, as the government now sponsors annual contests for the development of Korean characters .

If consensus can ever be reached, it would be that through the tireless efforts of Japanese publishers and their counterparts, and readers in other East Asian countries, manga has overcome very strong opposition from many quarters to become the most popular and most read literature in the region, possessing many appealing characteristics and viewed as having had impacts (mostly negative) on cultural values, national identities, indigenous comics markets, and artistic and other creative styles.

Interviews

Cha, Ae-ock (1994, July 2). Interview with the author, Seoul, Korea.
Cheng Wen (1992, July 10). Interview with the author, Taipei, Taiwan.
Cho Kwan Je (2003, August 16). Interview with the author, Seoul, Korea.
Choi Suk Tae (1994, July 3). Interview with the author, Seoul, Korea.
Fang Wan-Nan (1992, July 10). Interview with the author, Taipei, Taiwan.
Hwang Kyung Tae (1994, July 2). Interview with the author, Seoul, Korea.
Jung Joon-young (1994, July 3). Interview with the author, Seoul, Korea.
Kid Jerry (1992, July 9). Interview with the author, Taipei, Taiwan.
Ki, David (1992, July 13). Interview with the author, Hong Kong.
Kim Mun-Hwan (1994, July 7). Interview with the author, Seoul, Korea.
Kim Nak-Ho (2003, August 17). Interview with the author, Seoul, Korea.
Kwong Nam Lum (1992, July 14). Interview with the author, Hong Kong.
Lee Won-Bok (1992, July 2). Interview with the author, Seoul, Korea.
Lim Bum (2003, August 16). Interview with the author, Seoul, Korea.
Liu Sui Yin (1992, July 13). Interview with the author, Hong Kong.
Ma Shuk Chu, Ronnie (1992, 14 July). Interview with the author, Hong Kong.
Pak Jae-Dong (1992, July 7). Interview with the author, Seoul, Korea.
—— (1994, July 3). Interview with the author, Seoul, Korea.
Pang, C. Ming (1992, July 12). Interview with the author, Hong Kong.
Seon Jeong-U (2003, August 17). Interview with the author, Seoul, Korea.

Wan, Alan Wai Lun (1992, July 13). Interview with the author, Hong Kong.
Yuen Kin To (2002, July 12). Interview with the author, Hong Kong.
Zhong, Meng Shun (2005, July 28). Interview with the author, Taipei, Taiwan.

References

"Ambassadors Manga and Anime" (2007). *Japan Times*, http://search.japantimes.co.jp/cgi-bin/ed20070325a1.html.

Barmé, Geremie R. (2002). *An Artistic Exile: A Life of Feng Zikai (1898–1975)*. Berkeley and Los Angeles: University of California Press.

Cha, Kai-Ming (2007). "The Golden Age of Hong Kong Comics." *Publishers Weekly* 22.

Chang, Winnie (1992, January). "From Knights Errant to Errant Couples." *Free China Review*, 4–17.

Chen Yueh-yun (1981). "Thirty Years of Cartoon's Vicissitude." *Commercial Times* 9–10.

Chi En-ping (1980, January 12). "Compilation Committee Makes Mistakes Again." *Taipei Weekly*.

Clements, Jonathan (1996, Fall). "Hong Kong Comics: The Second Wave." *Anime Fx*, 18–21.

"Dirty Strips" (1980, December). *Asian Mass Communications Bulletin*, 17.

Harbsmeier, Christophe (1984). *The Cartoonist Feng Zikai: Social Realism with a Buddhist Face*. Oslo: Universitetsforlaget.

"It's Not So Funny" (1986, January). *Media*, 6.

Iwabuchi, Koichi (2001). "Japanese Popular Culture and East Asian Modernities." *Media Development* 3: 25–30.

"Japanese Cartoons Flood Korea" (1991, April 20). *Newsreview*, 28.

Lee, Wood-hung, and Yomei Shaw (2006). "A Textual Comparison of Japanese and Chinese Editions of *Manga*: Translation as Cultural Hybridization." *International Journal of Comic Art* 8(2): 34–55.

Lent, John A. (1993)."The Renaissance of Taiwan's Cartoon Arts." *Asian Culture* 21(1): 1–17.

—— (1995). "Korean Cartooning: Historical and Contemporary Perspectives." *Korean Culture* 16(1): 8–19.

—— (1999a). "Local Comic Books and the Curse of Manga in Hong Kong, South Korea and Taiwan." *Asian Journal of Communication* 9(1): 108–28.

——, ed. (1999b). *Pulp Demons: International Dimensions of the Postwar Anti-Comics Campaign*. Madison, NJ: Fairleigh Dicknson University Press.

—— (2004). "Far Out and Mundane: The Mammoth World of Manga." *Phi Kappa Phi Forum* 84(3): 38–41.

Lent, John A., and Hong-Chi Shiau (2008). "Seeking Inwards, Looking Outwards: Taiwanese Cartoonists' Quest To Transcend Japanese Influence." *International Journal of Comic Art* 10(2): 718–36.

Lu Li-chen (1990, August). "When Chu-ko Szulang Meets City Hunter." *Sinorama*, 33–41.

Nakamura, Mayumi (2005, December). "Doraemon Charms the World." *Asia-Pacific Perspectives*, 2–3.

Ng, Wai-ming (2003). "Japanese Elements in Hong Kong Comics: History, Art, and Industry." *International Journal of Comic Art* 5(2): 184–93.

Noh, Sueen (2004). "The Gendered Comics Market in Korea: An Overview of Korean Girls' Comics, *Soonjung Manhwa*." *International Journal of Comic Art* 6(1): 281–98.

Walsh, David (2007, April 23). "Forget Manga. Here's Manhwa." Business Week.com, http://www.businessweek.com/innovate/content/apr2007/id20070423_634051.htm.

Wong, Wendy Siuyi (2006). "Globalizing Manga: From Japan to Hong Kong and Beyond." *Mechademia* 1: 23–45.

Yamanaka, Chie (2006). "Domesticating Manga? National Identity in Korean Comics Culture." In *Reading Manga: Local and Global Perceptions of Japanese Comics*, edited by Jaqueline Berndt and Steffi Richter, 191–202. Leipzig, Germany: Leipziger Universitätsverlag.

19

The Manga Publishing Scene in Europe

Paul M. Malone

In *Popular Culture, Globalization and Japan,* Matthew Allen and Rumi Sakamoto write, "Our central thesis is that there are many 'insides' ('localities') and many more 'outsides' ('extra-localities') which inform the production and consumption of 'Japanese popular culture'" (2006, 3). This is true outside of Japan as well; the European manga industry, like a series of Chinese boxes, defies the thesis that globalization entails homogenization.

Manga entered Europe later and more slowly than in America (see Goldberg, this volume); nonetheless, in Western Europe, as in the United States, it was television — specifically, the broadcast of Japanese *anime* (animation) for young viewers — that began creating an audience for manga. Unlike in America, however, this process was also bound up with a collective transformation of the media landscape: the privatization of the broadcast media. Tim Pilcher and Brad Brooks allude to this phenomenon in discussing the Italian comics scene; they do not, however, draw more than an indirect connection to the rise of manga as they comment, "Until 1976, the Italian government had a monopoly on the country's TV output, with the state effectively controlling what the people could watch. When a loophole in the legislation was found, a multitude of private TV stations suddenly erupted, flinging the comics market into turmoil. Where people had been coming to comics for their daily entertainment, TV could now provide a free alternative 24 hours a day. Many comics disappeared overnight, and the only survivors were those who could offer something different" (2005, 186).

Manga would be one such "something different," and these developments would expand far beyond Italy. At the same time, however, the various national comics industries operated under different conditions, setting up localized crises at different times. In Italy, for example, the comics scene was greatly reduced in the late 1970s, as described above; in Spain, the comics industry had stagnated thanks to the virtual monopoly of Bruguera Editorial, which would be broken in part by future manga publishers in the 1980s (Pilcher and Brooks 2005, 193–94); in France, the 1990s brought an "inbred and nostalgic" comics culture dependent upon past glories to a financial and artistic crisis (Beaty 2007, 171–73); and in Germany, where there had never been a vibrant indigenous comics production, a similar financial catastrophe was exacerbated by too-rapid expansion in the early 1990s (Knigge 2004, 69–70). Moreover, all of these local crises coincided with the passing of the first great generation of European comics artists, or the franchises they had founded. It is in this context that the import of Japanese manga, with its prolific creators and huge back catalogs, became attractive to European publishers.

TELEVISED ANIME AS WESTERN EUROPEAN HARBINGER OF MANGA

Some of the early anime series imported to Europe were the same shows broadcast in America: Tezuka Osamu's[1] *Janguru Taitei* (Kimba the White Lion), for example, was shown in Spain in 1969 (retitled *Kimba, el león blanco*), and in France in 1972 (as *Le Roi Léo*; Clements and McCarthy 2006 474). Other series were chosen for their appeal to a specifically European audience — most famously the 1974 version of *Heidi*, an anime retelling of Johanna Spyri's 1880 Swiss novel (and an early notable effort of Takahata Isao and Miyazaki Hayao).[2] This series became enormously popular due in part to its overarching plot, spanning over fifty-two episodes, which was still unusual in Western animated children's series (Baglini 1998, 48). *Heidi*'s success led to a wave of Western-inspired literary anime series, including adaptations of *The Dog of Flanders* (1975), *Anne of Green Gables* (1979), and *The Swiss Family Robinson* (1981), among many others; so that the European idea of anime is more likely to be colored by these shows than by the science-fiction action series famous in North America (Clements and McCarthy 2006, 730; Moliné 2002, 58).

Europe did not lack such programs for long, however: 1978 saw the simultaneous arrival of Nagai Gō's *Majingaa Zetto* (Mazinger Z) in Spain, and his *UFO Robo Gurendaizaa* (Grandizer) in France (renamed *Goldorak*) and Italy (retitled *Atlas UFO Robot*, but better known as *Goldrake*). The popularity of these series in Spain and Italy led to a wave of Nagai's robot series, but *Goldorak* alone became a true cult hit in France (Clements and McCarthy 2006, 474). Young female viewers in France and Italy were not neglected; in 1978, Mizuki Kyōko and Igarashi Yumiko's *shōjo* (girls') soap opera *Kyandii Kyandii* (Candy Candy) also hit their television screens. The next year saw the arrival in both France and Italy of Matsumoto Leiji's *Uchuu Kaizoku Kyaputen*

Haarokku (Space Pirate Captain Harlock; rechristened *Albator* in France, to avoid confusion with Tintin's associate Captain Haddock; "Classement Manga de A á Z" 2005, 334). Again, most of these series appeared on state-owned networks such as TVE in Spain, France's Antenne 2, or the Italian Rete 2. From this point, however, Italy, the first European country to permit private broadcasting companies — with their need to fill programming schedules and sell advertising time — saw a sudden boom of 183 anime series imported between 1978 and 1983 (Baglini 1998, 48; Moliné 2002, 68).

The success of so many Japanese television productions led to licensed spin-off comics drawn by Western artists, usually working in anonymous collectives. Among the first of these was the adaptation of the anime series *Heidi*, drawn and published in Spain by Ediciones Recreativas, beginning in 1975;[3] comic versions of other such series followed, marked by slavish reproduction of the simplified character designs of the original cartoons, guaranteeing recognition for marketing purposes (Dolle-Weinkauff 1990, 251). The close connection to the televised series, however, also made it difficult for these comics to continue once the respective series ended its broadcast run (Dolle-Weinkauff 1990, 252) — though the German edition of *Heidi* lasted four years and 179 issues ("Heidi" 2009).

Once this method of adaptation had been established for anime not based on a work of Japanese manga, it was simply transferred to anime that had such a basis: European publishers tended to ignore the original manga, with its problems of translation and adaptation, preferring to license locally produced equivalents. Thus an Italian *Goldrake* comic was issued by Edizioni Flash in 1978 and lasted for ninety-six weekly issues, in conjunction with monthly titles from the same series (Baglini and Zacchino 1999, 64); despite the poor quality of the story and art, French editions of both this version and another *Goldrake* adaptation published by Giunti Marzocco appeared simultaneously, though at least some of the latter were drawn by French artists as well ("Goldorak — Le robot de l'espace" 2009). An entirely French endeavor was Dargaud's 1980 eight-issue edition of *Albator* (*Captain Harlock*), drawn by Five Star Studios ("Albator" 2009). Likewise, a version of *Mazinger Z* was published in Spain by Ediciones Junior, with art by Estudio Beaumont (Moliné 2002, 176–77).

Some comics were samplers of several series; in 1980, *Albator* also appeared with several French series in the *Journal de Captain Fulgur* (Fulgur being another science-fiction hero, but of French provenance; *Albator*'s popularity kept Fulgur from appearing on his own cover). In Italy, Edizioni TV's 1981 magazine *Noi Supereroi* (Our Superheroes) offered locally drawn stories about Captain Harlock as well as *Capitan Futuro, Gundam, Daitarn 3, Gaiking* and *Grand Prix*. The artists' fidelity to the anime designs, rather than to the respective original manga works, was meant to appeal to young television viewers just as the *Heidi* adaptations had (Baghini and Zacchino 1999, 64–66; Castellazzi 2004, 105–6).

In 1979, however, Italy's Fabbri Editori had begun publishing Nagai Gō and Ota Gosaku's original *Gureeto Majingaa* (Great Mazinger) — albeit translated, censored, "flipped" to read left to right, and colorized — under the title *Il grande Mazinga/Mazinger*; it lasted for twenty-five weekly issues (Baglini and Zacchino 1999, 67). Fabbri also launched a weekly *Candy Candy* magazine in 1980, using Mizuki and Igarashi's original manga, again censored, flipped, and colorized. When the Japanese material was exhausted after seventy-seven issues, Fabbri hired an Italian team, Staff di If, to carry on; and the series lasted 326 issues in all, first as *Candy Candy TV Junior* and then as the hyperbolic *Candyissima*, until 1986 (Castellazzi 2004, 30).[4] As a backup feature, the Italian *Candy Candy* also contained other shōjo manga, most notably *Lady Oscar* (Ikeda Riyoko's *Berusaiyu no Bara*, or Rose of Versailles), which appeared from 1982 to 1984 as a sixteen-page supplement to *Candy Candy* before being reissued in a sixty-four-page magazine format (Baglini and Zacchino 1999, 71). *Lady Oscar* never matched *Candy Candy*'s phenomenal success, though it was published in conjunction with the 1982 broadcast of the anime adaptation on the newly launched commercial network Italia 1. While both versions of Lady Oscar were censored for young Italian audiences, the manga suffered censorship so rigorous that entire pages of Ikeda's original were sacrificed, though the heroine herself was not: in the Italian version, unlike the original, Oscar and her beloved André live happily ever after (the anime, by contrast, kept its tragic ending intact).

Aside from the aforementioned publications geared for younger readers, the only other European venue for Japanese work was offered by expatriate Atoss Takemoto (*né* Takemoto Motoichi) in his Swiss-published manga anthology *Le cri qui tue* (The Scream that Kills), aimed at adult comic connoisseurs. *Le cri qui tue* appeared in six issues from 1979 to 1981 before going under — though Takemoto had given a small Francophone audience a glimpse of the work of Tezuka Osamu, Ishinomori Shotaro, Saitō Takao, and others (Bastide and Prezman 2006, 20; Moliné 2002, 68). In 1980, Takemoto also licensed works by *gekiga* (more realistic, adult-oriented Japanese comics) pioneer Tatsumi Yoshihiro to the Spanish publisher Ediciones La Cúpula for publication in *El Víbora*, most important of the new generation of Spanish comic magazines (Pilcher and Brooks 2005, 194); these stories were popular enough that three years later, La Cúpula issued an entire album of Tatsumi's work, *Qué triste es la vida y otras historias* (How Sad Is Life, and Other Stories; see Bastide, n.d.; Moliné 2002, 68–69).

TENTATIVE STEPS TOWARD A GENUINE MANGA MARKET

By the early 1980s, then, locally produced adaptations of Japanese anime series had become routine in Western Europe, and the public had to some degree become accustomed to their aesthetic and dramaturgical conventions; moreover, a small number of authentic Japanese manga had also been translated and published. The full-scale entry of real manga, however, would still require several attempts.

One of these attempts was the translation and import of Nakazawa Keiji's seminal manga *Hadashi no Gen* (Barefoot Gen; see Moliné 2002, 69). The prevailing antinuclear sentiment in Europe seemed fertile ground for Nakazawa's autobiographical description of the Hiroshima bombing, particularly in Germany, where it was the first manga to appear, in 1982; however, the German *Gen* was published by Rowohlt Verlag — not a comics publisher — in a series generally earmarked for straightforward political texts; and no context was given to reconcile the horrors depicted with the cartoony style. The resulting poor response meant that only one volume of Nakazawa's epic series was published (Jüngst 2004, 86). A year later, *Gen* appeared in France, published by the science-fiction-oriented independent publisher Les Humanoïdes Associés; here, too, publication ceased after a single volume ("Gen d'Hiroshima" 2009).

The ice began to break only in the early 1990s, with the almost simultaneous arrival of Ōtomo Katsuhiro's *Akira* in Spain (Ediciones B, 1990), France (Glénat, 1990), Italy (Glénat Italia, 1990), and Germany (Carlsen, 1991). To reduce the risk of publishing such a work, all these editions were simply licensed from the 1989 American Marvel/Epic edition, already assimilated to Western tastes by being both flipped and colorized (Castellazzi 2004, 9; Jüngst 2004, 89). *Akira* sold successfully in most countries, notwithstanding initial doubts within the respective publishing houses (Knigge 2004, 67;Vignol 2005, 205).[5]

Up to this point, the strategy of assimilating Japanese cultural products to conform to Western expectations had generally worked well, as had the locally produced versions that substituted for the works of the Japanese creators. This same tactic had been used successfully with the comics of Walt Disney, for instance: Italian, Danish, Dutch, and French artists had been rendering Mickey Mouse, Donald Duck, and friends in licensed local editions for decades. The licensing of the Americanized version of *Akira* had only been a variation on this strategy. The drawback to making manga in imitation of Western comics, however, was that by definition, they failed to reach readers outside the established — and aging — comics audience (Jüngst 2004, 89).

SPAIN: TAKING AN EARLY LEAD

This situation was about to change, however, and once again television played a major part — by now, private and regional commercial television channels had become common throughout Western Europe. The same year that *Akira* arrived, Spain's regional channel TV3 began broadcasting the anime version of Toriyama Akira's *Dragon Bouru* (Dragon Ball) in Catalan. The series became such a hit that other Iberian independent channels took it up, leading to a brisk underground traffic in photocopies of the original Japanese manga (Moliné 2002, 69–70). In turn, Spanish nationwide channels were inspired to program Kurumada Masami's *Seitoushi Seiya* (Saint Seiya; retitled *Los Caballeros del Zodiaco* and shown on state-run TVE) and Takahashi Yōichi's *Kyaputen Tsubasa* (Captain Tsubasa, which appeared as *Campeones* on the new private channel Tele 5), both with considerable success (Moliné 2002, 70).

The previously moribund Spanish comics industry was also showing signs of regeneration at this time, as new, fan-oriented publishers began to fill the void left by the decline of Editorial Bruguera, which had enjoyed a profitable but ultimately stultifying "virtual monopoly" in Spanish comics publishing from the 1960s to the early '80s (Pilcher and Brooks 2005, 193), finally going under in 1986. La Cúpula, for instance, had taken up publishing manga periodically in *El Víbora* again in 1991, including Tanaka Masashi's *Gon*, but it was 1992 before the first freestanding Spanish editions of Japanese manga appeared, when relative newcomer (and Spanish Marvel licensee) Planeta-DeAgostini published Hara Tetsuo and Buronson's *Hokuto no Ken* (Fist of the North Star; retitled *El puño de la Estrella del Norte*) and Koike Kazuo and Ikegami Ryōichi's *Kuraingu Furiiman* (Crying Freeman), followed by Toriyama Akira's *Dragon Ball* — in both Spanish and Catalan editions; Norma Editorial, which had previously specialized in European comics, followed with Shirow Masamune's *Dominion* (Dominion/Dominion Tank Police) in 1993 and Hojo Tsukasa's *Shitii Hantaa* (City Hunter) — one of the first manga titles in Spain to be printed right to left, in Japanese fashion — in 1994 (Moliné 2002, 70, 111). Over the next few years, a variety of manga-oriented but generally short-lived fanzines and magazines also came and went, including Glénat's *Kabuki*, Norma's *Otaku*, Camaléon Ediciones' *Neko*, and Ediciones Inu's *Kame*,[6] followed by a string of magazines from Ares Informática (of which *Minami* is the only survivor; Moliné 2002, 71).

The indigenous comics scene in Spain has not yet recovered from the declining years of Bruguera dominance; while the younger firms attempt to promote Spanish artists, it is largely the imports of American comics and particularly of manga that keep today's publishers afloat (Pilcher and Brooks 2005, 195). Today, Glénat, Norma, and Planeta-DeAgostini remain the major players in Spanish manga publishing, with the more manga-specialized

Mangaline Ediciones, Editorial Banzai, and Editorial Ivrea (an Argentine company) occupying smaller shares of the market.

ITALY: MORE THAN A FISTFUL OF MANGA

Italy also moved quickly into manga after the appearance of *Akira*. Here, the anime shown on Italy's private broadcasting channels had fallen subject to increasing censorship in the late 1980s, resulting in an infantilizing domestication that made it difficult to take it seriously;[7] *Akira*, however, served to counteract the declining interest in Japanese popular culture. Luigi Bernardi had founded Granata Press in 1989;[8] in 1990 he launched the magazine *Zero*, containing chapters of Hara Tetsuo and Buronson's *Hokuto no Ken* (Fist of the North Star, retitled *Ken il guerriero*) and Kanzaki Masaomi's *Xenon*. Unlike *Akira*, the manga in *Zero* were uncolorized; Bernardi hoped to prove the artistic worth of manga on its own terms. *Zero*'s stories were taken from American versions by VIZ Communications, however, so that they were already flipped left to right (Baglini and Castellazzi 1999, 125). *Zero* did well enough that a companion periodical, *Mangazine*, was born in 1991, featuring Takahashi Rumiko's *Urusei Yatsura* (retitled *Lamù*) and Shirato Sanpei's *Kamui Den* (Legend of Kamui, retitled *Kamui*). Takahashi's *Ranma ½* would also appear here (Castellazzi 2004, 109). The following year saw Granata issue albums of manga such as Kurumada Masami's *Seitoushi Seiya* (Saint Seiya; retitled *Cavalieri dello Zodiaco*) and Manabe Jōji's *Autorandaazu* (Outlanders; see Baglini and Castellazzi 1999, 126).

At the beginning, Granata had had no competition, but in 1991 Play Press attempted several manga series with adult themes under the banner Japan Comics, including Terasawa Buichi's *Gokuu* (Midnight Eye Goku) and *Kobura* (Space Adventure Cobra). None of these was successful, and Play Press moved into erotic manga such as Inui Haruka's *Ogenki Kurinikku* (Ogenki Clinic, retitled *La clinica dell'amore*; see Baglini and Castellazzi 1999, 126; Corno and Castellazzi 1999, 147); the mainstream acceptability in Europe, and particularly in Italy, of adult comics with nudity and sexual themes undoubtedly contributed to this decision. Then Star Comics, another young company, launched *Kappa*, a rival magazine directed by former Granata employees and armed with Kodansha licenses, including Fujishima Kosuke's *Aa Megamisama* (Oh My Goddess! retitled as *Oh mia Dea!*) and Shirow Masamune's *Koukaku Kidoutai* (Ghost in the Shell, retitled *Squadra speciale Ghost*).[9] Granata now had to increase its offerings to compete, and in 1993 it acquired Nagai Go's *Debiruman* (Devilman); followed up with his classics *Mazinga Z* and *Il grande Mazinga*; reissued old favorites *Lady Oscar* (now uncensored) and *Captain Harlock*; and published Miyazaki Hayao's *Nausicaä*, all in album form. Over the next two years, Takahashi Rumiko's

Lamù and *Maison Ikkoku* also appeared in this format.

In 1995, however, Star Comics acquired the rights to Toriyama Akira's *Dragon Ball*, which Japanese rights holder Shueisha insisted be printed from right to left; Star acquiesced, and was rewarded with record sales. That very same year, Star also started a shōjo magazine, *Amici*, and licensed Takeuchi Naoko's *Bishoujo Senshi Seeraa Muun* (Sailor Moon). Increasingly, the company moved from printing unprofitable comic-style anthologies to paperbacks similar to Japanese *tankōbon* ("single book," a collection of several previously published manga chapters in paperback book form) — a development that occurred throughout Europe, as it had in the United States (Castellazzi 2004, 128; Moliné 2002, 70). The year 1995 also saw the entry of U.S.-owned Marvel Italia into the Italian manga market, with Asamiya Kia's *Sairento Mebiusu* (Silent Möbius) and *Seijuu Denshou Daaku Enjeru* (Dark Angel) and Inoue Takehiko's *Suramu Danku* (Slam Dunk), Italy's first sports manga title.[10]

In 1996 Granata Press folded, leaving Star Comics and Panini/Planet Manga to take over its unfinished series (Baglini and Castellazzi 1999, 128–29). Planet Manga was even able to publish the two missing volumes of *Akira* in 1997 (Rumor 1999, 119). Nagai Go, however, whose own series had also been left stranded, founded his own imprint, Dynamic Italia (later Dynit; a subsidiary of his existing Japanese studio Dynamic Planning) to publish not only his own work but also that of other Japanese artists, including Egawa Tatsuya's *Gouruden Boui* (Golden Boy). Smaller firms also arose, such as Hazard, specializing in Tezuka Osamu's more adult works, and Comic Art, which published much of Tezuka's other work, as well as Aoyama Gosho's *Meitantei Konan* (Detective Conan; see Rumor 1999, 130). Comic Art's demise in 2001 left Hazard, Kappa, Dynit and Play Press as the major small publishers between the two giants, Star Comics and Panini/Planet Manga. Play Press now publishes teen-oriented manga, having passed its erotic licenses to the oddly named [nu] Hunter Edizioni. Altogether, a relatively small number of publishers manages to supply Europe's largest manga market — presumably quite profitably (Bouissou et al., this volume).

FRANCE: NEGOTIATING WITH THE FRANCO-BELGIAN TRADITION

Meanwhile, in France, both Kurumada Masami's *Seitoushi Seiya* (Saint Seiya; retitled *Les Chevaliers du Zodiaque*) and Toriyama Akira's *Dragon Ball* had already become popular in 1988, when they were broadcast with other anime series on the newly privatized channel TF1 as part of *Club Dorothée*, an afternoon children's program hosted by the eponymous singer-actress (née Frédérique Hoschedé). La Cinq, France's first private commercial broadcaster, countered with its own afterschool show, *Youpi! L'école est finie* (Yippie! School Is Finished), which also showcased anime, including Takahashi Yōichi's *Kyaputen Tsubasa* (Captain Tsubasa; retitled *Olive et Tom*), Koizumi Shizuo's *Atakka Yuu!* (Attacker You! retitled *Jeanne et Serge*) and Matsumoto Izumi's *Kimagure Orenji Roudo* (Kimagure Orange Road; retitled *Max et compagnie*).

The popularity of this new wave of anime — which led French fandom to define itself in terms of the older *génération Albator* and the nascent *génération du Club Dorothée* (Vignol 2005, 205) — alarmed French parents and authorities, however, who remained suspicious of anime's supposedly violent tendencies;[11] accordingly, the major French comics publishers boycotted manga until the demand became impossible to ignore (Bouissou 2006, 154). Thus, it took until 1993 for Glénat to follow up *Akira* and publish *Dragon Ball*. In 1992, rival Casterman had issued Tanaka Masashi's *Gon* and Taniguchi Jiro's *Aruku Hito* (Walking Man; retitled *L'Homme qui marche*), conservatively pursuing a policy of publishing manga that conformed closely to the Franco-Belgian *bande dessinée* tradition. Glénat decided to concentrate instead on manga familiar from television; after the huge success of *Dragon Ball*, Takahashi Rumiko's *Ranma ½* followed in 1994 and Takeuchi Naoko's *Bishoujo Senshi Seeraa Muun* (Sailor Moon) in 1995. All these editions were thoroughly domesticated; though not colorized, they were flipped and used character names from their French-dubbed anime counterparts (Vignol 2005, 206).

The year 1994 saw the founding of Éditions Tonkam, the country's first specialized manga publisher, which deliberately focused on manga unknown in France; its first effort was Katsura Masakazu's *Den'ei Shoujo* (Video Girl Aï). Over the next few years, Tonkam also pioneered printing manga unflipped, with CLAMP's *Seiden RG Veda* (RG Veda) and *Toukyou Babiron* (Tokyo Babylon; see Vignol 2005, 206–7). In 1995, *Manga Player* magazine began publishing manga volumes under its own imprint (later to become Pika), beginning with Mochizuki Minetaro's *Doragon Heddo* (Dragon Head). Competition from these niche publishers forced Glénat to venture into untelevised territory with Kishiro Yukito's *Gunnm* (Battle Angel Alita) in 1995 and Hagiwara Kazushi's *Basutaado!! Ankoku no Hakai Shin* (Bastard!) the following year (Vignol 2005, 207).

The year 1996 also saw two more long-established comics publishers found manga imprints: J'ai lu set up J'ai lu Manga, while Dargaud gave birth to Kana. Both concentrated on shōnen titles that were well known from television — a safe decision, since 90 percent of the readership at this time was male — with J'ai lu advertising the connection by keeping the French anime titles as subtitles (thus, *Les tribulations d'Orange Road: Max et compagnie* and *Captain Tsubasa: Olive et Tom* were among their first releases).

Kana struck gold with *Les Chevaliers du Zodiaque*, and went on to publish *Détective Conan* and Togashi Yoshihiro's *Yu Yu Hakusho* (Vignol 2005, 207–8).

During this period there were also various attempts to establish manga magazines, but as in Spain, these ventures were usually short-lived; neither the cheap paper nor the massive circulations of the Japanese equivalent could be transferred to the European context, so that neither Glénat's *Kameha* (1994), Manga Player eponymous magazine (1995), its successor Pika's *Shōnen* (2003) nor Tonkam's *Magnolia* (2003) could establish a foothold (Engelbrecht 2005, 260–63). These economic obstacles similarly spelled doom for most European attempts to publish manga in comic anthology form rather than in thick pocket-size paperbacks.

In 1997 *Club Dorothée*, which had introduced many anime series to a young television audience for over a decade, left the air; despite the loss of this test bed, however, the manga market now took off independently, experiencing particular growth in the adult-oriented sector. The big four French manga publishers, Glénat, J'ai lu, Kana and Tonkam, supplied about 80 percent of the available output; niche markets such as erotic manga were served by newcomers like Dynamic Benelux (Dybex), another Nagai Gō concern (Vignol 2005, 208–9). In 2000 Panini subsidiary Génération Comics added another major firm to the list, and the early part of that decade saw the birth of several smaller publishers, such as Éditions Asuka and Kurokawa. J'ai lu ceased publishing manga in 2006, leaving Glénat, Pika and Kana as the market leaders.

France currently has the continent's largest concentration of manga publishers, thanks in part to the number of well-established bande dessinée concerns (Casterman, Dargaud, et al.) that print manga, either directly or through subsidiaries, in addition to European and American comics. Consolidation is ongoing, however, within the French market: Tonkam, for example, is now owned by Delcourt alongside Delcourt's original manga imprint, Akata, while Pika has sold out to Hachette. Smaller firms continue nonetheless to be founded at a surprising pace (Bouissou et al., this volume); it remains to be seen which of these will survive independently in the long term.

GERMANY: MANGA TO THE RESCUE

In Germany, by contrast, the success of *Akira* had had even fewer repercussions. Schreiber & Leser, a small comics publisher, had published Ikegami Ryōichi's *Kuraingu Furiiman* (Crying Freeman) in 1993; and Egmont Ehapa Verlag, one of the two major publishers and chief rival of *Akira* publisher Carlsen Verlag, had issued Shirow Masamune's *Appurushiido* (Appleseed) through its subsidiary Reiner Feest in late 1994 (Knigge 2004, 67). The real

German manga wave, however, did not begin until 1998, again with the aid of television: the private broadcaster RTL 2 scheduled Takeuchi Naoko's *Bishoujo Senshi Seeraa Muun* (Sailor Moon; beginning in May 1997) and *Dragon Ball* (in late 1998), both quickly becoming popular. In 1997, Carlsen brought out an edition of *Dragon Ball* translated directly from the Japanese and — again at Shueisha's insistence, and not without misgivings on Carlsen's part — printed the text right to left. The Feest edition of *Bishoujo Senshi Seeraa Muun* (beginning in September 1998), on the other hand, was domesticated — flipped left to right and translated from previous English or French editions (Jüngst 2004, 91; Knigge 2004, 71). Shueisha had in fact first offered *Dragon Ball* to Egmont, who had resisted the idea of publishing an unflipped edition. The Japanese firm then took its property to Carlsen and refused to deal with Egmont for several years (Rosenbach 2001, 78). Since the unreversed right-to-left printing quickly became a marker of "authenticity," however — as had already happened in other countries — Egmont soon switched *Bishouko Senshi Seeraa Muun* and its subsequent manga to the Japanese style; on these foundations both Carlsen and Egmont enjoyed a tremendous boom as they acquired ever more licenses (Knigge 2004, 82–83).

The major German comics publishers' aggressive cornering of the manga market is a stark contrast to both the situation in North America, where smaller publishers were established under the mainstream publishers' noses to serve the growing readership, and that in most of Europe, where the mainstream publishers were generally quicker to seize the opportunities offered by manga than their North American equivalents but niche publishers also sprang up in large numbers. In Germany, however, it has been almost exclusively large multinational firms that have entered the field from the beginning, since manga was seen as the savior of a beleaguered import-based industry rather than a threat to an established production industry, as was initially the case in France. The Italian-owned Panini Verlag, through its Planet Manga division, was the next to challenge Egmont and Carlsen, beginning with Asamiya Kia's *Seijuu Denshou Daaku Enjeru* (Dark Angel) in 2000; by contrast, smaller publishers such as BDErotix who attempted to enter the manga market at this time generally did not survive the comics market decline of 2000–1.

Both Carlsen and Egmont (though not Panini) have also attempted to maintain periodical manga magazines (Jüngst 2004, 99), though with little more success than in other European countries. Egmont published the bimonthly *Manga Power* in 1996–97, but poor sales forced its cancellation. When Carlsen founded the shōnen magazine *Banzai!* in 2001, however, Egmont revived *Manga Power* the next year. Carlsen's *Daisuki* — a shōjo counterpart to *Banzai!* — began appearing in 2003, and in the same year Egmont brought out *Manga Twister*, eventually dropping *Manga Power* again. *Manga Twister* combined shōjo manga (Watase Yuu's *Arisu Naintiinsu* [Alice 19th]; Kaho Miyasaka's *Sora wa Akai Kawa no Hotori* [Kare First Love]; and Shinohara Chie's *Sora wa Akai Kawa no Hotori* [Anatolia Story]) and shōnen manga (Aoyama Gosho's *Meitantei Conan* [reprinted as *Detektiv Conan*]); Hashiguchi Takashi's *Yakitate! Japan* (literally "Freshly-baked Japan," with a pun on *pan*, "bread," but known by its original Japanese title in both English and German; and Fukuchi Tsubasa's *Ueki no Housoku* [The Law of Ueki]), each taking up its own half of the magazine; *Manga Twister* had a front cover on either side, and could be turned over to suit the reader's taste — hence the magazine's name. *Manga Twister* folded as well after thirty issues, in October 2006. Carlsen's *Banzai!* had already ceased publication in 2005 — Shueisha had withdrawn its licenses — but *Daisuki*, whose contents are licensed from the Japanese Hakusensha, survives to the present.

Finally, in 2004 the creation of Tokyopop Germany added another major player to the German landscape, armed not only with the experience of its American parent company and its German director, former Carlsen head Joachim Kaps, but also with solid licensing agreements with Shueisha through VIZ Media in the United States (the arrangement that had doomed Carlsen's *Banzai!*). Tokyopop quickly zoomed past Panini to the number three spot behind Carlsen and Egmont, on the basis of popular series such as Kubo Tite's *Buriichi* (Bleach), Nonaka Eiji's *Sakigake!! Kuomati Koukou* (Cromartie High School) and Ohba Tsugumi's *Desu Nouto* (Death Note). In the shadow of the big four, firms such as Heyne and Schreiber & Leser publish relative handfuls of manga. Oddly, Germany may now actually have more publishers producing locally drawn pseudomanga — including Egmont, Carlsen, and Tokyopop, in addition to several smaller presses — than actual Japanese product; thus the German comics industry is dependent on manga, and particularly on shōjo manga, to a degree unique in Western Europe (Bouissou et al., this volume).

THE UNITED KINGDOM: LATE TO THE PARTY

If up to this point the United Kingdom has gone unmentioned, this is because for many years its manga was generally supplied by import from America, often at inflated prices; the readership was too small for British publishers to bother entering the market. When sales of manga increased sixfold between 2001 and 2005, however (Hollingworth 2006), this became the impetus for the British publisher Gollancz to launch the Gollancz Manga imprint via a licensing deal with VIZ Media ("U.K. Publisher Jumps Aboard Manga Craze" 2005). One of Gollancz's flagship offerings thus became Takahashi Kazuki's *Yu-Gi-Oh!* (Hollingworth 2006). Tokyopop had already set up a UK branch in 2003; once the boom took off, it was approached in 2006 by Pan Macmillan to set up an exclusive distribution deal for series like Murakami Maki's *Gurabiteeshiyon* (Gravitation; see "Pan Macmillan Goes Manga Crazy" 2006). In the same year, Random House established the Tanoshimi line to publish manga issued in the United States by Del Rey, such as CLAMP's *xxxHorikku* (xxxHOLiC) and Kobayashi Jin's *Sukuuru Ramburu* (School Rumble; see "Random House to Launch Manga List" 2006).[12] In the spring of 2007 Titan Books joined the fray, licensing several manga titles from Dark Horse in the United States, including Fujishima Kosuke's *Aa Megamisama* (Oh My Goddess!) and Otomo Katsuhiro's *Akira*. New entries were still coming in as of late 2007; in October of that year Little, Brown Book Group licensed manga from the new U.S. publisher Yen Press, including Okada Kazuto's *Sundome*.[13] However, so far it seems unlikely that these developments mark the birth of a genuine indigenous manga market; given the long head start of American publishers, the transatlantic conglomerate ties among so many firms, and the convenience of the common English language, there is little economic incentive for the British to reinvent the wheel. Although UK publishers are less given to censorship than their American counterparts, in most respects they will probably remain a manga colony of the United States as much as of Japan.

ELSEWHERE IN EUROPE

Other Western European countries have had trouble maintaining independent manga industries, with, for example, the active Scandinavian publisher Mangismo! ceasing its Norwegian activities in December 2006 and declaring bankruptcy in its Swedish and Danish branches during the summer of 2007. In eastern Europe, meanwhile, comics and manga alike are just getting off the ground; the signal exception is Poland, where the comics tradition is strongest among the former Warsaw Pact nations, and where pan-European concern Egmont set up in the mid-1990s as a major publisher of first comics and then a growing manga scene (Moliné 2002, 71; Pilcher and Brooks 2005, 202), to be joined by direct Japanese-run competition from Waneko and Japanica Polonica Fantastica (Bouissou et al., this volume). However, even Russia is slowly developing a taste for manga, despite long decades when comics of all kinds were scorned as capitalist decadence or children's entertainment, with pirated translations (Mikhailova 2006, 190) slowly being displaced by legal Russian editions from companies like the Sakura Press (established 2002), licensee of Takahashi Rumiko's *Ranma ½*, and Fabrika Komiksov (founded in 2006), which carries Akino Matsuri's *Pettoshoppu obu Horaazu* (Pet Shop of Horrors; retitled *Magazinchik uzhasov*), among other series.

CONCLUSION

In summary, it is fair to say that a certain degree of common trans-European manga culture is perforce created by the fact that Western Europe's comics publishing is largely in the hands of transnationals, which tend in the absence of other factors to pursue similar editorial and marketing policies across national and linguistic boundaries. At present, for example, the French-founded Glénat stretches from Spain through France to the Benelux countries, disseminating manga in Spanish, French, and Dutch/Flemish. In this sense, then, Allen and Sakamoto's "inside" and "outside" often do not coincide with national borders.

However, the situation is further complicated by these concerns' respective degrees of centralization, licensing agreements with their own territorial limits, ongoing mergers within the publishing sector, and the vagaries of local markets. Thus the Italian firm Panini is a major force in manga throughout Italy, Germany, Spain (as Planet Manga) and France (as Génération Comics) — but not in its many other countries of operation worldwide, where it concentrates on collectible stickers or reprinting American Marvel comics. In this way, manga's supposed global reach is complicated by local policies.

Within local markets, of course, these transnational firms compete not only with each other but also with smaller concerns either founded to deal only in manga or developed out of alternative comics publishers. These firms tend to be in constant flux; their size makes them more susceptible to insolvency (as in the case of Mangismo!) or absorption by larger companies (as has already occurred with many of France's small publishers).

Larger firms, however, are also not immune to acquisition. Until recently, the Swedish-based Bonnier Group published manga under its Bonnier Carlsen imprint in Sweden, as well as under the Carlsen name alone through its subsidiaries in Denmark and Germany, and in Finland by way of Sangatsu Manga;[14] and the Danish Egmont concern issued manga in Denmark, Germany, Finland, and Poland — but not in England, where it preferred to focus on the *Astérix* and *Tintin* properties. In June 2007, however, Egmont bought out the Bonnier Group, leading to the consolidation of several of their Scandinavian subsidiaries; fears that a merger of Egmont and Carlsen in Germany would lead to a near monopoly, controlling about 80 percent of both the manga and general comics market (Pasamonik 2007), have been stilled in the short term by the German Carlsen's exclusion from the deal to pursue independent policies, though it remains under the Bonnier umbrella ("Carlsen: Wirbel um ein Gerücht" 2007). The merger's implications for other markets are not yet clear.

In general, manga readers in the larger markets of Western Europe — though not yet in the eastern part of the continent — are well served; thanks to a preexisting comics culture that had always embraced more than funny animals, romance, and superheroes, this market by and large reveals much more depth and breadth than its North American equivalent, particularly so in those cases where multilingualism and geographical proximity allow readers to choose from the selections offered by neighboring countries as well as their own. The fears raised by the Egmont-Bonnier merger, however, illustrate one of the problems of the European manga industry, much of which teeters on the brink of bankruptcy while the rest verges on monopoly. The result may be a publishing scene of great complexity and diversity, both nationally and internationally; and yet — particularly given the nature of the comics industry as a niche market relative to larger and more profitable media — this diversity does not necessarily diminish its fragility.

Notes

1. Personal names in this chapter follow the traditional style of family name, given name.
2. *Heidi* began airing on Spain's TVE network in 1975, on Italy's RAI in 1976, on West Germany's ZDF in 1977, and on France's TF1 in 1981 — all, incidentally, state-owned at the time.
3. These stories were republished in Germany by Bastei Verlag from 1977, and in Italy by the publisher Ediboy from 1978 on.
4. A French version of this magazine, with varying formats, was also issued ("Classement *Manga* de A á Z," 333), as well as a Spanish edition, *Candy Candy Corazón*, published by Editorial Bruguera in 1984 (Moliné 2002, 99–100).
5. The Italian version, however, suffered from an irregular publication schedule (Baglini and Castellazzi 1999, 125), and was unable to reverse the decline of Glénat Italia, which folded in 1994, having published thirty-eight volumes of *Akira* — two short of the complete series (Rumor 1999, 119).
6. The latter two publishers are now defunct.
7. This was particularly true of the channels belonging to Silvio Berlusconi's Fininvest concern — namely, Canale 5, Italia 1, and Rete 4.
8. Bernardi had previously been head of Glénat Italia.
9. *Kappa* would become the longest-surviving Italian manga periodical (Castellazzi 2004, 95), finally ceasing publication at the end of 2006 after 173 issues. Kappa Edizioni lives on as a manga publisher.
10. Marvel Italia soon passed back into Italian ownership and reclaimed its original name, Panini; by 1997, it had its own manga imprint, Planet Manga (Baglini and Castellazzi 1999, 129).
11. From the beginning, Europe's private broadcasters have been criticized for their tendency to rely heavily on often sensationalistic programming.
12. Del Rey, like the aforementioned Heyne in Germany, is also a Random House subsidiary, and thus part of the German-based Bertelsmann AG concern.
13. The Yen Press, like both Gollancz and Little, Brown, is owned by the French Lagardère conglomerate, while Pan Macmillan is part of the German-based Georg von Holtzbrinck Publishing Group.
14. The connections among the many arms of conglomerates are sometimes complex; Sangatsu, for instance, is a branch of Kolibri Kustannus, owned in turn by Bonnier's Finnish representative Kustannusosakeyhtiö Tammi.

References

Note: In addition to the sources listed here, the websites of many of the publishers named and/or their parent companies were also frequently consulted.

"Albator" (2009). *Bédétheque.* Ed. Laurent Cirade. hhtp://www.bedetheque.com/serie-6333-BD-Albator.html.
Allen, Matthew, and Rumi Sakamoto (2006). "Inside-Out Japan? Popular Culture and Globalization in the Context of Japan." In *Popular Culture, Globalization and Japan,* edited by Matthew Allen and Rumi Sakamoto, 2–12. London: Routledge.
Aronson, Michael (2007, October 12). "PR: Yen Press Debuts." *Manga Life,* http://www.mangalife.com/news/PRYENPRESSDEBUTS.htm.
Baglini, Claudia (1998). "È un Uccello? È un aereo? È Goldrake!: Gli anime invadono le television italiane" [Is it a bird? Is it a plane? It's Goldrake! *Anime* invade Italian television]. *IF: Immagini & fumetti* 25(8): 48–57.
Baglini, Claudia, and Davide Castellazi (1999). "I manga occupano la penisola: Breve storia della seconda invasione" [*Manga* occupy the peninsula: a brief history of the second invasion]. *IF: Immagini & fumetti* 25(8): 124–31.
Baglini, Claudia, and Cristiano Zacchino (1999). "Manga Made in Italy: Le reviste degli anni settanta " [*Manga* made in Italy: the magazines of the 1970s]. *IF: Immagini & fumetti* 25(8): 62–73.
Bastide, Julien. "Atoss Takemoto, l'ambassadeur manga" [Atoss Takemoto, manga ambassador] AnimeLand.com, http://www.animeland.com/index.php?rub=articles&id=220.
Bastide, Julien, and Anthony Prezman (2006). *Guide des mangas: Les 100 séries indispensables* [Guide to manga: 100 indispensable series]. Paris: Éditions Bordas.
Beaty, Bart (2007). *Unpopular Culture: Transforming the European Comic Book in the 1990s.* Toronto: University of Toronto Press.
Bouissou, Jean-Marie (2006). "Japan's Growing Cultural Power: Manga in France." In *Reading Manga: Local and Global Perceptions of Japanese Comics,* edited by Jaqueline Berndt and Steffi Richter, 149–65. Mittledeutsche Studien zu Ostasien 11. Leipzig, Germany: Leipziger Universitätsverlag.
Bouissou, Jean Marie, Marco Pellitteri, and Bernd Dolle-Weinkauff, with Ariane Beldi (2010). "Manga in Europe: A Short Study of Market and Fandom." *Manga: An Anthology of Global and Cultural Perspectives.* Ed. Toni Johnson-Woods. New York: Continuum, 253–66.
"Carlsen: Wirbel um ein Gerücht" [Fuss over a rumor] (2007). Borsenblatt.net, http://www.boersenblatt.net/148688/.
Castellazzi, Davide (2004). *A–Z manga: Guida al fumetto giapponese* [Manga A to Z: Guide to Japanese comics]. Rome: Coniglio Editore.
"Classement Manga de A á Z" [Manga listings from A to Z] (2006). In *Le guide Phénix du manga 2005/2006.* Ed. Rodolphe Massé. Paris: Éditions Asuka. 297–579.
Corno, Mattia dal, and Davide Castellazi (1999). "Erotismo dal Sol Levante: Umorismo, Lolite e tentacoli" [Eroticism of the rising sun: Humor, Lolitas and tentacles]. *IF: Immagini & fumetti* 25(8): 146–47.
Dolle-Weinkauff, Bernd (1990). *Comics: Geschichte einer populären Literaturform in Deutschland seit 1945* [Comics: History of a popular literary form in Germany since 1945]. Weinheim, Germany: Beltz.
Engelbrecht, Hans (2005). "Les magazines manga en France" [Manga magazines in France]. In *Le guide Phénix du manga 2005/2006* [The Phénix guide to manga 2005/2006], edited by Rodolphe Massé, 260–63. Paris: Éditions Asuka.
"Gen d'Hiroshima" (2009). *Bédétheque.* Ed. Laurent Cirade. http://www.bedetheque.com/serie-6871-BD-Gen-d-Hiroshima.html.

Goldberg, Wendy (2010). "The Manga Phenomenon in America." *Manga: An Anthology of Global and Cultural Perspectives.* Ed. Toni Johnson-Woods. New York: Continuum. 281–96.

"Goldorak – Le robot de l'espace" (2009). *Bédéthèque.* Ed. Laurent Cirade. http://www.bedetheque.com/serie-8756-BD-Goldorak---Le-robot-de-l-espace.html.

"Heidi" (2009). *Deutscher Comic Guide.* Ed. Stefan Ungefroren, Lothar Schneider and Frank Bongartz. http://www.comicguide.de/php/detail.php?id=1744&?le=r&display=short.

Hollingworth, Will (2006, June 16). "British Publishers Soar in Face of 'Manga' Boom." *Japan Times,* http://search.japantimes.co.jp/print/nn20060616a7.html.

Jüngst, Heike (2004). "Japanese Comics in Germany." *Perspectives: Studies in Translatology* 12(2): 83–105.

Knigge, Andreas C. (2004). *Alles über Comics: Eine Entdeckungsreise von den Höhlenbildern bis zum Manga* [Everything about comics: A journey of discovery from cave paintings to manga]. Hamburg, Germany: Europa Verlag.

Massé, Rodolphe, ed. (2005). *Le guide Phénix du manga 2005/2006* [The Phénix guide to manga 2005/2006]. Paris: Éditions Asuka.

Mikhailova, Yulia (2006). "Apocalypse in Fantasy and Reality: Japanese Pop Culture in Contemporary Russia." In *In Godzilla's Footsteps: Japanese Pop Culture Icons on the Global Stage,* edited by William M. Tsutsui and Michiko Ito, 181–99. New York: Palgrave Macmillan.

Moliné, Alfons (2002). *El gran libro de los manga* [The big book of manga]. Barcelona: Ediciones Glénat.

"Pan Macmillan goes Manga Crazy" (2006, July 13). Macmillan, http://www.macmillan.com/13July2006PanMacmillanPressRelease.asp.

Pasamonik, Didier (2007, June 12). "Le groupe Egmont Media rachète plusieurs actifs stratégiques de Bonnier" [The Egmont Media group buys up several strategic assets of Bonnier] *Univers BD,* http://www.universbd.com/spip.php?article5313.

Pilcher, Tim, and Brad Brooks (2005). *The Essential Guide to World Comics.* London: Collins and Brown.

"Random House to Launch Manga List" (2006, March 21). Booktrade.info, http://www.booktrade.info/index.php/showarticle/8314.

Rosenbach, Marcel (2001, March 5). "Frische Ware aus Fernost" [Fresh goods from the Far East]. *Der Spiegel,* 77–78.

Rumor, Mario A (1999). "La testa di ponte in Occidente: Akira apre la porta ai manga" [The bridgehead in the Occident: *Akira* opens the door to *manga*]. *IF: Immagini & fumetti* 25(8): 118–21.

"U.K. Publisher Jumps Aboard Manga Craze" (2005, March 14). *Book Standard,* http://www.thebookstandard.com/bookstandard/news/global/article_display.jsp?vnu_content_id=1000837634. No longer active, archived at http://web.archive.org/web/20060111203216/http://www.thebookstandard.com/bookstandard/news/global/article_display.jsp?vnu_content_id=1000837634.

Vignol, Anne (2005). "Le marché du manga en France" [The manga market in France]. In *Le guide Phénix du manga 2005/2006* [The Phénix guide to manga 2005/2006], edited by Rodolphe Massé, 204–13. Paris: Éditions Asuka.

20

Globalizing Manga: From Japan to Hong Kong and Beyond

Wendy Siuyi Wong

INTRODUCTION

Many modern societies produce a form of visual and narrative art that contains a series of printed pictures, usually — though not always — with text. In English, readers may call it sequential art, comics, comic books, cartoons, cartoon strips, or graphic novels. The French term is *bande dessinee* (BD) — literally, "strip drawing." In Chinese, commonly used terms are *manhua, lianhuantu,* and *car-ton.* The written Chinese characters for *manhua* are the basis for both the Japanese and Korean terms for comics, which are, respectively, *manga* and *manhwa.*

No matter what it is called, this visual art form in various countries and languages has similarities and differences. Scott McCloud (1994) points out that this art form is a communication medium able to convey information and to produce aesthetic pleasure for the readers. As a part of the globalization of media, American comics and animation have a long history of exporting such works. Studies find that American comics played an important role in introducing modern comics to Asia, as in Hong Kong in the 1950s and '60s. In Japan, the great comics artist Tezuka Osamu openly acknowledged the influence of early Walt Disney and Max Fleischer animation in his work. Japan's comics and animation industry was the most developed among countries in Asia in the early 1960s. John Lent's (1998) study of the American animation industry and its offshore factory development in East and Southeast Asia confirm that Japan was the pioneer in the field in the region at that time. Indeed, when comics started to take off in Japan in the early 1960s, the influences of manga began to spread to its neighbors, and

American influence started to wane in the region.

Manga is "one of the features of mass culture in present-day Japan. In 1994, 2.27 billion manga books and magazines were published, making up 35 percent of all material published" (Grigsby, 1998, 65). The manga market in Japan is big, and genres are highly diversified. However, when examining the exportation of Japanese cultural products, including comics, the cultural economist Dal Yong Jin points out that these products "have hardly penetrated worldwide to the same degree as its [Japan's] economic power and the domestic culture market" (2003, 337). It was not until approximately fifteen years ago, partly because of Japan's economic recession, that the Japanese manga industry began to grant copyrights to overseas publishers in Asia and to explore the transnational development of its cultural products.

The influence of manga in the Southeast Asian societies is obvious. Outside Japan and Asia, the visibility of manga is clearly emerging into the mainstream media. Comics scholars and cultural studies scholars are optimistic that Japan can be "consider[ed] as another centre of globalization" (Befu, 2003, 19) because of the current global development of manga and *anime* (Japanese animation). This chapter aims to investigate the flow of manga as a cultural product in the global market, from its country of origin, Japan, to its neighboring region and then to the rest of the world. Because of the influence of American and Western comics in manga, one may find that works of Japanese manga are "undoubtedly deeply imbricated in U.S. cultural imaginaries, but they dynamically rework the meanings of being modern in Asian contexts at the site of production and consumption. In this sense, they are neither 'Asian' in any essentialist meaning nor second-rate copies of 'American originals.' They are inescapably 'global' and 'Asian' at the same time, lucidly representing the intertwined composition of global homogenization and heterogenization, and thus they well articulate the juxtaposed sameness and difference" (Iwabuchi, 2003, 16).

I am interested in exploring these globalization flows by focusing on manga. To begin the inquiry, I will open with a brief review of the concept of globalization.

GLOBALIZATION'S THEORETICAL ISSUES

Globalization is one of today's hottest buzzwords. Stuart Hall (1995) reminds us that this phenomenon is nothing new and can be traced back through the long history of Western imperialism. Following such imperialism, many people in non-Western countries had experienced different degrees of colonialization over the past few centuries. Anthony Giddens (1990) sees globalization as the consequence of modernity in which European nations employed their military and economic power to conquer and rule tribal societies and inferior countries, thus gaining raw materials and securing new markets. Because of its historical origins, globalization was dominated first by Europeans and later Americans. However, as "the emergence of new global communicational technologies has facilitated the questioning of the previously taken-for-granted Western cultural superiority" (Beynon & Dunkerley, 2000, 10), the stage of contemporary globalization that David Held *et al.* (1990) see is becoming possible. For people today, it is "becoming increasingly impossible for them to live in that place disconnected culturally form the world" (Beynon & Dunkerley, 2000, 10).

How has cultural globalization occurred in the contemporary context? Anthropologist Harumi Befu (2003), based on the Japanese example, sketches out the two routes that cultural globalization has taken. The first conduit of cultural globalization is through sojourners, people who leave their homelands and settle someplace else, such as emigrants, students and businessmen. These expatriates bring their native cultural sensibilities and traditions abroad with them, creating a global network of various ethnoscapes. This worldwide redistribution of people has played a major role in the process of cultural globalization. The second route of cultural exportation is through cultural products. Although this means of dispersion apparently occurs independently, without the need for a native carrier, Befu believes that these two routes are actually entwined together in a complex relationship, and need to be examined simultaneously in serious studies of cultural globalization.

Befu provides us another model for understanding the spread of cultural products outside of American and European influence. Globalization is "an outcome of capitalism in the modern period" (Beynon & Dunkerley, 2000, 4). Cultural products, often considered as additional consumer commodities, are being marketed and promoted like any other products. In the case of anime, Jiwon Ahn notes that it "can be more fully understood within the web of influences organized according to the successful 'media mix' strategy," which started,

> although not necessarily in a chronological sense, from the original manga (comic book) series, then the manga is adapted to animated television series or film features or both formats; also video production of the animated series follows. . . . Almost simultaneously, various goods related to the manga and anime, including original soundtrack CDs, paperback books, fanzines, and numerous character merchandises like action figures, toys, stationery goods, confectionary products, etc., are distributed in the market. Also, the release of computer games based on the manga and anime follows, which in turn increase the sales of the original manga series, magazines, books and videos, and spurs the creation extended. (Ahn, 2003, 12).

Similar "media mix strategy" analysis can be seen in the work of other scholars such as Susan Napier (1993), Mary Grigsby (1998), and Anne Allison (2000) on manga studies.

To study the global flow of cultural products such as manga, Befu reminds us that in "non-diasporic cultural globalization it is important to distinguish between the 'structural and institutional' and the 'agency' levels of discourse" (Befu, 2003, 4). "Structural and institutional" levels of discourse refer to "government regulations" and "a certain level of economic well-being and lifestyle, including middle-class aspiration and the availability of sufficient disposable income to enjoy imported cultural products" (Befu, 2003, 5). Arjun Appadurai (1990) identifies his five famous flows of structural and institutional factors: "ethnoscapes," "technoscapes," "financescapes," "mediascapes," and "ideoscapes." All these aspects, Befu points out, "constitute the structural backdrop for agents to act out their volition, [and] the two are interconnected and influence each other in the realm of cultural globalization" (Befu, 2003, 5).

Within these theoretical constructs of globalization, I am interested in exploring how the structural, institutional, and agency levels of discourse in manga interact with each other, in different cultural settings and societies, within the contemporary globalized environment. What made manga able to travel from Japan to the rest of the world? What factors and elements made manga able to communicate across cultures? In Asia, "when considering Japan's globalization, one normally does not consider black markets. But the huge volume of black marketeering of Japanese products suggests the importance of this process. Copyright infringement is a great loss to the Japanese economy, but it is an aspect of Japan's globalization" (Befu 2003, 11). However, in North America and Europe, that case may not be applied. Consider the recent phenomenon of "Asianization of the West," in which we "witness japonisme — diffusion of manga and anime, Japanese cuisine, karaoke, and the like. There is no name for this phenomenon, but it is an obverse of 'Japanization of the West'" (Befu 2003, 20). "Precisely how power is woven into the globalization of Japanese-made images . . . are issues few have studied," Allison points out (2000, 70). The present study shares her view. With the understanding of "the assumption that globalization emanates from the West, and that the rest of the world is its recipient" (Befu 2003, 3), this chapter hopes to contribute "an empirically grounded approach that would avoid these Western-centered assumptions and relativize the overall view" (Befu 2003, 3).

ANOTHER CENTER OF GLOBALIZATION: THE CONTEXT OF MANGA IN JAPAN

Japan has long been open to outside influences, especially those of China. In the case of manga, Frederik Schodt points out, "no one knows exactly when the first Japanese tried his or her hand at cartooning" (1986, 28), but he sees the possibility that the adaptation of this art form was influenced by early Chinese civilization. The now widely used term for comics and cartoons, *manga*, came into popular use around the mid-1700s, with print artist Katsushika Hokusai's work *Hokusai Manga*. Western influences on manga can be traced back to when Japan opened up to the Western world in the Meiji period (1868–1912), in which the first Western-style humor magazine — *Japan Punch* — was published in Yokohama from 1862 to 1887 by a British artist, Charles Wirgman.

The modernization process in Japan began in the Meiji period, when the country began to look for advanced Western models to adapt for all walks of life. Various Western countries influenced the modern Japanese comics in the form of manga. Leading cartoonists traveled abroad frequently, mostly to the United States, but also to European countries. In an example from 1937 — "A New Year's Party for the World's Most Popular Comic Characters" — drawn by members of the New Cartoon Faction Group, we can see "Japanese artists were well acquainted with American comic strips." To Japanese readers, foreign comics represented exotic culture. It was the artists who learned from the foreign comics format and adapted them for readers. As Schodt points out, "Japan's relative cultural isolation has always allowed her to be more choosy about foreign influences and then to adapt them to her own tastes. . . . Foreign comics were exotic but, in the end, alien" (1986, 45) The most famous children's monthly magazine, *Shōnen Club*, was established in 1914; and *Shōjo Club* began publication in 1923. The prewar period marked the beginning of the modern comics of Japan — in a word, *manga.*

After World War II, manga picked up where it left off before the war and rose to a new height. This period (1950s to '60s) saw the flourishing of science fiction and the rise of "the God of manga," Osamu Tezuka. Tezuka's *Atomu Taishi* (Ambassador Atom), later changed to *Tetsuwan Atomu* (Mighty Atom, or Astro Boy) and then made into an animated television series (as *Astro Boy*), marked a milestone in manga history in Japan. This development "reflected the movement to a mass society and the influence of American culture and marked the rise of the manga of contemporary Japan" (Grigsby 1998, 64).

As Befu (2003) points out, manga culture in Japan is now highly developed, with a vast audience of readers of all ages and backgrounds, and widespread circulation of manga publications ranging from single storybooks to multiple-story magazines and series. Available genres fall into extensive categories and subcategories. These genres are classified according to the age and gender of the target readers, as well as personal preferences and tastes. Manga marketed to different readers by age include those for teenage boys (known as *shōnen manga*); for teenage girls (*shōjo manga*); for children (*yōnen manga*); for women (*josei, redikomi,* or *redisu manga*); and men (*seinen manga*). Other main genres included *garo* (alternative, underground, and avant-garde) manga, *gekiga* (dramatic pictures) manga, magical girl (*maho shōjo*) manga, *mecha* (giant robot) manga, *moe/maho kanojo* (magical girlfriend) manga, *shōjo-ai* (lesbian romance) manga, and *shōnen-ai* (gay romance) manga. All the genres appear in magazines containing multiple series of manga by various artists — and some become *tankōbon*, a compilation paperback-sized volume of a single series originally published in a magazine.

Within Japan, manga plays a role to "'release tension' from the controlled work/school environment" and "is a silent activity that can be carried on alone" in a relatively small space without bothering others (Cooper-Chen 2001, 106). As Grigsby observes, "There is a long tradition linking manga to the world that is separate from the rationalized work-a-day world and locating it in a space that is removed from the usual constraints of Japanese society" (Grigsby 1998, 62). She points out the social function of manga in Japan is to provide readers with "information about the beliefs, values and practices of the culture in which they are conceived, [and] it is important to recognize that the relationships of the creators and readers to the larger social, economic and political systems within which a given comic is created, published and made available for purchase are key elements in the production of the comic and in the reproduction of culture" (Grigsby 1998, 62).

Japanese manga publishers enjoyed huge domestic successes throughout the decades after World War II. They therefore had little incentive to develop international licensing systems for their manga. The successful exportation of manga within Asia first started in Hong Kong, Taiwan, Korea, and other Southeast Asian countries, and black markets operated in individual locales to distribute pirated copies. To most Asian nations, Japanese modern culture represents a hybrid identity of Western and Asian influences. Like other Japanese cultural products, such as Japanese *dorama* (dramas), manga offers "the possibility of modernity in an Asian image" and for the Asian audience "with a similar cultural-economic experience, these images become highly identifiable and accessible" (Leung 2002, 66).

It was not until the domestic market for manga started to decline in the mid-1990s that publishers began to search for a new market. With the initiation started by other Asian locales in the mid-1960s, Japanese publishers finally organized and made international licensing a part of their business with Asian partners in the late 1980s. Then, with the success of licensing in

Asia and Europe, publishers "started to focus on their last resort: entry into the remaining market, the United States, where the population of children is twice as big as Japan's" (Misaka 2004, 25). The following section investigates the different time frames of the transnational flow of manga as cultural products to the rest of the world.

MANGA IN HONG KONG AND SOUTHEAST ASIAN COUNTRIES

When studying the global flow of manga, one has to acknowledge that "a pure 'Japaneseness' has gone hand in hand with the acceptance of significant Western influence," and manga has the characteristics "representing the juxtaposed sameness and difference" (Iwabuchi 2002, 16). Thus, this feature contributed a great deal to the cultural flow globally of manga, but different readers may have different degrees of identification. For Japan's Asian neighbors, manga can be considered to represent the new image of what it means to be "Asian." Befu points out that the "similarity of the cultural assumptions and background-undeniably makes it easier for some Asian countries to understand and empathize with performances and characters. Physical or biological similarity between the Japanese and neighboring Asians also plays a part" (Befu 2003, 8). However, the spread of manga in this region was not smooth. As Leo Ching describes the tension surrounding Japanese mass culture in Asia, "Japan's economic expansion has brought fear to its Asian neighbors, mainly because of the great suffering Japan has inflicted on other Asian countries during World War II and because of Japan's persisting reluctance to face up to its wartime responsibilities. These concerns are genuine in light of Japan's prevailing prejudice and insensitivity toward its neighbors. Unlike the Germans, the Japanese government has never sincerely or formally acknowledged and apologized for its wartime brutalities and atrocities" (Ching 1994, 205). Because of this unsettled past, especially the Japanese government's nonadmission of guilt, both Taiwan and Korea banned major Japanese cultural products for decades, and so Hong Kong became the earliest outlet of the global flow of manga from Japan.

Hong Kong also benefited from being a British colony after the war; freed of political turmoil, capitalism was able to flourish. In the 1950s, the territory saw an influx of people, including talented artists and entrepreneurs, from the People's Republic of China. As the economy progressively recovered, newspapers became more affordable, and demand for four-panel cartoons strips in newspapers began to pick up. With the increasing demand for cultural products, the first comics boom in Hong Kong appeared in the mid-1950s to mid-1960s. The best-selling serial comics, known locally as *manhua*, were Wong Chak's *Loufuji* (Master-Q; 1964), Hui Guan-man's *Choi*

Shuk (Uncle Choi; 1958), Ng Gei-ping's *Tungjigwan* (Boy Scout; 1960), and Lee Wai-chun's *Sapsam Dim* (13-Dot Cartoons; 1966). Also, children's magazines such as *Yitung Lokyun* (Children's Paradise; 1953), *Siuonkei* (Little Angeli; 1954) and *Siupangjau Waabou* (Little Friends Pictorial; 1959) played an important role in Hong Kong's manhua history. This first boom was led mainly by local artists previously trained in mainland China, and influences by the United States and Europe. For example, the character of Little Angeli, created by the Bao brothers, was modeled after L'il Abner, Popeye, and other American cartoon characters. Lee Wai-chun, known as the "master of girls comics" in Hong Kong, admitted that she was not very keen on the "old-style" Chinese manhua drawing style. Instead, she modeled her main character Miss 13-Dot (see figure 20.1) after Western fashion magazines such as *Mademoiselle*.

The introduction of Japanese manga to Hong Kong began around the mid-1960s through pirated copies of the Chinese versions. Works such as Osamu Tezuka's *Tetsuwan Atomu* (Astro Boy), *Ribon no Kishi* (Princess Knight), and *Hi no Ton* (Phoenix), as well as Mikiya Mochizuki's *Wairudo Sebun* (Wild 7), Mitsuteru Yokoyama's *Tetsujin Nijuhachi-go* (Tetsujin 28-go), and many others were directly reproduced from the originals without mention of the artists' names or were completely redrawn by local artists. Many classic manga titles were introduced to Hong Kong through this channel. Fujiko Fujio's Doraemon was known as "Ding Dong" (in Cantonese) for a long time until 1999. Doraemon's first appearance was in *Yitung Lokyun* (Children's Paradise) in 1975, in which the manga was redrawn completely in full color and all the characters were given Chinese names. The 1970s saw the waning influence of American cartoons on Hong Kong's manhua and the emerging major role played by manga in both local artists and share of readership. Together with the worldwide "kung fu fever" led by Bruce Lee, the biggest hit from Wong Yuk-long (also known as Tony Wong) — *Siulauman* (Little Rascals) — became the unique Hong Kong martial arts-styled manhua. Wong was strongly influenced by Mikiya Mochizuki in drawing style, but like Japanese *mangaka* (manga artists), Wong learned the format and expression style from manga and gave the story a Hong Kong context to suit the local flavor.

After Wong Yuk-long's success, Japanese manga became the main inspiration source for local artists. The younger generation artists in the 1980s, such as Ma Wing-shing, Li Chi-tat, and Szeto Kimquo, were manga fans themselves and loved titles like *Kazuo Koike* and *Kuraingu Furiiman* (Crying Freeman), Shirō Masamune's *Kokaku Kidotai* (Ghost in the Shell), *Kido Senshi Gandamu* (Mobile Suit Gundam), Yoshiyuki Tomino's (Kidou Senshi Gundam — The Origin), and Katsuhiro Ōtomo's *Akira*. The kung fu genre started to decline in the mid-1990s, partly because Japanese publishers' international licensing system was well in place by the time and the genres of other locally produced manhua were becoming more diverse. New genre comics such as "car racing (e.g. *GT Racing*), soccer (e.g. *Monk Soccer*) and yoyo (e.g. *The King of Yoyo* and *The Star of Yoyo*) published since 2000 are modified from the best-selling Japanese manga, *Initial D*, *Captain Tsubasa* and *Beyblade* respectively" (Ng 2003, 189). "Elements of manga penetrate different forms of the comics industry of Hong Kong," Japanese studies scholar Wai-ming Ng has observed (2002, 31).

Major local manhua publishing companies owned by local artists, such as Wong Yuk-long's Jade Dynasty and Ma Wing-shing's Jonesky, also published licensed Chinese-version manga to diversify their revenue sources. The biggest of these publishers, Culturecom Comics, has published more than three hundred licensed manga titles since its establishment in 1992. Chinese-version manga has a significant market share in Hong Kong's manhua industry, and its influences have become more dominant. Typical Hong Kong manhua are published weekly, with an average of thirty-two to forty-eight pages in full color, on 7.5 x 10.75 inch paper. Now, more and more local artists have adopted the manga book format, with about two hundred pages, black and white, printed on 5 x 7 inch paper and published monthly. Also, various forms of manga culture, such as comic rental shops, comics Internet cafés, *dōjinshi* (amateur comics), and *cosplay* (costume play) are common in Hong Kong.

The other major consumption center, Taiwan, also has various forms of manga culture. Because of the government's official ban on Japanese songs, films, and other cultural products before the mid-1980s, the penetration of manga into Taiwan was later than in Hong Kong. However, in the 1970s, pirated Chinese-version manga were widely published and circulated in Taiwan. Some of the Taiwanese pirated titles traveled to Hong Kong, Singapore, and Malaysia as well. Thus, Taiwanese readers were familiar with Japanese manga though various unofficial channels. By the mid-1990s, "despite the official ban, Japanese songs and video programs [could] be heard and rented in every record and video rental store" (Ching 1994, 210). Top comics magazines featuring Japanese comics, such as *New Youth* and *Youth Express*, have circulations larger than 100,000 copies per issue. Unlike Hong Kong, Taiwan does not have long-running, locally produced comic titles like Wong Yuk-long's *Lung Fun Mun* (Oriental Heroes), formally known as Siulauman, or Ma Wing-shing's *Chungwah Yinghung* (The Chinese Heroes), or a unique comics style like the kung fu genre. For Ng, "Taiwan comics are the most Japanese of all Asian comics. Many Taiwanese comic artists copy the Japanese style faithfully and one can hardly find any Taiwanese elements in their work" (Ng 2002, 31). Perhaps the one outstanding exception is Zheng Wen, who "skillfully combined Japanese (particularly Ryōichi Ikegami and Goseki Kojima's), and Western comic styles with Chinese painting and calligraphic skills in his comics" (Ng 2002, 31). His best-known works are *Cike Liechuan* (Stories of Assassins; 1985) and *Dong Zhou Yingxiong Chuan* (Stories of Eastern Zhou Heroes) in 1990.

In Korea, manga are also widespread, even though the government's official policy stated that "production or distribution of Japanese dramatic movies, video films, comics, CDs, and records as well as the public performance of Japanese popular songs are not allowed" (Han 2001, 205). Like Taiwan, Korea was a Japanese colony; both are under strong Japanese influence, but at the same time are very cautious of being culturally colonized. As for decolonization, "sometimes it meant ruthless galloping into economic development in an effort to catch up and 'compete' with Japan" (Han 2001, 197). Despite that, pirated Korean-version manga still developed into major reading materials for the people. And locally produced Korean comics — manhwa — very much mimic Japanese manga in style and technique. Korean comics and animation artists learn skills firsthand from the Japanese through offshore animation factories. Both Taiwan and Korea have these factories, which provided opportunity for the local talent to learn from Japanese directly. With that skill set as the foundation, Korea is now eager to develop its own manga and animation. Korea is particularly successful with online animated short pieces such as *Mashimaro* and *Pucca*. These two product lines have become popular in Asia and competed with Japanese lines worldwide. Despite the competition, there is a trend for Korean and Japanese artists to collaborate in comics and animation. For example, *Comic Punch*, a Japanese comic magazine published by Shinchosha, started to publish in both Japanese and Korean in May 2001. And in 2002, leading manhwa artist Yang Kyong II collaborated with Hirai Kazumasa to produce *Shiryogari* (Zombie Hunter) in Japan.

Hong Kong, Taiwan, and Korea are the first group of countries to experience the transnational flow of Japanese manga outside Japan; the other Southeast Asian countries and the newcomer, China, make up the second group. More than 75 percent of Singapore's population is of Chinese origin, the rest being Malays, Indians, and others. According to Ng's March 1999 survey, 68 percent of Singaporeans prefer Japanese manga, 14 percent prefer Hong Kong manhua, 13 percent prefer English comics, and 5 percent favor Taiwanese manhua. Ng points out that "racial composition, cultural background, value system, religion, and state censorship" (Ng 2000, 55) all contributed to the different level of acceptance of manga in Southeast Asian countries. Before the legal licensing of the 1990s, Malaysia and Taiwan were the major sources of pirated Chinese-version manga in Singapore, starting in the early 1980s. Readers are familiar with classic titles like *Siufeihaap* (Astro Boy), *Siuseksi* or *Samlam Wongji* (Jungle Emperor), *Lammboushek Wongji*

(Princess Knight), *Siutimtim* (Candy Candy) and *Doraemon*. However, Hong Kong's kung fu manga also garnered significant attention from readers. Starting in the mid-1980s, Japanese manga began securing the leading role in the comics markets of Singapore and Malaysia.

One might wonder why Southeast Asian nations were slower to pick up manga. According to Ng (2000), Singapore and Southeast Asia have been strongly affected indirectly through Hong Kong and Taiwan rather than by Japan directly. In addition, Southeast Asian countries, except for the Philippines, do not have their own mature comics culture and local comics production tradition to counterbalance Japanese manga. Finally, the entry of animated TV series into cable and Malay channels occurred much later than in East Asia. As for China, the country has opened up only relatively recently after decades of communism and isolation, and its economy has been growing rapidly in recent years.

In contrast to Hong Kong's tradition of foreign influence, artists in the People's Republic of China (PRC) have not been able to freely embrace the influence of Japanese manga. Because of government's policy, the PRC's manhua artists "are under pressure from the government and publishers or production companies to cut down Japanese influence in order to develop Chinese-style comics and animation. Regardless of official policy to promote Chinese-style works, Japanese influence is getting stronger in Chinese comics and animation" (Ng 2002, 31). Chinese manga is becoming more accessible in the PRC, and artists are not shying away at all from having their work seen as mimicking Japanese manga.

Today the presence of manga in Asia is everywhere. In the area of heavy Chinese influence, such as Hong Kong, Taiwan, Korea, and to a degree Singapore, the concept of "cultural similarity" or "cultural proximity" can explain why manga is more popular there, "but for Southeast Asia it is not a convincing explanatory tool" (Befu 2003, 8). It is not known how much Chinese and non-Chinese manga readers in Asia look to Japanese manga, as Japanese readers do, for the release of tension because of work and societal stress, or how much they share the "beliefs, values and practices of the culture" that are projected in the manga. Harumi Iwabuchi provides the concept of something as "culturally odorless," as "Japanese media industries seem to think that the suppression of Japanese cultural odor is imperative if they are to make inroads into international markets" (Iwabuchi 2003, 94). He points out that "Japanese popular culture has been deeply influenced by American media. Rather than being dominated by American products and 'colonized' by America, Japan quickly localized these influences by imitating and partly appropriating the originals" (Iwabuchi 2003, 95) Thus, in general, Japanese cultural producers believe that the foreign influences of their products in Asia will eventually be integrated into locally produced

FIGURE 20.1: Lee Wai Chun, *Ms 13-Dot Cartoon*. © 1970/2003, Lee Wai Chun; used by permission.

ones. Cultural products such as manga and dorama are "the trans-local agents, breaking cultural boundaries as they bring to the fore the essential human desire for love, fantasy and aspiration, which might be veiled in the urban reality" (Leung 2002, 73). For most Asians, Japanese manga, like other Japanese cultural products, is the "hybridization of modernity (that has been stereotyped as 'Western') with more traditional attitudes (that are identified as 'Asian')," as well as "the representation of modern living" (Leung 2002, 73). Therefore, although Asians are in general cautious about Japan's past colonization in the region and the invasion of cultural imperialism, they feel they are "completely 'free' and apparently autonomous agents who make choices without any ideological assumptions in itself as ideology" (Ching 1994, 218).

THE PRESENCE OF MANGA IN EUROPE AND NORTH AMERICA

We can easily ascribe the reason for the popularity of manga in Asia to Japanese "cultural similarity" or "cultural proximity" to its Asian neighbors. However, this explanation cannot be applied to manga's penetration of non-Asian cultural markets, such as those of Europe and North America. For regions with strong Asian communities, like Hawaii, the west coast of the United States, and two major Canadian cities, Vancouver and Toronto, manga has been dispersed via Asian immigrants. In that case, the effects of cultural similarity can still apply to those Americans and Canadians with Asian ancestors. The nonsojourner route for the spread of manga beyond Japan and Asia into European and North American markets in the 1990s is interesting to study. Japanese media industries by that time had already utilized the "culturally odorless" principle in their manga and animation-related products in Asian markets, toning down the "Japaneseness" of their products. Now they were ready to explore the possibilities in non-Asian markets.

Non-English speaking European countries, such as France, Germany, Spain, the Netherlands, and Italy, have their own comic cultures and are relatively open to outside cultural influences when compared to the United States. In the mid-1990s, it was not a surprise when the Japanese company Bandai, handling *Bishojo Senshi Sera Mun* (Sailor Moon) distribution worldwide, became successful with animation and products in most of the European market. On the other hand, *Bishojo Senshi Sera Mun* (Sailor Moon) was considered "ultimately failed" in the U.S. market because "it never really registered with the tastes and desires of American girls. In short, *Sailor Moon* was perceived as being too 'different,'" Allison observes (2000, 78).

Without a doubt, the American market is less tolerant of "alien" cultural products, and almost all foreign cultural products must be adapted and altered to suit local tastes. Even though the Japanese media industries are well trained in "cultural odorless" awareness, it still requires a certain learning curve. As some prominent comic scholars point out, the acceptance of Japanese manga and animation by the American audience has been changing in recent decades. This trend reflects the successful marketing mix strategy employed by the Japanese cultural producers since the 1990s. It was also because the domestic manga market in Japan has been declining since the mid-1990s, making publishers seriously push for international licensing and start to focus on the U.S. market.

The new generation of Japanese publishers now has more conscious marketing strategy and is eager to build distribution networks with local comic publishers, which makes manga books and magazines more accessible to potential readers. Indeed, international licensing for translation in different languages and enhancement of distribution networks are important factors for the global flow of manga. In France, comics are highly respected as an art form and have a long tradition. With a strong and diverse comics market, there are more than ten established French-version manga distributors. Since the first years of the new millennium, manga has received more attention, and many titles have reached France. This market is not restricted to the more popular offerings, also including some nonmainstream genres in Japan. Independent mangaka, such as Jirō Taniguchi, are good examples of this phenomenon. In addition, there is a recent local movement, known as *la nouvelle manga* and started by Frederic Boilet, that combines French and Japanese comics tradition into his comics.

Germany also has German-language manga distributors in place, including Tokyopop Germany, established in summer 2004, and Carlsen Comics, which introduced Akira Toriyama's *Doragon Boru* (Dragon Ball) to Germany in 1997. The first German manga magazine targeted at boys — *Banzai!* — was published in autumn 2001, and the second manga, *Daisuki*, intended for girls, was published in the beginning of 2003. The April 2005 issue of *Banzai!* includes popular stories like Yoshihiro Togashi's *Hanta Hanta* (Hunter X Hunter), Hiroyuki Togashi's *Shaman Kingu* (Shaman King), Masakazu Katsura's *Aizu* (I's), Yumi Hotta and Takeshi Obata's *Hikara no Go* (Hikaru's Go), and Masahi Kishimoto's *Naruto*. Other manga-related activities such as fan clubs, fan art, and manga shops are active in Germany. Italy also has at least seven major Italian-language manga distributors. Spain has at least two Spanish-language distributors, with current popular titles including Masahi Kishimoto's *Naruto*, Masami Kurumada's *Saint Seiya*, Akimine Kamijyo's *Samurai Deeper Kyo*, and Rumiko Takahashi's *Inu-Yasha*, distributed by Glenat. Even a newly open Eastern European country like Poland has the most current popular manga titles available in Polish through the international licensing system.

In the United States there is a notable increase in licensing publishers and titles in response to the demands of the past five years. English-language manga titles, known as graphic novels, are now available not only from specialty stores but also in regular bookstores, typically with their own separate shelf and section. Los Angeles-based publisher Tokyopop released two hundred titles in 2002 and doubled its number of titles the following year. In November 2002, San Francisco-based VIZ Media, a major American manga publisher, published the first Japanese manga magazine in English, *Shōnen Jump*. Like its original Japanese counterpart, the magazine contains serial stories to build reader loyalty. The initial issue, which sold out 250,000 copies instantly, has seven serial stories, including three hit TV animation programs in the United States: *Dragon Ball Z, Yu-Gi-Oh!* (an alternate spelling of the Japanese title *Yu gi o*), and *Yu Yu Hakusho*. The May 2003 issue's distribution was 350,000 copies, and the magazine's overall circulation is expected to increase to one million readers in three years. The marketing objective of the American version of *Shōnen Jump* is to make manga another style of comic known to as many Americans as possible. For female readers, the first American shojo manga, *Shōjo Beat*, hit American newsstands in July 2005. That issue includes six of the hottest shojo manga from Japan: Yuu Watase's Zettai Kareshi (Absolute Boyfriend), Marimo Ragawa's Aka-chan to Boku (Baby & Me), Mitsuba Takanashi's Beni-iro Hiro (Crimson Hero), Kaori Yuki's Goddo Chairudo (Godchild), Taeko Watanabe's Kaze Hikaru, and Ai Yazawa's Nana. Both specialized American manga magazines continue the same formula used in Japan: when the serial stories are finished, an independent edition in the format of a "graphic novel" will be published for the fans to own the whole story in one volume (a tankobon), a strategy that has successful cultivated manga culture in Japan for decades. American comics publishers are now experiencing booming sales in graphic novel titles, and sales have been increasing rapidly since 2002.

Studies on how Japanese cultural products are consumed by non-Asian audiences beyond Asia are still limited. American scholars such as Susan Napier, Mary Grigsby, Anne Allison, Kaoru Misaka and Jiwon Ahn have contributed to an introductory understanding of how the American audience circulates and consumes manga and anime. To conclude the study of the growing popularity of anime in the United States, Allison (2000) cites Napier's findings on American fans who "are engaged in a relatively new form of spectatorship, that of the committed fan, whose interaction transcends issues of national boundaries," (p.84) and who unintentionally share experiences with the Japanese audience. Allison found that children in both Japan and the United States prefer manga characters and stories that they can identify with, and which are able to transport them into a fantasy or dream world. Her observation echoes Napier's findings that the "issue of Japaneseness is not the major attraction" (2000, 85) for most American manga fans.

In fact, less "Japaneseness" is better for the transnational circulation of manga and anime, which Japanese cultural producers learned from *Bishojo Senshi Sera Mun*'s failure and *Pokemon*'s triumph. As Allison observes, Japanese manga publishers strive for a culturally odorless feel in their products, a "creation of imaginary world(s) that strike fans with a mixture of familiarity as well as fantasy" (2000, 85). The American audience may well get a sense of de'ja vu from Japanese manga, as their individual imaginations and associations embedded within their own cultural context are stirred by the publications. Indeed, Japan has a long history of learning from and incorporating elements of American comics, cartoons, and animation. What matters is that manga appeals to audiences regardless of their cultural backgrounds. Like manga readers in Asian countries, both European and North American manga and anime audiences "can take on Japanese culture without loving Japan. This becomes clear when one realizes that Japanese presence and influence are structural phenomena. Loving or not loving Japan is a matter of individual response" (Befu 2003, 9). However, there is still no fixed successful formula on "familiarity and fantasy" that can be guaranteed to work every time. To Japanese cultural producers, the transnational flow of its products is still a hit-or-miss proposition, although success rates have been increasing.

CONCLUSION

To continue the inquiry into the cultures of globalization, Ahn seeks inspiration from Arjun Appadurai's "hopeful vision of the political future of the imagined communities of global media reception, which he believes to be capable 'of moving from shared imagination to collective action' and of 'creating the possibility of convergences in translocal social action that would otherwise be hard to imagine'" (Ahn 2002, 20). Indeed, we can now see the emerging global communities of manga where readers share certain collective action, such as reading the same manga titles at the same time, collecting the same trading cards, mimicking the hottest mangaka's work, and so on. According to Ahn, the medium of anime is "the most personal yet social activity, and the most schizophrenic yet possibly liberating experience in the context of globalization" (Ahn 2002, 20). Manga can certainly fit well into Ahn's observations. As well, Allison has discovered that American children who play with Japanese cultural products have "a greater openness towards, and awareness of, Japan" (Allison 2000, 87).

Given the long worldwide domination of American cultural products, the challenges being posed by manga and anime can be seen as a good sign that the world is developing more balanced and tolerant practices. At the moment, Japanese cultural products are the only major alternative choice outside the American cultural hegemony. Although the future of these cultural products seems promising, some critics, including Dal Yong Jin, are not too optimistic about the future of Japanese global cultural power. Jin has reviewed Japan's overall global economic power and concludes,

Japan's GDP stood in second place with $4.75 trillion in 2001, and Japan was the world's second largest exporter of high-technology products. In the 1998–99 fiscal year, Japan exported $126 billion worth of high-tech products, just behind the US with $206 billion. . . . Japan boasts the second largest cultural consumption market in the world. . . . Japanese cultural products, however, have hardly penetrated worldwide to the same degree as its economic power and the domestic cultural market. Japan's revenue from cultural product exports is relatively low compared to other Western countries and several East Asian [countries]. The general notion that cultural power is quite comparable to economic power does not seem to be applicable in the case of Japanese cultural influence in the global cultural market. (Jin 2003, 336–7)

Jin points out that "there are several reasons for the weakness of Japanese cultural power-political and economic as well as cultural reasons: Japan's experience of colonialism; the US's cultural dominance; language and limited diasporas; and the paucity of government cultural policy" (Jin 2003, 339). He sees that "there is only a slight possibility that Japanese cultural products would penetrate worldwide within at least 10 years, mainly because the Japanese economy is still in its worst economic recession. For the Japanese government, cultural product development and export are not a high priority. After the recovery of its economy, Japan's second major priority is preparing for the silver society," and "Japan will be on the edge of the global cultural business in the near future" (Jin 2003, 342–3). Jin does acknowledge, howver, that "Japanese cultural products have increased in their influence in international communication over the past decades" (2003, 342). Nowadays, it is safe to say, "Japan is a manga superpower. It has replaced the United States as the world's largest exporter of comics and animation" (Ng 2002, 30). It is still impossible for a lot of other Japanese cultural products, such as dorama, pop songs, and movies, to penetrate into the American market without severe alteration and localization. The global phenomenon of manga has triggered discussion of the possible Japanese challenge to American cultural hegemony. Here I share the view of Befu, who sees Japan as "another center of globalization," and I agree that "by examining Japan's cultural globalization we should be able to uncover processes of globalization that will help to build a general theory of how globalization occurs" (Befu 2003, 19). Like Befu, we should question "why 'universal theory' or concepts applicable globally must be born out of Western experience" (2003, 20) and why experiences and concepts originating in Japan are not applicable to the rest of the world. Befu argues that "'Japanization' is a unique concept with little use in analyzing other cases of globalization, but it is parallel with such concepts as 'Westernization' and 'Americanization', which have sometimes been equated with globalization. If they represent an aspect of globalization, so does Japanization" (2003, 20). He foresees that "sinicization" may be the next global cultural power after "Japanization," as China emerges as the next super economic superpower. His prediction of the penetration of Chinese cultural products in the global market may take some time to actualize. The role of Japanese manga in providing a counterbalance to Western cultural imperialism and understanding of globalization theory cannot be understated. More than just an alternative to the hegemonic position of the West, it is the new era of "imagined communities of global media reception" (Ahn 2002, 20). Without question, more studies on this aspect of globalization are needed.

References

Ahn, Jiwon (2002). "Animated Subjects: On the Circulation of Japanese Animation as Global Cultural Products." *Spectator — The University of Southern California Journal of Film and Television* 22(1), 10–22.

Allison, Anne (2000). A Challenge to Hollywood? Japanese Character Goods Hit the U.S. *Japanese Studies* 20(1), 67–88.

—— (2003). Portable Monsters and Commodity Cuteness: Pokemon as Japan's New Global Power. *Postcolonial Studies* 6(3), 381–95.

Appadurai, Arjun (1990). "Disjuncture and Difference in the Global Cultural Economy." In *Global Culture: Nationalism, Globalization and Modernity*, edited by Mike Featherstone, 295–310. London: Sage.

Befu, Harumi (2003). "Globalization Theory from the Bottom Up: Japan's Contribution." *Japanese Studies* 23(1): 3–22.

Beynon, John and David Dunkerley (2000). *Globalization: The Reader*. New York: Routledge.

Carlsen Verlag (n.d.). Carlsen comics and manga portal, http://www.carlsencomics.de.

Ching, Leo (1994). "Imaginings in the Empires of the Sun: Japanese Mass Culture in Asia." *Boundary* 2: 198–219.

Cooper-Chen, Anne (2001). "Sex, Violence, and Hierarchy in Japanese Comics." In *Comics and Ideology*, edited by Matthew McAllister, Edward Sewall, and Ian Gordon, 99–128. New York: Peter Lang.

"Franco-Belgain Comics" (2005). Wikipedia, http://en.wikipedia.org/wiki/Franco-Belgian_comics_.

Giddens, Anthony (1990). *The Consequences of Modernity*. Cambridge: Polity Press.

Grigsby, Mary (1998). "Sailormoon: Manga (Comics) and Anime (Cartoon) Superheroine Meets Barbie: Global Entertainment Commodity Comes to the United States." *Journal of Popular Culture* 32(1): 59–80.

Hall, Stuart (1995). "New Cultures for Old." In *A Place in the World? Places, Cultures, and Globalization*, edited by Doreen Massey and Pat Jess, 175–214. Oxford: Oxford University Press.

Han, Seung-mi (2001). "Consuming the Modern: Globalization, Things Japanese, and the Politics of Cultural Identity in Korea." In *Globalizing Japan: Ethnography of the Japanese Presence in Asia, Europe, and America*, edited by Harumi Befu and Slyvie Guichard-Anguis, 194–208. London: Routledge.

Held, David, Anthony McGrew, David Goldblatt, and Jonathon Perraton (eds.) (1999) *Global Transformations: Politics, Economics and Culture*. Stanford: Stanford University Press.

Iwabuchi, Harumi (2002). *Recentering Globalization: Popular Culture and Japanese Transnationalism*. Durham, NC: Duke University Press.

Jin, Dal Yong (2003). "Globalization of Japanese Culture: Economic Power vs. Cultural Power, 1989–2002." *Prometheus* 21(3): 335–45.

Lent, John (1998). "The Animation Industry and Its Offshore Factories." In *Global Production: Labor in the Making of the "Information Society,"* edited by Gerald Sussman and John Lent, 239–54. Cresskill, NJ: Hampton Press.

Leung, Lisa Yuk Ming (2002). "Romancing the Everyday: Hong Kong Women Watching Japanese Dorama." *Japanese Studies* 22(1): 65–75.

"Manga" (2005). Wikipedia, http://en.wikipedia.org/wiki/manga.

McCloud, Scott (1994). *Understanding Comics: The Invisible Art*. New York: Harper Perennial. Sagebrush Education Resources.

Misaka, Kaoru (2004). "The First Japanese Manga Magazine in the United States." *Publishing Research Quarterly*, Winter, 23–30.

Napier, Susan (1993). "Panic Sites: The Japanese Imagination of Disaster from Godzilla to Akira." *Journal of Japanese Studies* 19(2): 327–51.

Ng, Wai-ming (2000). "A Comparative Study of Japanese Comics in Southeast Asia and East Asia." *International Journal of Comic Art*, Spring, 45–56.

—— (2002). "The Impact of Japanese Comics and Animation in Asia." *Journal of Japanese Trade and Industry*, July–August, 30–33.

—— (2003). "Japanese Elements in Hong Kong Comics: History, Art and Industry." *International Journal of Comic Art*, Fall, 184–93.

Sabin, Roger (1993). *Adult Comics: An Introduction*. New York: Routledge.

Schodt, Frederik. 1986. *Manga! Manga! The World of Japanese Comics*. New York: Kodansha International.

VIZ Media (2005). " Viz Announces The Launch Of Shojo Beat Magazine," http://www.viz.com/news/newsroom/2005/02_shojobeat.php.

Wong, Wendy Siuyi (2002). "Manhua: The Evolution of Hong Kong Cartoons and Comics." *Journal of Popular Culture* 35(4): 25–47.

—— (2003). "An Illustrated History of 13-Dot Cartoon: The Work of Lee Wai Chun." Hong Kong: Ng Hing Kee Book and Newspaper Agency.

—— (2004). "Hong Kong Comic Strips and Japanese Manga: A Historical Perspective on the Influence of American and Japanese Comics on Hong Kong Manhua." *Design Discourse*, inaugural preparatory issue, 22–37.

Notes on Contributors

Jason Bainbridge is senior lecturer and head of media studies at Swinburne University, Australia.

Ariane Beldi is a doctoral student in media and communication studies at the University of Geneva, Switzerland.

Jean-Marie Bouissou is a senior researcher at the Fondation Nationale des Sciences Politiques in Paris.

Lorie Brau is an associate professor of Japanese in the department of Foreign Languages and Literatures at the University of New Mexico.

Philip Brophy creates and critiques across three disciplines — music, film, and print. He is the curator of the critically acclaimed *Tezuka: The Marvel of Manga* exhibition that has traveled from Melbourne to various cities in the United States.

Mio Bryce is a senior lecturer and head of Japanese studies at Macquarie University in Sydney, Australia.

Neil Cohn is currently a doctoral student in Cognitive Psychology at Tufts University in Boston.

Sara Cooper is an associate professor in Spanish and multicultural and gender studies at California State University–Chico.

N. C. Christopher Couch teaches in the Program in Comparative Literature, Department of Languages, Literatures, and Cultures, at the University of Massachusetts Amherst, and at the School of Visual Arts, New York.

Tania Darlington is a PhD candidate in English at the University of Florida with an emphasis on cultural and media studies.

Jason Davis is a liaison librarian at Macquarie University in Sydney, Australia.

Bernd Dolle-Weinkauff is a senior researcher and director of the comics archive at the Institute for Research in Children's Literature, Goethe-Universität Frankfurt am Main, Germany.

Angela Drummond-Mathews is a professor of American literature at Paul Quinn College in Dallas, Texas.

Wendy Goldberg is a PhD candidate in English at the University of Connecticut.

Marc Hairston is a space physicist at the University of Texas–Dallas, where he also teaches anime and manga in literature courses.

Emma Hayley is the director of London-based publishing house SelfMadeHero and publisher of the *Manga Shakespeare* series.

Toni Johnson-Woods is a senior lecturer in the school of English, Media Studies and Art History at the University of Queensland.

John A Lent has been a professor of communications at Temple University in Philadelphia since 1974.

Mark McLelland is a sociologist and cultural historian of Japan at the University of Wollongong, Australia.

Paul M. Malone is an associate professor in the Department of Germanic and Slavic Studies at the University of Waterloo, Canada, where he teaches German film, culture, and language.

Craig Norris is a lecturer in journalism, media, and communications at the University of Tasmania.

Marco Pellitteri is a sociologist, at the University of Trento, Italy, and essay director for Tunué Publishing.

Jennifer Prough is assistant professor of the humanities and East Asian studies at Valparaiso University in Indiana.

James Rampant is a postgraduate student in translation studies at Monash University, Melbourne, Australia.

Wendy Siuyi Wong is an associate professor in the Department of Design, Faculty of Fine Arts at York University in Toronto, Canada.

Index

Names are presented in Japanese order – family name first. References to manga, anime, books, films and other fictional works are in *italics* – names of magazines and authors are in plain text. References to images are in **bold**.